Beyond the
Troubled Water of *Shifei*

SUNY series in Chinese Philosophy and Culture
Roger T. Ames, editor

Beyond the Troubled Water of *Shifei*

From Disputation to Walking-Two-Roads in the *Zhuangzi*

Lin Ma and Jaap van Brakel

Work on this book is supported by the Chinese Fund for the Humanities and Social Sciences, the Fundamental Research Funds for the Central Universities, and the Research Funds of Renmin University of China. 18WZX010

项目名称: 从比较哲学的角度探究先秦思想中的"是非"

Cover art: Lu Zhi (1496–1576). *Zhuangzi Dreaming of a Butterfly*. Ming dynasty, mid-sixteenth century.

Published by State University of New York Press, Albany

© 2019 State University of New York

All rights reserved

No part of this book may be used or reproduced in any manner whatsoever without written permission. No part of this book may be stored in a retrieval system or transmitted in any form or by any means including electronic, electrostatic, magnetic tape, mechanical, photocopying, recording, or otherwise without the prior permission in writing of the publisher.

For information, contact State University of New York Press, Albany, NY
www.sunypress.edu

Library of Congress Cataloging-in-Publication Data

Names: Ma, Lin, 1970– author. | Brakel, J. van (Jaap), author.
Title: Beyond the troubled water of Shifei : from disputation to walking-two-roads in the Zhuangzi / Lin Ma and Jaap van Brakel.
Description: Albany : State University of New York Press, 2019. | Series: SUNY series in Chinese philosophy and culture | Includes bibliographical references and index.
Identifiers: LCCN 2018036000 | ISBN 9781438474830 (hardcover : alk. paper) | ISBN 9781438474823 (pbk. : alk. paper) | ISBN 9781438474847 (ebook)
Subjects: LCSH: Zhuangzi. | Methodology. | Philosophy, Comparative.
Classification: LCC BL1900.C576 M29 2019 | DDC 299.5/1482—dc23
LC record available at https://lccn.loc.gov/2018036000

Photogragh taken by Ma Lin in Kunming, Yunnan, China. Text on top reads: *Renjian youjing* 人間幽境 "A place of tranquility in the human world." Calligraphy by Yang Shen 楊慎 (1488–1559, Ming dynasty), who resided in Yunnan for thirty years.

Contents

Acknowledgments		xi
Note on Referencing		xiii
Introduction		xix
1	Preliminaries	1
	Necessary Preconditions of Interpretation	1
	Against the Ideal Language Assumption	3
	Underdetermination of Meaning and Interpretation	8
	Would "On Its Own Terms" Be Possible?	9

Part I
The Troubled Water of *Shifei*

2	Projection of Truth onto Classical Chinese Language	15
	The Harbsmeier–Hansen Dispute	15
	Looking for the "Is True" Predicate in Classical Chinese	18
	Conceptual Embedment of *Shi* 是 and Its Congeners	19
	Transcendental Pretense in Projecting "Theories of Truth"	21
	The Later Mohist *Canons*	25
3	Competing Translations of *Shifei* 是非	31
4	Variations of the Meaning of *Shi*	39
	Shi as a Demonstrative	39
	Shi as Meaning both "This" and "Right"	41
	Modifiers of *Shi*	43

5	Dissolution of Dichotomies of Fact/Value and Reason/Emotion	49
	Are There Dichotomies in Classical Chinese?	49
	Fact/Value Dichotomy in Western Philosophy	54
6	Rightness and Fitting	57
	Nelson Goodman on Rightness and Fitting	57
	Setting up the Quasi-universal of *Yi* 宜 and Fitting	62
7	*Shi* and Its Opposites and Modifiers in the *Qiwulun* 齊物論	67
	Non-English Translations of *Shifei*	67
	Bi/Ci (彼/此) and *Shi/Fei*	74
	Shibushi 是不是, *Ranburan* 然不然, *Kebuke* 可不可	78
	Qing 情 and *Shifei*	82
	Modifiers of *Shi* in the *Qiwulun*	85
	Graham's Contrasting between *Yinshi* 因是 and *Weishi* 為是	89
	Translations of *Yinbi* 因彼, *Weishi*, and *Yinshi*	95

Part II
From Disputation to Walking-Two-Roads in the *Zhuangzi*

8	Is Zhuangzi a Relativist or a Skeptic?	109
	Zhuangzi and Relativism	109
	Relativities versus Relativism	114
	Hansen and Graham's Relativistic Interpretations of the *Zhuangzi*	118
	Zhi 知 and Skepticism	121
9	Zhuangzi's Stance	129
	Stance Instead of Perspective or Set of Beliefs	129
	No Fixed Meanings (*Weiding* 未定)	135
	Walking-Two-Roads (*Liangxing* 兩行)	141
	Doubt and Rhetorical Questions	149
	Buqi Erqi 不齊而齊: Achieving Equality by Leaving Things Uneven	155
10	Afterthoughts	161
	Do the Ruists and Mohists Really Disagree?	161
	Is Zhuangzi's Stance Amoral?	170

Appendix	179
The *Zhuangzi*—Key Notions	179
Zhuangzi's Text(s): What Are the Authentic Chapters?	180
The Big (*Da* 大) and the Small (*Xiao* 小): Early Interpretations and Disagreements	184
The *Qi* 齊 and *Lun* 論 of *Wu* 物	188
The Sages	193
Dao 道, *Tian* 天, and "the One"	198
Ziran 自然 and *Hundun* 渾沌	201
Wuwei 无為 and *Wuyong* 无用	203
Notes	209
Works Cited	253
Name Index	271
Subject Index	277

Acknowledgments

We would like to thank two anonymous reviewers for their patience in reading an earlier draft of the manuscript and for providing numerous comments that have helped improve the text. We also thank our acquisitions editor at SUNY Press, Christopher Ahn, for helpful suggestions concerning the organization of the book. We are grateful to Professor Roger Ames for his continuous support for our work.

Note on Referencing

This book consists of ten chapters and some subsidiaries in an appendix. There are about forty sections, which are numbered by adding letters a, b, c, ... to the chapter number (but this letter is not used in the title of the section). The symbol "§" (plural: §§) followed by a number and a letter is used to refer to sections, for example, "§7c" refers to the third section of chapter 7. The sections in the appendix are numbered as §A1, §A2, §A3, ...

Author-Year Reference System

In this book, sources are usually referred to in accordance with the author-year system, except that we do not always mention the year of publication if there is only one entry under the author's name in the list of works cited. Chinese, Japanese, and Korean authors are referred to by last name followed by given name(s); other authors only by last name. Subsequent references to the same work of the same author in the same continuous text only give the page number in parentheses. In appropriate cases, a work is listed under the year of initial publication. Then the publication year of the edition consulted is given after the name of the publisher in the list of works cited. In a few cases, a text is available only on the internet (as indicated in the list of works cited); hence, no pagination is available. This applies to Hansen (2015), Sturgeon (2014), and Ziporyn (2009b), in particular. Similarly, a reference to a database on the internet does not include a year of publication. The following three abbreviations are used for the databases most often referred to:

- CTP (*Chinese Text Project*, http://ctext.org/);
- TLS (*Thesaurus Linguae Sericae*, http://tls.uni-hd.de/); (Harbsmeier and Jiang Shaoyu 2013);

- *Ricci* (*Le Grand Dictionnaire Ricci de la langue chinoise* [Ricci 2001]), also referred to as the *Grand Ricci*. http://chinese referenceshelf.brillonline.com (Le Grand Ricci Online).

The dictionaries we have consulted include, for classical Chinese: CTP, Ricci, TLS, *Erya* 爾雅, *Shuowen jiezi* 說文解字, and *Kangxi zidian* 康熙字典; for modern Chinese: *Wenlin*; for Dutch: *van Dale*; for English: *Oxford English Dictionary* and *Merriam-Webster*; for French: *Larousse* and *Ricci*; for German: *Langenscheidt* and *Wahrig*. They are not mentioned in the list of works cited, as there are many different editions.

The following abbreviations are used for the publications of A. C. Graham: G89 for Graham (1989); G91 for Graham (1991); G59 for Graham (1959), G60 for Graham (1960), that is, his translation of the *Liezi*; G78 for Graham (1978), that is, his translation of the later Mohist *Canons*; and for various renditions of the *Zhuangzi*: G69 for Graham (1969/70), G81 for Graham (1981), and G82 for Graham (1982).

Chinese Characters

On first occurrence in each chapter, Chinese words or phrases in the main text are given in *pinyin* (without tone marks), followed by traditional Chinese character(s). When the *pinyin* corresponds to only one character in a particular chapter, the character is given only on first occurrence. If two or more characters with the same *pinyin* appear in the same chapter, the character is included on each occasion. For longer citations no *pinyin* is given. Names of classical Chinese scholars are given in *pinyin*, followed by traditional characters. The Index may indicate more places where the use and meaning of a particular Chinese character is elucidated.

In other scholar's translations, we may substitute a word in pinyin to replace the corresponding English word.

"Chinese characters (words, concepts)" refers to Chinese texts of the classical period, here defined as dated from 500 BCE to 100 CE (roughly corresponding to the Warring States Period, often dated from 475 BCE to 221 BCE). Throughout this book, when we only write *shi*, it refers to *shi* 是; if not, we add the relevant character other than 是. In classical Chinese, most words were monosyllabic, and there was a close correspondence between characters and words. However, Chinese characters lack inflection; there is no conjugation or other modifications of a "word," which alone may serve as verb, noun, adverb, and so on. The number of different "particles" (function words, "empty words," 虛詞 xuci) is much larger than in English and they partly resolve issues such as lack of inflection.

Quasi-Universals

Revisable quasi-universals are working hypotheses that connect conceptual schemes from a limited number of traditions (§1a).[1] We refer to them with the following conventions. In constructions such as {zhi 知 ⇔ know(ing)}, "⇔" indicates a relation of family resemblance ("is similar to"). An alternative construction is to write the quasi-universal as zhi/know(ing). We assume that an English word occurring in a quasi-universal includes all kinds of inflections of the word. For example *know* includes knowledge, knows, known, knew, knowing, know-how, know about, know that, know of it, and so on. However, zhi/understand(ing) would be a different quasi-universal and zhi/understand–know is again different.

References to Chinese Texts

For references to Chinese texts, we follow the sequence numbering of TLS.[2] It is not the best, but it is freely and easily accessible on the internet.[3] The *Zhuangzi* is referred to by the abbreviation "ZH," followed by the TLS sequence number; and the relevant page number in Graham (1981, chapter 8) if Graham considered a passage occurring in the outer and miscellaneous chapters as "related to the inner chapters" (Graham, 100–11). In chapters 7 to 10 and the appendix, which focus on Zhuangzi, the abbreviation ZH is omitted. References to the later Mohist *Canons* follow Graham (1978) and not the TLS. Publication details of translations can be found in the list of works cited under the name of the translator.

Citations

Usually a citation consists of two parts: first, the Chinese original plus TLS sequence number in brackets; then, usually starting on a new line, the translation followed by the name of the translator in brackets and, if needed to disambiguate, the volume number or year of publication of the translation. If the citation is very brief, both Chinese and English may be placed on the same line. All translations from Dutch, French, German, and postclassical Chinese into English are of our responsibility. Translators may decide on different parsing of the text. We follow the punctuation of sources cited and we refer to clauses only, not to sentences. With very rare exceptions, we do not consider different "original" texts. Unless explicitly noted otherwise, we follow the Chinese editions used in TLS and/or CTP.

Punctuation in Chinese text is different from that in English. Originally classical texts did not contain punctuation, but punctuation was later added and occurs in all published editions. We follow the punctuation of Chinese text and its translations, except for adding a Chinese full stop (。) or a "Western" full stop at the end of citations rendered in Chinese or a Western language respectively.

Translations of the *Zhuangzi*

Translations of (part of) the *Zhuangzi* used include, for Dutch: Schipper (2007); for English: Billeter (1998), Chan Wing-tsit (1969), Cleary (1999), Eno (2010), Feng Youlan (1928), Feng Gia-Fu and English (1974), Giles (1889), Graham (1981), Harbsmeier (1992), Kjellberg (2001), Legge (1891; in CLT), Lin Yutang (1957), Mair (1994), Muller (2016), Wang Rongpei (2003), Watson (1968), and Ziporyn (2009a); for French: Billeter (1994; also in Billeter 2016, 117–22), Lafitte (1994), Levi (2010), and Wieger (1913); for German: Schuhmacher (2006) and Wilhelm (1920); for modern Chinese: Cao Chuji (2000), Chen Guying (2007), Qin Xuqing and Sun Yongchang (2003), Si Lü (2013), and Zhang Gengguang (1993). Watson is the default for translations of passages in the *Zhuangzi* if only one translation is given. Even if a reference to Graham (1981) is included for "passages related to the inner chapters," the default translation is still Watson. Translations of the *Zhuangzi* (and of the *Mengzi*) are referred to only by name of the translator (no year of publication or page number is given). Graham mentioned as translator of the *Zhuangzi* without year of publication refers to the translation in Graham (1981). Translations of passages from the commentaries of Guo Xiang 郭象 (252–312) and Cheng Xuanying 成玄英 (flourished mid-seventh-century CE) in the *Zhuangzi zhusu* 莊子注疏 are our own.

Other Translations

Translations of other classical text are referred to by name of the translator and page number. These translations include: Lau (1963) for the *Daodejing*

道德經; for the *Mengzi* 孟子: Eno (2016), Lau (1983), Legge (1869; in CLT), Levy (2003), and Van Norden (2001); Bullock (2011) for the *Yangzi fayan* 揚子法言; Crump (1979) for the *Zhanguoce* 戰國策; Forke (1907) for the *Lunheng* 論衡 (by Wang Chong 王充); Harbsmeier (in TLS) and Liao (1939, 1959) for the *Hanfeizi* 韓非子; Hawkes (1985) for the *Chuci* 楚辭; Knoblock (1988, 1990, 1994) for the *Xunzi* 荀子; Knoblock and Riegel (2013) for the *Mozi* 墨子; Legge (1869) for the *Zuozhuan* 左傳; Legge (1885) for the *Liji* 禮記; Liu An (2010) for the *Huainanzi* 淮南子;[4] Hightower (1952) for the *Hanshi waizhuan* 韓詩外傳; Malmquist for the *Guliang zhuan* 穀梁傳; Pokora (1975) for the *Xinlun* 新論; Rickett (1985, 1998) for the *Guanzi* 管子; Tjan Tjoe Som (1949, 1952) for the *Baihutong* 白虎通; Watson (1993) for the *Shiji* 史記; and Zhai Jiangyue for the *Lüshi chunqiu* 呂氏春秋. When referring to these works as reference, the titles are not italicized and the year of publication of the translation may be omitted.

Occasionally an isolated translation is cited. In this case year and page number of the relevant publication are included. This group includes: Coutinho (2015), Harbsmeier (1998), Liu Xiaogan (2015b), Pulleybank (1995), Reding (1985, 2004), Roetz (1993), and Waley (1939).

Index

In alphabetizing the subject index and list of works cited, articles and particles are overlooked. However, names with prefixes, such as *de*, *da*, *van*, and *von*, are alphabetized under the prefix. Adjectives are usually to be found under the nouns they modify. Expressions consisting of two nouns are usually listed under the last word. However, Chinese phrases consisting of two or more characters are listed under the first character. Chinese words in the Index are given in *pinyin* followed by character(s), but no English translation is offered, so as to avoid isolated context-free translation. We have attempted to make the book accessible to readers who are not familiar with the Chinese language. However, in a few cases, the Index must be consulted in order to find locations where the character is discussed. All abbreviations are given in the Index.

Miscellaneous Conventions

We will use the word "concept" in the sense of the meaning and use of a word in English, or of one or two characters in classical Chinese. Usually we do not use italics or quotation marks when mentioning (instead of using) a term or phrase. The difference will be clear from the context, or circumlocutions are used such as: the word philosophy, the expression *zhexue*, and so forth. Unless otherwise noted, emphases in citations are from the original. Square brackets in citations surround our additions. If square brackets already occur in the citation, they have been changed to braces.

Apart from a few conventional uses of a slash (for example, "and/or"), we use the slash for dichotomies; that is, two poles that exclude each other, for example "fact/value." The slash is also used in referring to quasi-universals; for example, "*zhi* 知/knowing–understanding." The en dash, as used in the last expression between knowing and understanding, indicates that "knowing" and "understanding" are either alternative renderings of *zhi* or refer to a hybrid concept to which the concepts of both knowledge and understanding contribute (and perhaps more). In our view, when translating Chinese characters, constructing hybrid concepts makes more sense than presupposing alternative meanings.

Introduction

In our earlier work *Fundamentals of Comparative and Intercultural Philosophy* (Ma Lin and van Brakel 2016a), we have formulated a new theory of interpretation for comparative and intercultural philosophy. The present book can be considered as an exemplification of this theory as well as an extensive elaboration of the subsection "Truth and Rightness" in the earlier work (289–93). It lends further support for our arguments *against* the ideal language assumption, and goes a step further in undermining the claim for the need of universal concepts as a necessary condition for comparative or intercultural philosophy.

Through a focused study of the meaning and interpretation of *shi* 是 and *shifei* 是非, in the inner chapters of the *Zhuangzi*, in particular, this book exemplifies in detail our approach to comparative philosophy. The most common translation of *shi* is "this" or "right" (§4ab), and the most common translation of *shifei* is "right/wrong" (chapter 3, §7a). However, other varied translations, in particular the ones in French, problematize such received wisdom. Although this book focuses on Zhuangzi, our discussion has relevance beyond Chinese and comparative philosophy, because it is an application of our general theory of interpretation. For example, we often appeal to the notion of quasi-universal (see §1a), which is crucial for any scholar involved in translation or interpretation of whatever texts.

In 1957, Martin Heidegger remarked: "European thinking is threatening to become planetary, in that contemporary Indians, Chinese, and Japanese can usually bring to us what is experienced by them only through our European way of thinking" (145). In recent decades, some Chinese scholars have expressed similar concerns insofar as they consider that Chinese classics have been forced into systems of classification prevalent in Western philosophy and thus have imperceptibly transformed the Chinese classics into examples illustrating Western themes.[5] This book purports to contribute to redressing such situation through the studies carried out in it.

In the first part of the book, we take as the guiding line the complexities involved in translating the characters *shi* 是 and *shifei* 是非 in the Warring States texts, the *Zhuangzi* in particular, so as to illustrate methodologies that may help avoid the above problems. We take into account not only English, but also other Western language translations such as French, German, and Dutch. We show that *shi* and *fei* apply to both descriptive and prescriptive language use; they do not presuppose any fact/value dichotomy (§5b). Further, we propose that *shi* can be understood in terms of a generic pre-philosophical notion of rightness and we substitute the quasi-universal {*yi* 宜 ⇔ fitting} for the "is true" predicate.[6] In the Western context, truth is subordinate to rightness. In the classical Chinese context, there is no clear difference between true and right. The two traditions can be connected via the quasi-universal of fitting.

In the latter half of this book, we discuss important features of Zhuangzi's stance with regard to language–meaning (*yan* 言), knowledge–doubt (*zhi* 知–*yi* 疑), equalizing (*qi* 齊), and his well-known deconstruction of the discourse in ancient China on what is *shi* and what is *fei*.[8] As the most significant ingredient of Zhuangzi's stance, we highlight his idea of "walking-two-roads" (*liangxing* 兩行). Furthermore, we emphasize that all of Zhuangzi's positive recommendations are presented in a language in which the meaning of words–characters is not fixed; and that every stance he conveys to his readers remains subject to fundamental doubt as a way of life.

According to most interpreters, Zhuangzi considers the debates on what is *shi* and what is *fei* to be futile, because there exist no universal criteria for making judgments as to whether "it" is *shi* or *fei*. We claim that, for Zhuangzi, the lack of universal criteria leads neither to a Chinese variant of relativism, which implies making all perspectives "equal," nor to mysticism, which enshrines the universal One *Dao* as the final arbiter.

In the "Subsidiaries," we elaborate such key notions as *dao* 道, the One, *tian* 天, and the various sages in the inner chapters of the *Zhuangzi*.[8] These discussions are comparable with working notes that serve as background or cross-reference for our more detailed discussions of specific issues in the main chapters of the present book. In what follows we offer a more detailed overview of the contents of the respective chapters and sections.

In chapter 1, we summarize our earlier work that is directly relevant to this book. We emphasize that, strictly speaking, interpreting a text or a notion from a different cultural tradition "on its own terms" is not possible (§1d) because of the necessary and inherent features of interpretation (§1a). An interpretation cannot avoid being tied to a modern language. One of the necessary conditions of interpretation is that virtually *all* concepts in *all* languages are family resemblance concepts. This proviso is to replace the still common "ideal language" assumption (§1b). On the basis of cross-cultural family resemblances as grounded in the mutual recognition of human practices, we can establish quasi-universals that "connect" concepts from different traditions (§1a). There are many options for the choice or construction of quasi-universals because of "underdetermination" of meaning and reference (§1c).

As background for investigating the meaning and interpretation of *shi* and *shifei* in subsequent chapters, in chapter 2, we first discuss the issue whether there exist correlates in classical Chinese to the Western "is true" predicate. We follow Chad Hansen in arguing that there is no such correlate (§2a). There is a large range of Chinese concepts that seem to convey the notion of truth in some contexts, for example, *shi* 是, *ran* 然, and *dang* 當 (§2b), but there is no specific counterpart to the "is true" predicate.[9] From the perspective of the English language, notions such as *shi* and *shifei* can be seen as hybrid or cluster concepts (§2c), but there is no character in classical Chinese that can be considered as the counterpart of "is true." In addition, we discuss some examples of transcendental pretense involved in projecting theories of truth on classical Chinese texts (§2d). We also criticize the tendency in the secondary literature to treating the later Mohist *Canons* as if it is part of contemporary logic and analytic philosophy (§2e).

In chapter 3, we trace different uses of *shi(fei)* in classical Chinese texts. The meaning of *shi* and *fei* in these texts appears to be similar to that of a range of dichotomies in Western languages such as true/false, right/wrong, correct/incorrect, and good/bad. There is no consensus among translators and commentators on this issue. In the introductions and overviews in English language books, we rarely find "true/false" as a possible translation of *shifei*, though often translators have chosen it to render concrete occurrences of *shifei*. There does not seem to be a simple explanation for this inconsistency.

In chapter 4, we consider various uses of *shi* (and *fei*) and the meaning of its combination with a number of modifiers. *Shifei* can be understood as either one or two words. As one word, it can refer to *shifei*-judgments or *shifei*-debates. As two words, it can refer to three different connections: *shi* and *fei*, *shi* or *fei*, or *shi* versus *fei*. *Shi* and *fei* can also be used individually as verbs: to *shi* something and to *fei* something. Because *shi* is also used as a demonstrative (§4a), the translation "this" (and "not-this" for *fei*) is sometimes added (§4b). Hence, some scholars advocate that *shi* has "double meaning": "this and right." However, whether "right" is to be understood as morally right or factually correct, or some other kind of (normative) rightness, this is not always clear. In §4c we discuss the meaning of *shi*'s combination with a number of modifiers. In the Warring States texts, it is typically assumed that *shi* is subordinate to a higher-order standard of correctness, for example, *zhen* 真. But this is much less obvious in the case of the *Zhuangzi* (§7a).

Shifei is also a phrase in modern Chinese; but its meaning and use is not exactly the same as in classical Chinese. This has prevented Chinese commentators from questioning the use and meaning of *shifei* in classical texts because usually the old meaning of *shifei* (whatever it is) is not "translated" into modern Chinese.

It has often been said that dichotomies such as fact/value and reason/emotion are "absent" in classical Chinese (§5a). This suggests a "fusion" of true and right in the case of *shi*. In chapter 5, we formulate arguments, following Hilary Putnam, that aim to undermine the assumption of a fact/value dichotomy (§5b). This would allow easier access to Warring States texts. We suggest that *shi* and *fei* apply to both descriptive and prescriptive languages (in the Western sense); they do not presuppose any fact/value dichotomy.

Nelson Goodman has proposed a generic notion of rightness in terms of fitting, considering truth as a subsidiary of this generic rightness (§6a). In chapter 6, we extend Goodman's proposal to the intercultural situation and attempt to establish the quasi-universal {*yi* 宜 ⇔ fitting} (§6b). We propose that *shi* can be understood in terms of a pre-philosophical (or pre-conceptual) notion of fitting (*yi* 宜).

That translations or interpretations by different scholars can differ widely, and can even be contradictory, is well accepted. This is not our primary concern. What we want to emphasize is that almost all the anglophone translations of the *Zhuangzi* render *shifei* in a similar manner: "right and wrong." In contrast, translations in other languages raise serious doubts about the omnipresent translation of *shifei* as right/wrong in the English-language literature (§7a).

Zhuangzi uses *shi* as the correlate to a couple of words such as *bi* 彼 (that), *bushi* 不是 (not-this), and *fei* 非. Therefore, one cannot simply claim that *shi* and *fei* constitute a pair of exclusive opposites like right/wrong or true/false. In the *Zhuangzi*, the difference between *shi* 是, *ran* 然, and *ke* 可 may not be as large as what is generally assumed in connection with the "standardized" translations as "right," "so," and "permissible" (§7b). This is the same case with *shibushi*, *ranburan*, and *kebuke*, which are more interdependent in the Chinese language of the classical period than their translations would suggest (§7c). A possible ambiguity is discussed in §7d. Should one read "是非 . . ." not as "*shifei* . . ." but as "this [*shi* 是] is not [*fei* 非] . . ."? Zhuangzi seems to avoid commitment to higher-order standards to evaluate *shifei* disagreements (§7e). We show that binomes modifying *shi* are much less common in the inner chapters than in other Warring States texts.

In chapter 7 we also discuss *yinshi* 因是 and *weishi* 為是. We present Graham's proposal to understand *yinshi* as adaptive *shi* and *weishi* as contrived *shi* in §7f. In §7g we discuss alternative translations of the passages in which *yinshi* and *weishi* occur in the inner chapters. We conclude that Graham is right to highlight the distinction between actions based on the changing situation and actions based on inflexible principles. However, this can be supported without imposing Graham's cumbersome translations of *yinshi* ("'that's it' which goes by circumstance") and *weishi* ("'that's it' that deems").[10]

In chapter 8, we suggest that we distinguish between relativism and relativities (§8ab). We show that influential sinologists such as Hansen and Graham, who have advocated relativistic interpretations of the *Zhuangzi*, present much more nuanced analyses than what has been generally assumed by their critics and what their own wording may suggest (§8c). We suggest that Zhuangzi neither constructs skeptical arguments nor draws skeptical conclusions. Instead, for him, raising doubt is a way of life (§9d). Relativism only becomes a "threat" for an observer who is committed to the ideal language assumption (§1b) or for a disputer who opposes Zhuangzi's idea that the meanings of words are not fixed (indeterminate, *weiding* 未定). In chapter 8, we also scrutinize Zhuangzi's usage of the character *zhi* 知 (§8d), which differs from the usage in other classical Chinese texts.

We propose to understand Zhuangzi's most important views and commitments not as a tenet in the sense of a doctrine, a coherent theory, or a set of beliefs, but in terms of a stance. As to this particular notion of stance, we follow van Fraassen (§9a). A *stance* includes a set of beliefs, but it also includes attitudes, commitments, comportments, emotions, and other factors that cannot be completely reduced to beliefs.

Contrary to the position held by some authors, we argue that Zhuangzi does not set himself against the use of language in general, but only against a specific form of language, namely, the ideal language that assumes fixed meanings of words and phrases and rigid *shifei* distinctions. We discuss his view concerning the use of language, and his idea that the meaning of words or what-is-said (*yan* 言) is "unfixed" in §9b. Because meanings are not fixed (*weiding*) and always keep on changing, there are no atemporal *shifei* distinctions.

We advocate that the approach of "walking-two-roads" (*liangxing* 兩行)—of *ren* 人 and of *tian* 天 (of humans and of heaven–nature)—constitutes the most significant ingredient of the commitments embodied in the inner chapters of the *Zhuangzi* (§9c). The commoners and inferior scholars consider themselves as the arbiters of right–true–correct and wrong–false–incorrect (*shifei*), and are immersed in parading their proffered disputations (*bian* 辯). By contrast, the sage (*shengren* 聖人; cf. §A4) harmonizes with both *shi* and *fei*, and takes his or her abode in the light of Heaven (*yiming* 以明). Hence, the sage walks two roads simultaneously. On the one hand, he or she merges with the ordinary (*yong* 庸) to comply with the *shi* and *fei* of things themselves; on the other hand, he or she rests at the center of the celestial potter's wheel (*tianjun* 天鈞).

In addition, we consider that doubt is an important feature of Zhuangzi's stance. Zhuangzi's doubt is neither to be seen as a label of skepticism, nor to be taken in the Cartesian sense. It is rather similar to Peirce's "reasonable doubt." Zhuangzi uses what we call "contradictory rhetorical questions" to raise doubt (and surprise) and to highlight the interdependence of concepts (§9d). Zhuangzi's doubt is directed not only at other schools such as Mohists and Ruists, but *at himself as well*. We do not agree with ascribing to Zhuangzi a general skeptical attitude concerning *zhi* (as displayed in, say, the *Daodejing*). He does raise doubts (§9d), but refrains from reaching a general negative conclusion about *zhi*, not even therapeutically.

In the last section of chapter 9, we include a particular interpretation of Zhuangzi's idea of *qiwu* 齊物 ("equalizing things") in terms of *buqi erqi* 不齊而齊 (§9e), which has been strongly recommended by Zhang Taiyan.[11]

In two items of afterthought (chapter 10), we address the question as to whether Ruists (Confucians, *rujia* 儒家) and Mohists "really" disagree with one another in their notorious *shifei* debates (§10a), and consider the contention about Zhuangzi's (alleged) amoralism (§10b). According to Zhuangzi, debates in terms of what is *shi* and what is *fei* are fundamentally inconclusive and for this reason pointless. However, *we* do not reject *shifei* discussions altogether (§10a). Does undermining the sense of the *shifei* binome or dichotomy lead to incommensurability and/or amoralism? It does not, if the ideal language assumption, so characteristic of the later Mohist *Canons* (§2e), is absent. Zhuangzi's doubts only concern the commitment to a theoretical approach that aims at universally valid principles and concepts.

Chapter 1

Preliminaries

Necessary Preconditions of Interpretation

In this section, we briefly review some of the necessary preconditions of any interpretation, which constitutes the theoretical guide for our study in this book. These conditions have been argued for in detail in our *Fundamentals of Comparative and Intercultural Philosophy*.[1] One precondition we must highlight in particular is the family-resemblance-principle. This principle consists of two parts.[2]

First, for interpretation to be possible, one *must* assume family resemblance of forms of life (which include philosophical traditions).[3] Similarities and differences are grounded in mutually recognizable human practices. We should keep in mind that the idea that different parties notice similarity of practices does not mean that both sides (or a third party) are seeing "the same" practices. However, there is family resemblance between, for example, "games" and *youxi* 游戲, or between contrasting pairs such as that/this and *bishi* 彼是, other/I and *biwo* 彼我, or good/bad and *hao'e* 好惡. The mutual recognition of human practices in relation to various pairs of languages or traditions makes it quite easy to gain an inkling of the miscellaneous stories Zhuangzi tells involving "dukes," disabled people, craftspeople, birds, fish, and so on. Mutually recognizable practices even give access to metaphorical language and rhetorical questions.

Second, for interpretation to be possible, one *must* assume that *all* general concepts or conceptual schemes in *all* languages are family-resemblance-concepts without any hard-core, clear borders, or unchanging essence. Consequences of the necessity of assuming family-resemblance-concepts include the practice of extending these concepts across languages and traditions as well as the necessary construction of quasi-universals. Revisable quasi-universals are working hypotheses that connect conceptual schemes from a limited number of traditions. Hence, they are *not* universals in the sense of being valid for all traditions (cultures, forms of life). However, they fulfill a necessary role in interpretative practice. The projection of quasi-universals cannot be avoided, lest interpretation be impossible. The first access to unfamiliar conceptual schemes is via extension of conceptual schemes of the interpreter. A quasi-universal connecting, for example, modern English and modern Chinese, has two sides in English and Chinese respectively. English "games" and Chinese *youxi* are not the same concept or practice, but they share family resemblance that allows extending "games" to include much of *youxi* and extending *youxi* to include much of "games."

It needs to be emphasized that people deploy indefinite manifolds of perspectives or conceptual schemes simultaneously and participate in manifolds of forms of life, manifolds that can neither be described nor formalized in their totality. What human beings share are broadly similar responses to a diversity of forms of life.[4] From the point of view of *one* language or *one* form of life, practices or forms of life always show certain similarities (because they are *human* practices). It is a necessary precondition for interpretation that these similarities appear to be there (with overwhelming empirical support as well).

A further precondition is the necessity of presupposing a principle of mutual attunement, including the supposition that the behavior of humans (including speech acts) is somehow consistent with their environment (both natural and cultural).[5] Therefore, we may expect much agreement across human traditions, in particular agreement on the appearance of humans and their environment. For interpretation to be possible, it is *necessary* to presuppose that in the early (radical) stages of linguistic interpretation one *must* assume that "the other" is *usually* sincere, consistent, and right.

In addition to these *necessary* preconditions, there are a few *unavoidable* constraints, in particular the influence of globalization on all human languages and the "hermeneutic relativity" of the interpreter (including commitment to particular epistemic virtues).

While arguing for these preconditions and constraints, we emphatically deny the need for the ideal language assumption, the requirement of a common language, or the presupposition of a large number of universals shared by all humanity. Dropping these assumptions allows us to dissolve the "either universalism or relativism" issue,[6] and to replace it by the family-resemblance-principle and the construction of quasi-universals. The family-resemblance-principle is a feasible alternative to the "not-so-necessary" ideal language assumption.

Against the Ideal Language Assumption

We have opposed what we call the ideal language assumption. According to the ideal language approach, communication is identical with information exchange wherein meaning is understood in terms of semiotic codes or in terms of a formal theory of information processing systems. In our earlier book we have discussed the ideal language assumption and its congeners at length.[7]

The idea of an ideal language traces back to the early history of Western philosophy. According to Aristotle,[8]

> Just as all men have not the same writing, so all men have not the same speech sounds, but the mental experiences, which these written and spoken words directly symbolize, are the same for all [humans], as also are those things of which our experiences are the images.

In modern terms, we can paraphrase Aristotle's "isomorphy thesis" as follows: the structures of humanity's universal innate concepts are isomorphic with the fundamental structures of reality, whereas these isomorphic structures can be described in an ideal language (of thought) into which, allegedly, all human languages are translatable. As Graham has shown, traces of the ideal language assumption can be found in ancient China as well (G89, 404).

> The Mohist *Canons*, which consistently use only one particle for one function, and the same word in the same sense in syntactically regular sentences which sometimes defy current idiom, is plainly the result of a deliberate decision, like the cleaning up of English in the 17th century by the Royal Society.

Perhaps the most significant feature of an ideal language as proposed by Frege (1892) is that precise meanings are possible and should be strived for. In our view, the notion of precise meanings makes no sense for natural languages such as Chinese and English, including philosophical language. It is possible to propose definitions specifying necessary and sufficient conditions for the use of a word, but one cannot give such definitions for all the words that are used in the definitions. This is an example of the *problem of complete description*.[9] That is, it is impossible to provide, once and for all, all the necessary and sufficient conditions for the knowledge or application of a concept or a rule, or for the cause of a particular event, or for the style of a work of art, and so forth. Something like "the one correct true description, translation, or interpretation" does not make sense, not even as an ideal.[10]

There are many other issues closely related to the ideal language assumption, including the following:

1. All kinds of universals are congeners of the ideal language paradigm. Linguistic, cognitive, cultural, or philosophical universals provide the meaning of the words and grammar of the (universal) ideal language.

2. The idea of a complete description of the world in an ideal language is basic to the logical atomism of Russell and Wittgenstein in the 1920s. Today, this assumption may still be evident in what is sometimes called metaphysical realism, which holds that there is exactly one true and complete description of what the world is like (even if we can never achieve this goal).[11]

3. In linguistics, Chomsky assumed a rich and invariant conceptual system, which is prior to any experience (1988, 28). In cognitive science, Fodor used the expressions "modularity of mind" (1983) and "Language of Thought" (1975) to refer to an (innate) ideal language of thought. In recent decades, cognitive science has exerted a dominant influence on much of Western philosophy and its presence is also felt in Chinese philosophy.[12]

4. Global processes of standardization pull natural languages in the direction of a universally shared "ideal" language. For example, the ideal language assumption is in full force in the development of the so-called Web Ontology Language: "Ontology specifies terms with unambiguous meanings, with semantics independent of reader and context" (Siddiqui and Alam 2011, 48).

5. Both universalist and relativist are committed to the ideal language assumption. According to the isomorphy thesis, at some fundamental level, there is always an isomorphy (that is, being of identical or similar form, shape, or structure) between language, thinking, and world. This is the universalistic view, if it is assumed that there is only one way of mirroring the world in language. The isomorphy model is used by the relativists as well, except that languages or traditions mirror domains of reality in different ways and may have

different ways of ordering domains. Both the universalist *and* the relativist deploy the same metaphor that language is a mirror of the world.

Any discussion about artificially constructed ideal (formal, symbolic) languages is embedded in a natural language. Imagine that European and Chinese philosophers each develop an ideal language for conducting comparative philosophy. When they should meet, they would have to use an "ordinary" natural language, such as Chinese or English, to discuss their respective ideal language proposals. No natural language is, nor can be, an ideal language (Tarski 1931).

In the remaining part of this section, we present an example illustrating that, even for the most everyday words, one cannot assume there are neatly corresponding words in all languages. In the sequel, we use small capitals to indicate that the word written is not actually a word of the English language, but a word in a veiled universal ideal meta-language into which all natural languages presumably could be translated.[13] BLUE is such a word. It is represented in English by "blue," in French by *bleu*, in German by *blau*, in Dutch by *blauw*, in modern Chinese by *lan* 藍;[14] yet it is not easy to find a single classical Chinese character corresponding to BLUE. This shows the weakness of assuming such a universal language. Consider the following example from the first chapter of the *Zhuangzi*. There it is reported that the (mythical) bird Peng 鵬, who "measures I don't know how many thousand li [里] across" (ZH 1.1.1), sees the "blue sky" below him.[15] This seems to suggest that *cang* 蒼 means "blue."

天之蒼蒼，其正色邪？其遠而无所至極邪？ (ZH 1.1.3)

The sky looks very blue [蒼蒼]. Is that its real [*zheng* 正] color, or is it because it is so far away and has no end? (Watson)

We do not know whether the blueness of the sky is its original [*zheng* 正] color, or is simply caused by its infinite height. (Feng Youlan)

Is the azure of the sky its true [*zheng* 正] colour? Or is it that the distance into which we are looking is infinite? (Graham)

And the blue on blue of the sky—is that the sky's true [*zheng* 正] color? Or is it just the vast distance, going on and on without end, that looks that way? (Ziporyn)

Is azure the true [*zheng* 正] color of the sky? Or is the sky so distant that its farthest limits can never be reached. (Mair)

Is the blueness of heaven its real color? Or does it look like that just because it is so far off? (Muller)

Translators all agree about rendering *cang* 蒼 as blue, which is confirmed by the TLS.[16] However, two "paragraphs" later we read:

適莽蒼者，三餐而反，腹猶果然。(ZH 1.1.5)

If you go off to the green [蒼] woods nearby, you can take along food for three meals and come back with your stomach as full as ever. (Watson)

He who goes to the grassy suburbs, taking enough food for three meals with him, comes back with his stomach as full as when he started. (Feng Youlan)

Someone off to the green of the woods, with enough for three meals will be home with his belly still full. (Graham)

If you go out on a day trip, you can return with your belly still full. (Ziporyn)

If you're going on an outing to the verdant suburbs you only need to take along three meals and you'll come back with a full stomach. (Mair)

Someone who takes a day trip to the local meadow has three meals and comes back home with his stomach still full. (Muller)

The conclusion that *cang* means blue does not seem right, since, apparently, it also means green.[17] That *cang* can be translated as either blue or green (in some contexts) is confirmed by many sources.[18] According to Chen Yinchi (2016, 65), *cang* in "*tian zhi cang cang* 天之蒼蒼" means dark blue, but he does not discuss the use of *qing* 青 in the same chapter (nor *cang* signifying *green* woods).

Should we say that *cang* covers all the layers of meaning of the "modern" notions of blues and greens (plus some other contextually determined meanings)? Saying so does not tell the whole story. In many respects, *qing* 青 is a near-synonym of *cang*.[19] Immediately after the blue sky of *cang*, we read about the blue sky in terms of *qingtian* 青天.

> 故九萬里,則風斯在下矣,而後乃今培風,背負青天而莫之夭閼者,而後乃今將圖南。(ZH 1.1.4)

> Therefore when the P'eng rises ninety thousand li [里], he must have the wind under him like that. Only then can he mount on the back of the wind, shoulder the blue sky [*qingtian*], and nothing can hinder or block him. Only then can he set his eyes to the south. (Watson)

> So it is only when the bird is ninety thousand miles high, with the wind underneath it, that it rests its weight on the wind and it must have the blue sky on its back and a clear view ahead before it will set course for the South. (Graham)

> That is why he needs to put ninety thousand miles of air beneath him. Only then can he ride the wind, bearing the blue of heaven on his back and unobstructed on all sides, and make his way south. (Ziporyn)

The expression *qingtian* (blue sky) is repeated in ZH 1.1.9. Like *cang*, *qing* also covers the green of vegetation.[20]

> 受命於地,唯松柏獨也在冬夏青青。(ZH 5.1.7)

> Though all life-forms receive their vitality from the earth, it remains constantly replete only in the pine and the cypress, so they remain lush and green [*qingqing*] both summer and winter. (Ziporyn)

> Of those that receive life from the earth, the pine and cypress alone are best—they stay as green as ever in winter or summer. (Watson)

> Among all that owe the earth, only the pine and cypress are due on course; winter and summer they are the same green. (Graham)

Another character that may, for modern eyes, possibly refer to blue in some contexts is *xuan* 玄.[21] According to Baxter (1983), *xuan* 玄 was put into use earlier than *cang* to cover "dark-cool black/green/blue." Other reported uses of *xuan* include: dark blue, color of the sky, brown/black (metallic), purple; reddish black, black tinged with glimmerings of red; hence derivatively: distant, mysterious and unfathomable; any dark/gloomy color.

We conclude that *cang* and *qing* are very similar in their usage in the Warring States period. Both cover the blue sky and the green of vegetation. Perhaps the only difference is that *qing* (and *xuan*) has a closer association with the connotation of mysterious than *cang*.[22] More importantly, these examples show that COLOR is not a universal category. Although regarding modern Chinese and English *yanse* 顏色/color is a respectable quasi-universal, when it comes to classical Chinese, *se* 色/appearance is a more plausible quasi-universal than *se*/color.[23]

Underdetermination of Meaning and Interpretation

The *cang/qing* example also shows that one is never interpreting one thing at a time. One is always interpreting abundant things at the same time. As a result, an interpretation is highly underdetermined by "the data." Ascription of beliefs, meanings, concepts, emotions, logical principles, and so on are all involved in the process of interpretation. Every particular interpretation depends on innumerable other interpretations, every particular one of which can be wrong, but many have to be right. Every interpretation is relative to a context or background that cannot be described completely.[24]

There are always numerous reasonable interpretations, but there is not a single best interpretation. Underdetermination of interpretation is already apparent from the fact that an experienced scholar such as the late A. C. Graham has changed his fairly idiosyncratic translations of the second chapter of the *Zhuangzi* for at least three times (G69, G81, G89). This does not imply that his earlier translations were "wrong," but that there is a wide range of indeterminacies.

We will speak of the underdetermination of an interpretation by the "evidence" (that is, "the data") and about the indeterminacy of meanings (indeterminacy of reference and translation).[25] Indeterminacy is more fundamental than underdetermination. In the case of underdetermination, meanings are fixed; while in the case of indeterminacy, meanings are not fixed (*weiding* 未定). Both indeterminacy and underdetermination entail that a variety of translations or interpretations (instead of a single "correct" one) are possible, but they should be differentiated from incommensurability according to which, strictly speaking, *no* translation is possible.[26] The "causes" of underdetermination of an interpretation by the data include:

choice of texts, incomplete or battered sources, commitment to particular epistemic virtues, and other aspects of unavoidable hermeneutic relativity (Ma Lin and van Brakel 2018).

A number of features of interpretation counteract underdetermination, including the mutual recognition of human practices and the choice of quasi-universals. In addition, the interpreter *must* choose a number of epistemic virtues, which curtail underdetermination and ties a particular interpretation to a particular interpreter and her/his choice of epistemic virtues.[27]

Would "On Its Own Terms" Be Possible?

For over a century, there has been a debate on the identity of *zhongguo zhexue* 中國哲學 (Chinese philosophy).[28] In recent decades, one still finds in Chinese-language literature such remarks as the following:[29]

> Since the 1990s, everyone has been deeply disturbed by the adverse effects caused by the use of Western paradigms to explain Chinese learning.

In this book we make an attempt to take such concerns seriously. We adopt the following strategies:

1. As far as possible we use ordinary (that is, "common sense") language and try to avoid (Western) philosophical concepts loaded with a long history of usage (such as truth) so as to militate possible distortions.

2. We scrutinize a large variety of translations of relevant Chinese characters so as to highlight what may have been distorted in translations.

It is a good idea to try to avoid Western (philosophical) concepts and paradigms in comparative and Chinese philosophy. But here is one important proviso. Strictly speaking, there is no such thing as explanation (or understanding, letting speak, etc.) *on its own terms*. In the case of classical Chinese texts, such an expression would mean being able to think and to write in classical Chinese. That is to say, one would be expected to elaborate the meaning of characters or phrases in the way classical literati or dictionaries such as the *Shuowen jiezi* 說文解字 did.

The phrase "on its own terms" in the context of comparative and Chinese philosophy seems to originate with Ames and has been used by a number of other scholars.[30] For example, Rosemont (2016) writes in the *Stanford Encyclopedia of Philosophy* (on the internet): "the Chinese do their work in accordance with their own 'grammar,' their own questions, definitions of problems, methodology, patterns of argument and standards of justification." But he assumes that the meaning of English concepts such as "argument" and "justification" are universals.[31]

Also consider the following attempt to explain Chinese notions "on their own terms." Ames and Rosemont (1998, 311) propose translating *ren* 仁 as "authoritative conduct" instead of "humanity," *zheng* 正 as "correct conduct" instead of "rectification," *chi* 恥 as "shameful conduct" instead of "shame." Is this a case of translating "on its own terms"? The proposed translations may be better than the "traditional" translations, but they presuppose a unifying (pragmatic) notion of conduct as a universal. One may even worry that the notion of human conduct in the work by Dewey (1922) and G. H. Mead has been projected onto classical Chinese texts.

No matter how familiar an interpreter is with the relevant embedding concepts of an older or dead language, he or she remains tied to a modern language.[32] Embedding characters among their "own" concepts has to stop somewhere. For example, explaining *qing* 情 "on its own terms" remains relative to some quasi-universals for which reasonable cross-cultural extensions of family-resemblance concepts are hypothesized. Eventually, the connection with the interpreter's language has to be made directly by claiming for instance that *qing* can be embedded in the following quasi-universals: FR(*yu* 欲) ⇔ FR(desire), FR(*xin* 心) ⇔ FR(embodied mind), FR(*xing* 性) ⇔ FR(human nature), and so forth.[33] To make this more precise, one might restrict one's account of *qing* 情 to a particular source text, for example, the inner chapters of the *Zhuangzi* (§7d). In addition, one may set out to explain, say, *xing* 性 "on its own terms," but this explanation must depend on constructing other quasi-universals so that the classical and modern language could be connected. This would require a hybrid language (as is used in most publications on Chinese or other non-Western philosophies).[34]

The following example, although the author, Kim Myeong-seok (2014), does not claim to interpret Chinese texts "on its own terms," also illustrates that no matter how many Chinese notions/characters are brought into the discourse, in the end, an assessment is made in terms of the interpreter's language. The latter may be adjusted in light of the investigations, but hermeneutic relativity can never be overcome completely.

Kim aims to explain Xunzi's views on the "ideal state for humans" by discussing the meaning and interrelation of, primarily, *zhi* 指, *li* 理, *he*

和, and *yi*—as well as *lun* 倫, *fen* 分, *zhidao* 治道, and *dali* 大理. However, this cannot be a "pure" case of interpreting "on its own terms." The broad context of the discussion is framed by philosophically loaded English phrases such as "ethical thought," "ideal state for humans," and "personal interactions." Translations and interpretations of the relevant expressions in the *Xunzi* are discussed in English, which involves comparison of classical Chinese concepts and modern English concepts. It is true that something is said about the interrelationship of the characters mentioned. However, in the final analysis, Xunzi's "own terms" are explained in the "own terms" of modern (philosophical) English or Chinese. We are not claiming that this methodology is wrong, but it should not be called "interpreting on its own terms."

Interpretation is complicated further by the possibility (plausibility?) that the author, say Zhuangzi, is using some characters "in his own way." Some characters may not occur in other (extant) philosophical texts, or Zhuangzi is allegedly using some characters in an idiosyncratic way. In the latter case, the meaning and use of the character concerned is highly underdetermined by the limit of the available texts. The *Zhuangzi* can be made sense of only if, first, a sufficient number of characters can enter into family-resemblance-relations with the use of these characters in other Warring States texts. Second, mutually recognizable human practices and relevant quasi-universals make the connection with modern languages, taking into account the views of many translators and commentators. This brings Zhuangzi's text into modern discourse.

The focus on relations between Chinese concepts in original texts is a major improvement compared with interpreting a text already translated into a modern language. However, it is a mistake to assume that one can let these "own terms" speak for themselves without the interference of quasi-universals either chosen or constructed by the interpreter, which connect the classical text with modern discourse.

Part I
The Troubled Water of *Shifei*

Chapter 2

Projection of Truth onto Classical Chinese Language

The Harbsmeier–Hansen Dispute

It has long been suggested that all traditions have a concern with the "truth," "correctness," "real-ness," "appropriateness," and so on of objects, persons and their actions, utterances, and inscriptions. In the analytic tradition of philosophy, the predicate "is true," as applied to sentences, was promoted to be the only form of (semantic) truth, which is the successor of the traditional correspondence theory of truth. Such a notion of truth has been supported by the success of science.[1] In the continental tradition, the focus has been more on truth as a notion in metaphysics (Being and Truth), which is also said to be the primary focus of Indian philosophy. On the other hand, Chinese philosophy of the Warring States Period is often associated with a focus on the true person and a (virtual) lack of what has been called semantic truth (that is, as a predicate of "truth-apt" entities: sentences and "derivatives" such as beliefs).

Many sinologists are implicitly or explicitly committed to a variant of the correspondence theory of truth.[2] Hansen's view (1985, 2007), and perhaps our view, can be considered as a commitment to either the coherence or the pragmatist theory of truth.[3] Hall and Ames (1995) could also be understood as being committed to a pragmatist theory of truth.[4]

In the critical discussion in this chapter, we focus on implicit variants of the correspondence theory. Current analytic philosophy proposes theories of truth that are different from the "old" competitors (correspondence, coherence, pragmatist), including "redundancy" theories of "truth" or deflationism. It sounds plausible to appeal to intuitions such as: a true sentence or utterance says things the right way; it shows how things hang together; it corresponds with how things are; it expresses a commitment to what has been said. However, what conditions need be met to prevent these definitions from becoming circular?[5]

In 1985, Hansen presented an "argument for urging translators not to use 'true' as a translation for any single word of classical Chinese" (Hansen 2007, 490n18).[6] In response, Harbsmeier wrote:[7] "I have demonstrated through examples that the classical Chinese applied verbs meaning *something like* 'be true' to sentences, and that in this sense they had a concept of semantic truth" (202, emphasis added; cf. 199, 200).[8] Hansen dismisses this critique on the ground that Harbsmeier's supporting evidence "consists of supplying a long list of passages of classical texts with his question begging translations" (Hansen 2007, 490n18). That is to say, Harbsmeier presents translations of passages using the word true (in the Western sense) in his translations. He assumes that the reader would agree that his translations are "good" translations. Hansen considers this methodology to be begging the question, because it already assumes that the meaning of "is true" is self-evident and is a cross-cultural universal.[9]

According to Hansen, classical Chinese does have resources to express the idea of truth: "*zhen* 真 is just such a resource" (1985, 504).[10] However, there are no theories in classical Chinese in which *zhen* fulfils that conceptual role. *Zhen* may mean something like "true," but that is so in the non-semantic sense, as in *zhenren* 真人 (true–real–authentic–genuine person).[11]

The semantic predicate "is true" applies to sentences. The disagreement between Hansen and Harbsmeier already starts at this level.[12] Harbsmeier defines the semantic concept of truth as: "that a sentence, statement, or claim is true" (196).[13] He suggests, citing Wang Chong 王充, that the distinction between *zi* 字 "character, word," *ju* 句 "sentence," and *zhang* 章 "paragraph" shows that *ju* refers to a sentence (183). However, "phrase" would do as well as a translation of *ju* and can be inserted in the "hierarchy" between character (*zi*) and paragraph (*zhang*). Harbsmeier (179) also says that *judou* 句讀 means "stops and commas."[14] As far as we know, the expression *judou* does not systematically occur in pre-Han texts and only came into use during the Song dynasty.[15]

According to Graham, the later Mohists used *ci* 辭 as a technical term for propositions or sentences and argues that they shifted attention to the sentence (G89, 153–55, 394; cf. G78, 25, 469). Hansen agrees that *ci* could denote "what we would call a compound word, a noun- or verb-phrase, duplicated verbs, whole sentences, and even pairs or groups of related sentences" (1992, 45; cf. 1985, 496). In addition, Hansen acknowledges that the Mohists *did* discuss word order and its importance, as Graham has shown, but he emphasizes that they did not make a clear distinction between sentences, phrases, and compound terms.[16]

Harbsmeier supports Graham, finding more (alleged) support for translating *ci* as sentence. However, he also remarks that *ci* "invites the translation 'sentence,' but 'formulation' would do as well" (182). If that were so, the proper conclusion would be to say that *ci* does not have a counterpart in English. The ground of the "invitation" is the hope to find the notion of sentence in classical Chinese.

Brandom (1983; 1994, 173–75) has suggested that we had better speak of being true as applied to assertions (instead of the Tarski-inspired focus on sentences). Some sinologists, in particular Fraser (2012, 2015) and Saunders (2014), have followed the influential publications of Brandom in analytic philosophy and found semantic concern in classical texts (in particular in the later Mohist *Canons*). Fraser and Saunders focus on assertions instead of sentences.[17] Certainly, it would seem to be easier to find assertions rather than sentences in classical Chinese, in particular if one ponders Brandom's suggestion.[18]

> Whether or not one claim justifies another, for example, is not determined by some objective semantic content or relations the sentences have and which the community must try to live up to or reflect in their social practices of recognizing some claims as justifying others. Rather, a justification is whatever the community treats as one—whatever its members will let assertors get away with. (Brandom 1983, 644)

Brandom proposes that the function of the concept of truth is expressive: it allows us to say and do things with language that we would otherwise be unable to. This moves "being true" toward "being permissible," which resembles Hansen's emphasis on the pragmatic commitments of Chinese scholars.[19]

We consider that the debate between Hansen and Harbsmeier has missed important facets of agreement between them by narrowly focusing on a rigidly defined concept of semantic truth. Perhaps truth as a property of (Tarskian?) *sentences* was not explicit in Chinese texts, but this did not prevent the occurrence of a wide range of notions which mean something like right, sincere, authentic, and even "something like 'be true' " (Harbsmeier 1998, 202), though there is not one character or phrase that univocally corresponds to the Western "being true."

Looking for the "Is True" Predicate in Classical Chinese

It is not uncommon in Chinese and comparative philosophy to start from a central concept in modern philosophy and check whether there are "corresponding" Chinese characters in classical Chinese. A well-known example is "to be." There seems to be a dominant view that there is no character for "to be" in classical Chinese,[20] whereas the issue of the truth predicate is a matter of debate.

According to Roetz, the range of the truth predicate in modern English is covered in classical Chinese by such characters as *cheng* 誠 (sincerity), *dang* 當 (adequacy to facts), *ran* 然 (being so, suchness), *shi* 是 (normative rightness), *shi* 實 (accordance with facts, actual situation, objective conditions),[21] *xin* 信 (veracity, trustworthiness),[22] *zhen* 真 (genuineness), *zheng* 正 (correctness, whether truth-related or rightness-related), and perhaps a few more other words (Roetz 1993, 85–96).[23] Roetz shares Harbsmeier's view that there is a range of characters in classical Chinese that "imply the claim to truth" (1998, 96), but they do not fully agree on which characters can fulfill that requirement.[24]

According to Graham, Chinese concepts comparable with "Truth" in its various usages include *dang* (fit the fact), *ran* (so), *shi* 是 (is this), *xin* (trustworthiness), *cheng* (integrity), *zhen* (genuine), and *ke* 可 (admissible). His list is a bit shorter, but otherwise similar to Roetz's (G89, 498), except for the addition of *ke*. The first three items in Graham and Roetz's list (*dang, ran, shi* 是) are considered by other sinologists as well to be prominent candidates for the "expressive function of truth" (Fraser 2012, 362).

McLeod (2011, 39) lists the following words as the Chinese equivalents of "is true": "*ran* (然), *shi* (是), *you* (有), *shi* (實), etc."; *dang* is not among them. Sturgeon (2014, 35) adds *ke* (acceptable) to *dang* (fitting), *ran* (so, this way), and *shi* (so, correct). According to Reding, "each of these terms [for him: *shi/fei*, *you/wu* 有/無 or 有/无,[25] *ran*, and *dang*] can be made to express in turn predication, truth or existence" (2004, 194). Perhaps the most noticeable *possible* "inconsistency" in these lists is that Roetz renders *shi* 是 as "normative rightness" and Graham as "is this" (cf. §4b). Otherwise, it seems to be fair to conclude that there is near-consensus that *shi, ran,* and *dang* are most akin to "true." There is no agreement as to whether *ran,* or *dang,* or *shi* should come first as a "truth-candidate."

Differences between Roetz's and Harbsmeier's lists draw attention to suppressed issues of translation and classification. Roetz's list of characters overlaps with the synonymy group for "true" in the TLS. Broadly speaking, Harbsmeier follows TLS (of which he is the director).[26] However, a few characters Roetz lists occur in other synonymy groups in the TLS. This explains why Harbsmeier does not list some characters listed by Roetz. These are: *bei* 誖 (self-refuting, consistency), *gu* 固 (certainty), *ke* 可 (normative admissibility or objective possibility), *ming* 明 (clearness, evidence), *qing* 情 (apprehension of the really given), *yi* 宜 (normative appropriateness).

Like Harbsmeier, Roetz argues against Hansen's "pragmatism." Instead, Roetz takes speech act theory or ideal speech situation as used by Habermas to be universally valid.[27] He argues that, as far as graphs, phonemes, and words are concerned, Hansen's "reduction" of "is true" to correctness or appropriateness is often all right. But as far as "sentence meaning and mode" are concerned, truth, rightness, and sincerity are needed (77–78). According to Roetz, Hansen leaves us "without transcultural criteria of validity" (103).

That such a disagreement between Hansen, Harbsmeier, and Roetz is possible and taken seriously is a sufficient hint that "is true" does not easily qualify as a quasi-universal.[28] This is further confirmed by the observation that although some characters can be translated as "true" *in some contexts*, these translations are open to criticism of being biased toward trying to find "the same." Each of the characters in Harbsmeier's and Roetz's lists can be translated as "being true" in some (rare) contexts, but none of them has as its core meaning IS TRUE. An alternative translation is always possible. This reinforces our general point that even if one can find similarities that allow for family-resemblance extensions, it makes no sense to look for identity of concepts, in particular not for concepts that have a technical philosophical meaning and a long history in a Western context.

We agree with Hall when he wrote,

> Modern Chinese-English dictionaries will increasingly include the word "true" or "truth" as one of the English meanings of Chinese terms. This should not be taken as indicative of the effective presence of the idea of truth in the Chinese intellectual tradition. It is, rather, an illustration of the linguistic contortions sometimes required to import exoteric notions from one culture into another. (Hall 2001, 286)

Conceptual Embedment of *Shi* 是 and Its Congeners

There are quite a number of characters in classical Chinese that can, sometimes, be translated as "(is) true." This offers the inkling that there is no one-to-one translation. It supports our view that there is no direct counterpart to (Western) "is true" in classical Chinese. Instead of looking for characters that can be brought into direct "correspondence" with English concepts on a one-to-one basis, we suggest that it is more appropriate and more productive to focus on clusters of concepts,[29] for example,

cluster of {shi 是, ran, dang, zhen, zheng, cheng, you, shi 實, xin, . . .}
⇔ cluster of {true, being so, right, correct, fitting, genuinely, trustworthy, sincere, . . .}

A somewhat different approach is to leave *shifei* untranslated and consider it as a hybrid of possible one-word translations of the pair *shi* and *fei*, for example,

{shifei} ⇔ {right/wrong, true/false, yes/no, affirm/deny, approve/disapprove, that's it/that's not, this/not this, . . .}

In practice, such clusters would rarely be made explicit, but they *do* play a role in the interpreter's discourse.

In the examples just given, "⇔" should be read as "has a family resemblance with," that is to say, a relation of similarity or of family resemblance between clusters of family-resemblance-concepts in different languages. The choice of clusters to be compared depends on various factors, in particular on the general goal and presuppositions of the investigation. In addition, the choice of concepts embedded in a cluster depends on how the interpreter situates the cluster in the broader context of the language being considered.[30] For example, should *ke* be added to the *shi*-cluster? (See §7c.)

Different clusters result when starting from *shi* 是 instead of from "true." The cluster that contains *shi* may even omit "true": *Shi* often refers to persons or objects.[31] In English, persons or objects can be right or wrong (with respect to a situation or an action), but not true or false. If issues surrounding *shifei* were addressed in Japanese, Japanese clusters would be involved. In this sense, an interpretation is always relative to the language of the interpreter unless one presupposes a universal "ideal language," which assumption cannot be warranted (§1b).

The role of clusters of concepts is already apparent within one language. They influence how the interpreter would form the cross-culturally relevant clusters. In the above examples, we started from *shi*, on one side, and "true," on the other side. On the side of English, we could start instead from a cluster embedding the more generic concepts of rightness (to be developed in section §6a). In a more generic sense, "being right" can be used as a synonym for a large range of words, for example: being considered to be correct, appropriate, valid, consistent, coherent, genuine, good, proper, real, preferable, successful, in harmony, in accordance with what is just, and also with being true. This will influence the choice of characters listed on the Chinese side.

Closely related to the cluster concept is the notion of hybrid concept.[32] A concept on one side may perhaps be "defined" in terms of a hybrid of concepts from the other side. Many characters that are translated differently in different contexts may often be considered as hybrid concepts, as seen from the European side.[33] For example, instead of translating *cheng* in different contexts as sincerity, creativity, reality, faithfulness, truth, integrity, earnestness, genuineness, self-realization, straightforwardness, correctness, or some other concept from the Western philosophical tradition, one may try to express something "intermediate" between all of them, which constitutes a new hybrid concept (from the perspective of the interpreter). In such a case, one might use "cheng" as a word of the English language, emphasizing that the English concept "cheng" is different from the Chinese concept *cheng*. This approach is often better than imposing different translations in different contexts (as interpreted in the language of the interpreter). However, the new hybrid concept is inferior to the Chinese concept, because it misses full embedment in the Chinese intellectual history. Being too eager to render *cheng* intelligible in English leads to statements such as, "sincerity is the most important moral precept that underpins, motivates, and governs the thought and action of a Sinic soul" (Jung Hwa Yol 2013, 473). What the author means is that *cheng* "is the moral fiber that produces the fabric of Confucian philosophy" (ibid.). It is not correct to suggest that the *English* concept of sincerity plays such an important role in Confucian philosophy.

We conclude that considering *clusters of concepts*, instead of single characters or words, helps dealing with divergences "in the large." Similarities in the small can often be found in particular contexts when an appropriate translation based on family resemblance suggests itself.[34] However, differences or divergences in the large may be hidden behind prima facie similarities. Focusing on similarities in the small, we may be struck by the close resemblance of *you* 有 and "there is" (as well as resemblance to the logical quantor "∃x").[35] However, when our focus moves to the wider context of how these notions are embedded in their surrounding forms of life, issues may arise such as the interpretation of *you* in chapter 11 of the *Daodejing*.[36]

Transcendental Pretense in Projecting "Theories of Truth"

Transcendental pretense manifests itself when particular concepts are taken to be universals with a unique characteristic (the "essence"). It is assumed that, by proceeding with such (home-grown) universals, truth (or whatever) in other traditions can be revealed. This idea can be considered as a mixture of essentialization and standardization and is apparent in the common practice of applying a fixed system of philosophical branches and a determinate set of basic philosophical terminology to classical Chinese texts and philosophers,[37] such that Laozi is viewed as a metaphysician, and Zhuangzi a relativist.

An extreme form of transcendental pretense ascribes to the later Mohists the belief that "language can be used to establish objective truth and that the way to do this is to follow logic" (Cheng Chung-ying 2003, 353). This approach is particularly disturbing if the author, who writes in English, cites (or offers) English translations of classical sources without giving (or consulting) the original text. Our methodological advice is that, in translating and interpreting "alien" texts, philosophically loaded words should be avoided insofar as it is possible, that is to say, "ordinary language" should be used if at all possible.[38] We strongly disagree with the scholars who simply take it for granted that the "universals" from the history of Western philosophy, such as "objective truth," can be presupposed to be indigenous to classic China as well. It follows that we should be sensitive to the use of certain words *when they are used to describe the features of classical Chinese*.

Now we first consider a concrete case of projecting "theories of truth" onto classical Chinese scholars. In McLeod's *Theories of Truth in Chinese Philosophy* (2016), the author ascribes a pluralistic theory of *shi* 實 (translated as true or truth) to Wang Chong 王充 (27–ca. 100 CE), the alleged author of the *Lunheng* 論衡.[39] McLeod presupposes that truth is a universal, foundational, abstract, informative, normative, and shared concept of human thought.[40] He discusses concepts and theories of truth he finds in texts by Confucius (Kongzi 孔子), Mencius (Mengzi), Mozi, Xunzi, Zhuangzi, Wang Chong, and others.[41] The author's main proposal is that "the summit of pre-Buddhist Chinese thought on the concept of truth" (144) can be found in the *Lunheng*.[42]

In the exchange between McLeod (2011, 2015), Brons (2015), and Mou (2015), it transpires that their disagreement does not concern so much with Wang's *shi* 實 as with Wang and other scholars' *theories of truth*, as if Wang Chong is a contemporary analytic philosopher. Why would *shi* (實), *shi* (是), and *ran* (然) be *truth*-related properties? McLeod asks himself whether perhaps "Chinese thinkers *did* have a radically different understanding of truth" (2015, 182). This is not the right way of putting the matter, because it already presupposes that "truth" or the predicate "is true" is a universal. That Wang Chong and the *Lunheng* are immersed in modern discourse is apparent from passages such as the following:

It is a brute fact about humans that we do seek properties such as 是 *shi* and 然 *ran* when we appraise sentences and accept or believe statements based on whether or not we have reason to think they are *ran* or *shi*. (2011, 56; also in 2016, 161)

Why didn't Wang simply say that the purpose of the *Lun-Heng* is to *uncover the truth*, to help us distinguish between *shi* 實 and *xu* 虛, which seems his main purpose as he describes it in other passages? (2011, 52; 2016, 158, emphasis in original)

McLeod discusses "theories of truth" because that is a fashionable issue in analytic philosophy. McLeod says that Forke (1907) translates *shi* 實 as true. But Forke does not always do so. Sometimes he translates *shixu* 實虛 or *xushi* 虛實 as full and hollow or reality and emptiness (which are the more common translations of these characters). *Shi* 實 on its own is sometimes translated as reality. Further, *shifei* is not the only word rendered as right and wrong. Forke sometimes translates *zhenwei* 真偽 as right and wrong, sometimes as true and false, sometimes as truth and falsehood. *Zhen* on its own is also translated as true or truth.

McLeod (2015, 2016) rightly notes that the character *shi* 實 has a central role in the *Lunheng* (being used 647 times according to the database of the Chinese Text Project), and so do *shi* 是 and *ran* (occurring 719 and 635 times, respectively). However, the author provides no support for his suggestion that the *Lunheng* has something to say about the *relation* between the "first-order" *shifei* and *ranfou* 然否, on the one hand, and the "second-order" *shi* 實 and *xu*, on the other. Hinting at a second-order concept allegedly serving as the "criterion" for *shifei* (or for *ranburan* or for *kebuke*) assessments of first-order concepts can be found, tacitly, in many texts from the Warring States Period, not just in the *Lunheng*.[43]

The projection of truth or the truth-predicate onto classical text is not the sole case of transcendental pretense. Transcendental pretense is rampant whenever labels of abstract Western philosophical concepts are employed when translating Chinese characters. Another example is translating *lei* 類 as category. Consider

今且有言於此，不知其與是類乎？其與是不類乎？ 類與不類，相與為類？(ZH 2.5.1)

Now suppose that I speak of something, and do not know whether it is of a kind [*lei*] with the "it" in question or not of a kind. If what is of a kind and what is not are deemed of a kind with one another, there is no longer any difference from an "other." (Graham)

Now I am going to make a statement here. I don't know whether it fits into the category [*lei*] of other people's statements or not. But whether it fits into their category or whether it doesn't, it obviously fits into some category. (Watson)

Now I will try some words here about "this." But I don't know if it belongs in the same category [*lei*] as "this" or not. For belonging in a category and not belonging in that category themselves form a single category. Being similar is so similar to being dissimilar! So there is finally no way to keep it [that is, "this"] different from "that." (Ziporyn)

Suppose here is a statement. We do not know whether it belongs to one category [*lei*] or another. But if we put the different categories in one, then the differences of category cease to exist. (Lin Yutang)

Graham is the only one who translates *lei* as "kind." Other scholars translate *lei* as "category." Admittedly, it is difficult to translate some phrases in this passage "literally," but preferably one should avoid the word "category" in translations of classical Chinese.[44] The comment by Guo Xiang concerning 2.5.1 shows that such a passage has to be regarded as applying to a particular example wherein the meaning of *lei* is contextually determined.

Now suppose [I want to] claim that there is no *shifei*, then [I don't know] whether this is similar or dissimilar with those who claim that there is *shifei*. If I want to say that they are similar, but I regard *wu shifei* [that there is no *shifei*] as *shi*, and they regard it as *fei*, then these are dissimilar [we hold differing positions]. However, although we hold different views on *shifei*, we both cannot avoid *you shifei* [taking a stance regarding issues of *shifei*]; hence we turn out to be similar. Hence it is said, being similar and being dissimilar turn out to be similar, and it follows that I do not differ from those [who claim the other way around]. (43)

That is to say, perhaps *lei* should be understood as being similar to the contextually determined thing. In the passage from chapter 2 of the *Zhuangzi* as cited, the specific statement that may be at issue is the apparent paradox of Zhuangzi *shi*-ing that there are no *shi* and *fei*, and *fei*-ing that there are *shi* and *fei*, which one may consider as the central theme of the *Qiwulun* 齊物論, the second chapter of the *Zhuangzi*.

We interpret Guo's comment as follows. The text would raise such a rhetorical question: Are Zhuangzi's "*fei*-ing *shifei*" and the "*shi*-ing *shifei*" of the Ruists and Mohists (*rumo* 儒墨) similar?⁴⁵ Or perhaps: Does Zhuangzi's "*fei*-ing *shifei*" constitute a contradiction? Is it correct to describe Zhuangzi's stance as one of *fei*-ing the activity of making *shifei* judgments? In §10a we suggest that Zhuangzi takes a negative stance toward the activity of making *shifei* judgments (which itself does not amount to making a *shifei* judgment).

We conclude that it is advisable to follow Hansen's suggestion (§2a) and never translate a Chinese character in a classical text as either "true" or "truth."

The Later Mohist *Canons*

In this section, we discuss some examples from the literature concerned with translating and interpreting the later Mohist *Canons*. Projection (transcendental pretense) is to some extent unavoidable, because one cannot completely sever oneself from the language in which one addresses contemporaneous scholars. However, most current translations depend perhaps too much on Western conceptual schemes. This is true even with translations into modern Chinese, for example, when *bei* 誖 in the Mohist *Canons* is translated as *zixiang maodun* 自相矛盾 (self-contradictory). The (Western) notion of self-contradiction is closely related to logic and the "is true" predicate; but it is not obvious that the same could be said of *bei*.⁴⁶ Translating it as "perverse" may be more appropriate.

The later Mohist *Canons* have been considered to be the best candidates for "finding" semantic truth in classical Chinese.⁴⁷ Consider the following translation by Harbsmeier (1998, 330) of canon A74:⁴⁸

辯，爭彼[fan 仮]也 。辯勝，當也。

Logical analysis (*bian* 辯) is contending over (claims which are) the contradictories of each other (*zhengfan* 正反). The alternative that prevails (*sheng* 勝) fits the facts (*dang* 當).

The use of the English phrases "logical analysis," "contending over claims" and "contradictories" may well suggest to the reader that the Mohists are contemporary analytic philosophers—yet another example of transcendental pretense.

Translations of *bian* include discriminate, dispute, argue, distinguish, discuss, and understand. Something is to be said about all of them, but a cluster or hybrid is preferable. However, Harbsmeier repeatedly refers to *bian* as formal or strict logical analysis, for example, when it occurs in A74, B35, and NO6 (330–31). He translates B35 as "To say that neither alternative prevails in logical analysis [*bian*] necessarily (*bi* [必]) does not fit the fact. Explained by: logical analysis" (331).⁴⁹

Most commentators follow Graham (G78) in translating *fan* 仮 (or *bi* 彼) as "contending over claims which are the converse of each other."⁵⁰ Harbsmeier translates *fan* in A73 and A74 as "contradictories" (1998, 217, 331). Recently, Saunders has pointed out that the text does not warrant more than speaking about disputing "opposites." Here are the translations of A74 by Graham and Saunders respectively.⁵¹

> 辯，爭彼 [*fan* 仮] 也。辯勝，當也。(辯)。或謂之牛，或謂之非牛，是爭彼 [*fan* 仮] 也。是不俱當，不俱當必或不當。

> *Bian* (disputation) is contending over claims which are the converse of each other. Winning in disputation is fitting the fact. One calling it "ox" and the other "non-ox" is "contending over claims which are the converse of each other." Such being the case they do not both fit the fact, and if they do not both fit necessarily one of them does not fit. (G78, 318)

> *Biàn* is disputing about opposites. Winning *biàn* is fitting. Explanation: Some say oxen, while others say non-oxen: this is disputing about opposites. Here, both do not fit. Not all fitting, some must not fit. (Saunders 2014, 221)

According to Saunders, *bi* (*fan*) applies to words, not to claims.⁵² *Bian* "is not disputing about converse claims or assertions, but simply disputing opposites."⁵³ Also note that Saunders translates *dang* as "fitting" but not as "fitting the facts."

However, it is noteworthy that Graham is not as sure about his translations as Saunders presumes. In other work, he offers alternative translations.

> Discrimination is contesting the other's case. Victory in discrimination is one's claim fitting the facts. [*Explanation*] One saying that it is an ox, the other that it is not, is "contesting

the other's case." Their claims will not both fit, and if they do not both fit one necessarily does not fit. (G69, 142)

"Argumentation" is disputing over the converse. To win in argumentation is to fit the fact. One calling it "ox" and the other "non-ox" is disputing over the converse. In this they do not both fit the fact, and if they do not both fit necessarily one of them does not fit. (G89, 167)

Revising one's own translations repeatedly indicates the irresolvability of practical underdetermination. Underdetermination leaves room for many plausible translations. However, in all cases there is the risk of assuming too much similarity. In his most recent translation of A74, Graham still uses the words "facts" and "converse."

Most translators do not use the word "true" (but "fitting") in translating *dang* in the *Canons*.[54] However, in discussing B71 and A32, Cheng Chungying uses the phrase "objective truth" five times and says that in an argument (*bian*) both sides aim for objective truth.[55] According to Cheng: "[The neo-Mohists] believe that language can be used to establish objective truth and that the way to do this is to follow logic and follow logical principles" (353). The projection of a correspondence theory of truth is even more explicit in the translation by Guo Weiwei (2007, 273), who, in his rendition of A74, uses the phrase "correspond to reality" (*correspondre à la réalité*).

Many commentators translate *bei* as self-contradictory or self-refuting.[56] There seems to be little doubt that the *Canons* give reasons (in the commonsense meaning of the word) why varieties of skepticism or relativism are "perverse" (*bei*).[57] Perhaps B79 is most explicit.[58]

非誹者誖，說在弗非。不非己之誹也，不非誹。非可非也，不可非也，是不非誹也。

To reject denial is self-contradictory. Explained by: he does not reject it.

If he does not reject his own denial, he does not reject denial. Whether his rejection is to be rejected or not, it amounts to not rejecting denial. (G78, 453)

Quite a few central Western conceptions are projected when one uses the words "logical" or "contradictory" with their association to sentences, being either true or false.[59]

Another example often discussed in connection with the translation of *bei* is B71.

以言為盡詩，詩。說在其言。以：詩，不可也。出入之言可，是不詩，則是有可也。之人之言不可，以當必不審。

> To claim that all saying contradicts itself is self-contradictory. Explained by: what he says himself. To be self-contradictory is to be inadmissible. If what this man says is admissible, there is saying which he recognizes as admissible (and so not self-contradictory). If what this man says is inadmissible, then to suppose that it fits the facts is necessarily ill-considered. (G78, 445)

Harbsmeier (1998, 345) follows Graham with minor modifications. Harbsmeier also cites Yang Xiong 揚雄 (53 BCE–18 CE), translating *bei* as "contradictory" (216).[60]

Again it should be noted that Graham does not seem to be confident about his translations (of B71), given that he renders *bei* as "mistaken" in 1969/70 and "inconsistent" in 1989.[61]

> One who considers all statements mistaken is mistaken. Explanation: His own statement. (G69, 95)

> To deem all saying inconsistent with itself is inconsistent with itself. (G89, 185)

Fraser refers to one calling it "ox" and the other "non-ox" in A74 as "two contradictory speech acts" (2012, 361), but it may be more neutral to speak of "contrasting speech acts" (as Fraser does on the previous page of his article).

Avoiding logical terminology, Hansen translates *bei* as perverse, or in more technical terminology as "self-defeating action-guides." His translation of B71 comes across quite differently from the translation by Graham cited above (Hansen 1992, 241–42).

> *Canon B 71*: To regard language as all *bei*^{perverse} is *bei*^{perverse}—the explanation is in its own language.

> *Explanation*: *bei*^{perverse} is *not-permissible*. If this person's language is permissible then it is not perverse and there is permissible (language). This person's language is not-permissible. He has obviously not examined deeply enough how it *dang* $^{\text{maps onto things}}$.

We conclude that students of Chinese philosophy should be much more wary and refrain from taking the universality of modern conceptual schemes for granted (*including* the conceptual schemes associated with modern logic). But, of course, a certain degree of "transcendental pretense" or hermeneutic relativity cannot be avoided when one is constructing quasi-universals.

Chapter 3

Competing Translations of *Shifei* 是非

In this chapter, we consider a large number of citations from classical sources and look at how (different) translators systematically render *shifei* as right and wrong, or alternatively as true and false, or vary their translations according to context.[1] The classical texts we cite include the *Guanzi*, *Hanfeizi*, *Hanshi waizhuan*, *Huainanzi*, *Liezi*, *Lunheng*, *Mengzi*, *Xunzi*, and the *Zhuangzi*. We refer to these works by their non-italicized titles, adding the TLS code for reference, name of the translator, and page number of the edition we consulted.[2]

Readers may be confused by the various ways in which commentators introduce the meaning of *shifei*. For example, in the glossary of *An Introduction to Classical Chinese Philosophy*, the author renders *shifei* as "this/not this," but in the index as "(admissible, not admissible)." In the main text, the author refers to *shi* and *fei* in terms of "right" and "wrong." In the meantime, the author also resorts to Graham's rendition of *shi* as "that's it" and *fei* as "that's not." No explanation is given for these different translations.[3]

The most common translation of *shifei* is right and wrong; the most common translation of *shi* is "(is)-this," but many other translations occur. Although in introductions and scholarly overviews "true and false" are rarely mentioned as a possible translation of *shifei*, such a rendition occurs in quite a number of translated texts.

In English translations, there is a strong preference for regarding *shifei* as meaning "right and wrong," but French translations usually favor *vrai* (true) or "*le vrai*" (the True) for *shi* and "*le faux*" (the False) for *fei*. In chapter 7, when discussing occurrences of *shifei* in the *Zhuangzi*, we will pay close attention to French translations of *shifei* as *vrai/faux* and *juste/faux* (true/false and correct/false). In French, German, and older English translations, "(dis)approve" also occurs as a translation of *shifei*.

In many contexts referred to in classical sources, *shifei* can only mean right/wrong, if the circumstances are judged with modern eyes. For example,

> 賞罰隨是非。(Hanfeizi 25.1.2)
>
> Rewards and punishments follow right and wrong. (Harbsmeier in TLS)
>
> 桀，天子也，而無是非。(Hanfeizi 25.5.3)
>
> The wicked tyrant Jié was Son of Heaven but he did not have a sense of right and wrong. (Harbsmeier in TLS)[4]
>
> ……推禮義之統分是非之分……(Xunzi 3.10.2)[5]
>
> ... derives guidelines from ritual and moral principles, makes sharp the division between right and wrong, ... (Knoblock 1, 179)

If the context is "danger and security" or "governing the state," true/false seems to be as relevant as right/wrong (as seen from a modern perspective), and *shifei* may involve both of them, although in such contexts the translations tend to have "right and wrong."

> 安危在是非。(Hanfeizi 25.5.1)
>
> Danger and security have to do with getting things right and wrong. (Harbsmeier in TLS)
>
> 與之參國政，正是非。(Xunzi 16.4.3)
>
> Join them in examining the administration of the state and in putting aright matters of right and wrong. (Knoblock 2, 242)
>
> 治國是非，不以術斷……(Hanfeizi 47.9.2)
>
> If the rights and wrongs in governing the state are not judged according to professional skill, ... (Harbsmeier in TLS)

However, true/false as a translation does occur. For example,

> 所謂是而無非，非而無是，是非有。(Guanzi 11.15/4)

> As for saying there is the true with no false, or the false with no true, since they both exist, they are certain to emerge interacting together. (Rickett 1985, 206)[6]

> 是非之所在……(Huainanzi 9.11.6)

> In deciding where truth or falsity lies, . . . [honor and status are simply irrelevant] (Liu An, 319)

> 見物然後知其是非之所在。(Xunzi 32.3.8)[7]

> Only after one has perceived the true [*ran* 然] state of things does one know where right and wrong lie. (Knoblock 3, 267)

Graham almost always translates *shi* and *fei* as that's it/that's not it, but here is an exception.

> 口之所欲道者是非，而不得言，謂之關智。(Liezi 7.7/3)

> What the mouth wishes to discuss is truth and falsehood, and if this is denied it, I say that the intelligence is restricted. (G60, 142)

Why did Graham choose "truth and falsehood" on this occasion?
 Chinese literati often worry that *shi* and *fei* be confused and are concerned that a sharp distinction be made; otherwise, anarchy may follow.[8] Translators can see the cause of confusion in either right/wrong or true/false.

> 熒惑諸侯，以是為非，以非為是。(Zhanguoce 19.3.5)[9]

> Su Ch'in dazzled and deceived the Lords, made what is true seem false and twisted wrong into right. (Crump, 294)

> ……使混然不知是非治亂之所存者。(Hanshi waizhuan 4.22/1)

> . . . causing them [the ignorant masses] in their confusion not to know wherein lie truth or falsehood, order or anarchy. (Hightower, 145)[10]

名實亂，是非之形不明。(Xunzi 25.37)

Names and their realities have become confused, and the boundary between right and wrong has become unclear. (Knoblock 3, 128)

今天下之人，皆惑于是非，昏于利害。(Liezi 3.8.3)

Nowadays everyone in the world is deluded about right and wrong, and confused about benefit and harm. (G60, 72)

Because of the dominant translation of one of Mengzi's "four sprouts" as right and wrong (judgment), usually the function of judging right/wrong is ascribed to *xin* 心 (mind-heart),

心將迷者，先識是非。(Liezi 4.10/1)[11]

The mind [*xin*] is about to go astray when it cannot recognize right and wrong. (G60, 84)

Mengzi expressed this idea in much stronger terms.

無是非之心，非人也。(Mengzi 2A/6)

Not to have a mind which calls things right or wrong is not human. (Pulleybank 1995, 86)

However, true/false associated with *xin* also occurs.[12]

心意之論，不足以定是非。(Huainanzi 6.3.5)

Discussions employing the mind and its conceptions are not adequate to distinguish true and false. (Liu An, 219)

In the classical texts, a variety of opposites are often enumerated in which *shifei* occurs. In such cases, *shifei* has always been translated as right/wrong. But would not true/false, (dis)approve, and so on, also be possible in such cases? Consider the following:

……察能分白黑，視醜美，而知能別同異，明是非者，何也？(Huainanzi 1.21.2)

. . . differentiate between white and black, discern ugliness and beauty; . . . , understand sameness and difference, and clarify right and wrong. (Liu An, 75)

……哀樂聲色臭味是非。(Liezi 3.8/5)

. . . joy and sorrow, music and beauty, smells and tastes, right and wrong. (G60, 72)

……賢愚、好醜、成敗、是非。(Liezi 7.14/2)

. . . worth and folly, beauty and ugliness, success and failure, right and wrong. (G60, 153)

是非……成未……俱適……存亡……姓故……貴賤。(canon A88)

Being this or not being it (/right or wrong), proved or not yet proved, both being complements, present or absent, surname or the thing itself, dear or cheap. (G78, 339)

Also consider:

是非相間革更其行也。(Baihutong 12.106.1)

As good and evil [*shifei*] alternate, so one's conduct can be changed. (Tjan Tjoe Som, 468)

Translating 是非 as "right and wrong" instead of "good and evil" would seem to be possible as well. That in many cases it is difficult to decide whether *shifei* should be translated as true/false or as right/wrong is confirmed by conflicting choices of anglophone interpreters concerning the same passage. Consider the following text from the *Xunzi*,[13]

是是非非謂之知。非是是非謂之愚。(Xunzi 2.3.1–2)

To recognize as right what is right and as wrong what is wrong is called "wisdom." To regard as wrong what is right and as right what is wrong is called "stupidity." (Knoblock 1, 153)

Numerous recent translations in English choose right/wrong to render *shifei* in this passage, for example,

> To treat right as right and wrong as wrong is called wisdom. To treat right as wrong and wrong as right is called stupidity. (Watson 2003, 27)

> To recognize right as right and wrong as wrong is called wisdom, to take right as wrong and wrong as right is called foolishness. (G78, 456)

> To consider as right what is right and as wrong what is wrong is called knowing; and to consider as wrong what is right and as right what is wrong is being ignorant. (Harbsmeier in TLS)

Harbsmeier (1993, 12), who speaks of "Xunzi's puzzling definition," also translates it as[14]

> Considering this (or what is right (shi)) as this (or: right), and considering not-this (or: what is wrong (fei)) as not-this (or: wrong) constitutes knowing. Considering this as "not-this" and considering what is not-this as "this" is making a fool of oneself.

Sturgeon (2014, 23) explicitly makes a distinction between the first and the second shi (and fei). . . . shi-ing shi and fei-ing fei is what is meant by knowledge. He distinguishes between (subjectively) taking as shi (that is, endorsing) those things that are objectively shi. But now consider Reding's rendition.[15]

> To consider what is true as true and what is false as false, that is what is called "knowledge." To consider what is true as false and what is false as true, that is what is called "ignorance." (2004, 193)

Why does Reding choose to translate shifei as true/false? The reason is that his writings are embedded in French sinology (see further §7a).

Somewhat similar but less frequent ambiguity in translation can be found in the case of *ranburan* 然不然 or *ranfou* 然否. Usually it is translated as "so or not so," but the translation right/wrong occurs as well.[16]

> 辯然否，謂之士。(Baihutong 1.3.4)

> He who distinguishes between right and wrong is called a shi 士. (Tjan Tjoe Som, 221)

A "fusion" of true/false and right/wrong under the influence of *shifei* can be found in Wardy's translation of a passage in the *Minglitan*《名理探》, published in Hangzhou in 1631.[17]

> ……辨是與非，辟諸迷謬，以歸一真之路。(Furtado and Li Zhizao 李之藻 1959, 8)

> [Aristotle] distinguished right/true [*shi* 是] and wrong/false [*fei* 非], and banished and deluded error so that we might return to the road of unique correctness [真]. (Wardy 2000, 97)

Perhaps in this case the motivation to write right/true and wrong/false is to have it both ways: "true" to be true to Aristotle's text, "right" to acknowledge how Aristotle's *shi* might have been understood by the intended audience of the text.[18] Wardy suggests: "both these extremely common graphs [*shi* and *fei*] occur with either meaning [that is, true/right and false/wrong], the ethical sense is uppermost, and often a choice between them is difficult *or even ill-advised*" (97, emphasis added). In his monumental *The Discovery of Chinese Logic*, Kurtz (2011) writes in his introduction: "standards of right/true (*shi*) and wrong/false (*fei*) were discussed along all ideological divides" (3). However, when he cites the same passage from the *Minglitan* that Wardy cites, Kurtz (21) translates the clause that defines logic as[19]

> [guiding] humans in advancing their intellects, distinguishing between right [*shi* 是] and wrong [*fei* 非], preventing error and delusion, and leads them back on the path to the one and only Truth [真].

Perhaps the *Minglitan* can be considered as the point where the Aristotelian notion of true/false is "added" to the meaning of *shifei*.[20] However, the citations from Wardy and Kurtz show that a strict correspondence between *shifei* and Western logic is not at all obvious.[21]

Commentators are not always very careful in distinguishing between true/false and right/wrong, which may be taken as support for blurring the distinction between fact and value; hence, one may speak of value–fact or fact–value as each a single word (see §6b). In elucidating a passage from the *Lunheng*, Harbsmeier seems to have fused true and right, when he says concerning incompatible statements that they "could not at the same time be true, in the sense that if one was right (*shi*) the other had to be wrong (*fei*) and *vice versa*" (1998, 215).[22] However, elsewhere he uses "right/true" in the translation of a passage from the *Lunheng*,[23]

文不稱實，未可謂是也。(Lunheng 14.2.3)

When written statements do not correspond to reality, they cannot be called right/true [*shi*]. (Harbsmeier 1998, 195)

When introducing *shifei*, Kim Myeong-seok mentions "this" and "right," but not "true." However, he continues to claim that *shifei* involves a "judgment, rather than merely a feeling about the way things are, with full commitment to *truth*" (2014, 53–54, emphasis added). It seems that there is no consensus as to how to translate *shifei*. In most cases one might think that the translation is chosen on the basis of what "fits" the context that is created in English.

Some of the preceding observations are further supported in §7a when focusing on passages in the *Zhuangzi*. Each of the translations mentioned in this chapter would require separate discussion in view of both narrower and wider context. Often, *prima facie*, both true/false and right/wrong are possible translations. Many uses could mean either or both. Instead of translating *shifei* as right/wrong or true/false depending on the context or on the fancy of the translator, it is more appropriate to envisage *shifei* as a hybrid concept (as judged from the side of English), which cannot be completely captured by yes/no, this/not-this, assent/dissent, affirm/deny, (in)correct, true/false, right/wrong, (dis)approve, good/bad, and so on.

Chapter 4

Variations of the Meaning of *Shi*

Shi as Demonstrative

It is often said, correctly, that one of the most common translations of *shi* in classical Chinese is as a demonstrative, in particular if *shi* occurs at the beginning of an utterance. For example,[1]

是非必也。(canon A51)

That it is this or is not is necessary [is certain]. (G78, 300)

是非類與乎。(Hanshi waizhuan 2.2/5)

Is this not the same sort of thing? (Hightower, 40)

是非美。(canon B3)

It is not the case that this is beautiful. (G78, 354)

The use of *shi* as a demonstrative (including "it" and "such") may be quite hidden.

是非君子之道。(Mengzi 3B8)

Such is not the way of a good man. (Legge in CLT)

That was not the behavior of a true aristocrat. (Levy)[2]

子之歌詩，何故若是？(ZH 6.10.2)

What do you mean—singing a song like that! (Watson)

The verse you were singing, what did you mean by it? (Graham)

The evolvement of the meaning of shi can be summarized as follows: Shi started as a demonstrative in the Pre–Warring States Period. Later, the meaning of assent was added to it. The history of fei followed a somewhat different path before the Warring States Period: on oracle bones it means disapproval or disagreement; on bronze it signifies mistake or error as well (Ricci 2001).[3] That is to say, originally shi and fei were not used as a pair. Because fei was used in the same grammatical constructions for denial instead of assent, shi and fei "came to be regarded as opposites and were used in the sense of 'right' and 'wrong,' 'to call right' and 'to call wrong'" (Pulleybank 1995, 86).[4]

It has been argued that both ran 然 and shi 是 are originally demonstratives. Although shi and ran have been distinguished from each other on grammatical grounds, actual translations overlap. Recent literature does not always agree on the details of these grammatical differences concerning how shi and ran function.[5]

Most translators draw a distinction between shi and ran. Early on, Graham distinguishes between ran (so, like this) and shi (this, the thing said) (G78, 575, 577). But sometimes he renders ran as true (and shi as true as well), for example, ranhuzai 然乎哉？(ZH 2.6.4) "is this true" (of a loach, of a monkey)?[6] Graham considers that ran functions as a response to action, to a verb (riding a horse, climbing a tree), and shi functions as a response to a noun (being a white horse, being a stalk).[7] He also argues that the later Mohists made a distinction between nominal elements (terms) and verbal units (predicates), to which shi and ran apply respectively. According to Graham, this is the case with the Zhuangzi as well. Hansen partly agrees with Graham on this point (1985, 510n24). More recently, Sturgeon (2014, 20–23) makes the suggestion that ran and shi are two different ways of "being so": "ran: so, this way"; "shi: so, correct" (35). That is to say, he sometimes translates shi as "so."

Graham thus explains the difference between ci 此, shi, and ran in his translation of canon B2.[8]

此然是必然……(canon B2)

If what is so of the thing here is necessarily so of the thing it is judged to be . . . (G78, 120)

Ran is usually translated as "(is) so" or "such," but the translations "this" or "true" also occur;[9] *Shi* is usually translated as this or right, but "such" and "true" also occur. *Ran* is usually considered to be "more objective" than *shi*, and *shi* is sometimes identified as "regard as *shi*."

We believe that underdetermination and lack of consensus concerning the grammar of classical Chinese is the source of differing translations; Nevertheless, the (alleged) difference between *shi* and *ran* may be less than is generally assumed. That is to say, the standardized translations of (not-)so and (not-)right suggest more difference between *shi* and *ran* than is warranted.

Shi as Meaning both "This" and "Right"

In recent years, commentators have tended to offer "this" and "right" as the alternative or the "double meaning" of *shi*. Typographical conventions differ: "this/right" (Fraser 2015); "right/wrong, this/not-this" (Fraser 2011, 103); "this:right" (Hansen 1992, 104, 427); "*shi*/this:right:assent" (Hansen 1983b, 34); "this (or: right)" (Harbsmeier 1993, 12); "being this or not being it (/right or wrong)" (G78, 339); "contrast between, on the one hand, what is and what is right, and, on the other, what is not, and what is wrong" (Lloyd 2004, 59).[10] Unfortunately, authors have not clarified their respective motivations for their choice of notations, which may well indicate their different stances concerning the use and meaning of *shi* in the *Zhuangzi* and elsewhere.

The phrase "double meaning" may be itself an example of "double meaning" (*double entendre*). Does it imply that meaning depends on context (meaning either this or that)? Is it a "mix" of both meanings in each context? Or is it even ambiguous (from a modern perspective) in such a way that it cannot be resolved by referring to the context? According to Ziporyn, *shi* "means both 'this' and 'correct.'"[11] He writes,[12]

> The *double meaning* of "this" and "right" is key to Zhuangzi's argument in chapter 2. (2009a, 217, emphasis added)

He also writes,

> "wrong [*fei* 非]," both in the sense of untrue (of an assertion) and in the sense of morally objectionable (of an action). (2009b)

> Graham has ingeniously covered both senses of the term by rendering it into the somewhat cumbersome English phrase,

"That's it!" which implies both correctly identifying something as what someone intended to refer to, and the affirmation of correctness. (2009b)

In his translation of the *Zhuangzi*, Graham often uses "That's it; that's not it" as a translation of *shifei*. However, perhaps after having read the review of Graham (1981) by Ames (1983),[13] Ziporyn does not follow Graham in using the "somewhat cumbersome" phrase "That's it!" but instead sticks to the "received" right/wrong throughout his translation of the *Zhuangzi*.

Some commentators explicitly "fuse" this and right. Kim Myeong-seok writes, "[Zhuangzi] presents an interesting view that fuses *shi* 是 as an indexical (that is, 'this') and *shi* in the sense of 'right' (adjective) or 'to consider (something) as right'" (2014, 75n34). Intuitively, making this connection seems to be natural. As Hansen puts it succinctly: "Finding a *this* is finding the *right* thing" (1992, 126).

It remains somewhat unclear how Graham wants himself to be understood. He seems to be saying that *shifei* should not be understood as morally right/wrong: "when [*shifei* is] translated [as] 'right' and 'wrong' [; this is] not to be confused with the moral concept *yi* [義], the 'right' as the socially fitting" (G89, 495). Perhaps *shifei* should be understood as judging "right and wrong alternatives in *bian* 'argumentation'" (G78, 120–21). This seems to suggest that right/wrong should be taken in a non-moral sense. An example of using *shifei* in a non-moral sense of rightness is,

先日所用，今或棄之；今之所棄，後或用之。此用與不用，無定是非也。(Liezi 8.5/6)

The method we used yesterday we may discard today and use again in the future; there are no fixed right and wrong to decide whether we use it or not. (G60, 163)

If rightness is assumed to cover any normative rightness, then it includes being true as well. Judging something to be true is a normative judgment.[14] Epistemic virtues are usually understood as "leading to truth." Many translations of *shi* as right seem to take it as referring to socially appropriate or morally right action, which is often supported by the context (as seen from a modern perspective).[15] For example, Sturgeon (2014) remarks explicitly: "'*Shi* (是)' and '*fei* (非)' are ethically loaded terms" (20). Referring to Mengzi (2A6, 6A6), Roetz (1993, 86) claims: "*shi* and *fei* denote the 'right' and 'wrong' in the moral meaning that every man knows by virtue of this innate 'good knowledge.'" McLeod writes: "Non-moral statements cannot be 是 *shi*, just as moral principles cannot be 然 *ran*" (2011, 54).[16]

It seems that, without further explanation, "right" is often understood as "morally right." But "right" may also mean "correct" (which may or may not include "morally right"). While some commentators emphasize that *shifei* is morally loaded,[17] others distinguish *shi* 是 rightness from *yi* 義 rightness. There is no consensus in the Anglophone literature on how to understand the word "right" when it occurs in translations of *shifei*. We will use the English words "value" and "right(ness)" emphatically in the sense of *all kinds of* rightness and values. For example, scientific knowledge is relative to epistemic *values* such as consistency and faithfulness to the text. Therefore, we conclude that in interpreting *shifei*, we should think of a generic notion of rightness, which, as seen from a modern perspective, ranges across the rightness of facts and values as well as other uses of "right," including normative rightness that is not always moral rightness (see §6b).

Modifiers of *Shi*

In this section, we address a rather neglected issue. We show that most philosophers in the Warring States Period make an implicit demarcation between "everyday" *shifei* judgments and higher-order criteria of what we call "correctness" that are assumed to govern the *shifei*-ing in everyday *shifei* judgments. These higher-order standards can be found in *tian* 天, *dao*(s) 道, *qing* 情, the sage-kings, and so on. Characters such as *zhen* 真 and *zheng* 正 are occasionally used to point to these higher-order standards as well.

Zhen and *shi* are often clearly distinguished in terms of genuine and true.

故知眾瑞皆是，而鳳凰、騏驎皆真也。(Lunheng 16.4)

Hence we know that the omens are all true, and that phoenixes and unicorns are likewise all genuine. (Forke 1, 373)

Zhen on its own is sometimes translated as "the True" (capitalized).[18]

概塵垢之枉攘兮，除穢累而反真。(Chuci 14.1)

I have brushed away the dust and disorder, purged unclean attachments and returned to the True. (Hawkes, 267)

是謂反其真。(ZH 17.1.38)

This is what I mean by returning to the True.

However, most commonly, *zhen* is used as a modifier of *shi*. For example,[19]

此真是非也。(Huainanzi 11.27.4)

This is genuine [*zhen*] "right" and "wrong." (Liu An, 417)

彼无為謂真是也。(ZH 22.1.7/14)

Do-Nothing-Say-Nothing is the one who is truly right.

而義真是也。(ZH 29.2.1) Then righteous conduct is the real key.

而信真是。(ZH 29.2.2) Then trust is the real key.

In these phrases, *zhen* seems to point to a higher-order rightness, but it is also possible that it is used merely as emphasis. Double negation can also be used as emphasis of *shi*, and this kind of emphasis may be doubled or tripled. For example, Forke translated 無不然真是 as "absolutely true" (Forke 2, 240). Sometimes *zhenshi* is simply rendered as "true." On the other hand, when *zhen* is added to *shi*, it is sometimes unclear whether the translation "true" derives from *zhen* or from *shi*.

苟信一文，使夫真是幾滅不存，睹真是之傳。(Lunheng 16.1.1)

People lightly believe in this statement, and consider it as true, whereas the truth is nearly forgotten. (Forke 1, 454)

In all such situations, *zhen* as translated as true or genuine is ranked higher than the translation of *shi* as right (or true, etc.). A similar "higher standard" with respect to *shifei* is found in certain usages of *cheng*, *zheng*, *dang*, *qing*, *guo* 果, and other characters.

Chengshi 誠是 is quite common. It has been translated as "genuinely like this," "truly right," or more idiosyncratically "true and right."

己誠是也，人誠非也……(Xunzi 4.3.4)

Considering that he alone is truly right and others are truly wrong . . . (Knoblock 1, 187)

掩之，誠是也……(Mengzi 3A/5)

If [merely] covering them (i.e., the bodies of dead parents) were really right . . . (Pulleybank 1995, 86)[20]

傷誠是之不察兮。(Chuci 11.1/8)

It grieves me that what is true and right should not be examined. (Hawkes: 241)

Zheng occurs in a number of combinations.

彼正正者……(ZH 8.1.6). He who holds to True Rightness . . .

正是非。(Xunzi 16.4.3)

Putting aright matters of right and wrong. (Knoblock 2, 242)

正直者順道而行。(Hanshi waizhuan 7.21/1)

The correct and upright act in accordance with the True Way. (Hightower, 245)

行必正直。(Guanzi 59.1/1)

Their conduct is certain to be correct and straightforward. (Rickett 1998, 285)

正直為正。(Zuozhuan 9.7.6/3)

The rectification of one's self is real rectitude. (Legge 1869, 432)

The most convincing example of *zheng* being used as a "standard" for *shifei* judgments is perhaps the following passage from the *Xunzi*.

無隆正則是非……天下之大隆是非之封界。(Xunzi 18.9.1)

If there are no such high standards of correctness then truth and falsity cannot be separated. . . . The highest standards are those that establish the boundary between truth and falsity. (Knoblock 3, 46)

Various other combinations also occur. For example,[21]

> 聖人也者……當是非。(Xunzi 8.11.1)
>
> A sage . . . is absolutely accurate in regard to right and wrong. (Knoblock 2, 81)
>
> 誰使正其真是兮。(Chuci 13.3/2)
>
> Who can any longer tell what the truth was? (Hawkes, 250)
>
> 苟信是…… (Guanzi 11.15/5)
>
> If a [prince] believes that he is [always] right . . . (Rickett 1985, 206)
>
> 是信情乎。(ZH 17.1.14) Is this a true statement? (Watson)
>
> 果是 (Lunheng 9.12.3) accord with reality; proved true (Forke 1, 179)

These examples suggest that no matter how *shi* or *shifei* is translated, it always refers to local standards for evaluative judgments, which are subject to higher-order distinctions or criteria. The higher-order standard can be associated with *zhen*, *zheng*, *qing*, and other modifiers. The Ruists may invoke their own "higher standards."

> 俄而原仁義分是非。(Xunzi 8.4.3)
>
> Yet suddenly I might find the wellspring of humanity and justice and so be able to divide right from wrong. (Knoblock 2, 73)

Elsewhere in the *Xunzi*, *shifei*, and *ranburan* are contrasted as subsidiaries of *qing*.

> ……不卹是非然不然之情 (Xunzi 8.3.3; cf. 23.8.3)
>
> . . . in being indifferent to the real nature [*qing*] of truth and falsity [*shifei*] and the true nature of what is the case and what is not [*ranburan*] (Knoblock 2, 71)

After having cited Aristotle's *Metaphysica* 1051b2–5,²² Harbsmeier wonders: "The question is whether we have statements of this sort in ancient China. We do" (1998, 194). He cites Xunzi for support.²³

是謂是，非謂非曰直。(Xunzi 2.3.2)

We call it "being straightforward" to declare something "this (or: right)" if it is this (or: right), and to declare something "not-this (or: wrong)" if it is not-this (or: wrong). (Knoblock 1, 153)

However, given the "important contrasts" (194) between Aristotle and Xunzi's formulations, Harbsmeier's conclusion that their statements are of the same sort does not seem to be convincing. As Harbsmeier himself points out, Aristotle focuses on "being in accordance with the truth [*aletheia*]," whereas Xunzi focuses on "being straight [*zhi* 直], telling the truth, getting things straight" (194). In the citation from the *Xunzi*, *zhi* seems to be used to point to a higher-order standard.

A somewhat different example of a possible higher-level evaluation can be found in McLeod (2011; 2015; 2016, 152–64), who argues that in the *Lunheng* by Wang Chong, *shi* 實 and *xu* 虛 are higher-order concepts, but not *ran* and *fou* or *shi* and *fei*.²⁴

The characters *shi* 實 and *xu* 虛 have been translated in a variety of ways.²⁵ According to McLeod, *shi* 實 is what makes a statement (*yan* 言) either *shi* 是 or *ran* 然. He suggests that Wang Chong distinguished *shi* 實-making properties of moral statements from *shi* 實-making properties of nonmoral statements, that is, *shifei* and *ranfou*, respectively (2011, 53). They are the *same* way of exemplifying *shi* 實, the "general truth property" (2015, 172), which is itself an evaluative term that is fundamentally open.²⁶

However, there can be alternative ways of explaining the function of *shixu*. Perhaps such concrete notions can be interpreted as a "model" (metaphor, analogy) of more abstract concepts. Similarly, abstract binomes such as *shifei* can be drawn into comparison with concrete binomes, which are often taken from the practice of using tools such as the marking line. For example, the expression *quzhi* 曲直 (crookedness versus uprightness or straightforwardness) is perhaps used as an "explanation" of *shifei* in the following passage:²⁷

然而猶有能分是非、治曲直者邪？若夫非分是非，非治曲直……(Xunzi 21.9.6)

> This being so, although they have ability, could they properly separate the right from the wrong or determine what is straight and what crooked? If they cannot separate things as right and wrong, cannot determine what is straight and what crooked . . . (Knoblock 3, 111; cf. 2, 155)

In this section, we have shown that there are a large variety of higher-order modifiers of *shi* (and *fei*). Different scholars may use different notions (characters) as higher-order modifiers. In §9d we will see that Zhuangzi is an exception insofar as he tries to avoid considering a higher-order standard for *shifei* judgments.

Chapter 5

Dissolution of Dichotomies of Fact/Value and Reason/Emotion

Are There Dichotomies in Classical Chinese?

In this chapter, we argue that we should give up the "universal" fact/value dichotomy with respect not only to classical Chinese texts but also with regard to Western philosophy. In the same vein, the "metaphysical" distinction between factual truth and moral rightness, which has been prevalent in the Western tradition in recent centuries, should be dissolved. This also holds for other dichotomies. To achieve this goal, we first discuss the relevant work by the American pragmatists Hilary Putnam and Nelson Goodman in this and the next chapter.[1]

We reserve the word "dichotomy" for the division of the whole of reality into exactly two well-defined and non-overlapping parts, as formulated in Western metaphysics. Primarily we are concerned with the fact/value dichotomy because of its association with *shifei*, which is translated sometimes as true/false and sometimes as right/wrong.[2] We also briefly touch on the reason/emotion dichotomy (because *shifei* sometimes occurs as one of the components of *qing* 情).

All languages have opposite terms such as dark/light and high/low. Most of the time they can be considered quasi-universals.[3] In addition, all languages employ something like indexicals, that is, those words whose meanings depends on the location of the speaker, such as "this" and "that." Such contrasting "binaries" are not dichotomies.

Quite a few sinologists have been cited as opposing "such dichotomies as fact/value, moral/aesthetic, rationality/spontaneity, absolutism/relativism"

(G89, 320).⁴ Rosemont (1992, 34) cites from the index of Graham's *Disputers of the Tao* and remarks,⁵

> Under "fact" we find "fact/value dichotomy; its absence in classical Chinese thought." Under "ought" we find "ought and is; no word comparable with 'ought' distinguishing prescriptive utterance in classical period."

Examples of dichotomies "denied" to (classical) Chinese include: description/prescription, thinking/acting, nature/culture, fact/value, reason/intuition, competition/cooperation, individualism/collectivism, resistance/accommodation, denotation/connotation, subject/object. Sometimes Western dichotomies are replaced by Chinese indigenous "dichotomies." For example, Hansen "replaces" the fact/value dichotomy with (in)constant and (un)conventional (1992, 127).

Probably the vast majority of contemporary sinologists and Chinese philosophers would agree that dichotomies such as fact/value or reason/emotion are not "present" in classical Chinese, or are only present in a "weak form" (whatever this phrase may mean).⁶ However, a few scholars take a different view. According to Nivison, the fact/value dichotomy "is natural to most of us" (1991, 140).

Our focus in this section falls on scholars who assume a fact/value dichotomy in their meta-language, relative to which the "ambiguity" of classical Chinese is reported. That is to say, when doubt concerning the "presence" of dichotomies in Chinese is raised, such a view is stated with the assumption of metaphysical dichotomies such as fact/value in the meta-language the interpreter uses. We also address the question as to whether the fact/value dichotomy is actually an indisputable feature of modern thinking (see §5b).

Consider some of the following common ways of indicating "absence" of a fact/value dichotomy in classical Chinese (emphasis added):

> Talk of *shi–fei* distinctions tends to *mix* descriptive and normative issues. (Fraser 2012, 355)

> They are working with a more fundamental notion of correct distinction drawing that *covers both*. They tend to assume the two *coincide*. (Fraser 2012, 358)⁷

> . . . collapsed the distinction between the normative and the descriptive. (McLeod 2016, 66)

> Ethical norms are derived directly from this *fusion* of "is" and "ought." (Ziporyn 2013, 24; cf. 23, 37; 2008, 5)

> The *isness* of anything and the *oughtness of the thing* are everywhere and always *conjoined*. (Berthrong 2011, 85, concerning Confucianism)

> There is a true nature of things for Zhuangzi that *involves* both facts and values. (Kjellberg 2007, 288)

Furthermore, consider the following:

> It may be that the two related but *distinct* senses of the word may to some extent *impinge* upon one another and potentially shape discourse about *shi-fei*. (Sturgeon 2014, 22, emphasis added)[8]

Speaking of two distinct senses is how it may look from a modern perspective. Saying that *shi* can mean either "this" *or* "correct" may be wrong if *shi* should only have *one* meaning. It is not self-evident that the *classical Chinese* word has two senses.

One can see that commentators speak of the mixing, collapsing, fusing, conjoining, coinciding, impinging of factual *and* normative issues.[9] Our concern is not with the occurrence of the words fact and value in the (contemporary) meta-language of these scholars, but that such wording assumes that these concepts were already there, and that the pre-Qin scholars fuse or mix these concepts. If these concepts were not there, one could not fuse or mix them. Such wording also suggests, perhaps not intended by the writer, that *classical Chinese scholars* should be able to consider *fact* and *value* inseparable. There is nothing wrong with using the words *fact* and *value* and presupposing the understanding of the dichotomy *in contemporary philosophical discourse*. However, these words are neither acceptable as quasi-universals, nor needed to interpret classical sources. That is to say, there just exist no counterparts of these words in classical Chinese terms.

These hidden projections of Western conceptual schemes are exacerbated when the fact/value dichotomy figures in translations. Consider,

> The Li [理] of a thing is both "what makes it so" (所以然之理 *suoyiran zhi li*) and "how it should be" (當然之理 *dangran zhi li*). (Ziporyn 2013, 23f)

Translating *dangran* is difficult, but it may be better not to use the word "should." *Suoyiran* can be translated as "the reason for this," which avoids commitment to an is/ought dichotomy.

Consider, finally, the translation of part of 2.6.4 from the *Zhuangzi*.[10]

四者孰知正味？

Of these four, which knows how food ought to taste? (Watson)

Which of the four has a proper sense of taste? (Graham; similarly, Eno)

Among these four, who knows the right taste? (Feng Youlan; similarly Chan Wing-tsit, Lin Yutang, Kjellberg)

Of these four, which "knows" the right thing to eat? (Ziporyn; similarly, Mair)

There is no basis in the Chinese original to introduce the English word "ought," as Watson does (all the other translators have not done so).[11]

In support of his view that the Chinese philosophical tradition "dissolves what we would call the fact/value dichotomy into a matter of degree of constancy and naturalness" (1992, 128),[12] Hansen draws attention to an interesting passage from the *Mozi*.[13]

今王公大人之政也，或殺人，其國家禁之，此蚤越有能多殺其鄰國之人，因以為文義，此豈有異蕡白黑、甘苦之別者哉？ (Mozi 7.3 or 28.7)

Now the kings, dukes, and great men in their exercise of government forbid, with battle-axes and halberds, anyone from killing a person within their state. But they call those in neighboring states capable of killing many people very righteousness. How is this different from obscuring the difference between black and white or the difference between sweet and bitter? (Hansen 1992, 128)

Mozi's text should *not* be understood as lending support for the analogy of moral and factual judgments. The text shows that this distinction simply does not (or rather, cannot) arise. From a Western perspective, particular *shifei* judgments may seem to be more subjective or more objective depending on whether they concern the so-called values or facts. But in Chinese there is just one thing: *shifei* judgments of some situation (which some Western discourses may label as either prescriptive or descriptive).

Now we turn briefly to another dichotomy. In interpreting words such as *xin* 心 and *qing* 情 in classical Chinese texts, relevant scholars take it for granted that they echo the rather recent Western dichotomy of reason and emotion. Consider the following passage in which Zhang Dainian cites Zhu Xi 朱熹 (1130–1200), who defines *qing* 情 as:

恻隐、羞恶、辞让、是非，情也。(Zhang Dainian 1989, 197)

Compassion, shame, yielding, distinguishing right and wrong are emotions. (Zhang Dainian 2002, 387)[14]

Zhu Xi borrows his list of four "germs" from Mengzi, where the Chinese words that Zhang Dainian considers as "emotion" words are mentioned as the germ (*duan* 端) of benevolence–humanity (*ren* 仁), righteousness (*yi* 義), rites–decorum–propriety (*li* 禮), and wisdom (*zhi* 智), respectively.[15]

Zhang Dainian comments: "Zhu Xi could not avoid, particularly in the fourth case [that is, *shifei* judgments], confusing the rational and the emotional spheres" (387).[16] Zhang seems to assume that the list of 情 *qing* is a list of (Western) emotions. This gives rise to his criticism that Zhu Xi was confused. Such adjudication is derived from the presumption that Western conceptual schemes are universal, and sources that do not comply with Western standards are simply wrong or confused.

As in the case of *shifei*, many commentators who take the view that the reason/emotion dichotomy cannot be found in classical Chinese nevertheless retain this dichotomy in their meta-language. For example, Fraser (2011, 104, emphasis added) says,

For the *Zhuangzi*, there is probably no strict distinction between cognitive, evaluative, and affective attitudes. . . . Emotions are *intertwined with* and grounded in cognitive judgments.

The view expressed in the citation seems to belong in the margin of cognitive science, which focuses on a universal theory of "the mind." Similarly, Marchal (2013, 204) says: "Confucians don't draw a clear distinction between reason and emotion." If such distinctions, let alone dichotomies, do not exist in (or behind) classical Chinese texts, then it does not make sense to claim that Chinese philosophers fuse or confuse these alleged distinctions.

In order to get beyond the discourse of exclusionary contrasting terms, it is necessary to raise the question of whether such dichotomies as fact/value are justified in the Western discourse. We now turn to this issue.

Fact/Value Dichotomy in Western Philosophy

In the previous section, we have seen that, although students of Chinese philosophy tend to acknowledge that the well-known Western dichotomies such as descriptive/evaluative (fact/value) do not inform the classical texts, they still tend to retain these dichotomies as part of the modern meta-discourse of the investigator. In this section, we discuss Hilary Putnam's arguments that aim to undermine the fact/value dichotomy.

The assumption of a clear-cut distinction between facts and values is commonplace in modern thinking (philosophy, sciences, humanities, ordinary language). Just like other "traditional" dichotomies such as objective/subjective or cognitive/affective, the fact/value dichotomy has a firm grip on intellectual and academic discourse. However, the so-called American pragmatists have radically undermined the fact/value dichotomy. Therefore, it should not be taken for granted that such dichotomies still dominate all areas of current Western discourse. Concerning this issue, the classical Chinese tradition can be invoked as support for pragmatism (and vice versa).

In recent decades, Putnam has written at length arguing that scientific "facts" depend on values (such values are called epistemic virtues or values), that defining the rational is as difficult as defining the moral, that *both* facts *and* values satisfy human needs. Putnam does not claim that there is *nothing* that warrants speaking of facts, on the one hand, and values, on the other. What is wrong is the essentialization of this (metaphysical) distinction. It is an artifact of Western history of ideas, which has led to the situation where the only rationality left is instrumental rationality. There are many other philosophers who have raised questions about the fact/value dichotomy, in particular in the pragmatist tradition. Putnam reminds us that Dewey has already drawn a distinction between "ordinary" distinctions and metaphysical dichotomies.[17]

The fact/value dichotomy is part of what may be called the absolute dichotomy. One of the clearest defenses of the absolute dichotomy is Williams's bipartition of the (universal) "we" of science and logic and the parochial "us" worrying about moral matters. Related dichotomies are the empirical/transcendental dichotomy, Kant's distinction between "the laws of the intellect" and "the laws of our actions," Nagel's distinction between the objective and the subjective, and Sellars's distinction of the manifest and the scientific image. On the other hand, Sellars's scientific image corresponds to Eddington's viewpoint of no one in particular, to Nagel's view from nowhere, and to Williams's absolute conception of the universe, that is, a conception of the world as it is independently of our inquiries or experiences. Nagel's view from nowhere is the view in which facts are sharply distinguished from "the laws of our actions."[18]

We shall briefly review Putnam's very detailed and explicit arguments undermining the fact/value dichotomy, though focusing on the philosophy of science. Science ("facts") and ethics ("values") is probably the most dominant dichotomy that has motivated Western thinking to be committed to the absolute belief in the fact/value dichotomy. Putnam's arguments can be structured in terms of five observations.[19]

First, the rules that are used to establish the (scientific or other) facts are values; epistemic virtues are also values. To say that truth is the goal of scientific or philosophical inquiry is a normative judgment. The activity of justifying factual claims presupposes value judgments (which must be regarded as right). "Value judgments are essential to the practice of science itself" (2002, 135).

Second, to justify what is the best conception of rationality is as difficult as to justify what the best ethical system is. Rationality transcends what can be said about it (Putnam 1988). The idea that there is a sole scientific method (which establishes the facts) has been cast away (Lacey 1999, 216–23). Various attempts to make a clear distinction between epistemic, pragmatic, moral, and other norms of evaluation and justification of values have failed. Many non-descriptive statements are objective in the sense of "under rational control."

Third, in practice, facts and values cannot be kept apart. The same applies to the distinction between rationally-acceptable and interest-relevant. One cannot place oneself outside one's tradition: "the cat sits on the mat" is a "fact,"[20] but it presupposes the relevance of *particular* classifications. All truths, norms, and values are on a par in having to show their possibility to function in practice. There are no descriptive sentences that are true for *everyone*, while it is not true that there is *always* less controversy about facts than about values. Ethics and science are as entangled as value and fact are; "evaluation and description are interwoven and interdependent" (Putnam 2002, 3).[21] A word such as "cruel" allows itself to be used sometimes for a normative purpose, sometimes as a descriptive term, and sometimes both simultaneously. Here, the fact/value dichotomy collapses. The same is true of crime, rude, and other "thick" ethical concepts, and even of the taste of chocolate (which is both subjective *and* objective).[22]

Fourth, people are too realistic about physics and too subjectivist about what cannot be reduced to physics. Should all meaningful languages be similar to the language of physics? If values are subjective, then the following should be subjective as well: color (perception), counterfactuals, causality, talk of reference, and much more. Values are not reducible to sentiments (such as approval and disapproval),[23] desires, utility, or happiness.

Fifth, facts *and* values both satisfy human needs. People *do* find something reasonable, disgusting, good, bad, and so on. On the other hand, scientists do *not* agree on the best model for the universe. Putnam points out that the idea of a future only makes sense if many of one's factual *and* moral beliefs are true. Neither for facts nor for values are there absolute foundations. In both cases, one appeals to the authority of a continuing human community.[24] In addition, to understand what other people say is in the first place a moral matter, as there is always an implicit appeal to a community.[25]

Finally, to put it in Putnam's own words, "The fact that there are many kinds of value judgment that are not themselves of an ethical (or 'moral') variety tends to get sidelined in philosophical discussions of the relation between (so-called) values and (so-called) facts" (2002, 19).

Putnam argues that what went wrong in the history of Western philosophy is that rationality (in the sense of criteria for truth, objectivity, and good reasons) separated itself from ideas of the good. The fact/value dichotomy is a product of the Enlightenment and has been raised to its present dominant status by empiricism and logical positivism. According to Putnam, all values (including facts) are founded in what the Greeks called *eudaimonia* (which means happiness, well-being, the idea of the Good, "having the right reasons and preferences").[26]

The strict distinction between facts and values is no longer as plausible as it once seemed. Facts and values, rationality and morality are warp and weft to one another. Factual and normative, epistemic and moral-political aspects cannot be separated. Putnam asks: Why could we not have a reasoned (and reasonable) discourse concerning both cognitive and social values and give up the distinction as a general dichotomy? He concludes that the fact/value dichotomy distorts and impoverishes our thought.

Chapter 6

Rightness and Fitting

Nelson Goodman on Rightness and Fitting

In this section, we first discuss Nelson Goodman's arguments to the effect that the applicability of "truth" is severely limited and that we should replace "knowledge" with "understanding." Instead of focusing on "truth," Goodman proposes a generic notion of rightness or correctness, to be understood in terms of working and fitting. Thus, truth becomes a subsidiary notion relative to rightness. We extend Goodman's proposals (which are restricted to the Western tradition) to the cross-cultural situation and suggest that (generic) rightness is a matter of "fitting." We claim that there is a close family resemblance between fitting as understood by Goodman and the Chinese notion of yi 宜, which is often translated as appropriate.[1] Putnam argues that facts and values are intertwined. This is similar to Goodman's contention that all conventions depend on fact, yet all facts are conventions. "Facts, after all, are obviously factitious" (Goodman 1978, 93). The scientist "as much decrees as discovers the laws he sets forth, as much designs as discerns the patterns he delineates" (18).[2]

As Putnam points out, facts are subsidiary to values because there can only be facts *given* that there are concepts and epistemic virtues.[3] This is rather similar to Goodman's argument that truth is subsidiary to rightness except that Goodman uses a provocative discourse in terms of making worlds. According to Goodman, two contradictory statements cannot be both true in the same world, but each can be true in a different world. The question of whether the earth is moving or not is one of his favorite examples. There seem to be two conflicting versions: the scientific version according to which the earth moves (around the sun), and the manifest version according to which the earth is at rest (and the sun rises every day). Goodman's first step is to say that both ways of thinking are appropriate–right. The apparent contradiction (the earth is and is not moving) does not imply that one version has to go. This has nothing to do with relativism. Surely, we cannot let the earth move in any way we like. It is also wrong to say: "the earth is at rest" was true long ago and now "the earth is moving" is true. *Both* versions are true, but each is true for *different worlds*. A true version is true in some worlds, but in no world is a false version true. Which world is the right one does not depend on one being true and the other not, but on fitting into the context of use that brings a version (and a world) with it.[4]

For Goodman, "everything" is made: scientific theories, interpretations of classical texts, artworks. A right work of art makes a world (for example, a painting by Paul Klee or the causeway in West Lake designed by Su Shi 蘇軾 [also called Su Dongpo 蘇東坡]),[5] just as a good interpretation of a text (for example, the *Qiwulun*) or a scientific theory (for example, quantum mechanics) makes a world. Artwork, interpretation, and theory offer the possibility of new worlds. Even stars are made.[6] How is this possible? Stars have been around long before there were any human beings. Of course, Goodman agrees with the last statement: stars have been made by a version that situates itself later in time than the stars. Look at the sky in a clear night at the place where one sees a particular star, ★. Write down what you see, call this version A. Look in an astronomy book to see what it says about ★, call this version W. According to W, the star ★ doesn't exist anymore, but its light will reach the earth until at least the year 3000. Version W, which has become available only recently, situates the existence of ★ in the past, but in version A, ★ is still shining. Both A and W are equally objective or equally "irrealistic" (Goodman's word)—such philosophical labels are of no significance.

In principle, there is no difference between making a work of art and making a scientific theory, or, for that matter, making concepts, interpretations, conventions, facts, and so on. Hence, there is no difference between things made and interpretations; interpretations are simply more things made. Making new (world) versions is difficult, because the only thing we have is the scrapyard of old versions. Worlds are relative to versions, but that does not mean that any version would do.

Putnam argues that "being (not) true" is equally applicable to factual and evaluative utterances. Goodman does not disagree, but he would add that truth has a limited area of applicability. A more generic notion is rightness. "Truth is often inapplicable, is seldom sufficient, and must sometimes give way to competing criteria . . . The whole truth is too vast, variable, and clogged with trivia" (Goodman 1978, 107; 19). Much of knowing aims at something other than true. The truth alone would not be enough; even for true versions, rightness may matter more. For example: The officer ordered the soldier to shoot the prisoners if they were to move. As soon as the officer had finished giving the order, the soldier shot all the prisoners. When asked to justify his action, the soldier said that all prisoners were moving around the sun at high speed. His statement is true but not right on that occasion.[7]

How can a version be wrong about a world it makes? "We must obviously look for truth or rightness not in the relation of a version to something outside that it refers to but in characteristics of the version itself and its relations to other versions" (Goodman 1984, 37). There are many situations where we can speak of rightness but not of truth. For example, with respect to demands and queries, orders, validity of (deductive, inductive, abductive) inferences, categorizations, all kinds of interpretations, samples, exemplifications, analogies, maps, illustrations, paintings, musical scores and performances, poems, pictures, diagrams, designs, as well as all kinds of "experiments," in short, wherever "symbols" are used (Goodman and Elgin 1988, 155–56). "Right" and "wrong" apply to symbols of all kinds, verbal and nonverbal. Arguments to the effect of ascribing a particular conceptual scheme to authors or texts in another tradition cannot be based on its being true, since a conceptual scheme has no truth value. Instead, the efficacy of a conceptual scheme in worldmaking and understanding should be taken into account.[8]

Goodman's position can be considered as a specimen of relativism. This is most apparent from Elgin's exposition. Consider the following (emphasis added):[9]

> The right facts—ones that are *relevant*, apt, and suited to our purposes . . . (Elgin 2007, 12)

> Our antecedent *relevant* commitments, when assessed by currently acceptable standards of *relevance* and reasonableness. (15)

And also:

> We need to deploy *appropriate* categories. (12)

Asking what is relevant or appropriate and what not reveals the relativism hidden in these words.

Elgin acknowledges the need for "commitments about second-order matters such as the trustworthiness of methods" (17). Toward the end of her paper, she adds a universalistic claim.

> The categorical imperative and the principle of utility are universal in scope. (21)

One can see the same "secret" appeal to relevance among sinologists, for example, Callahan makes such claim (1998, emphasis added):[10]

> . . . to see the situation from the *relevant* perspectives. (183)

> A situation can have a myriad of *relevant* distinctions. (185)

> In this way we can assume all the *relevant* perspectives from which the *shi* and *fei* of the situation were distinguished. (190)

Similarly, the use of words like "efficacious" and "appropriate" presupposes the notion of relevance, as in the following citations (emphasis added):

> The sage's mind is mature and his thinking *efficacious*. (Hansen 1992, 373)

> Zhuangist criteria for harmonious, *efficacious* dào-following . . . the ability to adapt fluidly, creatively, and *efficaciously* to changing conditions, such that we can spontaneously find *effective* paths to follow in our activity. (Fraser 2014, 562, 556)

> The structure of any given situation determines the *shi/fei* distinctions (*bian*) needed to *efficaciously* (*de* 德) navigate it. (Williams 2017b, 6; cf. 2017a, passim)

> The sage hits in any particular situation on that single course which is uniquely *appropriate* yet fits no rules. (G89, 188)

According to Goodman and Elgin, in order to avoid the accusation of relativism (and hence be irrelevant), comparative and Chinese philosophy should focus on understanding, not on concern with knowledge and truth, which have only limited application and results in a *reductio ad absurdum* (that is to say: relativism is self-refuting). Goodman follows Peirce in "replacing" knowledge by understanding.[11] According to Goodman, understanding means abilities to inquire and invent, to discriminate and discover, to connect and clarify, to order and organize, to adopt or reject. Understanding can also mean the processes of using such skills for making and remaking worlds. This would be a Goodmanian description of the practice of comparative and Chinese philosophy.

In the Western tradition, one can say that truth is a subsidiary of rightness. In the Chinese tradition, there are no clearly recognizable subdivisions of generic rightness. It seems more plausible to say that there we find interrelated clusters without a hierarchical structure, and different writers may select different characters (words) to fulfill a more generic role (cf. §4c and §7e).

So, we are left with the commonsense notion of rightness concerning the descriptive and prescriptive and concerning the rightness of moral and non-moral evaluative judgments. What then is the basis for a version being right if there is nothing except versions? What are the criteria for rightness? Goodman replies: We *make* rightness.[12] Rightness is primarily a matter of fit, a matter of fitting together (ranging from concrete fitting in space-time and metaphorical extensions of conceptually fitting), which in the end is rooted in traditions. Goodman writes,

> Rightness is a matter of fitting and working. . . . A fitting *into* a context or discourse or standing complex of other symbols. . . . What counts is not so much the working of what is fitted in as the working of the resultant whole. . . . The working is also a kind of fitting—fitting into a going operation or process or endeavor. Moreover, even what constitutes fitting and working may undergo change, may itself have to be adjusted in order to fit and work. (Goodman and Elgin 1988, 158–59)

Criteria for rightness (fitting and working) are similar to epistemic virtues. Goodman lists the following "attractive" virtues of a version (theory, interpretation, and so on): fitting in with the rest of knowledge and understanding in a tradition, increasing understanding of all versions (that is, theories, interpretations, and stories), structural coherence, initial credibility, future value, usefulness, relevance, informativity, and simplicity. Note that something like "correspondence with facts" is conspicuously missing. Goodman's "final" word is (McCormick 1996: 207), "What is sought is not a simple overall definition of rightness, but a pluralistic treatment that allow rightness to have species, to vary with context, and sometimes to be graded or comparative."

In the next section, we suggest that Goodman's notion of rightness in the sense of fitting offers a suitable quasi-universal for *shi* 是.

Setting up the Quasi-universal of *Yi* 宜 and Fitting

We choose *yi* 宜 as the counterpart to the Goodmanian notion of fitting (*dang* 當 can be an alternative).[13] The scope of *yi*/fit covers what in English may be called being true, being right, being correct, being appropriate, and other similar cases of "fitting." It also includes "it is this," "approve it," and "affirm it," because "it" fits. The commonsense family resemblance of "fitting" across traditions can make a much stronger claim to the validity of cross-cultural quasi-universality than the rather "provincial" notion of truth (this is even more so when truth is understood as semantic truth).

We suggest that one should not focus on a single all-purpose functional translation of *shifei* in English. *Shi* 是 should not be understood as *either* true *or* right *or* whatever, but as a more generic notion of rightness or correctness in the sense of "fitting." *Shi* implies fitting (*yi* 宜), *fei* implies not fitting (fitting or not fitting the circumstances, the situation, the rules of proper behavior, the tradition, and so on).

We suggest that Goodman's concept of rightness could be a suitable model for constructing and interpreting a generic notion of (pre-philosophical) rightness or correctness (understood in terms of fitting).[14] This notion covers epistemic, moral, and other kinds of normative rightness, including the rightness of "fitting the facts" (fitting experience, "saving the phenomena"). In Chinese, *yi* 宜 can be a useful translation of the Goodmanian notion of fitting; that is to say: *yi* 宜 shows similarities with fitting as judged from the perspective of English conceptual schemes; fitting shows similarities with *yi* 宜 as judged from the perspective of Chinese conceptual schemes.[15] Fitting can serve as a philosophically unloaded quasi-universal.[16] In Chinese, *yi* 宜 could fulfill this role. Hence: {*yi* 宜 ⇔ fitting}.

Yi 宜 often occurs in classical texts. The most common translations include: fitting, appropriate, and proper. It can be said of words, place, time, custom, tool, use, government, law, regulation, offering, carriage, business, person, name, occupation, debate, response, demeanor, and so on. It refers to something fitting the situation or circumstances, whether physical or social. The expression *buyiyihu* 不亦宜乎 regularly occurs in many sources.[17] It is often translated as either "is it not right?" or as "is that not fitting?"

As Goodman also stresses, what fits is not something timeless and objective, but *yi*/fitting points to the flexible judgments that fit ever-changing situations, which is described in terms of all the aspects that may cause situations to differ.[18] Hence, *yi* 宜 contrasts with the exact and the necessary (as in the *Canons* [G78, 571]). The word "circumstances" is often used in the translations specifying *yi* 宜.

君王宜。(Shiji 97.10.7) It is proper under such circumstances. (Watson)

……審權勢之宜。(Shiji 6.58.8)

[The gentleman] perceives what is fitting in the light of circumstances. (Watson)

……宜次之……(Liji 10.1/7)

... their appropriateness to circumstances ... (Legge 1961)

曲因其當。(Huainanzi 1.15.13)

He [the *shengren* 聖人] does in every way what is fitting to the circumstances. (Harbsmeier in TLS)

As Graham recalls: *yi* 義 ("rightness") is often explained in terms of *yi* 宜.[19] In early Chinese texts, *yi* 義 and *yi* 宜 are often used interchangeably.[20] The *Zhongyong* 中庸 states explicitly: 義者宜也, "righteousness is (the accordance of actions with) what is right."[21] This statement was often repeated and embellished by other scholars.[22]

義者，宜也。(Baihutong 30.195.2)

Yì "sense of the correct principles" means yí "proper." (Tjan Tjoe Som, 565)

義者，各處其宜也。(Guanzi 36.1/35)

"Duty" refers to doing what is appropriate in each situation. (Rickett 1998, 77)

義者，謂其宜也，宜而為之。(Hanfeizi 20.4.2)

"Moral Principle" refers to this appropriateness. Regarding something as appropriate one does it. (Harbsmeier in TLS)

The *Shiming* 釋名 states the purpose of *yi* 義 as[23]

……義，宜也。裁制事物，使合宜也。(Shiming, "Shiyanyu" 釋言語)

. . . to divide and regulate things and events so as to make them accord with one another.

The relation between the two *yi*'s, on the one hand, and right and fitting, on the other, is rendered somewhat differently by different commentators, but they are always using the terminology of fitting or appropriate. When the two *yi*'s need be distinguished, the translations "righteousness" and "fitting" are used respectively.

We think that the two *yi*'s are not as different as is often assumed. Ames writes: "The subjective and objective are inseparable aspects of 'knowing our way around' (*dao*) that in coalescing culminate on the objective side in what is optimally fitting (*yi* 宜), and on the subjective side in what is morally appropriate (*yi* 義)" (Ames 2015, 102). However, we do not think that it is a good idea to assign *yi* 義 and *yi* 宜 to two sides of an objective/subjective split. Karlgren's glosses suggest that both *yi*'s have a prescriptive and descriptive aspect.[24]

Among the many meanings of *yi* 義 and *yi* 宜, the *Grand Ricci* lists the possible translation *approprié* for both of them. The connotation of both *yi*'s includes the notion of appropriateness. What fits is appropriate. Hence, it is right.

Yi 宜, when translated as fitting, appropriate, or proper, usually refers to a type of social or moral situation.

……父子之宜。(ZH 25.1.8)

. . . proper relationship between father and son.

其霸也宜哉。(Xunzi 7.1.5)

That he became lord–protector was altogether fitting and proper. (Knoblock 2, 58)

國亡宜矣。(Hanfeizi 19.5.4)

No wonder their states are doomed to ruin. (Liao 1939, 163)

It is only right and proper that their states should be ruined. (Harbsmeier in TLS)

然則為鄭伯者宜奈何。(Guliang zhuan 1.1/14)

Since this is so, what course of action would have been proper for the earl of Jenq? (Malmqvist 1971, 70)

However, when translated as fitting, yi 宜 may as well refer to the facts of the situation. For example, with reference to the suitability of soil (for various crops, etc.).

觀地宜。(Guanzi 4.7/3; Liji 10.1.4)

Observe the suitability of land [for certain crops]. (Rickett 1985, 107)

Each soil [has] its appropriate produce. (Legge 1961)

察於土地之宜……(Hanfeizi 37.13.5)

[If] the qualities of the soil are examined . . . (Liao 1959, 168)

If one clearly understands what is appropriate for the soils, . . . (Harbsmeier in TLS)

Ziporyn's sophisticated interpretation of li 理 as a "second-order coherence between found coherence in the world and coherent clusters of human evaluation" (2013, 27–28) may be seen as a possible theoretical background for yi/fitting because "coherence" can be considered as a kind of (appropriate) fitting.

We conclude that fitting/yi 宜 is the most suitable quasi-universal to cover notions that in English is indicated with words such as true (truth), right(ness), correct, and, of course, fitting, and that in Chinese is indicated with words such as dang 当, shi 是, zhong 中, yi 儀, ke 可, fu 符, and, of course, yi 宜.

Chapter 7

Shi and Its Opposites and Modifiers in the *Qiwulun* 齊物論

Non-English Translations of *Shifei*

In chapter 3 we looked at a great variety of renditions of *shifei* in the Warring States texts. While the existing translations tend to exhibit a bifurcation between right and true (thus entailing the fact/value dichotomy), *shi* is not implicated with such a dichotomy. We concluded that *shi* should be considered as a hybrid concept that cannot be easily rendered into English. It is best to understand *shi* as a case of fitting/*yi* 宜.

In this section, we provide more textual evidence—now specifically from the inner chapters of the *Zhuangzi*—that support the hybrid nature of *shi* (as judged from the perspective of the English language). We focus on translations that deviate from the dominant translations by Watson, Graham, and Ziporyn. In this chapter, we also consider in more detail the difference between *shifei* and *shibi* 是彼, and the interdependence of *shi*, *ran*, and *ke*, as well as the presence or absence of higher-order modifiers of *shi*.[1] In the last two sections of this chapter, we discuss Graham's interpretation of *yinshi* 因是 and *weishi* 為是.

First, consider the following famous passage from the *Qiwulun*.[2]

道隱於小成，言隱於榮華。故有儒墨之是非，以是其所非，而非其所是。欲是其所非，而非其所是，則莫若以明。(2.3.5)

When the Way [*dao* 道] relies on little accomplishments and words [*yan* 言] rely on vain show, then we have the rights and wrongs [*shifei*] of the Confucians and the Mo-ists. What one calls right [*shi*] the other calls wrong [*fei*]; what one calls wrong [*fei*] the other calls right [*shi*]. But if we want to right [*shi*] their wrongs [*fei*] and wrong [*fei*] their rights [*shi*], then the best thing to use is clarity [*yiming* 以明].

Note that Watson translates all occurrences of *shi* and *fei* as right and wrong.[3] One reason translations of 2.3.5 differ is because the meaning of *qi* 其 leaves undetermined whether "the one" and "the other" refer to the Ruists and Mohists, or to "they" (that is, Ruists and Mohists) and "you" (or Zhuangzi), or to you and somebody else.[4]

In 2.3.5, the *shifei* of Ruists and Mohists has been variously translated as the affirmations and denials of the Ruists and Mohists (Feng Youlan), their rights and wrongs (Ziporyn), their dichotomous evaluations (Coutinho 2015, 114), their controversies (Chan Wing-tsit, Mair), their quarrels (Billeter, Levi), their dissension (Wang Rongpei), as well as their judgments (Cleary). As can be seen from this list, many different translations have been given, but note that true/false is missing, although there are exceptions. Anglophone translators render most occurrences of *shifei* in the *Qiwulun* as "right and wrong."

The last clause of 2.3.5 is saying that the best thing is to use clarity (Watson, Hansen 1983b), the light of reason (Feng Youlan), the Illumination of the Obvious (Ziporyn), illumination (Graham, Coutinho 2015, 184), lucidity (Mair), clear understanding (Billeter), or a tranquil mind (Wang Rongpei). As Coutinho rightly emphasizes, Zhuangzi gives a "radical reinterpretation" of the Mohists' metaphor of clarity: "To see clearly is to see the ever-present possibility of indeterminacy, of paradox and contradiction" (Coutinho 2004, 154).

Reding (2004, 193) translates the middle part as follows:

……以是其所非，而非其所是……(2.3.5)

. . . to want to consider as true what they consider false and consider as false what they consider as true by considering as true what they consider as false and by considering as false what they consider as true . . . (Reding)

Reding's translation suggests a different parsing, and he translates *shi* and *fei* as true and false. Consulting the bibliography in Reding's publication (2004), one can see that there are quite a few references to literature in the French language.[5] Hence, it seems that francophone translators may choose true/false (or correct/false or correct/incorrect) for what anglophone translators usually render as right/wrong (except for Graham's "That's it/not").⁶ Billeter and Levi, two other francophone translators, render 2.3.5 as⁷

> Thus it is that quarrels arise between the Confucianists and the Mo-ists, one side regarding as correct what the other side regards as incorrect, and *vice versa*. {Hence}, rather than defending the point of view that the other side rejects, or rejecting the point of view that the other side defends, . . . (Billeter)

> Thus the quarrels of the Confucianists and the Mo-ists develop. Some hold for true what others hold for false and vice versa. Rather than . . . (Levi)

Billeter translates *shifei* as correct/incorrect (elsewhere correct/false) instead of true/false (as Levi does). The reason he gives is

> I propose "correct" rather than "true" as it seems to me to be useful to distinguish between a logic of denomination, which says of a term that it is "correct," and a propositional logic, which says of a proposition that it is "true." (Billeter 1998, 32n20)

All French translations of *shifei* in the *Qiwulun* we have consulted (Billeter, Lafitte, Levi, Reding, Wieger) differ from the English translations. There are eight occurrences of *shifei* and a few related occurrences of *shi* and *fei* separated by a few characters (cf. citation of 2.3.5 above). On three occasions Levi translates *shifei* as *vrai* and *faux* (true and false),⁸ on three other occasions as *affirmation* and *négation* (affirm and negate).⁹ On one occasion, Levi translates *shifei* as *approuver* and *condamner* (approve and condemn), *juste* and *fausse* (correct and false), and *de ce qui est (n'est pas)* [that which is (not)]. *Shi* on its own is translated three times as *vérité* (truth) and three times as *approuver* (approve).

On one occasion Levi translates *shifei* as "le bien et le mal" (good and evil), as does Schipper in a Dutch translation (*goed en kwaad*). Compare the following:

仁義之端，是非之徒，樊然殽亂。(2.6.6)

> The distinctions between justice and kindness [or: charity], between good and evil [*shifei*] may only sow disorder and confusion. (Levi)¹⁰

As I see it, this also applies to the principles of humanity and justice as well as the differences between good and evil [*shifei*]. These are so terribly confused. (Schipper)[11]

The principles of Goodwill and Duty, the paths of "That's it, that's not" [*shifei*] are inextricably confused. (Graham)

The rules of benevolence and righteousness and the paths of right and wrong [*shifei*] are all hopelessly snarled and jumbled. (Watson)

The *Grand Ricci* supports the translations *vrai* and *fausse* (true and false), in particular with reference to the *Zhuangzi*. According to this source, *shi* is a demonstrative on oracle bones (*ceci, ce, ces, ceux-ci*). The occurrence of *shi* in the *Zhuangzi* is explicitly referred to as: "*vrai* (opposite of *Faux fei*)."[12] *Fei* on oracle bones and bronzes is rendered as negation; in the earliest written sources negation or bad or false; in the *Zhuangzi* it is specified as "*Le Faux* (the opposite of *shi* 是 *Le vrai*)."

As far as the meaning of *shifei* in modern Chinese is concerned, English and French dictionaries specify *shifei* differently. English dictionaries highlight "right and wrong" and "quarrels." The French *Grand Ricci* dictionary lists these as contemporary meanings of *shifei*: distinguish between good and bad, distinguish between true and false; affirm or deny, yes or no; critiques, quarrels, discord, annoyance, complications, affairs, and gossip. Note that the *Grand Ricci* does not consider right/wrong as an option for translating *shifei*.

Further support can be found in Jullien's works. For example, one reads in the English translation of one of his books (Jullien 2014, 80): "The Chinese have effectively handled disjunctive judgment: 'it is this' and 'it is not this' (*shi* and *fei*: true or false, good or bad)."[13]

The "alternative" translations by francophone sinologists are not restricted to the *Zhuangzi*.[14] For example, Levy translates *shifei* in Mengzi's famous remarks in 2A6 and 6A6 as good and bad (*du bien et du mal*).[15]

是非之心，智之端也。(Mengzi 2A6)

The conscience of good and bad is the beginning of wisdom. (Levy)[16]

是非之心，人皆有之。(Mengzi 6A6)

The conscience of good and bad, all men have it. (Levy)[17]

English translators usually prefer either right and wrong or (dis)approve.[18]

無是非之心，非人也。(Mengzi 2A6)

The feeling of approving and disapproving is essential to man. (Legge, in CLT)

Not to have a mind which calls things right or wrong is not human. (Pulleybank 1995, 86)

Whoever is devoid of the heart of right and wrong is not human. (Lau)

Anyone who lacks a sense of right and wrong cannot not [sic] be a person. (Eno)

If one is without the heart of approval and disapproval, one is not a human. (Van Norden)

Without having consciousness of good and bad, one would not be a human being. (Levy)[19]

The difference between anglophone and francophone translations is undeniable.

In one of the most authoritative German sources, we find that *shi* and *fei* are possible answers to a yes/no question (Unger 2000, 106):[20]

"Correct [*richtig*]" and "false [*falsch*]." The answer to a yes/no question . . . and further "right [*Recht*]" and "wrong [*Unrecht*]."

The feature of affirm/deny (yes/no) is more prominent in German. One can see this by comparing Schuhmacher's German translation of Mair's English rendition of the Chinese original. What Mair translated as affirm and deny, Schumacher sometimes renders as "yes and no" or the corresponding German verbs ("yes-ing" [*bejahen*] and "no-ing" [*verneinen*]).[21]

They invariably affirm what their opponents deny and deny what their opponents affirm. If one wishes to affirm what others deny and deny what others affirm, . . . (Mair 2.3.5)

Was der andere verneint, bejaht man; was jener bejaht, verneint man. Weit besser als das Streben, jedem Nein des anderen ein Ja und jedem Ja des andern ein Nein entgegenzusetzen, . . . (Schuhmacher 2.3.5)

Shifei is translated in German translations as *richtig* or *falsch* and sometimes as *recht* or *unrecht*. The German word *richtig* often corresponds to "correct" or "right." Authoritative German dictionaries provide rather different entries for *richtig*.[22] Prima facie *richtig* suggests the side of true (though "correct" comes nearer). However, German also has the word *korrekt* and "to be correct" translates as *recht haben*). *Recht* suggests the side of right (including some uses of correct and often having the connotation of justice).[23] Both *richtig* and *recht* have a wide range of meanings and they overlap one another. Unger (2000, 106) suggests that *richtig* and *falsch* is the more basic meaning of *shifei*.

Another suitable example for comparing modern translations is the first occurrence of *shifei* in the *Qiwulun*.[24]

其發若機栝，其司是非之謂也。(2.2.2)

. . . plagues like the trigger of the crossbow in order to approve or condemn. (Levi)[25]

They strike like the crossbow's {bolt} when judging of true and false. (Billeter)[26]

They bound off like an arrow or a crossbow pellet, certain that they are the arbiters of right and wrong. (Watson)[27]

. . . urteilen [judge] über Richtig und Falsch. (Schuhmacher)

. . . Richter sein [being a judge] über Recht und Unrecht. (Wilhelm)

. . . manipulation of "that's it, that's not." (Graham)

Wilhelm, who was a Protestant minister, more often translates *shifei* as morally right and wrong or as justice and injustice (*Recht* and *Unrecht*).

Recent translations in English tend to decide on a single translation of *shifei* for all the occurrences in the *Zhuangzi*. The most common rendition is right and wrong (see Watson and Ziporyn). Mair, Feng Youlan, and Lin Yutang do the same, except for one occasion.[28] Graham has his own idiosyncratic translations. Early English translations as well as French and German versions chose different translations of *shifei* on different occasions. It is not clear whether this development on the English side is based on solid investigation and reflection or is merely a consequence of a general trend toward standardization. In older translations, in addition to affirm and reject, (dis)approve or (dis)like also occur. These two pairs may have been "imported" via the translation of the famous passage from the *Mengzi* concerning the four sprouts, *shifei* being the sprout or seed of wisdom. Translating *shifei* in this passage as (dis)approve or (dis)like may be related to the assumption that *shifei* judgments are considered as *qing* (cf. §7d).

Giles sometimes used the expressions contraries or likes/dislikes, which are not favored by later translators. Legge chose a variety of translations for *shifei* in the inner chapters, perhaps with some preference for approval and disapproval, as in (already partially cited above).[29]

自我觀之，仁義之端，是非之徒，樊然殽亂，吾惡能知其辯！(2.6.6)

As I look at the matter, the first principles of benevolence and righteousness and the paths of approval and disapproval are inextricably mixed and confused together—how is it possible that I should know how to discriminate among them? (Legge, in CLT)

A comparison of French, German, and English translations is made difficult because there are few words that directly overlap.[30] *Vrai* and *faux* tend to correspond to true and false. *Richtig* and *falsch* can cover true and false (but *wahr* and *falsch* is more explicit, having the association with bivalent logic), though *richtig* and *falsch* can also mean (in)correct (as *juste* and *fausse* can).

Most discussions in modern Chinese simply use *shi* and *fei* without particular attention to the possible differences between classical and modern Chinese.[31] Limiting the discussion to modern English (or modern Chinese) has led interpretations toward a global English discourse, which is not representative of French, classical Chinese, and all other languages.

As already argued in §2c, we advocate that we consider a word like *shi* (in contrast with *fei* or *bushi*) as a cluster concept, although this would lead to cumbersome translations such as

以是其所非而非其所是。欲是其所非而非其所是。(2.3.5)

What one calls this–right–true–yes–that's it–what is, the other calls that–wrong–false–no–that's not–what is not. What one calls that–wrong–false–no–that's not–what is not, the other calls this–right–true–yes–that's it–what is (what one approves–affirms, the other disapproves–denies–negates).

This is not very practical. A translator would almost always be obliged to stipulate (and hopefully to explain) a conventional one-word translation. A translator may leave some words–characters untranslated, but even then the word occurs in an alien grammatical context (cf. the use of *shi*-ing).

We conclude that the varying translations into French and, to a lesser extent, into German and Dutch, support our claim that *shifei* covers a cluster of English concepts, including true and false, right and wrong, good and bad, correct and incorrect. Hence, it is inappropriate to fix the meaning of *shi* (or *shifei*) in terms of a single notion in a Western language.

Bi/Ci (彼/此) and *Shi/Fei*

Many commentators have suggested that Zhuangzi's radical remarks about *shifei* were induced by the ambiguity in classical Chinese of the use and meaning of *shi*. Billeter remarks (1998, 24),[32]

> In [Zhuangzi's] language, the same *shi* was used to express, when functioning as a verb, the positive judgment "it is that" (in contradistinction to *fei*, "it is not that") and, when functioning as a pronoun, the relationship of proximity "this" (in contradistinction to "that").

In this section, we examine the binomes *shibi*, *biwo*, *cibi*, and *shifei* (是彼, 彼我, 此彼, 是非). We first present a succinct overview of most of the relevant passages, which are followed by the translations by Billeter.

非彼无我，非我无所取。(2.2.4)

物无非彼，物无非是……彼是方生之說也。(2.3.6)

方可方不可，方不可方可；因是因非，因非因是。(2.3.7A)

[……亦因是也] 是亦彼也， 彼亦是也。(2.3.7B)[33]

彼亦一是非，此亦一是非。果且有彼是乎哉？ 果且无彼是乎哉？ (2.3.8)

Shi and Its Opposites and Modifers in the *Qiwulun* 齊物論 / 75

But for such {phenomena} there would be no self; but for the self {these phenomena} would have nothing on which to take hold. (2.2.4)

Everything is at times a "that" and at times a "this" . . . This is why one says that the "this" and the "that" come into existence at the same moment. (2.3.6)

At the moment when {a designation} is {still} applicable it is {already} no longer so; and at the moment when {a designation} is {still} not applicable, it {already} is. {Thus, a given designation [dénomination]} is now correct and now incorrect, while {another} is now incorrect and now correct [*juste* and *faux*]. (2.3.7A)

A "this" is thus a "that," and a "that" a "this." (2.3.7B)

There are the correct and incorrect [*juste* and *faux*] from the point of view of the "that," and those from the point of view of the "this." But, this being so, are there, in the last analysis, a "this" and a "that"? (2.3.8)

The English translator of Billeter's French version renders *shifei* as correct and incorrect.

The first thing to notice is disagreement about parsing. The phrase marked 2.3.7B is part of 2.3.7 in TLS and other sources. However, Billeter considers it as the first characters of 2.3.8. Such translators as Billeter, Kjellberg, Mair, and Ziporyn insert a break at this point; some others do not (Watson, Lin Yutang, and Levi). However, these differences have not influenced the translation of 2.3.7B: "This too is that, that too is this." Sometimes, although there is a break, the passages are connected by a "therefore" or by a similar word. Here are a few alternatives.

亦因是也 [break?] 是亦彼也彼亦是也 (2.3.7B)

For one may base it on this, yet this is also that and that is also this. (Lin Yutang)

He too recognizes a "this," but a "this" which is also "that," a "that" which is also "this." (Watson)

. . . accepting "this" for what it is. [break] "This" is also "that"; "that" is also "this." (Mair)[34]

> Therefore [*donc*] each "this" is a "that," each "that" is a "this." (Levi)³⁵

In the *Zhuangzi*, the distinction between *shibi* and *shifei* is clearly made in 2.3.8. See above and the following:³⁶

> His "that" has both a right and a wrong in it; his "this" too has both a right and a wrong in it. So, in fact, does he still have a "this" and "that"? Or does he in fact no longer have a "this" and "that"? (Watson)

Note that the change from *shi* 是 ("this") to *ci* 此 ("this"), going from 2.3.7B to 2.3.8, is not noticeable in English.³⁷

Regarding 2.2.4, many translators opt for "I and other," for example: "If there is no other, there will be no I" (see Feng Youlan and similarly Mair, Levi, Schipper, and Kjellberg). Exceptions are: "that and me" (Ziporyn), "other and self" (Graham, Cleary). Contextualizing 2.2.4 in the light of a list of "emotions" in the lines before, Lin Yutang translates it as: "But for these emotions I should not be. Yet but for me, there would be no one to feel them" (referring back to the "ever-changing moods" in the previous clauses).³⁸ Combining the insight of all these translators, we could get the following:

> If there were no Other–them–that, there would be no I–self–me.
> If there were no one–me–I, there would be nobody to make–choose–select distinctions. They (views, identities, emotions) cannot exist without one another.

Sinologists agree to translate *wo* 我 as I–self–me, but there are several indications that suggest that *bishi* and *biwo* are "close" in meaning (Billeter 1998, 24; Cheng Xuanying 2001, 34). The position of the "I" is "this"; the position of the "other" is "that."

Translations of the first two clauses of 2.3.6 are similar except for Graham's version.³⁹

> Everything has its "that," everything has its "this." (Watson)

> No thing is not that, no thing is not this. No thing is not "other," no thing is not "it." (Graham)

As to 2.3.7, most translations of *ke* are similar: acceptable (Watson), admissible or allowable (Graham), possible (Feng Youlan, Lin Yutang), okay (Kjellberg).⁴⁰ Ziporyn approaches the existing translations of *shifei* by translating *kebuke* as affirm/negate (although he chooses right and wrong for *shifei*). Wang Rongpei translates (*bu*)*ke* as (dis)approval, which also brings *ke* and *shi* together.⁴¹ Chen Guying (2007, 69n5) says explicitly: "*ke* means *shi*; *buke* means *fei*. This proposition shows the infinite relativity of value judgment."

Levi highlights the distinction between naming and attributing.⁴²

> Each correct designation of naming [*denomination*] is at the same time incorrect [*fausse*] and, reversely, each incorrect designation is at the same time correct. So that each designation of attribution [*qualification*] is at the same time correct and incorrect and incorrect and correct. (Levi 2.3.7)

That is to say, *juste* and *fausse* are used for both *kebuke* and *shifei*, but a distinction is made between naming and qualifying. Mair (and hence Schuhmacher) splits the mentioning of *kebuke* and *shifei* into three parts.

> Every affirmation is a denial of something else, and every denial is an affirmation of something else. "This" and "that" are mutually dependent; right and wrong are also mutually dependent. (Mair 2.3.7)

> Jede Bejahung ist die Verneinung von etwas anderem, und jede Verneinung ist die Bejahung von etwas anderem. "Dies" und "Das" sind voneinander abhängig; Richtig und Falsch sind ebenfalls voneinander abhängig. (Schuhmacher 2.3.7)

As to 2.3.8, most translators assume that *either* "that" and "this" embodies *shifei* in its own discourse. However, Ziporyn, who integrates 2.3.7B and 2.3.8, almost treats this/that as corresponding to right/wrong.⁴³

> "This" is also a "that." "That" is also a "this." "THAT" posits a "this" and a "that"—a right and a wrong—of its own. But "THIS" also posits a "this" and a "that"—a right and a wrong—of its own. So is there really any "that" versus "this," any right versus wrong? Or is there really no "that" versus "this"? (Ziporyn)

Concerning the cluster of *shifei*, *shibi*, and *kebuke*, we conclude as follows:

1. Depending on context, the characters *shi* 是, *wo* 我, and *ci* 此 are interchangeable. Ziporyn comes nearest to considering

kebuke, shifei, and shibi (or cibi) as a single cluster of family resemblances.

2. A range of options exist for translating qi 其: other, they, he, its, this, . . .

3. Zhuangzi was aware of the ambiguity of shi in classical Chinese and played with it.

4. It is noteworthy that the passages concerning shibi (2.3.6–8) come *after* the major passage on shifei (2.3.5). Although shibi and shifei bear similarity, Zhuangzi has separate arguments for each of them. Some translators come close to identifying shifei with shibi; others blur the distinction between biwo, bishi, and shifei.

5. The similarity between kebuke and shifei is captured in Ziporyn's translation of kebuke as affirmability and negatibility.[44] We suggest that kebuke also belongs to the cluster that includes shibushi and ranburan (see next section).

Shibushi 是不是, Ranburan 然不然, Kebuke 可不可

In this section, we consider further indications that, for Zhuangzi, the difference between shi, ran, and ke may not be as large as is generally assumed. The following passage has a number of interesting features.

> 是不是，然不然。是若果是也，則是之異乎不是也，亦无辯；然若果然也，則然之異乎不然也，亦无辯。(2.6.21)

> When the issue is to discuss what is and what is not, or to decide whether something is thus rather than otherwise, by approving what the other approves, it becomes impossible to distinguish the true and the false, even if they are different; saying that that is such when the other judges it is thus, it becomes impossible to distinguish between what is thus and what is not, even if they are different. (Levi)[45]

> Right is not right; so is not so. If right were really right, it would differ so clearly from not right that there would be no need for argument. If so were really so, it would differ so clearly from not so that there would be no need for argument. (Watson)

Shi and Its Opposites and Modifers in the Qiwulun 齊物論 / 79

Right may be not right, so may be not so. (Mair)

Referring to the right and the wrong, the "being so" and the "not being so": if the right is really right, we need not dispute about how it is different from wrong; if the "being so" is really being so, we need not dispute about how it is different from "not being so." (Feng Youlan)

Treat even what is not this as "this," even what is not so as "so." If what is this is ultimately this and what is so is ultimately so, there is no difference for disputation between this and not this, so and not so. (G78, 455; G89, 184; cf. G81, 60)[46]

Affirm 是 what isn't, and attribute 然 what isn't so! If This were really This, then there would be no disputing the difference between This and not This. If So were really So, then there would be no disputing the difference between So and not So." (Coutinho 2015, 185)

There is the affirmation and the denial of it; and there is the assertion of an opinion and the rejection of it. If the affirmation be according to the reality of the fact, it is certainly different from the denial of it—there can be no dispute about that. If the assertion of an opinion be correct, it is certainly different from its rejection—neither can there be any dispute about that. (Legge)

Graham remarks concerning this passage (2.6.21): "we shall not attempt to analyze this utterance" (G89, 184). This is reflective of the degree of complexity of this passage, which gives rise to such wide-ranging variations in translation.

First, it should be noted that this is a unique occurrence of *shibushi* 是不是 in the *Zhuangzi*. In checking other classical sources, we come across only one more occurrence of *shibushi* in the *Lüshi chunqiu*.[47]

說淫則可不可而然不然，是不是而非不非。 (Lüshi chunqiu 16.8.1.1)

If the evil sayings are spread, what is allowable [*ke*] becomes not allowable [*buke*]; what is true [*ran*] becomes false [*buran*]; what is right [*shi*] is taken as the wrong [*bushi*]; what is wrong [*fei*] is taken as the right [*bufei*]. (Zhai Jiangyue)

Second, Watson renders *shibushi* and *ranburan* as two straightforward contradictions. This may be right if the idea is that a sage harmonizes or equalizes true and false, right and not right, so and not-so. But most other translators attempt to nuance the connection between A and not-A by using such expressions as "is also" (Ziporyn), "be really" (Lin Yutang), "may be" (Mair), and "treat even as" (Graham).[48] Coutinho (2004) regards *shibushi* and *ranburan* as contradictions, but he makes a distinction between *shi* and *ran* in terms of affirming and attributing respectively.[49] Alt (2000) correctly points out that Graham, Watson, and Mair all parse the phrase *shibushi ranburan* into English as a conjunction of two grammatically complete sentences. According to Alt, Graham's translation conjoins two imperatives; Watson's is a conjunction of two self-contradictory claims, and so may be Mair's.

Hence, translators tend to read the first two clauses as a conjunction suggesting contradictions. Alt refers to Feng Gia-Fu and English (1947), who give a translation assuming a topic-comment structure: The topic is "Consider right and wrong, being and non-being: [followed by] If right is indeed right, there need be no argument about how it is different from wrong. If being is really being, there need be no argument" (46). According to Alt, this translation avoids the implication of anti-rationalism and suggests that, if so really *is* so, arguing about it is a waste of time.

As can be seen from the citations listed above, Feng Youlan and Levi also assume a topic-comment structure. Zhuangzi employs a sophisticated use of contradictions (§9d), but he does not consider "simple" contradictions such as stating that *shi* is (the same as) *bushi*. In our view, *shibushi* and *ranburan* (as well as *kebuke* and *feibufei*) in the passages above do not involve contradictions.

Third, what is also noteworthy is the parallel construction between *bushi* and *buran* in 2.6.21. Zhuangzi uses this kind of parallel construction regularly.[50] The only other text in which such a construction occurs a few times is the *Lüshi chunqiu*.[51] A similar parallel construction in the case of *ke* and *ran* can be found in the following:[52]

> 可乎可，不可乎不可。道行之而成，物謂之而然。惡乎然？然於然。惡乎不然？不然於不然。物固有所然，物固有所可。无物不然，无物不可。(2.4.2)

Allowable?—allowable. Unallowable?—unallowable. The Way comes about as we walk it; as for a thing, call it something and that's so. Why so? By being so. Why not so? By not being so. It is inherent in a thing that from somewhere that's so of it, from somewhere that's allowable of it; of no thing it is not so, of no thing it is unallowable. (Graham)

What is acceptable we call acceptable; what is unacceptable we call unacceptable. A road is made by people walking on it; things are so because they are called so. What makes them so? Making them so makes them so. What makes them not so? Making them not so makes them not so. Things all must have that which is so; things all must have that which is acceptable. There is nothing that is not so, nothing that is not acceptable. (Watson)[53]

The possible is possible. The impossible is impossible. The *Tao* makes things and they are what they are. What are they? They are what they are. What are they not? They are not what they are not. Everything is something and is good for something. There is nothing which is not something or is not good for something. (Feng Youlan)

In his comment on the passage concerning the quarrels between Mohists and Ruists (2.3.5), Cheng Xuanying uses the expression *biwo shifei* 彼我是非. This implies that *biwo* (that and I, that and this) and *shifei* may be closely related in this context. Perhaps *biwo* "means" that and this, and *wo* 我 cannot be regarded as a personal pronoun. In his subcommentary on the passages from the end of chapter 5 of the *Zhuangzi* cited in the next section, Cheng Xuanying extends this blurring of distinctions even further.

吾所言情者，是非彼我好惡憎嫌等也。(Cheng Xuanying, 122)[54]

[W]hat I speak of as *qing* is *shifei*, that and this [*biwo* (that and I)], like and dislike (*hao'e*), hate (*zeng*), hate–doubt (*xian*), and so on.

The variety of parallel constructions in the *Zhuangzi* may be more than a stylistic embellishment. When the same is predicated of two or more contrasting pairs, it may be that Zhuangzi is implicitly adding "and this applies to other distinctions as well."[55] Hence, the relevant passages would be about "these kinds of contrasts."

We conclude that the difference between *shi*, *ran*, and *ke* may not be as large as is generally assumed in connection with the "standardized" translations "right," "so," and "permissible." As yet Zhuangzi's use of the ordinary characters *shi*, *ran*, and *ke* may not have received the attention it deserves.

Qing 情 and *Shifei*

The meaning of *shifei* (typically when it occurs at the beginning of a "sentence" that looks like a statement) is often underdetermined (as judged in the English language). This gives rise to divergent translations taking it as either "that/this is not" or as "right and wrong." An example can be found in a famous passage at the end of chapter 5. We first present the relevant parts of the dialogue between Hui Shi 惠施 (370–310 BCE) and Zhuangzi.⁵⁶

……无人之情，故是非不得於身……惠子謂莊子曰：「人故无情乎？」莊子曰：然！惠子曰：「人而无情，何以謂之人？莊子曰：道與之貌，天與之形，惡得不謂之人？惠子曰：既謂之人，惡得无情？莊子曰：是非吾所謂情也。吾所謂无情者言人之不以好惡內傷其身。(5.5.5–5.6.6)

Since he [the *shengren*] doesn't have the feelings of a man, right and wrong cannot get at him. . . . Hui Tzu [Huizi, Hui Shi] said to Chuang Tzu [Zhuangzi], "Can a man really be without feelings?" "Yes," said Master Chuang. Hui Tzu: "But a man who has no feelings—how can you call him a man?" Chuang Tzu: "The Way gave him a face; Heaven gave him a form—why can't you call him a man?" Hui Tzu: "But if you've already called him a man, how can he be without feelings?" "That's not what I mean by feelings. When I talk about having no feelings, I mean that a man doesn't allow likes or dislikes to get in and do him harm."

The translations of the penultimate clause, 是非吾所謂情也, fall into two groups. The first group are as follows:

What you mean by passions is not what I mean. (Giles)

You are misunderstanding what I mean by passions and desires. (Legge)

These passions is [*sic*] not what I mean. (Wilhelm)⁵⁷

That is not what I mean by affection. (Feng Youlan)

Shi and Its Opposites and Modifers in the Qiwulun 齊物論 / 83

You do not understand what I mean when I say "passionless." (Waley)[58]

That's not what I mean by feelings. (Watson)

That is not what I mean by emotions. (Mair, Schuhmacher)

That's not what I mean by *qing*. (Chong Kim-chong 2010, 32)

That which you mention here is not what I understand as "feelings." (Schipper)[59]

This translation is supported by a modern Chinese explanation of the classic text:[60]

> 是,此。指惠子所说的人情。
>
> *Shi* [是], means *ci* [此]. Referring to what Huizi [Hui Shi] speaks of as human *qing*. (Cao Chuji 2000, 69)

Alternatively, *shifei* is read as a binome.

Right and wrong (approval and disapproval) are what I mean by passions. (Lin Yutang)

Judging between right and wrong is what I refer to by "what is genuinely man." (G67, 261)

Judging "That's it, that's not" is what I mean by "the essentials of man." (Graham)

Rights and wrongs are what I mean by "essence." (Kjellberg)

Affirming some things as right and negating others as wrong are what I call the characteristic inclinations. (Ziporyn)

Distinguishing "right" and "wrong" is what I mean by dispositions. (Puett 2003, 258)

I call "feelings" the faculty of judgment. (Levi)[61]

Judging "it is so" or "it is not so," there it is what I call "being essentially human." (Reding 1985, 283–84)[62]

What I call passions (*qing* 情) are positive and negative affirmative evaluations of things. (Machek 2015, 531)

Judgment of "what is and what is not" is what I mean by "human characteristic." (Anne Cheng 2004, 52)

This translation is also supported by a modern Chinese rendition of the classic text. Si Lü (2013, 61) places a comma after *shifei* in the original (是非, 吾所謂情也), giving it the meaning: "*shifei*, that is what I mean by *qing*." Nevertheless, Si's translation in modern Chinese is: "This is not therefore what I say *qing* is. (这不是我所说的情。)"

In the first group, there is almost unanimity in translating *qing* as emotion–passion. The second group presents at least five different translations of *qing*. The translators in the first group have Zhuangzi say that he does not mean by *qing* what Hui Shi thinks he means. However, unfortunately, Hui Shi does not say much about what he means by *qing* 情. He seems to suggest that *qing* is the "essence" of *ren* 人 (human beings, and sages?), but the contents of *qing* is not specified.[63] The first group of translators may seem to be right and supported by Chinese readers, but the disadvantage of this interpretation is that we do not know what Hui Shi considers to be the contents of *qing*. The concern that *shifei* or *hao'e* would enter into the body may suggest that these binomes do not originate from *xin* 心 or *xing* 性, but from education and other external factors.

The translators of the second group have Zhuangzi take the view that by *qing* Zhuangzi refers to *shifei*. In the preceding "paragraph," Zhuangzi had already said that because the sage has no *qing* 情, *shifei* cannot get at him, which utterance is repeated a bit farther down in terms of *hao'e* 好惡 (instead of *shifei*). Zhuangzi does not seem to clearly distinguish between *shifei* and *hao'e*.[64] Compare:

无人之情，故是非不得於身。(5.5.5)

Since he doesn't have the feelings of a man, right and wrong [是非] cannot get at him.

吾所謂无情者言人之不以好惡內傷其身。(5.6.6)

When I talk about having no feelings, I mean that a man doesn't allow likes or dislikes [好惡] to get in and do him harm.

Compare also the commentary by Guo Xiang and another remark by Zhuangzi.

以是非爲情則無是無非無好無惡者。(Guo Xiang 2011, 122)

If one regards *shifei* as *qing*, then there is neither *shi* nor *fei*, neither like nor dislike.

而好惡是非，直服人之口而已矣。(27.2.3)

Your "likes" and "dislikes," your "rights" and "wrongs" are merely something that commands lip service from others, that's all. (G81, 102)

We suggest that on the one hand this may be an indication of a close connection of *shifei* and *hao'e*, which is supported by francophone translators who sometimes render *shifei* as good and bad (*bien et mal*) (In contrast, anglophone translators typically use "good and bad" for *hao'e*). On the other hand, we may extend this connection and presume that what is said about *shifei* and *hao'e* could be said about all distinctions. For example, as Graham's translation of part of 27.1.6 goes: *all* the distinctions "are merely something that command lip service from others."

As there are many different specifications of *qing* 情, this may be an extra reason why considering a sage or human as having no *qing* remains undetermined. There is no consensus as to whether Zhuangzi is committed to the idea that a sage lacks *qing*. Perhaps he is only thinking of lacking certain kinds of *qing*, or perhaps a sage may have many subdued emotions, but *shifei* (or any other "conventional" emotions?) is not one of them.

In comparing the two groups of translations of *shifei*, it should also be kept in mind that Zhuangzi is talking about a sage (*shengren* 聖人), not about ordinary human beings. Further, if it is assumed that *qing* can be translated as emotions or passions (which is not at all obvious), it needs to be explained why *shifei* is an emotion; even *hao'e* in the sense of good and bad is not a prototypical emotion, though like/dislike might be considered an emotion.[65]

Modifiers of *Shi* in the *Qiwulun*

In §4d we have discussed the possible higher-order usage of *zhen*, *zheng*, and other characters, but this kind of higher-order usage is not common in the inner chapters of the *Zhuangzi* except for rare exceptions. The following binomes do not occur in the inner chapters, although they do occur in other classical sources: *chengshi* 誠是, *dangran* 當然, *dangshi* 當是, *qingshi* 情是, *shishi* 實是, *yinshi* 信是, *zhenshi* 真是, *zhengshi* 正是, and *zhengzhen* 正直.[66] However, in the inner chapters, there are a few indications of higher-order judgments involving the characters *guo* 果 and *zheng* 正.[67]

……果…… necessarily right (2.6.17), really right (2.6.21)

果孰是邪？(24.5.5)

Now which of you is in fact right? (Watson)

[W]hich is really "it"? (G81, 101)

Guo can be used for emphasis ("really"). Zhuangzi seems to use it as part of an argument *ad hominem*.

The only sign of the presence of something "above" *shifei* in the inner chapters seems to be the use of *zheng* when it is translated as proper, standard, or true.[68]

三者孰知正處？(2.6.4)

Of these three creatures, then, which one knows the proper place to live? [a rhetorical question in reply to two explicit rhetorical questions]

四者孰知天下之正色哉？(2.6.5)

Of these four, which knows how to fix the standard of beauty for the world?

惡能正之？(2.6.19) How can he decide?

Preceding the last citation, we find *guoshi* (and *guofei* 果非) and *zheng*.

既使我與若辯矣，若勝我，我不若勝，若果是也，我果非也邪？我勝若，若不吾勝，我果是也，而果非也邪？(2.6.17)

Suppose you and I have had an argument. If you have beaten me instead of my beating you, then are you necessarily right and am I necessarily wrong? If I have beaten you instead of your beating me, then am I necessarily right and are you necessarily wrong?

Shi and Its Opposites and Modifers in the Qiwulun 齊物論 / 87

> 其或是也，其或非也邪？ 其俱是也，其俱非也邪？我與若不能相知也，人固受黮闇，吾誰使正之？ (2.6.18)

> Is one of us right and the other wrong? Are both of us right or are both of us wrong? If you and I don't know the answer, then other people are bound to be even more in the dark. Whom shall we get to decide what is right?

Zhen 真 regularly occurs in the Zhuangzi and is often translated as "true," sometimes as "the Truth."

> 人特以有君為愈乎己，而身猶死之，而況其真乎！(6.2.1)

> If he is willing to regard the ruler as superior to himself and to die for him, then how much more should he be willing to do for the Truth!

But zhenshi does not occur. However, via zhenwei 真偽, zhen may also assume a higher-order status. Zhuangzi contrasts the binomes shifei and zhenwei in 2.3.4 (our translation).

> 道惡乎隱而有真偽？ 言惡乎隱而有是非？

> How come that Dao becomes concealed and thence arise zhen and wei? How come that words become concealed and thence arise shi and fei?

Zhenwei and shifei are usually translated as true/false and right/wrong, respectively (Chan Wing-tsit, Cleary, Feng Youlan,[69] Legge, Mair, Roetz, Schipper, Wang Rongpei, Watson, and Ziporyn). Levi translates zhenwei as "the dichotomy between true and false [le vrai et le faux]" and shifei as affirmation and negation.[70] Graham translates zhenwei as "genuine and false." Ziporyn translates it as "genuine and fake."[71] The last is perhaps the most literal translation. "(In)authentic" also occurs as translation of zhenwei. Guo Xiang and Cheng Xuanying thus paraphrase and explain as follows:[72]

> How can Dao not exist?! How come that words become concealed and hidden and thence arise zhen and wei, and the names of shi and fei arise one after the other? (Guo Xiang)

> The empty and open Dao is neither zhen nor fei [feizhenfei 非真非]. Whence does it escape and hide itself and thence arise

zhen and *wei*. . . . The supreme teaching and supreme words *fei* what is *fei* and *fei* what is *shi* as well [*feifeifeishi* 非非非是]. How come that they become concealed and hidden, and hence arise *shi* and *fei*? (Cheng Xuanying)

As *zhenwei* is related to *dao*(s) and *shifei* to *yan*, *zhenwei* would seem to refer to a higher-order standard that can evaluate *shifei* standards.[73] Because *shifei* is translated as right/wrong, true/false becomes available for translating *zhenwei*. However, as we see from the above list of optional translations, *zhenwei* can be translated differently, which makes true/false free to translate *shifei*.

Alternatively, the *zhenwei* of *dao* and the *shifei* of *yan* can be considered to be a case of *huwen xianyi* 互文見義, a form of mutual reference or predication, which is a rhetorical device in classical Chinese.[74] We find a typical use in 2.3.4.

道惡乎隱而有真偽？言惡乎隱而有是非？(2.3.4)

How does it come about that the Way hides itself and that {the opposition between} the true and the false is born [*le vrai et le faux*]? How does it come about that language grows opaque and that we have {the opposition between} the correct and the incorrect [*le juste et le faux*]? (Billeter)

In the English translation there are two clauses: one about *dao* being *zhenwei* and one about *yan* being *shifei*. Being interdependent means that both *zhenwei* and *shifei* are predicated of both *dao* and *yan*. What is said of the first and of the second respectively applies to the other topic as well.

Zhuangzi uses *zhenwei* only once. But there are similar occurrences in other classical texts. For example, in the *Yangzi fayan* 揚子法言, the translator renders *zhenwei* as true/false.

真偽，真偽則政核。如真不真，偽不偽，則政不核。(Yangzi fayan, Foreknowledge 17; in CTP)

Discriminating the true and the false. If you can discriminate the true and the false, then you have grasped the core of governance. But if the true is not considered true, and the false not considered false, then governing will have no core. (Bullock)

Zhenwei has also been translated as right and wrong.[75]

天道有真偽。(Lunheng 8.5.1)

The laws of Heaven can be applied in a right and in a wrong way. (Forke 1, 377)

……訂其真偽，辯其實虛。(Lunheng, chapter 2; not in TLS; see Forke)

. . . the object of defining right and wrong and distinguishing between truth and falsehood. (Forke 1, 87)

If there is a plurality of *daos* in the *Zhuangzi*, as Hansen advocates, then different *daos* may come into conflict. Hence, we must draw on a certain higher standard to tell us which *dao*(s) should be used in cases of conflict. Hansen (2015) writes,

> We presuppose a *dao* when we interpret (or select) a *dao* . . . Thus, selecting a discourse *dao* is applying *shi-fei*$^{\text{this-not this}}$ 是非 to *daos*. . . . 仁 ren^{humanity} works as a kind of *dao* of *daos*, i.e. a *dao* or way of formulating and settling disputes about *dao*. . . . The *Zhuangzi* raises the obvious question: What is the correct standard (*dao*) to use in choosing and interpreting a *dao* and what is the correct *dao* of practical interpretation of that standard?

Although we are sympathetic to Hansen's proposal of translating 道 as *daos* (since there are many *daos*; cf. §A5), here he is perhaps over-interpreting by reading his own view into the text. We do not think that the question of how to evaluate and resolve conflicts between *daos* is very important for Zhuangzi. On his stance there is no need for such things as higher-order standards. What is relevant is to spontaneously go along with *dao*—whether the latter is understood as THE DAO or as *daos* is less important. Furthermore, if there is no strict boundary between *shi* and *fei*, there is no need for a common "universal" standard for making rigid *shifei* judgments.

Graham's Contrasting between *Yinshi* 因是 and *Weishi* 為是

In his commentary to his first translation of the *Qiwulun*, Graham drew attention to "two unobstrusive phrases" (G69, 143; G89, 297–301): *yinshi* 因是 and *weishi* 為是, which he translated as "adaptive *shi*" and "contrived *shi*" respectively. Later he translated them as "'that's it' that goes by circumstance" and "'that's it' that deems."[76] *Yin* means "to base one's actions on the changing situation, to adapt to circumstances without imposing fixed principles."[77] In contrast, *wei* is "to act on inflexible principles, forcing one's will against the spontaneous course of things" (G69, 143–44).[78] Hence, Graham suggests that *yin* and *wei* point to opposite kinds of *shi*; *weishi* is associated with opposing doctrines (such as those of the Ruists and Mohists), fixed perspectives, making and preserving distinctions. In contrast, *yinshi* is associated with adapting and responding appropriately to the changing situation (context, circumstances).

Graham draws on his translation and "ordering" of the later Mohist *Canons* (G78, 214–15) to suggest that we should consider *yinshi* in a "highly technical sense" (215). The "explained by: the criterion" (Graham's words, following the *Canons*) by which to judge is an example of *yin* being the "standard" to be used in *shifei* judgments; for example, the eyes are the criterion by which to judge whether it is (or is not) a blind horse. Graham translates all the occurrences of *yinshi* in the inner chapters by the same English phrase.

In addition, Graham points to Zhuangzi's use of *gongshi* 公是 "universally recognized *shi*" (G81, 101 [24.5.3]) and *yishi* 移是 "shifting *shi* (G81, 104 [23.7.4–7]).[79] Both *gongshi* and *yishi* Graham associated with *yinshi* (G69, 143). Here is an occurrence of *gongshi* 公是:

莊子曰：天下非有公是也，而各是其所是，天下皆堯也，可乎？ (24.5.3)

Chuang Tzu said, "If there is no publicly accepted 'right' in the world, but each person takes right to be what he himself thinks is right, then everyone in the world can be a Yao—all right?" (Watson, cf. G81, 101)

Yishi 移是 occurs in 23.7.4–6. Ziporyn follows Graham: "The definition of what is right adopts the shifting rightness of 'this.'" The issue of translating *yin* also arises with other sources. For example:

故有道之主，因而不為…… (Lüshi chunqiu 17.5.3.3)

A ruler who possesses the Dao, therefore relies on others and does not act. (Zhai Jiangyue)

Therefore the prince who has the Way adapts and does not contrive. (G69, 143)

The "classical" translation of *yinshi* is "to rely on." Using "to adapt" or mentioning circumstances in the translation of *yin* follows Graham.

In his translation of early commentators' explanations of the *Qiwulun*, Harbsmeier (1992) systematically translates *yin* as "adapt" or "adaptation." For example, concerning Jiao Hong 焦竑 (1540–1620), who comments on 2.4.4, Harbsmeier remarks that "[Jiao Hong] makes the critical link to the notion of *yin* 因 'adaptation'" (98).

寓諸庸因乎人也。(Jiao Hong)

Lodging in what is ordinary/mediocre is adapting to people. (cited and translated in Harbsmeier 1992, 98)

Throughout his translations, Harbsmeier renders *yinshi* in terms of adaptation.

是非兩存即因是也。(Chen Shen 陈深)

The coexistence of {considering as} right and wrong is the adaptive considering as right and wrong. (cited and translated in Harbsmeier 1992, 100)

但能因是則世目無爭奏。(Lin Xiyi 林希逸; 1193–1270?)

If only one is capable of the adaptive considering as right then there is no strife in the world. (cited and translated in Harbsmeier 1992, 103)

When commentators use *yin'er* 因而, Harbsmeier also translates it in terms of adaptation.[80]

因而然之不然之可也。(Luo Miandao 羅勉道; fl. ca. 1270)

By way of adaptation to consider them as so or not so is acceptable. (cited and translated in Harbsmeier 1992, 94)

達者因而不作……不知所以因而自因耳。(Guo Xiang)

The person of far-reaching understanding [達者] adapts but does not create. . . . He does not know why he adapts and adapts of himself/spontaneously, that is all. (cited and translated in Harbsmeier 1992, 100)

Concerning Chen Shen, Harbsmeier says (again) that Chen "shows the link with the notion of *yin* 因 'go by, take as one's standard.'" And he translates Chen Shen as follows:

故人曰可，吾因而可之。人曰不可，吾因而不可之。(Chen Shen)

Therefore, he says that when people call it acceptable then by adaptation I call it acceptable. When people call it not acceptable then by way of adaptation I treat it as not acceptable. (cited and translated in Harbsmeier 1992, 93)

Some commentators use *yinxun* 因循, which Harbsmeier does not seem to associate with adaptation.

因循萬物。(Cheng Xuanying)

He [the *zhiren* 至人] keeps in accordance to the ten-thousand-things. (cited and translated in Harbsmeier 1992, 101)[81]

We suggest that the phrase "following circumstances," "following the situation," or "following the things' own *shifei*" may be the most appropriate translation for *yinshi*. Consider Cheng Xuanying's comment on 2.4.5.

故能因是非而無是非。(Cheng Xuanying)

Therefore [the person of far-reaching understanding, *dazhe* 達者] is able to adaptively consider as right and wrong without considering as right and wrong. (cited and translated in Harbsmeier 1992, 100)

Many Western commentators have followed Graham's proposal of considering *yinshi* and *weishi* as "technical" terms in the sense as defined by the *Canons*.[82] On the other hand, many translators do not seem to accept Graham's idiosyncratic renditions.[83] One problem of interpretation is the question whether *shi* in these cases should be regarded as a noun or as a verb.

Roth was influenced by Graham's interpretation in translating *yinshi* and *weishi* as "fixated cognition" and "flowing cognition." For him, *yinshi* "involves a complete freedom" from attachment to one perspective: "a freedom to act spontaneously as the situation demands" (2003, 22). Slingerland (2013, 77) employs a rendition of *yinshi* as "following 'this is,'" but also resorts to the flow metaphor (as Roth does). In his interpretation of

Graham's interpretation of *yinshi*, Coutinho (and Billeter as well) is thinking primarily of the sages who display "pragmatic sensitivity to ever changing circumstances; being flexible, responding naturally, unmediated by conscious analysis" (Coutinho 2015, 167). Billeter makes the interesting suggestion that in the *yinshi* situation, "the words act back upon the situation" and thus modify the situation (1998, 24–25). Sellmann (1998, 164) suggests understanding *yinshi* as "active participatory harmony." Peterman (2008) criticizes Graham's translation and proposes "flexible, contextual 'that's it'" and "inflexible, non-contextual 'that's it'" as translations of *yinshi* and *weishi* respectively (379).[84]

Although most commentators, including Graham, propose that we inquire into classical Chinese thinking in relation to context that keeps changing, they in the meantime assume that at any moment context is determinate and that only *one* (spontaneous, *dao*-following) response is possible for a particular situation. Even if they acknowledge the existence of a plurality of *daos*, they still assume that there is only a single *dao*-following response for each situation. However, it is possible that the same situation allows for different spontaneous responses following different *daos*.[85]

Graham connects *yinshi* to spontaneity, a major theme he focuses on (cf. §A6). We suggest that spontaneity does not necessarily entail that there is only *one* unique response for each situation. Graham remarks: "the good is *the* spontaneous reaction" (G89, 209; emphasis added).[86] This would be all right if the good is taken to be plural. Graham says that following *dao* "is the direction to tend spontaneously if you mirror the concrete situation clearly and react to it spontaneously" (G81, 13). This would be all right if *dao* is understood to be plural. We should not exclude the possibility that there may be different sage-like responses in relation to *one* context, all of which are spontaneous. That is to say, there may be *different* spontaneous responses to the same event.

The *Zhuangzi* does not provide justification for the assumption that all sages are (or are not) identical. However, one can argue that in the ideal situation, there is only *one* possibility, namely the possibility "given" by *dao* or *tian* (or by the great sage [*dasheng* 大聖]). For example, Roth (2008, 25n29) explains why all sages would respond in the same way: "each and every thing contains the Way [*dao*] within it; and they are unified in that, from the perspective of the Way within, each thing is seen to be equal. Because they attain this Way, sages can have the exact same perspective." However, if we take *dao* to be a plural noun (*daos*), there may be different responses to the same situation, not only a plurality of *daos* for a plurality of situations. Even if some situation could be approached with perfect clarity (not achievable for humans), two sages may respond differently. After the response, doubt may remain, or conflict may ensue. Therefore, Graham may be wrong to speak of a "*single* course which is *uniquely* appropriate yet fits no rules" (G89, 188, emphasis added).

There are not many publications in which the possibility of "two sages respond differently to the same situation" is taken seriously.[87] We propose that this possibility should be taken into account.[88]

A general weakness of Graham's "technical" distinction between *yinshi* and *weishi* is that this distinction is not apparent from the wording in the inner chapters. For example, almost all the occurrences of *shifei* in the *Qiwulun* are situated in a context that makes it clear that the use of *shifei* by nearly everybody except sages is a case of rigid *shifei* inasmuch as such a use presupposes fixed classifications. However, the phrase *weishi* is never used on such occasions, although all these uses of *shifei* convey Graham's interpretation of *weishi*. For example, 2.2.2 (the arbiters of *shifei*), 2.3.1 (insist upon your *shifei*), 2.3.5 (the *shifei* of the Ruists and the Mohists), 2.4.8 (because *shifei* appeared, *dao* was injured),[89] and 2.6.6 (the paths of *shifei* are all hopelessly snarled and jumbled).[90] The reader of the *Qiwulun* cannot miss Zhuangzi's concern about the futility of *shifei* debates, which are based on a commitment to rigid meanings and rigid criteria of evaluation. This is clear without resorting to a "technical" distinction between *yinshi* and *weishi*.

In addition, the contrast between sages and the commoners is highlighted without using Graham's distinction of *yinshi* and *weishi*.[91]

聖人懷之，眾人辯之以相示也。(2.5.8)

The sage embraces things. Ordinary men discriminate among them and parade their discriminations before others. (Watson)

The sage hides in its embrace, while the mass of people debate it, trying to demonstrate it to one another. (Ziporyn)

The sage keeps it in his breast, common men argue over alternatives to show it to each other. (Graham)

The sages embrace all things, but ordinary people dispute over them to show off to each other. (Mair)

眾人役役，聖人愚芚，參萬歲而一成純。萬物盡然，而以是相蘊。(2.6.12)

Ordinary men strain and struggle; the sage is stupid and blockish. He takes part in ten thousand ages and achieves simplicity in oneness. For him, all the ten thousand things are what they are, and thus they enfold each other. (Watson)

While the mass of men are beleaguered and harried, the sage is dim and dense, standing shoulder to shoulder with the sun and the moon, scooping up time and space and smoothing them all together, leaving them all to their own slippery mush so that every enslavement is also an ennobling. He is there, taking part in the diversity of ten thousand harvests, but in each he tastes one and the same purity of fully formed maturation. For to him each thing is just so, each thing is right, and so he enfolds them all within himself by affirming the rightness of each. (Ziporyn)

The two passages cited are clear enough without using the "technical" terms *yinshi* and *weishi*.

Translations of *Yinbi* 因彼, *Weishi*, and *Yinshi*

In this section, we discuss the appropriateness of Graham's translations of *weishi* and *yinshi*. Later (§9c), as an alternative to Graham's focus on *yinshi* and *weishi*, we highlight Zhuangzi's notion of "walking-two-roads" and the contrast between, on the one hand, the sage (*shengren* 聖人 or *zhenren* 真人) and, on the other hand, the ordinary people (*zhongren* 眾人) and inferior scholars (such as the Ruists and Mohists). We begin with the binome *yinbi* 因彼, which occurs only once in the *Zhuangzi*.

故曰彼出於是，是亦因彼。彼是方生之說也。(2.3.6)

So I say, "that" comes out of "this" and "this" depends on "that"—which is to say that "this" and "that" give birth to each other.

All the translators provide similar renditions, although they use different verbs.
    First clause: comes out of or from (G69, Cleary, Kjellberg, Legge, Wang Rongpei, Watson, and Wu Kuang-ming), emerges from (Harbsmeier, Ziporyn, and Coutinho 2004, 160), derives from (Mair), emanates (Lin Yutang), proceeds from (Billeter), is born from (Levi), and is produced by (Chan Wing-tsit).

Second clause: depends on (Mair, Watson), adapts (G69), derives from (Billeter, Lin Yutang, and Wang Rongpei), follows from/on (Kjellberg, Ziporyn, and Wu Kuang-ming), is a consequence of (Legge), presupposes (Levi), on the basis of (Lin Yunming 林雲銘,[92] Cleary), accords with (Coutinho 2004, 160), and caused by (Chan Wing-tsit).

Third clause: the opinion (notion, theory, and reasoning) that "this" and "that" are born together, give birth (give rise) to each other (Wang Rongpei, Watson), are born simultaneously (G69, Cleary), come into existence at the same moment (Billeter); a case of simultaneous generation (Ziporyn), parallel birth (Kjellberg), cogenesis (Mair), co-birthings (Wu Kuang-ming), producing each other (Feng Youlan, Legge), engendering of *Other* and *This* (Coutinho 2004, 160, Levi[93]), interdependence (Lin Yutang), mutual generation (Guo Xiang in Liu Xiaogan 2015b, 208), mutual production (Chan Wing-tsit), and mutual production of complementary opposites (Schipper).[94]

Graham's translation is only minimally different,[95] which suggests that for him *yinbi* is nothing special, whereas *yinshi* is.

There are minor differences such as writing "this" and "that" with or without quotation marks. Most translators render *shi* in terms of this/that. Wang Rongpei's translation: this side, that side. Graham translates *shi/bi* as It/Other (Schipper: yourself/Other). Kjellberg is the only one who explicitly draws attention to the fact that "this" translates *shi* (and not *ci* 此).

> Hence it is said, "*Bi* 彼, 'that,' comes from *shi* 是, 'this,' and this follows from that." This is the doctrine of the parallel birth of "this" and "that."

In a paraphrase of 2.3.6, Cheng Xuanying suggests that the phrase is about both *bici* and *shifei*.[96]

Although the Chinese original uses two "verbs" for the relation between *bi* and *shi* (*yin* and *chu* 出 respectively),[97] and translators follow by choosing different verbs in the first and second clause of 2.3.6, we suggest that the relation between *bi* and *shi* is to be understood as symmetrical for the following reasons:[98]

1. If "this" and "that" give birth to each other (Watson), it is not clear why a difference is made between "that" *comes out of* "this" (*chu*) and "this" *depends on* "that" (*yin*). Symmetry is not denied, but verbs such as "depend on" may suggest a one-directional relation. If A depends on B in the sense

Shi and Its Opposites and Modifers in the *Qiwulun* 齊物論 / 97

   of A being determined by B, this is often understood as: B does *not* depend on A; B is *not* determined by A.[99]

2. The second clause says literally that it is *also* (*yi* 亦) like the former. There may be stylistic reasons why Zhuangzi uses different verbs in the first and second clause.[100]

3. All the translations we consulted rendered the third clause as stating a symmetrical relation; for example, by saying that *shi* and *bi* "produce each other" (Feng Youlan, Legge, Levi).

There are four occurrences of *weishi* in the inner chapters.[101] One phrase (為是不用而寓諸庸) occurs in two places (2.4.4; 2.4.11). To render *weishi* in the *Zhuangzi*, most translators choose because of, therefore, thus, so.[102] Many older-generation translators use similar renditions for all occurrences (Wu Kuang-ming, Feng Youlan, Lin Yutang, Watson, Mair, Chan Wing-tsit, Muller, Legge, and Schipper); whereas new different translations are offered by Graham, Ziporyn, Wang Rongpei, Eno, Kjellberg, and Levi. Here are a few examples for 2.4.4.

> 唯達者知通為一，為是不用而寓諸庸。(2.4.4)

Only the man of far-reaching vision knows how to make them into one. So he has no use {for categories}, but relegates all to the constant. (Watson)

Only the man who sees right through knows how to interchange and deem them one; the "That's it" which deems he does not use, but finds for them lodging places in the usual. (Graham)

Only the perceptive understand that all things join in Unity. For this reason they do not use things themselves but lodge in commonality. (Mair)

Only the penetrating person knows to comprehend them as one. Don't insist but lodge in the usual. (Kjellberg)

Although 2.4.4 and 2.4.11 contain the same phrase (為是不用而寓諸庸), translations may slightly differ, for example, Ziporyn and Eno.

Such a person would not define rightness in any one particular way but would instead entrust it to the everyday function {of each being}. (Ziporyn 2.4.4)

He makes no definition of what is right but instead entrusts it to the everyday function of each thing. (Ziporyn 2.4.11)

He asserts no "this is so." (Eno 2.4.4)

. . . does not confirm of anything "this is it." (Eno 2.4.11)

Almost all the translators speak of *buyong* in terms of "not using," but some add that it is the distinctions that are not to be used, which addition is not in the Chinese text (Feng Youlan, Lin Yutang, Wang Rongpei). For example,

> Only the truly intelligent understand this principle of the leveling of all things into One. They discard the distinctions and take refuge in the common and ordinary things. (Lin Yutang)

Most translations are similar to Lin Yutang's. A few do not include the word "One" in the translation, but instead use words such as uniformity (Wang Rongpei), unity (Cleary, Mair), or totality (Levi). *Weishi* also occurs in 23.7.5 and 27.1.2.

與己同則應，不與己同則反；同於己為是之，異於己為非之。(27.1.2)

What agrees with his standpoint he approves with a "That's it" which deems, what disagrees he rejects with a "That's not" which deems. (G81, 106)

Then men would respond only to what agrees with their own views and reject what does not, would pronounce "right" what agrees with their own views and "wrong" what does not. (Watson)

為是舉移是。(23.7.5)

A contrived "that's it" picks out a shifting "it." (G69, 143)

A "That's it" which deems picks out by a reference *it* as it shifts. (G81, 104)

The definition of what is right adopts the shifting rightness of "this." (Ziporyn)

And so for this reason you launch into your analysis. (Watson)

Ziporyn follows Graham, but the translation by Watson is very different. Graham's translations of *weishi* seem to be *ad hoc* choices when compared with the rather general consensus among the other translations. There is no need for assigning a technical meaning to *weishi*.

There are six occurrences of *yinshi* in the inner chapters. Interpretation may vary depending on what grammatical function is assigned to *shi* (noun, verb, demonstrative, . . .) and how it "connects" with the surrounding characters. The phrase 亦因是也 occurs twice.[103]

是以聖人不由，而照之於天，亦因是也。是亦彼也，彼亦是也。(2.3.7)

Therefore the sage does not proceed in such a way, but illuminates all in the light of Heaven. He too recognizes a "this," but a "this" which is also "that," a "that" which is also "this."

名實未虧，而喜怒為用，亦因是也。(2.4.6)

There was no change in the reality behind the words, and yet the monkeys responded with joy and anger. Let them, if they want to.

Some translators choose similar renditions for the same phrase, but the occurrence in 2.3.7 causes more problems than the one in 2.4.6. If 亦因是也 is read with *shi* referring back and *yin* as "based on this (*shi*)," then this is usually understood as recognizing things in their natural being-so. Feng Youlan simply skipped this phrase in his translation of 2.3.7. Instead of acknowledging severe underdetermination, many different translations have appeared for 2.3.7.

For one may base it on this, . . . (Lin Yutang)

. . . that also is an adaptive way of taking something to be "this" (Harbsmeier)

He [the sage] too recognizes a "this," . . . (Watson)

His too is a "That's it" which goes by circumstance. (Graham)

. . . accepting "this" for what it is. (Mair)

. . . consequently adapts his language to change. (Billeter)

He just goes along with things. (Kjellberg)

And that too is only a case of going by the rightness of the present "this." (Ziporyn)[104]

He conforms himself to the circumstances. (Levi)

. . . depend on affirmation. (Muller)

This is the reason. (Chan Wing-tsit)

Sometimes similar translations are given for 2.3.7 and 2.4.6 (in particular, Kjellberg, Levi, Ziporyn, and Graham). However, quite a few commentators give different translations for the occurrence in 2.3.7 and 2.4.6 (Feng Youlan, Chan Wing-tsit, Wang Rongpei, Watson, Mair, Muller, and Legge), for example,

seeks to recognize the true state of things. (Wang Rongpei 2.3.7)

followed the natural bend of the monkeys. (Wang Rongpei 2.4.6)

Perhaps consensus could be reached by suggesting that in both cases (2.3.7 and 2.4.6) the meaning of *yinshi* can be approximated by following the course of things or the circumstances while adapting to the situation.

The phrase *yinshi ye* 因是已 also occurs twice.

因是已。已而不知其然，謂之道。(2.4.5)

He relies upon this alone, relies upon it and does not know he is doing so. This is called the Way.

无適焉，因是已。(2.5.5)

Better not to move, but to let things be!

Shi and Its Opposites and Modifers in the *Qiwulun* 齊物論 / 101

There are two things to notice concerning the translation of these two occurrences of 因是已. The last character can be taken as "end of phrase marker" or as having the meaning "stop."¹⁰⁵ For the translators who opt for "stop here" (Lin Yutang) or similar dictions (for example, "Let us not proceed"), translations for 2.4.5 and 2.5.5 are rather similar (Muller, Legge, Feng Youlan, Lin Yutang, Legge, Muller, Schipper, Wu Kuang-ming, and also Graham). A minority of translators opt for something like "follow the course of things" (Levi, Cleary, Kjellberg, and Wang Rongpei). Some translators expand the occurrence in 2.4.5, as can be seen in comparison with the more "literal" translation they give to 2.5.5. For example,

> Go as far as whatever you happen to get to, and leave it at that. It is all just a matter of going by the rightness of the present "this." To be doing this without knowing it, and not because you have defined it as right, is called "the Course." (Ziporyn 2.4.5)

> Rather than moving from anywhere to anywhere, let us just go by the rightness of whatever is before us as the present "this." (Ziporyn 2.5.5)

> It is all a result of their understanding the mutual dependence of "this" and "that." To have achieved this understanding but not be conscious of why it is so is called "The Way." (Mair 2.4.5)

> We need not proceed at all if we understand the mutual dependence of "this" and "that." (Mair 2.5.5)

Watson's translations are brief and also quite different.

> He relies upon this [that is, 2.4.4] alone. (2.4.5)

> . . . but to let things be. (2.5.5)

Chan Wing-tsit combines the options (except for Graham's) by adding alternative translations in his notes.¹⁰⁶ *Yinshi* also occurs in 25.9.2 (G81, 108).

We conclude that there is not much support for Graham's translation of *yinshi* as " 'that's it' that goes by circumstance." We prefer Chan's "let us let things take their own course" (2.5.5).

Yinshi also occurs twice in the following passage:¹⁰⁷

[方生方死，方死方生。方可方不可，方不可方可] 因是因非，因非因是。是以聖人不由而照之於天，亦因是也。是亦彼也，彼亦是也。(2.3.7)

> But where there is birth there must be death; where there is death there must be birth. Where there is acceptability there must be unacceptability; where there is unacceptability there must be acceptability. Where there is recognition of right there must be recognition of wrong; where there is recognition of wrong there must be recognition of right. Therefore the sage does not proceed in such a way, but illuminates all in the light of Heaven. He too recognizes a "this," but a "this" which is also "that," a "that" which is also "this." (Watson)

In the TLS version of Watson's translation, Harbsmeier has added the Grahamian variants to the translation by Watson, specifying *shi* in terms of either adapting *shi* or rigid *shi*.

With a few exceptions, most translators unanimously render the third and fourth clause as "because of this [that is, what is stated in the first two clauses after the addition in square brackets], the sage does not follow this path, but focuses on the light of heaven." These translators include: Watson, and similarly Legge, Wilhelm, Feng Youlan, Kjellberg, Ziporyn, Muller, Chan Wing-tsit, and Eno. Graham also agrees with such renditions. Some add the clarification "rejects distinctions" (of this and that) (Giles, Feng Youlan, and Lin Yutang). Francophone translators provide significantly different translations.

> Each predication [*qualification*] is at once correct and incorrect and incorrect and correct. (Levi)[108]

> Thus, a given designation [*denomination*] is now correct and now incorrect, while {another} is now incorrect and now correct. (Billeter)

Only Ziporyn follows Graham in using the word circumstantially.

因是因非，因非因是. (2.3.7)

> If going by circumstance that's it then going by circumstance that's not, if going by circumstance that's not then going by circumstance that's it. (Graham)

Shi and Its Opposites and Modifers in the *Qiwulun* 齊物論 / 103

> What is circumstancely right is circumstancely wrong and vice versa. (Ziporyn)

All the other translators either seem to overlook the character *yin* or convey a sense of "dependence" between *shi* and *fei*. Early translators render *shifei* as affirm/deny (Cleary, Giles, Legge, Wilhelm, Lin Yutang). More recently, Eno and Muller have followed this rendition. Most of the influential translators modify the apparent contradiction of 因是因非因非因是 by nuancing the dependence of right and wrong. As we consider that this is an important observation, we cite some examples.

> (The disputants) now affirm and now deny; now deny and now affirm. (Legge)

> Where there is recognition of the right there must be recognition of the wrong; where there is recognition of the wrong there must be recognition of the right. (Wang Rongpei)

> "This" and "that" are mutually dependent; right and wrong are also mutually dependent. (Mair)[109]

> If they are right in a way, they are wrong in a way. If they are wrong in a way, they are right in a way. (Kjellberg)

> Because there is a "yes" there is also a "no" and opposite the "not" there is always a "yes." (Schipper)[110]

> Because there is right, there is wrong. Because there is wrong, there is right. (Feng Youlan)

> Because of the right, there is the wrong, and because of the wrong, there is the right. (Chan Wing-tsit)

> Following the right, there comes the wrong; and following the wrong, there comes the right. (Guo Xiang, translated by Liu Xiaogan 2015b, 208)

That is to say, many translations convey the idea that *shi* and *fei* cannot exist without the other being present as well. Chen Guying (2007, 69n6) explicitly articulates this idea in assuming that this passage expresses a similar idea as 2.3.6: "This means that *shi* and *fei* generate one another, when there is *shi*, there would be *fei*; when there is *fei*, there would be *shi*" (following Chen Qitian 陈启天).

Graham and Ziporyn's translations cited above come nearest to presenting two contradictions.[111] And perhaps the following also presents a contradiction:

> To rely on what we assert is to rely on what we deny; to rely on what we deny is to rely on what we assert. (Eno)

Harbsmeier (1992) follows Graham's terminology, but removes any trace of apparent contradictions.

> But then, one moment there is life; one moment there is death. One moment there is death, one moment there is life. One moment it is acceptable, the next moment it is not acceptable. One moment it is not acceptable, the next moment it is acceptable. Going by {some} circumstances it is right, going by {other} circumstances it is wrong. Going by {some} circumstances it is wrong, going by {other} circumstances it is right. Therefore the sage does not go by {these concepts of right and wrong [that is *yinshi* and *weishi*]}, but takes the perspective of Heaven. But that again is a case of adaptive considering as right. "This" is also "that." "That" is also "this."

Some translators seem to have tried to be neutral (with respect to the question of whether the original states a contradiction).

> Affirmation is based upon denial, and vice versa. (Lin Yutang)

> Depending on affirmation, depending on rejection; depending on rejection, depending on affirmation. (Muller)

Translations in modern Chinese show interesting differences with translations in modern English. Consider the following:

> Although this is the case, in all kinds of situations when there is birth, it will be accompanied by death; when there is death, it will be accompanied by birth; when there is rightness [*dui* 對] there will occur wrongness [*cuo* 錯]; when there is wrongness there will occur rightness. Hence, the sages do not pursue the way of discussing *shifei* and *bici*. (Qin Xuqing and Sun Yongchang)

Even if so, things are always coming to an end while coming into birth, and coming into birth while coming to an end. When one aspect is affirmed, there is always another aspect that is negated; when one aspect is negated, there is always another aspect that is affirmed. When there is *shi* there is *fei*; when there is *fei* there is *shi*. Both *shi* and *fei* appear in mutual relation with each other. Hence, the sages do not follow the way in which *shifei* are opposed. (Si Lü)

The translation by Qin and Sun illustrates that some translations into modern Chinese *do* translate *shi* and *fei* as *dui* 對 and *cuo* 錯, respectively. But in the next sentence they "translate" *shifei* as *shifei*. Si Lü sticks to *shi* and *fei*. Qin and Sun "forget" translating the clause 方可方不可方不可方可, or perhaps they take it to be of similar meaning with 因是因非因非因是. In contrast, Si inserts an extra sentence (not in the original) to elucidate the meaning of 因是因非因非因是 : "Both *shi* and *fei* appear in mutual relation to one another."

Si Lü translates the clause Qin and Sun leave out in terms of negate/affirm, which has also been used as a translation of *shifei*. It is difficult to say whether the modern Chinese translation reflects an implicit contradiction. But both sources are explicit about what the course is that sages are *not* following: the sages do not follow the way in which *duicuo* (or *shifei*) are opposed, and they do not pursue the way of discussing *duicuo* (or *shifei*) and *bici*. But the functioning of *shifei* in classic texts disappears from sight when *shifei* is translated as *duicuo*.

It is noteworthy that Graham's "innovation" does not seem to have provided an explanation why sages do not follow the course of *yinshi* and *yinfei*, as 2.3.7 suggests (see, for instance, citation from Harbsmeier a few paragraphs back). Graham's translations would possibly lead to the conclusion that a sage does *not* follow the road of going along with the circumstances. He is right to highlight the "distinction" between actions based on the changing situation and actions based on inflexible principles. The relevance of the "distinction" (which Graham calls "opposite kinds of *shi*") is important, but the translations of *weishi* and *yinshi* he proposes seem to be highly speculative when compared with other translations. Moreover, insofar as *yin* in the sense of "following along with the course of things" is supportive of the "distinction," this idea can already be found in older commentaries (Guo Xiang, Cheng Xuanying, Lin Xiyi). Instead of Graham's proposal, we opt for highlighting Zhuangzi's notion of "walking-two-roads" and the contrast between sages and humans (see §9c).

Part II

From Disputation to Walking-Two-Roads in the *Zhuangzi*

Chapter 8

Is Zhuangzi a Relativist or a Skeptic?

Zhuangzi and Relativism

The debate as to whether skepticism and/or relativism are appropriate labels for Zhuangzi has attracted much attention in recent years in the anglophone literature.[1] We take the view that this scholastic fervor stems primarily from the domination of Anglo-American philosophers in the English scholarly circle. Given the variety of relativisms, it is impossible for us to make any general statements about the relevant notions and theses.[2] Meaning, reference, truth, ontology, metaphysical commitment, reality, epistemic values (virtues), moral values, and aesthetic values, each of these notions can be said to be relative to one or to a few items from such a list: language, conceptual scheme, theory, scientific paradigm, version, description, culture, community, and individual (Haack 1998, 149). Each combination characterizes a particular brand of relativism.[3]

Among sinologists, Graham and Hansen are typically regarded as having ascribed relativism to Zhuangzi, and their writings may seem to support this. For example, Coutinho (2015) discusses what he considers as the relativistic interpretations of Hansen and Graham in much detail before coming to his own views. He does not flatly deny ascribing relativism (or skepticism) to Zhuangzi, but he prefers highlighting other features of the *Zhuangzi*, for example, Zhuangzi's stance with respect to language (see §9b). Assuming that Hansen or Graham's interpretation of Zhuangzi is correct (within the linguistic confines of English), we argue that the form of relativism they ascribe to Zhuangzi can hardly be called by that label. One can claim relativism on Zhuangzi's behalf in a most minimalistic sense of relativism provided that this is only one aspect among numerous features of Zhuangzi's stance. Instead of focusing on applying labels such as relativism and skepticism, we prefer highlighting Zhuangzi's stance of doubt (§9d).

We do not deny that there are quite some passages in the inner chapters that may suggest a sense of relativism or skepticism, in particular to an innocent reader; but the apparent relativism or skepticism may disappear when we take into account a wider context. For example, Liu Xiaogan (2015b) cites about ten passages from the *Zhuangzi*, each of which, when taken in isolation from its immediate textual context, can be characterized in Western terms as a "typical statement of the relativist argument" or "clearly an ethical relativist position" (208–9).[4] However, as Liu correctly points out, each passage is then followed by phrases such as "Dao makes all into one"[5] or by similar phrases involving a sage, the One, *tian*, or *Dao*.[6]

It is noteworthy that Liu does not explicitly mention the quarrels between the Ruists and Mohists in 2.3.5. However, he writes,

> The "this" has one standard of right and wrong, and the "that" also has a standard of right and wrong, which is clearly an ethical relativist position if we were to encounter it as isolated statement. (209)

Liu makes this statement with respect to 2.3.8, but it can as well be applied to 2.3.5. Moreover, 2.3.5 is *also* followed by a "solution," namely using *ming* 明 ("if we want to right their wrongs and wrong their rights, then the best thing to use is clarity").[7] However, this is a minor point. On the whole, we agree with Liu that only when passages are considered in isolation do hints at relativism or skepticism arise.

More generally speaking, we suggest that the concepts of and discussions concerning relativism and skepticism only make sense on the assumption of a large number of rigid notions of classification, truth, justification, and so on. These notions are not applicable to Zhuangzi who enjoys free use of language. The labels of relativism and skepticism are not helpful (because of the multifarious meanings of these labels), and irrelevant (because they are not classical Chinese concepts) to promoting our understanding of Zhuangzi. Many interpretations have been based mainly on a few brief passages severed from context.

Ascribing relativism to Zhuangzi may have been influenced by the dominating influence of Guo Xiang's commentary. (Guo also composed the earliest extant edition of the *Zhuangzi*.) Guo Xiang wrote the following:

> Everything is what it is. The opinions of the one and the other are different; that they both have opinions is the same. (cited in Feng Youlan 1928, 39)
>
> Let everything enjoy its own nature, and have its own satisfaction. (cited in Feng Youlan 1928, 51)

Given the distance in time and language, perhaps these passages should not be interpreted as a straightforward illustration of relativism. However, Feng Youlan's comments on his translation of the inner chapters into English (Feng Youlan 1928) may be considered as articulating an explicit form of relativism.

> The different opinions are like the different noises of wind. . . . They are equally right and good. (11)
>
> But all of them are equally natural, equally good. So the different things and opinions mentioned in what follows are also equally natural, equally good. (40)
>
> There is a variety in the ways of living, just as there is a variety in things. These different ways are of equal value. (51)

We can see from these citations from Feng Youlan, and perhaps also from Guo Xiang, that the *Zhuangzi* easily suggests to the "modern" reader a form of relativism.[8]

In recent secondary literature concerning Zhuangzi's stance, the word perspectivism is often used, in particular when discussing *zhi* 知 (knowledge–understanding),[9] as is apparent in titles such as "Perspectivism as a Way of Knowing in the *Zhuangzi*" (Connolly 2011) and "*Zhuangzi*, Perspectives, and Greater Knowledge" (Sturgeon 2015). The term perspectivism is often used as a "soft" name of relativism (Hansen 2015; Ziporyn 2009b). However, this term does not occur in translations of the *Zhuangzi*, though occasionally it does occur in translations of other Warring States texts. However, when this happens the word perspective is obviously added by the translator, because there is no Chinese character in classical times that directly stands in a family resemblance relation with the recent Western notion of perspective.[10]

Relativisms, at least in their radical forms, have often been charged with being self-refuting. Because of the charge of self-refutation, there are not many scholars who would openly declare themselves to be relativists. Instead, they tend to accuse some of their opponents as relativists. Putnam considers Rorty to be a relativist (see also §10b), whereas Putnam's "internal realism" has often been regarded as a form of relativism. However, both Putnam and Rorty stress that relativism is self-refuting.[11]

> That (total) relativism is inconsistent is a truism among philosophers. (Putnam 1981, 119)

> Relativism is the view that every belief on a certain topic, or perhaps about any topic, is as good as every other. No one holds this view. (Rorty 1982, 166)

An additional problem is that different relativistic views are incomparable (as a Zhuangzian could say concerning the views of Mohists and Ruists). There are no criteria for judging who is right (2.6.17–19). However, the so-called incommensurability only arises when an ideal language is assumed.[12] Furthermore, the thesis of incommensurability cannot prevent one from first learning and then evaluating the allegedly incommensurable views. Feyerabend, the author of *Against Method* (1975), remarks in retrospect.

> Incommensurability is a difficulty for philosophers, not for scientists. Philosophers insist on stability of meaning throughout an argument while scientists are experts in the art of arguing across lines which philosophers regard as insuperable boundaries of discourse. . . . Relativism flounders because one "stage" or "form of life" blurs into another. Most groups, societies, traditions not only interact, they are built for interaction. (Feyerabend 1999, 123–27)

We agree with Feyerabend's assessment. Incommensurability is a common phenomenon, but this does not entail strict boundaries, which is only set up by philosophers. Perhaps the strongest reason why no view should be labeled as (self-refuting) relativism is that every type of relativism is grounded in universalism, which we discuss in the chapter on preliminaries (§1a). For example, one can only judge a passage in the *Zhuangzi* to be "relativistic" by first translating it into English. Any actual translation presupposes mutually recognizable human practices and other basic traits of humans, including apparently trivial ones (for example, that the authors(s) and compiler(s) of the *Zhuangzi* are human beings who belong to a community, or communities[13]). A particular statement is *always* relative to a community simply because the language has to allow for a sufficient number of quasi-universals to be mutually understandable (§1a).[14]

Authors who discern relativistic tendencies in Zhuangzi typically take as universalistic their *claim* that Zhuangzi is a relativist. Allowing "exceptions" also reduces relativism to the claim that *some* judgments are not universalistic. For example, Hansen (2015) suggests: "possibly, some views are unwarranted from *any* perspective (for example, logical contradictions and counter-intuitives)." That is to say, Hansen assumes that there is universal agreement, for example, on what is and what is not "counter-intuitive."[15]

David Wong, the author of *Natural Moralities: A Defense of Pluralistic Relativism* (2006), is often mentioned when discussing moral relativism. However, he does not claim that all views are equally good (as Feng Youlan does on behalf of Zhuangzi). Wong holds the view that there is a universally fixed set of moral principles, and different scholars weigh these principles differently such that a single principle becomes dominant.[16] His version of relativism is a meta-model related to a number of current views. It does not embrace all possible views. Rather than relativism, it is better to consider this idea as a form of pluralism against the background of a fixed universalistic set of moral principles.

Most sinologists distinguish between relativism and pluralism, regarding the former as "bad" and the latter as "good." For example, Rosemont writes (2014, 153n5, 208–9),

> I allow there to be more than one very good reading of a work, and of differing ways of life. This however, makes me a pluralist, not a relativist. For me there can be no best interpretation (by whose cultural criteria would it be evaluated?), but it doesn't follow that I can't distinguish better or worse interpretations (or ways of life). . . .
>
> I can live easily without "true" and "false" while interpreting, translating, and writing, using "better" or "worse" instead.

But it is not clear whether invoking a distinction between better and worse interpretations can resolve the problem of criterion.[17] To judge whether one interpretation is better than another, one needs a standard for such a judgment, and the standard must be "universally valid" in order to bind everybody to accept the (allegedly) better interpretation. The factors contributing to hermeneutic relativity (Ma and van Brakel 2018) would influence the judgment of what the better stance is with respect to evaluating competing interpretations, for instance, of a certain passage from the Quran or from the Bible.

Although some commentators agree that Guo Xiang has presented a "relativistic" interpretation of the *Zhuangzi*, their interpretation is embedded in universalistic statements as well, in particular those concerning mutually recognizable human practices.

> Everything (people) considers itself to be right and others wrong, itself to be beautiful and others to be ugly. Everything is what it is. (Guo Xiang cited in Feng Youlan 1928, 39)

> Following what is of nature . . . is the source of all happiness and goodness; following what is of man is the source of all pain and evil. (Feng Youlan 1928, 130–31)

Both Guo Xiang and Feng Youlan presuppose a commonsense meta-language containing quasi-universals such as beautiful, ugly, happiness, goodness, pain, evil, small, big, wind, laughing, eel, monkey, and so on.

We conclude that the "weakness" of relativism (such as the alleged incommensurability and the charge of self-refutation) only arises when an ideal language is presupposed.

Relativities versus Relativism

When the conceptual schemes (theories, languages) of two people(s) in communication are different, we should distinguish between relativities on the one hand and relativisms on the other.[18] When it comes to relativities, meanings are relative to language, and distinctions may depend on an objective standard (similar to standards of measurement). That is to say, if, with some effort, one learns the other language and its distinctions or standards, then the differences would turn out to be primarily conventional, and explainable with reference to the natural embedment of each language in its own tradition. If the *prima facie* conventional differences come into conflict with irreconcilable beliefs, one could consider it as a case of relativism. Alternatively speaking, one could define relativism as an account of the (apparent) presence of unbridgeable (and to some extent incomprehensible) differences in beliefs. However, whether the idea of unbridgeable or irreconcilable beliefs is imaginable is disputable (This issue is further discussed in §10a). Furthermore, if there is no sharp boundary between relativities and relativisms, their separation is in itself a matter of interpretation.

There are a large variety of relativities, but, in our view, many relativities are hardly significant exemplifications of relativism; rather, they are trivial and innocent. Consider the following variety of relativities that do not bear on relativism:[19]

1. The relativity of standards of measurement does not exemplify relativism.[20]

2. The relativity of high(er) and low(er) does not lead to relativism. One only needs to understand the notion of comparison.

3. The relativity of this and that does not involve relativism. Starting from a "this," one can imagine a "that."

4. The relativity of concepts to a particular conceptual scheme is not necessarily a case of relativism. Accepting alternative "incommensurable" classifications does not entail relativism.

5. Differences "caused" by differences of context cannot be counted as relativism. Each party (or a third party) can assess the other's claim of "relative to context."

6. The conventional character of (alphabetic) languages in itself does not entail relativism. In English, exchanging the meaning of the words wrong and right is changing a *conventional* determination, which does not bear on relativism.[21]

One may argue that there are no trivial relativities because each item in the list above can be "raised" to be a case of "strong" relativism by insisting that the differences between different stances concerning allegedly incommensurable conventions are "deep," "essential," "unbridgeable," and so on. Our view is that there are no such "strong" cases of relativism. Each proffered case of strong relativism is embedded in a language in which the "strong" case of relativism is described. When one claims that one does not understand a language, such a claim admits that what one does not understand is a *language* (as distinct from the peeping of baby birds [2.3.3]). The relativities listed do not jeopardize understanding across languages and traditions. Pragmatically steered discussions concerning practical (dis)advantages of each stance or convention are always possible. Relativities are always open to evaluation by outsiders, although in practice there may be massive confusion because different interlocutors use the same word for different concepts.

We reserve the term relativism for the following situations: (1) when citing other authors, and (2) when there is disagreement at a "deep" level when interlocutors allegedly see no way out of the unavoidability of *agreeing to disagree* on a particular utterance (§10a).

It may be interesting to compare the views of the Strong Program (SP) with that of Zhuangzi. SP can be considered as a form of relativism that defends the thesis that the objectivity of a belief (or a web of beliefs) can only be grounded in (contingent) social institutions in which that belief finds its place. This type of relativism is based on the following premises:[22]

1. There are different opinions–beliefs on every topic.

2. The opinions–beliefs that are present within a certain context are a function of the circumstances in which those opinions have been formed.

3. All the beliefs claiming credibility are on a par.

The last postulate has been called the postulate of symmetry or equivalence. It means that, in a certain domain of research, the causes of the credibility of beliefs and ways of reasoning are to be studied irrespective of whether the SP-er thinks that the beliefs under consideration are right or wrong or meaningless. SP does not state that all opinions are equally true or false, but it does say that the local causes of their credibility must be studied. SP-ers do not accept the concept of truth, whereas scientists whose practice SP-ers study may employ such a concept. SP-ers replace "true" with "credible."

Peterman's criticism of *shifei* relativisms can well be addressed to SP (2008, 372):

> If it is true that "all judgments of *shi* and *fei* are relative to existing community practices," then this claim itself must be "*shi*-ed" only from a particular community practice. That is, if it is true, then it is only relatively true and may also be relatively false.

SP-ers may reply that they engage with their opponents, asking them which stance is pragmatically more satisfying.

SP is *not* the same as "anything goes" relativism. The SP-ers do not wish to deprive science of its scientific character, but they analyze this character in a different manner from mainstream scholars. Scientific research is ruled by conventions that have to meet criteria of social credibility and practical use, but in order to fulfill these conditions, one does not need a notion of universal truth or rationality. SP disavows a universal rationality and a ready-made world. The postulate of symmetry is a conclusion empirically grounded in successful case studies. These case studies show that if one examines the practice of scientific change sociologically (that is, empirically), the difference between "rational" opinions, which would be self-explanatory, and "irrational" opinions, which need a causal explanation, is nowhere to be found.

SP assumes that opinions and actions of scientists are natural phenomena in need of causal explanation in terms of social circumstances in the life-world of the particular scientific discipline. According to SP, there is no rigid distinction between reasons and beliefs that cannot be explained by reasons (except by sociological causes). Thus, the distinction between "giving reasons" and "being caused by some social mechanism" as understood on the received view becomes blurred. The criteria for giving reasons are intertwined with social processes.

Zhuangzi's and SP's views are somewhat similar, except that SP focuses on modern science:[23]

1. Classifications are not determined by how the world is, but are convenient ways in which the world can be presented.

2. The focus is more on *natural* causes, as Guo Xiang had already emphasized, than on argumentation.

3. Intellectual schools differ due to different circumstances (for example, being educated into a group).

4. There is no true or false, that is, no *shifei*.

5. The symmetry thesis can be ascribed to Guo Xiang and perhaps to Zhuangzi as well.

The disagreement between SP and other philosophers and historians of science shows similarities with the disagreement between Zhuangzi and other contemporaneous schools in his time. Both parties have their own concepts that exclude the other's concepts. A difference is that the notion of walking-two-roads (§9c) cannot be found in SP. Perhaps the weakness of SP is that they treat the equivalence postulate as a methodological postulate, which one could consider as an extreme case of value-free positivism. This is similar to Zhuangzi's alleged amoralism (§10b).

Neither Zhuangzi nor SP is a self-acclaimed relativist. SP carries out empirical research that is governed by strict rules, for example, the rule of avoiding bias (that is, preventing research results from the influence of personal preferences). There is no "anything goes" relativism in SP-research. Rather, SP adheres to rigid rules. Zhuangzi is not a relativist either. Although he does not subscribe to strict rules, he is committed to a range of beliefs and stances, which will be elaborated in the next chapter.

Hansen and Graham's Relativistic Interpretations of the *Zhuangzi*

Ascribing relativism to Zhuangzi has perhaps become a common practice in certain circles, but if one looks at the textual details, one wonders whether the word "relativism" is in any way appropriate. In this section, we consider the work by Graham and Hansen, two prominent scholars who have been regarded as offering relativistic interpretations of the *Zhuangzi*, and whose texts may seem to support this.[24]

Over a period of three decades, Hansen has developed the most detailed discussion of Zhuangzi in terms of relativism and skepticism (1983ab, 1992, 2015). According to him, Zhuangzi's discourse involving *bian* and *shifei* approximates Western discourse of judgment, thought, and inference. In his early work, Hansen preferred the label skeptical perspectivism or indexical relativism.[25] In his later work, he changed his ideas concerning what the best label is to be ascribed to Zhuangzi. Most recently, he has spoken of a combination of relativism, skepticism, and pragmatism, in sum: "skeptical relativism." Hansen (2015) associates skeptical relativism with "an argument for political neutrality and its associated toleration of different concepts of the good life" in ancient China.[26]

Although Hansen ascribes a so-called skeptical relativism to Zhuangzi, he acknowledges that in the *Zhuangzi* there is judgment-making, and that it is not the case that every *dao*[guide] is correct or all are equal. Every judgment depends on a certain other norm, which should not be considered to be absolute. He writes (2015),

> I therefore construe the Zhuangzi text as drawing a still weaker conclusion. It would accept, . . . that we are permitted to make judgments and to "deem" ourselves right in doing so. Still, we acknowledge that in our deeming, we have depended on some other norm that we acquired . . . in happening to be raised and exposed to one of many possible paths. We are not so confident as to make us stop listening to and discussing with others or to warrant using coercion to eliminate other daos.

This could be regarded as one of the plausible interpretations of Zhuangzi's text, perhaps except for the last sentence, which conveys Hansen's commitment to a form of liberalism. However, we think that Zhuangzi's stance should not be labeled as skepticism or relativism. We need to bear in mind that some passages in the *Zhuangzi* that appear to be supporting different versions of relativism or skepticism are actually at the service of undermining the ideal language assumption (which we take to be the opposite pole of *weiding* [§9b]).

We now turn to Graham. It is true that he writes "skepticism and relativism as extreme as Zhuangzi's are not in themselves unfamiliar to a modern reader, far from it" (Graham 1983, 7).[27] It is not clear why he uses phrases such as "relativism as extreme as Zhuangzi's." When there is hardly any context for his claim (as is the case with the foregoing citation), Graham seems to be appealing to a sort of consensus among sinologists. When there is context, he actually sketches a much more nuanced picture than what is suggested by such general claims.

For example, Graham's use of the phrase "bottomless skepticism" (G81, 4) is often cited as his representative view. But in the same paragraph where this expression appears, he mentions *eight* other characteristics of Zhuangzi's writings, including "invulnerable confidence" and "down-to-earth observation." Although Graham remarks that the debates between the Ruists and the Mohists "encouraged [Zhuangzi] in uncompromising moral relativism" (G81, 4), in a later publication he points to something that transcends relativism (G89, 193): "At the rock bottom of skepticism there remain spontaneity and a single imperative to guide it: 'Mirror things as they are.'" Hence, Graham assumes an imperative guide (both for Zhuangzi and for himself).[28] Finally, when Graham claims that Zhuangzi "*professes* a boundless skepticism about the possibility of ever saying anything" (G89, 199), this is contrasted with his being "a master of sophisticated argument, aphorism, anecdote, lyrical prose and gnomic verse."

In his *Disputers of the Tao*, Graham cites in translation all the passages that in some literature have been considered as an articulation of relativism.[29] But at those points, he does not really engage the issue of relativism. On the rare occasion where he explicitly discusses relativism in that work, he does not mention Zhuangzi (G89, 414–16, 428). Perhaps Graham's mistake was that he takes the Mohists as universalists (which is correct) and then draws on this to conclude that Zhuangzi must be a relativist.

Some commentators of Graham have ascribed to him the view that Zhuangzi is a relativist on dubious grounds. For example, Coutinho writes, "there are many things and many points of view, great and small; each has its own value, and none can be judged to be better or worse than any other" (2015, 161), which view he ascribes to Graham. However, this is Feng Youlan's view, and perhaps Guo Xiang's view, but not Graham's view.

Graham has argued for many years that Zhuangzi "discovered" conventionalism (G69, 141; G81, 10; G89, 177).[30] We might have named horses using the label "cows." Some scholars would consider this a case of relativism. Using "horse" as a label for horse is relative to the English language, in French the label is "cheval." But conventionalism is not the same as relativism. Graham says that conventional systems produce their own system of evaluation (G81, 11). This may be true of the normativity of meanings, but judgments of human actions are not part of language.

Graham considers the following passage as the prototypical illustration that Zhuangzi realizes that language is inherently conventional (24.5.1–3; G81, 101; cf. G89, 177):[31]

莊子曰：射者非前期而中，謂之善射，天下皆羿也，可乎？

Chuang Tzu said, "If an archer, without taking aim at the mark, just happens to hit it, and we dub him a skilled archer, then everyone in the world can be an Archer Yi—all right?" (Watson)

Said Chuang-tzu, "If archers who hit what they haven't previously specified as the target were to be called good archers, everyone in the world would be as great an archer as Yi—allowable?" (G81, 101)

It is correct that the first part of the passage cited can be read as an illustration of the conventionality of language. We could change the meaning of "skilled archer" in such a way that everybody is a skilled archer, though it would make this expression less useful in most societies. However, what is more important is, as Cheng Xuanying writes: "If each follows his own *shi*, then there is no universal *shi*" (440). Hence debate is futile.[32] Guo Xiang remarks (440): "If everybody is a Yao-sage, then why did the five scholars try to attack (*fei*) one another?" Cheng Xuanying continues: "If each affirms (*shi*) what he takes to be *shi*, then everybody would be a sage. Would this be possible? The reply is no."

We suggest that we distinguish between the indisputable conventionalism of language, on the one hand, and possibly irresolvable disagreement about right behavior (including actual employment of language), on the other.[33] Different conventions do not necessarily entail irresolvable disagreement, because new or other conventions can be learnt. Conventionalism as such is not relativism, though perhaps it may lead to (perceived) relativism.

Zhi 知 and Skepticism

Ascribing skepticism to Zhuangzi is even more common than ascribing relativism to him. This is not a "radical" skepticism which is self-refuting,[34] but, as the relevant authors point out, therapeutic skepticism as methodological doubt, as admitting mistakes, as releasing us from anxiety, or as continuous suspension of judgment (Kjellberg 2007; Raphals 1996).[35] As to suspension of judgment, Zhuangzi's stance is more fundamental than that of Sextus Empiricus (ca. 160 to ca. 210 CE), author of *Outlines of Pyrrhonism* (1976), who says the following:[36]

> Since the Dogmatists appear to have established plausibly that there really is a criterion of truth, we have set up counter arguments which appear to be plausible; and though we do not positively affirm either that they are true or that they are more plausible than their opposites, yet because of the apparently equal plausibility of these arguments and of those produced by the Dogmatists we deduce suspension of judgment.

Such a stance *suspends* judgment concerning the arguments of the Ruists and the Mohists. Zhuangzi does not just suspend judgment, but rather deconstructs *shifei* discourse (§10a).[37]

In this section we discuss the alleged skepticism of Zhuangzi. In a later section we address his stance of doubt, which we consider to be a different concern that does not bear on skepticism, nor is it a sort of methodological doubt (§9d). Authors referring to or discussing skepticism or relativism in relation to the interpretation of the *Qiwulun* start by saying things such as,

> The text [seems] to argue either for a skeptical denial that we could ever know the truth or for a relativistic denial that there is any truth to know. (Kjellberg and Ivanhoe 1996, xv)

However, the Western concept of "to know something" is not part of the classical Chinese language. This is a rather trivial observation, but it has not yet been taken seriously.[38] *Zhi* does *not* mean knowledge (understood as something like "justified true belief").

The idea of (non-propositional) know-how is often invoked to explicate *zhi* 知, and there is extensive literature on skill, ability, talent, ingenuity, art, craft, and so on, as illustrated by Cook Ding 丁 in the inner chapters. These skill notions are intimately connected with action. However, what can be noted here is that the character used to refer to these "knacks" of cook Ding in 3.2.2–4 is not *zhi*, but *ji* 技 (being able, being skillful).[39]

Zhi 知, a hybrid concept as judged from the side of English, can incorporate the senses of understanding, knowing, wisdom, discernment, comprehension, as well as consciousness of these and the know-how that follows (Ziporyn 2009a, 219).[40] Most uses of *zhi* and its translations can be summarized in terms of the quasi-universal *zhi*/knowing–understanding. Commonly used as a verb, only rarely is *zhi* used as a noun ("knowledge is . . ."). *Zhi* is sometimes translated as "wisdom," but the latter is usually considered to be the correlate of another *zhi*, 智. Pre-Han texts (including the Daoist texts) often use 智, but this character does not occur in the *Zhuangzi*. We consider that fallible knowledge is still knowledge, and uncertain *zhi* 知 is still *zhi* 知.

We agree with Sturgeon (2015, 892) that much self-evident knowledge is presupposed in the stories, parables, and dialogues in the *Zhuangzi*.[41] For example, all the stories in chapter 4 of the *Zhuangzi* presuppose mutually recognizable human practices: how to deal with people, how a disabled person survives, how a tree survives. It is the same case with other stories, including magical stories such as a sacred oak appearing in a dream (4.4.4).

The notion of *dazhi* 大知 has been analyzed in detail,[42] though it occurs only twice in the inner chapters.[43] Sturgeon noticed such a tension: "how the seeming endorsement of 'greater knowledge' [*dazhi*] squares with the seemingly negative stance much of the text takes toward knowledge in general" (904; cf. Allinson 2015).[44] The tension can be softened by noting that *dazhi* can be understood as "great understanding."[45] Translating *zhi* as understanding would avoid the usual connotations of the Western philosopher's concept of knowledge. *Dazhi* has also been associated with *wuzhi* 无知 (no-knowledge),[46] but there is not much evidence for this in the inner chapters.[47]

There are not many utterances in the *Zhuangzi* that are committed to an everyday understanding of *zhi*. In contrast, this is common in other classical sources, which justifies the quasi-universal *zhi*/know–understanding (which includes common and sophisticated uses of *zhi*/know). For example, the translator of the *Guanzi* (Rickett) speaks of acquiring, producing, developing *zhi*. The translator of the *Hanfeizi* (Harbsmeier) often uses "does not how to" constructions. In the *Canons*, one typically finds use of language such as the following:

知狗而自謂不知犬，過也。(canon B40)

If you know whelps, to say of yourself that you do not know dogs is a mistake of fact. (G78, 408)

Is Zhuangzi a Relativist or a Skeptic? / 123

Similar usages can be found in the *Liezi*, *Xunzi*, and *Hanshi waizhuan*:

而眾人皆愚而無知……(Hanshi waizhuan 3.28/1)

Since the people are all stupid and without knowledge, . . . (Hightower, 110)

齊智之所知，則淺矣。(Liezi 2.10/2)

What common knowledge knows is shallow. (G60)

是是非非謂之知。(Xunzi 2.3.1)

To consider as right what is right and as wrong what is wrong is called knowing. (Knoblock 1, 153)

However, such uses of *zhi* rarely occur in the *Zhuangzi*. When they do occur, they are meant ironically and/or ascribed to somebody else, for example,

是惡知禮意！(6.6.4)

What does this man know of the meaning of ceremony? [Ascribed to a Ruist.]

In the inner chapters, the dominating use of *zhi* is to state that something is *not* known (or not knowable). There are various rhetorical uses as well. The occurrence of *buzhi* 不知 abounds. For example, in the first and second chapter alone we come across the following expressions of not knowing something:

不知其幾千里也。(1.1.1)

I don't know how many thousand *li* [里] he [the bird Peng] measures.

朝菌不知晦朔。(1.1.6)

The morning mushroom knows nothing of twilight and dawn.

未有知其脩者。(1.1.8)

And no one knows how long [the bird Peng is].

……而莫知其所萌。(2.2.3)

. . . and no one knows where they sprout from.

而不知其所為使。(2.2.4)

I do not know what makes them the way they are.

終身役役，而不見其成功，苶然疲役，而不知其所歸，可不哀邪！(2.2.6)

Sweating and laboring to the end of his days and never seeing his accomplishment, utterly exhausting himself and never knowing where to look for rest—can you help pitying him?

我與若不能相知也……(2.6.18)

If you and I don't know the answer . . .

Generally speaking, not knowing something does not necessarily lead to skepticism. A skeptical argument suggests that there is *no way whatsoever* of knowing. In the main, Zhuangzi is considering concrete cases of "not knowing." Only rarely is there a sign of expressing doubts that could be considered skeptical, and this happens when dreaming and being awake are contrasted. For example,

不知周之夢為胡蝶與。(2.7.3)

He didn't know if he was Chuang Chou [Zhuang Zhou] who had dreamt he was a butterfly.

But this may still be a case of raising the question,

奚以知其然也。(1.1.6) How do I know this is so?[48]

There are a few emphatically negative statements concerning *zhi*.

而為知者殆而已矣。(3.1.1)

If you understand this and still strive for knowledge, you will be in danger.

名也者，相軋也；知也者，爭之器也。二者凶器，非所以盡行也。(4.1.9)

Fame is something to beat people down with, and wisdom is a device for wrangling. Both are evil weapons—not the sort of thing to bring you success.

However, we do not agree with ascribing to Zhuangzi an overall skeptical attitude concerning *zhi* (of the kind as displayed in, say, the *Daodejing*). He does raise doubts (§9d), but he refrains from reaching a general negative conclusion about *zhi*, not even for therapeutic purposes.

Wang Ni 王倪 is often cited as articulating skepticism when he is responding to a number of questions from Nie Que 齧缺 with the answer: "How could I know?" ("How would I know that?").[49] It is important to notice the continuation of the exchange (2.6.2–5).[50]

齧缺問於王倪曰：「子知物之所同是乎？」曰：「吾惡乎知之！」「子知子之所不知邪？」曰：「吾惡乎知之！」「然則物无知邪？」曰：「吾惡乎知之！」

雖然，嘗試言之。庸詎知吾所謂知之非不知邪？庸詎知吾所謂不知之非知邪？

且吾嘗試問乎女：「民溼寢則腰疾偏死，鰌然乎哉？木處則惴慄恂懼，猿猴然乎哉？三者孰知正處？民食芻豢，麋鹿食薦，蝍蛆甘帶，鴟鴉耆鼠，四者孰知正味？

猨猵狙以為雌，麋與鹿交，鰌與魚游。毛嬙麗姬，人之所美也，魚見之深入，鳥見之高飛，麋鹿見之決驟。四者孰知天下之正色哉？自我觀之，仁義之端，是非之徒，樊然殽亂，吾惡能知其辯！」

Nie Que asked Wang Ni, "Do you know what all things agree in calling right?" "How would I know that?" said Wang Ni. "Do you know that you don't know it?" "How would I know that?" "Then do things know nothing?" "How would I know that?

However, suppose I try saying something. What way do I have of knowing that if I say I know something I don't really not know it? Or what way do I have of knowing that if I say I don't know something I don't really in fact know it?[51]

Now let me ask you some questions. If a man sleeps in a damp place, his back aches and he ends up half paralyzed, but is this true of a loach? If he lives in a tree, he is terrified and shakes with fright, but is this true of a monkey? Of these three creatures, then, which one knows the proper place to live? Men eat the flesh of grass-fed and grain-fed animals, deer eat grass, centipedes find snakes tasty, and hawks and falcons relish mice. Of these four, which knows how food ought to taste?

Monkeys pair with monkeys, deer go out with deer, and fish play around with fish. Men claim that Mao-ch'iang and Lady Li [Mao Qiang 毛嬙 and Li Ji 麗姬] were beautiful, but if fish saw them they would dive to the bottom of the stream, if birds saw them they would fly away, and if deer saw them they would break into a run. Of these four, which knows how to fix the standard of beauty for the world?

As Graham points out, Wang Ni avoids making any statement that would be self-refuting (G69, 147). First, Wang Ni is studiously refraining from saying something general about *zhi* 知. Second, after making remarks that sound skeptical, Wang Ni continues to say something assuming knowledge about various "empirical" matters.[52] Wang Ni *does* know some things, as the subsequent paragraphs show.[53] Before making statements concerning skepticism, commentators should discuss whether 2.6.2 is not simply raising doubts as to whether those scholars who claim to know everything (all things together) and every thing (*wu* 物) (each particular thing) actually know.[54]

Perhaps 2.6.3 is more significant than 2.6.2 in that it undermines any statement involving *zhi*, including any skeptical argument raising doubt about the trustworthiness of *zhi*. In this respect Zhuangzi's doubt is more basic than skeptical doubt. In contrast, 2.6.4–5 pulls back to ordinary situations. The doubt in 2.6.3 is forgotten and some trivial relativities remain. It is too quick to consider the described situations as support for relativism (as distinct from relativities).[55] It is common sense that different *wu* 物 have different needs.[56] Perhaps what the simple examples in 2.6.4–5 are intended to say is: Surely you do not disagree. So how could you disagree with 2.6.3? We can say that Zhuangzi raises skeptical doubts about all the aspects of the ideal language assumption. But if we drop the ideal language assumption (that is, if we agree that meanings are underdetermined and/

or undetermined), ordinary and reflective *zhi* would arise without being tainted by skepticism.

Moreover, as Schipper points out, the crux of the text is in 2.6.6.

自我觀之，仁義之端，是非之塗，樊然殽亂，吾惡能知其辯！

The way I see it, the rules of benevolence and righteousness and the paths of right and wrong are all hopelessly snarled and jumbled. How could I know anything about such discriminations?

According to Schipper, 2.6.6 shows that Wang Ni is afraid that Nie Que wants to challenge him in a sophistic debate (2007, 67n61).

We conclude that, when taking some clauses from the inner chapters in isolation, they may look like skeptical (or relativistic) statements as seen from a Western perspective. However, if we consider the broader context, the alleged relativist or skeptic (including Zhuangzi) would always be happy to call on all kinds of knowledge. What makes a difference is that Zhuangzi raises doubt about rigid pigeonholing and universal principles governing *shifei* judgments. We think that Zhuangzi's attitude toward *zhi* is not as negative as is often assumed, because he associates *zhi* with rigid criteria. If one *does* ascribe a skeptical attitude to Zhuangzi, it would be the skepticism that concerns the meaning of words, that is to say: doubt is expressed before the issue of knowledge–understanding arises.

Chapter 9

Zhuangzi's Stance

Stance Instead of Perspective or Set of Beliefs

Philosophers often use the word stance, but it is rarely analyzed.[1] We employ the notion of "stance" in the sense as used by van Fraassen (2002; 2004) when advocating his stance (not doctrine) of empiricism. What may be innovative of our approach is that we extend his ideas to the areas of Chinese and comparative philosophy.

We will speak of Zhuangzi's *stance* instead of his beliefs, opinions, preferences, desires, commitments, and so on. A stance embraces all of these facets. It involves emotions and are influenced by moods. Word meanings are not fixed, partly because meaning is influenced by unpredictable mood changes. A stance includes the so-called facts and values, but they do not have a fixed boundary in a certain stance. In the philosophical literature, the notion of stance often appears indirectly when science and/or metaphysics are contrasted with art.[2] We claim that *every* view of some matter in the end depends on a (hidden) stance that is taken. Or, more generally speaking: *any* position (either Mohists', or Zhuangzi's, or contemporary sinologists', and so on), in the end, rests on a stance that cannot be justified in "standard" epistemological terms.

The word stance is often used in the literature on Chinese and comparative philosophy as a synonym for position, viewpoint, and so forth, but it has rarely been distinguished from a set of beliefs. Sometimes we recognize the idea of a stance without the word being used. For example, Chong Kim-chong says that Zhuangzi's "words have a certain metaphorical structure that enables him to resist being pinned down to any position"

(2006, 375). Similarly, we can say that Zhuangzi's stance cannot be pinned down to a position or a set of beliefs.

In his *The Empirical Stance* (2002), van Fraassen endorses an empirical stance that discredits metaphysics and admires science. In order for empiricism to avoid being accused of being a metaphysical position or belief (which van Fraassen aims to counter), it should be considered as a stance. Of course, the admiration for science cannot be easily associated with Zhuangzi. Van Fraassen's empirical stance as embedded in modern (analytic) philosophy of science is, understandably, a far cry from Zhuangzi's stance, but still we can discern similarities. A comparison of them may help us understand Zhuangzi's often (seemingly) contradictory utterances.

Roughly speaking, a stance is a set of attitudes.[3] The difference between a stance and a viewpoint that can be conveyed in terms of (propositional) beliefs is best illustrated by verbs (in English) that express attitudes. For example, van Fraassen writes,

> I listed the empiricists' calling us back to experience, their rebellion against theory, their ideals of epistemic rationality, what they regard as having significance, their admiration for science, and the virtue they see in an idea of rationality that does not bar disagreement.

As he correctly remarks, none of these factors are equitable with beliefs (47). The following is a similar list with phrases borrowed from the literature on Zhuangzi:[4]

> Zhuangzi is calling on one to accept the processes of life and death. He is calling attention to those individuals who can shift back and forth, in a playful way, between various perspectives and opinions. Zhuangzi is calling into question the assumption of an autonomous self, capable of achieving virtue (*de* 德). He questions distinctions.

> Zhuangzi admires skill but is not advocating a particular skill or a set of skills. He admires a lofty man who is different from the common people and all those whose virtue (*de*) is beyond the ordinary,

> Often reference is made to Zhuangzi's attitude toward language, his attitude toward distinctions and discriminations, his attitude toward the sage-kings, toward the working people, toward cripples, toward slave uprisings of his time, and so on.

Zhuangzi values Hundun's original state. He values a deep trust in life in its wholeness. Zhuangzi values "saying nothing." What he values is not simply freedom from constraints of conventions and rules but freedom of thought and action vital for authentic existence and self-development.

Zhuangzi engages in a metaphorical discourse. He engages in various modes of exposition to communicate his ideas that could not be said in ordinary words.[5] Zhuangzi engages Hui Shi on the limitations of his imagination.

Whether it is the list van Fraassen gives for the commitments of empiricists or our list of attitudes that have been ascribed to Zhuangzi, none of the things in these lists can be reduced to beliefs. Such attitudes may contain beliefs in order to achieve consistency, but there is more to it than can be expressed in a set of beliefs. A stance cannot be identified via its beliefs, and can persist through changes of beliefs. Neither can a stance be equated with making assertions nor captured in terms of dogmas.

Hence, a stance does not only consist of (propositional) knowledge. A stance includes: beliefs, attitudes, values, evaluations, opinions, goals, approaches, emotional commitments, and so on. Van Fraassen draws on Sartre to highlight the role of emotions and points out that we must figure out "how to view the role of emotion in . . . the epistemic enterprise as a whole" (108). Discussions concerning *shifei* involve beliefs, but these discussions also involve other attitudes such as emotional commitments. This is one of the reasons why adherence to a stance cannot be easily given up. Nonetheless, stances are not "irrational." They can be compared and discussed in terms of their fruitfulness, heuristic resources, and problem-solving abilities (in a certain particular situation).

Many disagreements cannot be reduced to disagreements of beliefs or perspectives. Rather, they are disagreements of stances. Nevertheless, as van Fraassen emphasizes, stances are subject to rational critique because they have consequences that involve beliefs. However, rejecting a belief that is part of a stance may not affect the stance.

Van Fraassen understands *rational* as a term that *allows* something, not as a term that *forbids* something. To explain this, he points to the distinction between "Prussian law" and "English law." The "Prussian" notion of law entails that what it is rational to believe is precisely what one is rationally forced to believe. Van Fraassen instead advocates the "English" notion of rationality: what it is rational to believe is everything that one is *not* forced *not* to believe. To say that you are rational is *not* to say that you are rationally (and "logically," "necessarily") *forced* to have the beliefs you have. One cannot expect that each "rational" person with the "same" experience (experiential input) should have the same beliefs. The constraints that rationality stipulates leaves much underdetermined and/or undetermined. Rationality, van Fraassen says, is bridled irrationality (2002, 92, 97): "an idea of rationality that does not bar disagreement" (47) and which includes "rational discourse . . . on matters that touch our values, attitudes, and commitments" (62).

Because of what van Fraassen (2002) has to say about the meaning of "stance" is mainly framed in negative terms, several commentators have tried to present a more detailed positive understanding of the notion of stance. Chakravarty (2004) proposes that stances can be considered as adopting a policy or a strategy regarding the generation of beliefs, or as being committed to a particular worldview (including clusters of beliefs, values, and attitudes). Values may be well- or ill-advised, but not true or false. Boucher (2014) suggests that stances should be understood as pragmatically justified metaphysical perspectives, or ways of seeing.

Van Fraassen offers the following characteristics of his stance of empiricism:[6]

1. There are no (formulations of) enduring criteria.

2. Stances are a mix of epistemic and evaluative factors (cf. §5b).

3. Stances require certain beliefs for their own coherence, but a stance is not equitable with beliefs.

4. Stances are dissatisfied with and disvalue explanation by postulate. Explanation demands are rejected: "I do not know" (cf. Wang Ni's "How would I know that?" [2.6.2]).

5. A stance calls us back to experience. It rebels against theories (that is, doctrines claimed to be universal).

6. It contains an idea of rationality that does not bar disagreement. How do we ever come to agreement in philosophy? We do not.

7. Certain types of paradoxes play a rhetorical role.

8. A stance exploits ambiguities and vagueness, without which progress would not be possible, whether scientific, poetic, or otherwise.

9. Stances may display gestalt shifts.

We suggest that there is a family resemblance between the notion of stance as elucidated by van Fraassen and Zhuangzi's "stance." We add the following features of a stance that are not explicitly mentioned by van Fraassen:

1. A stance is not possible without being committed to some rather rigid classifications at least for some domains and for some time. For example, Zhuangzi assumes rigid classifications for animals, trees and plants, and many other "ordinary" things.[7]

2. Many stances are part of the mutually recognizable human practices (§1a), but in the end they are not justifiable (in the sense of lacking a supportive argument), though they can be claimed to be "brute facts." This would apply, for example, to stances taken with respect to the practice of cook Ding and of many other characters that figure in Zhuangzi's stories.

3. A stance involves sensibilities, which result from character, education,[8] personal development, and mutual attunement.

We propose that *grosso modo* both lists (1–9 and 1–3) are applicable to Zhuangzi's stance. Further, being committed to a stance does not exclude engaging in a (meta-) *shifei* debate. On our interpretation of "walking-two-roads" (§9c), Zhuangzi could have entered into his own rational discourse trying to convince Ruists, Mohists, and others that *shifei* debates presuppose fixed meanings (§1b) and that therefore such debates are futile.

Interpreters, in particular those in English-language sinology, often express a concern about how to combine Zhuangzi's apparent skepticism and/or relativism with his positive recommendations of how to live a worthwhile life. We suggest that we could dissolve such problems by distinguishing between a *stance* and beliefs. Beliefs are embedded in the ordinary (modern) understanding of argumentative and justificatory discourse and similar commitments to propositional truth. On the other hand, emotions and spontaneous reactions cannot be reduced to "justified true beliefs." Different aspects of a stance, for example, Zhuangzi's overall stance, may be inconsistent when "translated" into *some* logically regimented languages. A stance cannot be considered as a specimen of skepticism or relativism because the latter only makes sense in the truth claiming justificatory discourse. Zhuangzi's stance includes: no fixed meanings (§9b), the principle of "walking-two-roads" (§9c), the principle of doubt (§9d), and equalizing things by leaving them uneven (§9e). We will highlight "walking-two-roads" as his main stance (§9c).

Zhuangzi has his own way of participating in the discourse of his contemporaries. So does van Fraassen.

> Since the differing stances also involve value judgments and attitudes toward life, love, and laughter, their basis may be thought to be purely subjective, and not susceptible to rational debate. . . . We need not look far to see that rational discourse is possible on matters that touch our values, attitudes, and commitments. (2002, 62)

We conclude that considering Zhuangzi's texts as expressing a stance (instead of a set of beliefs) may help make sense of apparent contradictions and inconsistencies in the inner chapters. Any "normal" human being could have many beliefs that are contradictory or inconsistent if strict standards are applied.

Zhuangzi's stance includes many views on a variety of matters. Most of his views are rather unique in that he is not following any of his predecessors or contemporaries. The wrong approach to his writings is to expect that it is possible to integrate everything into one vision. A stance includes visions and may contain numerous contradictions (in particular when one assumes that Zhuangzi wrote a "philosophical treatise").[9] Moreover, one should not employ contemporary Western abstract terms to characterize Zhuangzi's stance. His stance is best described in commonsense terms. For example, he raises doubts about "everything," including his own views (§9d).

Ziporyn lists about fifteen (Western) positions (mystic, skeptic, dualist, deist, and so on), for which one may seem to be able to find evidence in the inner chapters, and wonders (2009a, xviii): "Is there some coherent way to integrate all these different strands into one vision?" The answer should be: "No, of course not!" We agree with Wang Youru when he writes (2003, 147),

> Searching for the final meaning of Zhuangzi's words distorts Zhuangzi. Ask what particular position Zhuangzi holds among rival positions misses Zhuangzi's point. Expect Zhuangzi to clarify his intentions and his views will be disappointing.

Nevertheless, we have chosen four important characteristics of his stance to be highlighted in this chapter: meanings are not fixed, walking-two-roads, doubting every possible stance including his own, and achieving equality by leaving things uneven.

No Fixed Meanings (*Weiding* 未定)

In this section we consider the following passage:[10]

夫言非吹也。言者有言,其所言者特未定也。果有言邪?其未嘗有言邪?其以為異於鷇音,亦有辯乎,其无辯乎? (2.3.3)

> Speaking is not the same as breathing. When we speak, we speak of something, but what it is, is never determined. So then, are we speaking of something {when we are speaking}, or have we never talked of anything? If we take the view that our language is different from the twittering of birds, can we establish a clear distinction between the two or not? (Billeter)

Does this entail a dismissal of language? We do not think so. Sometimes Zhuangzi seems to be presenting an "anti-language" stance, but actually he is only criticizing certain kinds of high expectations for language.[11] Ascribing an anti-language stance would leave unexplained how he flourishes in using all kinds of devices of language such as lively stories, poetry, *as well as* subtle arguments.

In view of his advocacy that meanings are never determined (*weiding* 未定, "unfixed"),[12] we consider that Zhuangzi is an early opponent of the ideal language assumption. Apart from 2.3.3, Zhuangzi's discussion of *yuyan* 寓言, *zhiyan* 卮言,[13] and *chongyan* 重言 (27.1.4; G81, 106) may be considered as support for an anti-ideal-language stance and for our commitment to family-resemblance-concepts.[14] Schwitzgebel (1996, 88) suggests, "the alert interpreter has to admit that Zhuangzi does not always mean what he says." Instead we suggest that all of Zhuangzi's words are to be taken seriously. Zhuangzi does not present skeptical arguments in the Western sense because his words are only directed against certain types of exchanges between scholars.

The passage cited (2.3.3) is a rare case about which translators have few disagreements in that virtually all translations into English are very similar.[15] However, there is some difference with respect to the translations of *weiding* although the sense of the whole clause seems to be straightforward.[16]

It has been common to interpret 2.3.3 as interdependent with the *shifei* quarrels of Ruists and Mohists, which immediately follow this passage.[17] This is already apparent from the early commentaries by Guo Xiang and Cheng Xuanying.

Each has his own saying, hence it differs from wind. . . .What I call *shi*, the other sees as *fei*, and vice versa. Hence, it is said to be "unfixed" (*weiding* 未定). The unfixed instability stems from the one-sidedness of the sentiments of self and other.[18]

Though there are words different from the blowing of wind, everyone says that he is right and everyone says that the other is wrong. Since the preferences of the other and of mine diverge, there is no fixation (*buding* 不定). (Cheng Xuanying, 33)

Guo Xiang (33) and Cheng Xuanying (33) make many more comments concerning the text at this point, but seem to remain in doubt as to whether words have meaning at all. That is to say: the rhetorical question of whether there are words that are different from the sounds of baby birds remains unanswered.

Are there words? But there is no sufficient [basis] to determine. . . . Are there no words? But according to one there are already words. (Guo Xiang)

What this side takes to be *shi*, the other takes to be *fei* and what this side takes to be *fei*, the other takes to be *shi*. Hence, there is no fixation of *shi* and *fei*. How can words interpret them? Hence there is no sufficient basis to claim there are certainly words. However, each has its own prejudice and each adheres to what he/she takes to be *shi* and *fei*. These all proceed from one's own word. Therefore, it cannot be said that there are no words. . . . Words and the peeping sound are in accord. Whether there is disputation or not can really not be determined. The preferences in the world are not necessarily the same, and the words cannot possibly be different, hence *shi* and *fei* are confused and disorderly snarled. Nobody knows how to decide. . . . Each sticks to [his preference] and *shifei* cannot be determined, how is this different from the peeps of baby birds? There is only sound but no real differentiation (*bian*)! Hence, those who take words to be different from the peeps of baby birds, perhaps they do not have sufficient basis to make such a distinction. (Cheng Xuanying)

Although 2.3.3 may also be an example of "double rhetorical questions" (see §9e), we suggest that it should be taken at face value at the same time: There are meaningful words in a given situation, but there are no fixed meanings.[19] There is a difference between the meanings of words and the sounds of the pipes of earth (2.1.8) and/or the sounds of baby birds (2.3.3). Words have (local) meanings, but what one speaks about is underdetermined and/or undetermined.[20]

Many commentators have spotted the connection of 2.3.3 concerning words and the peeping of baby birds with moods and wind in the preceding text. Ziporyn (2009b) writes,

> What words *depend* on for their meaning, what they putatively refer to, is actually no more fixed than the shifting moods, the sounds of holes in a windstorm, or indeed, the chirping of baby birds.

Billeter discerns similarities between Zhuangzi's supposedly anti-language stance and the early Wittgenstein's stance (Billeter 2016, 113). He argues that we should turn away from language, which blinds us, and rediscover the source of vision located in our own activity. However, he also includes *ming* 明 and meditation as illustrating action leading to a view of the reality "that is vaster, more durable, and more fundamental than that normally perceived by the senses" (1998, 11).[21] Instead of highlighting trance states as illustrated in the *Zhuangzi*, we propose focusing on one of Billeter's other claims on behalf of Zhuangzi: "There is no meaning except in what is done {*en acte*}" (1998, 25), which may be associated with the later Wittgenstein's view that language is embedded in practice. Already in the 1920s and 1930s, Malinowski put forward such a view.[22]

> Words, which cross from one actor to another, do not serve primarily to communicate thought: they connect work and correlate manual and bodily movements. Words are part of action and they are equivalents to actions.

Any utterance, no matter how weighty, is only a moment in the continuous process of verbal communication. Language is not to be conceived as a closed system, nor as a subjectively expressive medium, but as the concrete and ceaseless flow of *utterances* produced in dialogues between speakers in specific social and historical contexts. The content of speech can be understood only in terms of the action that the speech performs. Speech acts, makes, produces, achieves, and means things.

Somewhat similar to Billeter and to our view, Coutinho interprets Zhuangzi as arguing for indeterminacy.

A discourser has a discourse, but what is said is exceptionally unsettled (indeterminate). . . . The categories in accordance with which we divide up the world are not fixed, but are conventional and variably fixed. (2015, 161; cf. 2004)

However, Coutinho seems to restrict indeterminacy to the "borders" of a concept (186).[23] This is not radical enough. We suggest that Zhuangzi also means to say that the core (essence) is not fixed; meanings of words can change, including the core ("essence") of their meanings.[24]

Zhuangzi's stance with respect to language can be compared with the later Wittgenstein's theory of meaning. Wittgenstein's later thought has been considered as radically opposed to the Western philosophical tradition inasmuch as it dismisses the conception of philosophy as offering a single totalizing theory in abstraction from the actual happenings of ordinary human life. Similarly, Zhuangzi sets himself opposed to abstract and rigid ways of thinking that, according to him, give rise to contentions such as that between the Ruists and the Mohists. In trying to release us from pursuing the illusory ideal of pure and frictionless conditions for philosophizing, Wittgenstein guides our attention toward the rough and plain ground of everyday life in dealing with seemingly grandiose philosophical matters. In a similar vein, in exposing the futility of allegiance to discriminative principles, Zhuangzi urges for a flexible comportment toward problems with varying complexities, which requires attending to the ordinary and concrete scenarios of human life.

Graham correctly points out that contradictions are "created" by relying on "fixed and clear concepts" (G69, 141). It is perfectly natural *and* rational to contradict oneself in a natural language. For instance, we may cite Graham himself when he remarks: "Like all great anti-rationalists, Chuang-tzu has his *reasons* for not listening to reason" (G89, 176, emphasis added).[25] We suggest that contradictions play an important role for Zhuangzi. There is more to Zhuangzi's contradictions than their drawing attention to the porous borders of meanings. It is not clear whether the corpse of a dead horse is a horse or not. This illustrates the vagueness of borders between meanings. However, Zhuangzi also uses contradictions to emphatically raise more serious questions and to express his own doubt about the so-called right answers.

Alt (2000) criticizes Graham, who seems to ascribe to Zhuangzi the stance of embracing contradictions and dismissing all distinctions.[26] According to Alt, Zhuangzi is *not* an anti-rationalist as Graham claims him to be (G89, 176). Alt acknowledges that Zhuangzi "tries to discredit disputation by the objection that at any moment of change both alternatives will be admissible," but he points out that anyone who should leave behind all distinctions would be unable to act. Perhaps Zhuangzi has meant to say that when acting no distinctions should be presupposed; of course, from a commonsense perspective, actions presuppose distinctions.[27] Chiu Wai Wai (2015, 267) suggests that Zhuangzi does not claim we should make no distinctions, but that he only aims to undermine our confidence in doing so.

Alt discusses several examples (translations by Watson, Graham, and Mair) showing that Graham interprets Zhuangzi as stating contradictions. In one out of three examples, in connection with 2.6.21, Alt makes a relevant observation concerning the need to consider the possibility of topic-comment structure (see §7c). However, in our view, Alt's two examples discussed below are based on implausible interpretations of the relevant texts.

One of Alt's examples concerns the following two clauses from 2.3.7.[28]

方生方死，方死方生。

But where there is birth there must be death; where there is death there must be birth. (Watson)

However, simultaneously with being alive one dies, and simultaneously with dying one is alive. (Graham)

Moreover, "when we are {still} alive we are {already} dead." At the moment when we are {still} dead we are {already} alive. (Billeter)

Nonetheless, from the moment of birth death begins simultaneously, and from the moment of death birth begins simultaneously. (Mair)

Even so, born together they die together. Dying together they are born together. (Kjellberg)

Although it be so, there is affirmed now life and now death; now death and now life. (Legge)

Nevertheless, when there is life, there is death, and when there is death, there is life. (Feng Youlan)

Nevertheless, life arises from death, and vice versa. (Lin Yutang)

Alt points out that we are all alive and dying, but no one is alive and dead at the same time. Then he speculates that Graham may consider that *sheng* 生 and *si* 死 function like contrary terms. Hence, the phrase may be considered to be stating a contradiction. We do not think that these considerations are relevant to the interpretation of the part of 2.3.7 cited. From the citations we can see that translators try to avoid stating a contradiction. Graham's translation, which Alt criticizes at length, is clearly inspired by his view that "in change contradictories are admissible at the same moment" (G81, 52; cf. G89, 178–79).

A similar issue arises with respect to the following:

辯也者，有不辯也。(2.5.7)

So {I say} those who divide fail to divide; those who discriminate fail to discriminate. (Watson)

To "divide," then, is to leave something undivided: to "discriminate between alternatives" is to leave something which is neither alternative. (Graham)

Therefore, wherever there is analysis, something is left unanalyzed. Wherever there is dispute, something is left undisputed. (Mair)

Alt objects that Graham's translation requires us to say that there is "something which is neither alternative," and he suggests that Mair's translation is better: when people claim the truth of some matter, their argument assumes the truth of other matters. But this seems to be too trivial a point to be ascribed to Zhuangzi. Instead, we suggest that in this passage Zhuangzi is refuting the later Mohists, who would argue that nothing is left out: either it fits, or it does not (§2e).

Graham claims that bivalence always leaves out something (G69, 145):[29] The separation of ox and non-ox leaves out something (that is, *dao*, which was already there before there were oxen and non-oxen). According to Graham, even the Mohists acknowledge that when "something" passes from being X (say being alive) to being non-X (say being dead), "at this moment it is *both* X and non-X."[30] The problem arises even more sharply in "not yet having begun having a beginning" (2.5.2). Graham argues convincingly, "Does it not follow that every statement at the moment when it becomes allowable is also unallowable?" (G81, 9–14). The example of the sun rising and declining at noon illustrates the point. We agree with Coutinho when he says,

> Thus, Zhuangzi does not praise contradictoriness *for its own sake*, but rather the fact that contradictions might well be *applicable in the penumbral borderlands*. In the borderlands, which might be

more extensive than we generally think, getting clear involves abandoning presuppositions of mutual exclusivity that refuse to make room for contradiction. (1994, 188, emphasis added)

The following passage may suggest that Zhuangzi aims to transcend bivalence (that is to say, he would not limit judgment to being either *shi* or *fei*):

其或是也，其或非也邪？其俱是也，其俱非也邪？ (2.6.18)

Is one of us right and the other wrong? Are both of us right or are both of us wrong?

We are not suggesting that Zhuangzi has preconceived paraconsistent logic,[31] but he did deny the exclusiveness of bivalence, although he formulated it as a rhetorical question. The emphasis of the passage is primarily that there is no way to establish who is right and who is wrong, that there is the possibility of the answer "neither" or "both."

Although Zhuangzi's remarks on "indeterminacy" are brief, we suggest that they are crucial to everything he articulates in language. For example, it follows that what Zhuangzi himself says is never fixed. Contraries and other concepts have no sharp boundaries, as Coutinho (2004, 2015) argues on behalf of Zhuangzi. We would add: There are only changing identities of the meanings of words. This correlates with other remarks about "missing" identities: the perfect person (*zhiren* 至人) has no self (1.1.13); the butterfly and/or Zhuang Zhou have no fixed identity (2.7.3); Ziqi 子綦 saying: "Now I have lost myself" (2.1.2: 今者吾喪我). Words have no identity; meaning changes with circumstances and is different at different times depending on and interacting with the particulars of the situation.

We conclude that Zhuangzi's (rather rare) statements about the nature of meaning and of language can be understood as rather similar to our stance of favoring ordinary language and the omnipresence of indeterminacy or underdetermination (§1c). We suggest that {*weiding* ⇔ indeterminacy and/or underdetermination} is a plausible quasi-universal. Meanings are not constant (*chang* 常), but they are not like the chattering of baby birds either. Imprecise open-ended quasi-universals can be grounded in the fact and necessity of mutually recognizable human practices (§1a).

Walking-Two-Roads (*Liangxing* 兩行)

Zhuangzi is perhaps best known for his deconstruction of *shifei* debates (see §7a and §10a). There are neither universal criteria for adjudicating apparently irresolvable disagreement, nor grounding standards for evaluating different stances in relation to one another. This deconstructive stance is compatible with Zhuangzi's stance concerning *weiding* (no fixed meanings; see previous section §9b) and his entertaining doubt as a way of life (see §9d)—even doubt concerning his own views. Zhuangzi's "arguments" in support of the irresolvability of *shifei* clashes seem to be irrefutable except that these "arguments" seem to be part of a *shifei* discourse. However, on several occasions in the *Qiwulun*, Zhuangzi does not stop at irresolvability, but goes a step further to invoke *yiming* 以明: the best thing is to use clarity or clear understanding. Primarily, *yiming* is the response to the *shifei* clashes between Ruists and Mohists (2.3.5).

Opinions differ on how to understand *yiming*.[32] We suggest that there are a number of interconnected ideas or expressions in the *Qiwulun* that give hints of how the sages (and we) can transcend *shifei* clashes in the "ordinary" world by employing *yiming*. Among these ideas, we highlight "walking-two-roads" (*liangxing* 兩行) of *ren* 人 (ordinary people) and of *tian* (heaven–nature) respectively. We advocate that "walking-two-roads" constitutes the most significant ingredient of the tenets embodied in Zhuangzi's stance. Although "walking-two-roads" is mentioned only once in the inner chapters, Chan Wing-tsit, among other scholars, ascribes primal importance to it (184): "The doctrine of following two courses at the same time has become a cardinal one in practically all Chinese philosophical schools."

The idea of "walking-two-roads" in 2.4.6 is closely related to the following notions: the "celestial potter's wheel" (2.4.6: *tianjun* 天鈞), heavenly equality, (2.6.21: *tianni* 天倪),[33] the "axis of *dao*" (2.3.8: *daoshu* 道樞), and "the everyday" (2.4.4, 2.4.11: *yong* 庸). Before discussing them in some detail, we give an account of their connections. The commoners and inferior scholars (*xiashi* 下士, prominently Ruists and Mohists)[34] take themselves to be the arbiters of right–true–correct and wrong–false–incorrect (*shifei*) and are committed to parading their proffered distinctions (*bian* 辯). The sage (*shengren* 聖人) does not proceed in such a way.[35] He transcends all *shifei* distinctions (2.4.4) and harmonizes both *shi* and *fei* (2.4.6) in order to achieve a clear understanding (*yiming*). Alternatively speaking, sages walk two roads (*liangxing*). On the one hand, they merge with the ordinary (*yong* 庸); on the other hand, they rest at the center of the celestial potter's wheel (*tianjun*).[36] As Jiao Hong 焦竑 (1540–1620) puts it, "the sage externally goes by others, making use of all sorts of rights and wrongs to harmonize with them, but internally he embodies Heaven the Potter's Wheel, free of all rights and wrongs" (cited in Ziporyn 2009a, 149).

Zhong Tai (2008, 47) claims: "The *Qiwulun* starts with deconstructing [*po* 破] the controversy concerning *wu* (吾) and *wo* (我),[37] *shi* and *fei*, and ends with complying with the use of *wu* and *wo*, *shi* and *fei*." Deconstruction concerns the passages referring to *yiming*: the best thing is to use clarity or clear understanding (2.3.5, 2.3.8, 2.4.9, 2.4.11). As we see it, complying is indicated by *yinshi* (2.4.5–6) and the introduction of the idea of walking-two-roads in 2.4.6.[38]

The sole occurrence of "walking-two-roads" (*liangxing*) in the *Zhuangzi* follows the story of the monkeys and the monkey keeper.[39]

是以聖人和之以是非,而休乎天鈞,是之謂兩行。(2.4.6)

So the sage harmonizes [和] with both right and wrong and rests in Heaven the Equalizer. This is called walking-two-roads. (Watson)

Therefore, the sages harmonize the systems of right and wrong, and rest in the evolution of nature. This is called following two courses at once. (Feng Youlan)

This is why the sage smoothes things out with his "That's it, that's not," and stays at the point of rest on the potter's wheel of Heaven. It is this that is called "Letting both alternatives proceed." (Graham)

The Sage uses various rights and wrongs to harmonize with others and yet remains in the middle of Heaven the Potter's wheel. This is called "Walking-two-roads." (Ziporyn)

As the different translations illustrate, there is no consensus regarding the precise relation of the sage and the world of ordinary *shifei* clashes. However, there is near-consensus on the translation of *liangxing*: walking-two-roads (Watson, Kjellberg). Similar phrases include: dual procession, following two courses at once, and "double walking" (Goulding 2007).[40] Older translations are slightly different.[41]

Translations of *tianjun* 天鈞 seem to derive from divergent speculations: Heaven the Equalizer (Watson), potter's wheel of Heaven (Graham, Harbsmeier, Liu Xiaogan, Mair, Ziporyn), Heaven's wheel (Kjellberg), celestial movement (Levi), heavenly balance (Eno, Lin Yutang, Muller, Wu Kuang-ming), natural equalization (Chan Wing-tsit), evolution of nature (Feng Youlan), equal fashioning of Heaven (Legge).

As Liu Xiaogan (2015b, 211) points out: "That the sage rests on the potter's wheel of Heaven is the same as standing with the axis of dao (*daoshu*

道樞) and he lets the wheel of right and wrong or any kind of conflict move around him with the mind remaining calm and transcendent at the center of the circle." Like *liangxing*, *daoshu* occurs only once.[42]

> 彼是莫得其偶，謂之道樞。樞始得其環中，以應无窮。是亦一无窮，非亦一无窮也。故曰莫若以明。(2.3.8)

> A state in which "this" and "that" no longer find their opposites is called the hinge of the Way [*daoshu* 道樞]. When the hinge is fitted into the socket, it can respond endlessly. Its right then is a single endlessness and its wrong too is a single endlessness. So, I say, the best thing to use is clarity.

Again, translators tend to agree on the same or very similar translations of *daoshu*: the pivot (hinge, axis) of the Way (Course, *Dao*).[43] We assume that one may think of the axis of *dao* (*daoshu*) as the axis of the celestial potter's wheel or the heavenly balance. It could be suggested that on the *dao*-axis (*daoshu*) there is no need for standards; in going along or merging with the "ordinary," we do not need them either (cf. §7d).[44]

Some translations of 2.4.4 bring out the idea that the sage who "stays at the point of rest on the potter's wheel of Heaven" (Graham 2.4.6) also merges with the common or the ordinary (*yong* 庸).[45]

> 為是不用而寓諸庸。(2.4.4)

> Instead of dwelling on distinctions of things, he [the sage] follows the ordinary course of things. (Wang Rongpei)

> [The sages] therefore do not make distinctions, but follow the common and the ordinary. (Feng Youlan)

> [The sages] discard the distinctions and take refuge in the common and ordinary things. (Lin Yutang)

Yong occurs for the second time in 2.4.11.[46] The two occurrences have partly similar context.[47] In 2.4.11 the sage relegates all "things" to the constant [*yong* 庸].

> 是故滑疑之耀，聖人之所圖也。為是不用而寓諸庸，此之謂以明。(2.4.11)

> The torch of chaos and doubt—this is what the sage steers by. So he does not use [*buyong* 不用] things but relegates all to the constant [*yong* 庸]. This is what it means to use clarity.

The first two clauses of 2.4.11 are translated in two quite opposite directions in the English translations we have been reviewing in this book.[48] Some translations tell us what the sage does or affirms.

> The sage steers by the torch of chaos and doubt (Watson)

> The Radiance of Drift and Doubt is the sage's only map. (Ziporyn)

> The torch of slippery doubt is what the sage steers by. (Kjellberg)

> What the sages aim at is the light out of darkness. (Feng Youlan)

> The scintillations of light from the midst of confusion and perplexity are indeed valued by the sagely man. (Chan Wing-tsit)

Some other translations tell us what the sage does not do or rejects.

> . . . discards the light that dazzles. (Lin Yutang)

> . . . to get rid of bewildering flamboyance. (Mair)

> Therefore the glamour of slippery uncertainties is something which the sage holds in low regard. (Harbsmeier)

> The glitter of glib implausibilities is despised by the sage. (Graham)

> The sage is wary of all disreputable and troubling flamboyance. (Levi)[49]

> . . . the true sage despises the bewildering arguments. (Wang Rongpei)

We would favor the negative reading, that is, the second group of translations. This is supported by most renditions in the Chinese language.[50] For example, Si Lü translates the part of 2.4.11 cited above into modern Chinese as follows:[51]

Therefore, the bombast that confuses the human heart is what the sage is to abandon. Hence, the sage does not use his/her own talent and disputation to show off to people, but rather dwells in the natural laws/rules of things. This is called *yiming* [以明]. (Si Lü 2013, 22)

According to Jiang Xichang 蔣錫昌,[52] sages would dispense with the illuminosity produced by disputations. *Guyi* 滑疑 refers to the speech of the disputers whose doctrines cause confusion and doubt to the human heart. Jiang suggests that *tu* 圖 is a loan word of *bi* 啚, and it means *se* 嗇, that is, frugal. This echoes the meaning of *buyong* in the next clause.[53]

Chu Boxiu 褚伯秀 (2014, 52) comments,

滑疑之耀 refers to the three scholars [that is, Zhao Wen 昭文, Shi Kuang 師曠, and Huizi 惠子, who are mentioned in 2.4.9] who use their skills to cause confusions to the world and to produce dubious and illusory perception for the people.

However, how to read the first two clauses is not such a big issue for the interpretation of Zhuangzi's stance. A more serious difficulty is the meaning of *yong* 庸. The translations of the phrase 寓諸庸 vary considerably.

. . . relegates all to the constant.[54]

. . . basing oneself on the people. (Harbsmeier)

Their everyday function is what works for them. (Ziporyn 2.4.4)

. . . instead entrusts it to the everyday function of each thing. (Ziporyn 2.4.11)

. . . finds for things lodging-places in the usual. (Graham)

. . . lodge in the usual. (Kjellberg)

. . . lodges in commonality. (Mair)

The exegeses of Guo Xiang and Cheng Xuanying are as follows:

. . . resides in the self-working of things. (Guo Xiang, 42–43)

. . . merges with the commoners. (Cheng Xuanying, 42–43)

We prefer the explanation by Guo Xiang and the translation by Ziporyn.

We suggest that the idea of "walking-two-roads" is closely connected to the contrast between *tian* (heaven–nature) and *ren* 人 (humans). This is already mentioned in the first chapter of the *Zhuangzi*. As Ziporyn points out: "riding upon what is true both to Heaven and to earth [1.1.13], [is] what he later calls 'Walking-two-roads'" (2009a, 5n10). The two roads can also be associated with being the companion of *tian* and *ren* respectively.

> 若然者，人謂之童子，是之謂與天為徒。外曲者，與人之為徒也。擎跽曲拳，人臣之禮也，人皆為之，吾敢不為邪！(4.1.20–21)

> A man like this, people call The Child. This is what I mean by being a companion of Heaven. By being outwardly compliant, I can be a companion of men. Lifting up the tablet, kneeling, bowing, crouching down—this is the etiquette of a minister. Everybody does it, so why shouldn't I?

> If I do what other people do, they can hardly criticize me. This is what I mean by being a companion of men. By doing my work through the examples of antiquity, I can be the companion of ancient times.

The approach of walking-two-roads is evident in many of Zhuangzi's stances, all of which could be compared to a *ren/tian* contrast just mentioned. For example, the monkey keeper walks two roads in that he goes along with preference of the monkeys and dwells at the non-position of the *dao*-axis or the celestial potter's wheel.[55] Further, as Billeter (1998, 30) correctly points out, we have to walk two roads in the sense of acknowledging that we have to simultaneously take into account the practical necessity of words as well as the fundamentally arbitrary nature of language. Since language is arbitrary (because it is conventional), it is inevitable that different people make different use of it, which would give rise to organized realities that are mutually incompatible.

The contrast (as well as the equivalence) between *ren* and *tian* is associated explicitly with the *zhenren* in the following passage (cf. §S5).[56]

> 故其好之也一，其弗好之也一。其一也一，其不一也一。其一與天為徒，其不一與人為徒。天與人不相勝也，是之謂真人。(6.1.15)

> Therefore, his liking was one and his not liking was one. His being one was one and his not being one was one. In being one, he was acting as a companion of Heaven. In not being one, he was

acting as a companion of man. When man and Heaven do not defeat each other, then we may be said to have the True Man.

In discussing 6.1.15, Feng Youlan (1928, 94) cites Guo Xiang.

> The true person unifies nature and man, and equalizes all things. . . . There is no natural conquest of nature and man. . . . He thus mysteriously unifies his own self with its other.

Hence, according to Guo Xiang and Feng Youlan, walking-two-roads can also be understood in terms of self and other.[57]

Zhuangzi often presupposes a nature/human (*tian/ren*) contrast or opposition, and yet he sometimes voices doubt about the *tian/ren* contrast.[58]

雖然，有患。夫知有所待而後當，其所待者特未定也。庸詎知吾所謂天之非人乎？所謂人之非天乎？(6.1.2)

However, there is a difficulty. Knowledge must wait for something before it can be applicable, and that which it waits for is never certain. How, then, can I know that what I call Heaven is not really man, and what I call man is not really Heaven?

According to Graham, the *tian/ren* contrast is "the most obstinate dichotomy Chuang-tzu strives to throw off" (G89, 195). Moreover, on a rare occasion (as Graham notes), Zhuangzi sides with humans instead of Heaven (*tian*). In a passage "related to the inner chapters," Zhuangzi says,

全人惡天？惡人之天？而況吾天乎人乎！(23.10.1)

The perfect man [*quanren* 全人] hates Heaven, hates what is from Heaven in man, and above all the question 'Is it in me from Heaven or from man?' (G81, 106)

The Complete Man [*quanren* 全人] hates Heaven, and hates the Heavenly in man. How much more, then, does he hate the "I" who distinguishes between Heaven and man. (Watson)

The highest man does not care about heaven in general and does not care about the heaven of the people in particular. (Schipper)[59]

The Whole Man hates the Heavenly, for he hates what other people {in contrast to themselves} as the Heavenly. How much more would he hate {identifying himself} as "the Heavenly!" or "The Human!" (Ziporyn)

Graham interprets this "extraordinary" passage as an indication that Zhuangzi is raising doubts about the "dichotomy" between *tian* and *ren* because he wants to deconstruct *all* dichotomies.⁶⁰ Some translators try to avoid a straightforward "hating of *tian*" by translating the first clause as "How would the perfect man know about heaven?"

Sometimes doubt may arise concerning the relation between sages and ordinary humans (*ren* 人). We assume that those passages suggesting that the sage is completely at the side of *tian* (heaven–nature) are not relevant to our vision of the sage (*shengren* 聖人 or *zhenren* 真人) serving as the role model for humans (see §S4). There is no sharp boundary between sages playing this role and humans.

夫卜梁倚有聖人之才而无聖人之道，我有聖人之道而无聖人之才，吾欲以教之，庶幾其果為聖人乎！(6.4.2–3)

Now there's Pu-liang Yi [Bu Liang Yi 卜梁倚]—he has the talent of a sage but not the Way of a sage, whereas I have the Way of a sage but not the talent of a sage. I thought I would try to teach him and see if I could really get anywhere near to make him a sage. It's easier to explain the Way of a sage to someone who has the talent of a sage, you know.

If there are stages on the way of becoming a sage, there are intermediate stages between human and sage.

We conclude that what is central to Zhuangzi's stance is the idea of "walking-two-roads," the road of *tian* and the road of *ren*. The ideal is to walk both roads at the same time. This is what sages do and all *ren* 人 should strive for. With respect to the road of humans, the sage merges with humans and "just goes along with things" (Kjellberg 2.3.7); with respect to heaven–nature–*dao*, the sage is placed at the center of the pivot or the potter's wheel of heaven–nature.

Doubt and Rhetorical Questions

Kjellberg writes: "Philosophically speaking, the *Zhuangzi* raises doubts, nothing more" (2007, 281).⁶¹ This assessment sounds fairly extreme. The author is probably aware of this, and so later in his article he adds: "There is a true nature of things for Zhuangzi." It is correct that there are quite some doubt-raising utterances in the inner chapters, but taking them at face value would risk neglecting Zhuangzi's positive claims and his subtle notion of knowledge–doubt, which implies that knowledge cannot be separated from doubt. One should not have "too much respect for the undoubted" (G81, 63).

A common opinion is that Zhuangzi uses rhetorical doubt to make the reader aware of taken-for-granted certainties. Zhuangzi's doubt is perhaps not a skeptical doubt of the kind we find in the case of Sextus Empiricus, neither is it a case of Cartesian methodological doubt. It is perhaps most similar to Peirce's "reasonable doubt."[62] Peirce (1905) argued that "complete doubt" (as for Descartes) is mere self-deception. Zhuangzi may agree with this claim. Peirce and Zhuangzi may also share the idea that doubt often brings about surprise. They differ in that, for Peirce, doubt is closely tied to the motivation to increase knowledge, whereas this is not Zhuangzi's concern, at least not if knowledge is understood in Peirce's sense. Perhaps one can say that Zhuangzi's doubt has the effect of increasing understanding instead of knowledge.

We suggest that Zhuangzi's stance concerning doubt is not part of a skeptical argument, but part of a reflective and yet natural way of living. Hence, we use the label "doubt as a stance." As already suggested at the end of chapter 8, our view is that *if* one should ascribe a skeptical attitude to Zhuangzi, it could only be the skepticism concerning the meaning of words.Graham moves a paragraph from the traditional chapter 32 to chapter 3. In the standard editions we find,[63]

> 以不平平，其平也不平；以不徵徵，其徵也不徵。(32.12.4)

> If you use unfairness to achieve fairness, your fairness will be unfair. If you use a lack of proof to establish proofs, your proofs will be proofless. (Watson)

But, in Graham, the transposed passage is longer.

> Why be bothered by doubts? If you use the undoubted to unravel the doubted and transfer it to the undoubted, this is to have too much respect for the undoubted. Use the unlevel to level and your leveling will not level, use the untested to test and your testing will not test. (G81, 63)

The part concerning "doubt" in Graham's translation is missing in the editions by Legge, Levi, Mair, Watson, and other translators. We cannot tell whether Graham's amendment of the text is correct.[64] But the spirit of not having "too much respect for the undoubted" is in accordance with other parts of Zhuangzi's text in the inner chapters. At the most fundamental level, we should not look for the undoubtable because it does not exist.

The Western bewitchment with perfection and completeness of knowledge may have effected translations of modifiers of *zhi* 知. Consider the following translations of the last part of 6.1.1:[65]

知天之所為，知人之所為者，至矣。知天之所為者，天而生也；知人之所為者，以其知之所知，以養其知之所不知，終其天年而不中道夭者，是知之盛也。(6.1.1)

To know what nature does and to know what humans do is to have *reached perfection*. Those who know what nature does live naturally. Those who know what humans do use what they know to nurture what they know they don't know. Living out their natural term and not dying along the way, this is the *flourishing* of knowledge. (Kjellberg, emphasis added)

He who knows what it is that Heaven does, and knows what it is that man does, has *reached the peak*. Knowing what it is that Heaven does, he lives with Heaven. Knowing what it is that man does, he uses the knowledge of what he knows to help out the knowledge of what he doesn't know, and lives out the years that Heaven gave him without being cut off midway—this is the *perfection* of knowledge. (Watson, emphasis added)

We have italicized the phrases Kjellberg and Watson use as translations of *zhiyi* 至矣 and *cheng* 盛. In addition to the difference of translating *tian* either as Heaven (Watson) or as nature (Kjellberg), Watson's translation of *zhizhicheng* 知之盛 as the perfection of knowledge may mislead Western scholars to think of perfect or complete knowledge. The first "perfection" (*zhiyi*, which Watson translates as "reaching the peak") does not directly bear on *zhi* 知 and is relatively innocent, but translating *zhizhicheng* as perfection of knowledge (Watson) is rather infelicitous. Translating *zhizhicheng* as the flourishing of knowledge (Kjellberg) is all right provided that *cheng*/flourishing is not interpreted as completeness.[66] For knowledge to flourish, it does not have to be complete. *Cheng* may indicate abundant flourishing but not completeness. Complete or perfect knowledge would require being able to provide "the one correct complete description" of the subject matter, which is not possible unless it can be assumed that an ideal language is possible and the frame problem can be resolved (cf. §1b).

Some commentators have focused on the incompleteness of knowledge as a source of doubt. Other commentators use phrases such as "ultimately correct" (Sturgeon 2015, 893, 906, 910) in connection with complete or perfect knowledge.[67] We consider that the notion of *complete* or *perfect* knowledge, or *ultimately* correct knowledge—in whatever context—makes no sense.[68] We consider that for Zhuangzi knowledge has no confines (3.1.1) and always remains subject to doubt.

Zhuangzi would never claim that *zhi* is incomplete. This is analogous to what we have called the "problem of complete description" (§1b). Even if commentators argue that complete or perfect *zhi* is unachievable, they still presuppose the idea of completeness. Instead, it is inherent to *zhi*/know(ing) that the notion of complete knowledge makes no sense. As Zhuangzi puts it,

吾生也有涯，而知也无涯。(3.1.1)

My life flows between confines, but knowledge has no confines. (Graham)

Your life has a limit but knowledge has none. (Watson)

If it is correct to consider Zhuangzi as an opponent of the ideal language assumption, it follows that his occasional references to "perfect knowledge" must be meant to be ironical, as in[69]

三子之知幾乎。(2.4.9)

The knowledge of these three was close to perfection.

The predominance of the stance of doubt is also apparent from the use of several types of rhetorical questions.[70] Ordinary examples of rhetorical questions in classical Chinese are as follows:

得乎哉！(Xunzi 2.1.2)

Would he be able to get his way? (Surely not!) (Harbsmeier in TLS)

鰍然乎哉？(ZH 2.6.4) Is this true of a loach?

There are many different particles used for rhetorical questions in classical Chinese. In the *Zhuangzi* we find in most cases *huzai* 乎哉 or *qi . . . hu*

其……乎. Zhuangzi does not express doubt in terms of *yi* 疑 or *luan* 亂 but by means of various rhetorical devices. A typical device is what can be called "contradictory rhetorical questions." This kind of use is rather unique. To emphasize its relevance, we cite a couple of examples.

> 其果有謂乎，其果无謂乎。(2.5.3)

> But I don't know whether what I have said has really said something or whether it hasn't said something.

> 果且有彼是乎哉？果且无彼是乎哉？(2.3.8)[71]

> So is there really a this and a that? Or isn't there any this or that? (Van Norden 2011, 145; following Kjellberg)

> Are there really It and Other? Or really no It and Other?" (Graham)

> Is there really a distinction between "that" and "this"? Or is there really no distinction between "that" and "this"? (Guo Xiang, cited in Liu Xiaogan 2015b, 209)

> 且方將化，惡知不化哉？方將不化，惡知已化哉？(6.7.3)

> Moreover, when he is changing, how does he know that he is really changing? And when he is not changing, how does he know that he hasn't already changed?

Questions may be raised concerning the predicates of accepted contrasts, as in the following:

> 予惡乎知說生之非惑邪！予惡乎知惡死之非弱喪而不知歸者邪！

> How do I know that loving life is not a delusion? How do I know that in hating death I am not like a man who, having left home in his youth, has forgotten the way back? (2.6.13)

We suggest that the contradictions should not be understood as really asking the reader to choose between the two options (like the use of *haishi* 還是 in modern Chinese when used as disjunction). Instead, we should read the cases of "contradictory rhetoric" as: "Is it A? Surely not. Is it not-A?

Surely not." That is to say, either Zhuangzi requests that we consider a third alternative, or he is proposing that such questions are pointless. The rhetorical message is raising doubt about the correctness of either side of an allegedly exclusive bivalence.

More complicated constructions may repeat the double rhetoric, adding either an example or a consequence.

果有言邪？其未嘗有言邪？其以為異於鷇音，亦有辯乎，其无辯乎。(2.3.3)

So then, are we speaking of something {when we are speaking}, or have we never talked of anything? If we take the view that our language is different from the twittering of birds, can we establish a clear distinction between the two or not? (Billeter)

... then do they [words] really say something? Or do they say nothing? People suppose that words are different from the peeps of baby birds, but is there any difference, or isn't there? (Watson)

果且有成與虧乎哉？果且无成與虧乎哉？有成與虧，故昭氏之鼓琴也；无成與虧，故昭氏之不鼓琴也。(2.4.8)

But do such things as completion and injury really exist, or do they not? There is such a thing as completion and injury—Mr. Zhao playing the lute is an example. There is such a thing as no completion and no injury—Mr. Zhao not playing the lute is an example.

若是而可謂成乎？雖我亦成也。若是而不可謂成乎？雖我亦成也。(2.4.10)

Can these men be said to have attained completion? If so, then so have all the rest of us. Or can they not be said to have attained completion? If so, then neither we nor anything else have ever attained it.

The rhetorical question may result from an extrapolation of the uncertainty of *zhi* 知 to a more abstract level.

雖然，有患。夫知有所待而後當，其所待者特未定也。庸詎知吾所謂天之非人乎？所謂人之非天乎？ (6.1.2)

Even so, there's a problem. Knowledge depends on something before it can be fitting. But what it depends on has not yet been fixed. So how do I know that what I call natural isn't really human and what I call human isn't really natural? (Kjellberg)

However, there is a difficulty. Knowledge must wait for something before it can be applicable, and that which it waits for is never certain. How, then, can I know that what I call Heaven is not really man, and what I call man is not really Heaven? (Watson)

Finally, the number of options may be increased, but the conclusion remains that none of them can be claimed to have provided the final answer to the question (cf. 2.6.18).

Given a context, a perspective, or a form of life, there is knowledge that is relative to what is valued. However, Zhuangzi's more fundamental stance is "doubt." It hovers in the background in debates concerning *shifei* (§10a) and concerning Zhuangzi's alleged amoralism (§10b). An attitude/stance of doubt may function in a therapeutic or a methodological way, but, after we have passed that point, it is not something to really worry about because it reflects the natural way of life.

We conclude that Zhuangzi stresses doubt (about anything he writes about), but it should not be considered as the kind of doubt that is associated with Descartes or Sextus Empiricus in the Western tradition. Zhuangzi's doubt is a way of life that touches everything.

Buqi erqi 不齊而齊: Achieving Equality by Leaving Things Uneven

In this section we focus on Zhang Taiyan's *Exegesis of the Qiwulun* written in 1910 (Zhang 1986).[72] In his interpretation of the *Qiwulun*, Zhang Taiyan highlights the difference between *qiqi buqi* 齊其不齊 and *buqi erqi* 不齊而齊.

> Trying to even out what are not even–equal [*qiqi buqi* 齊其不齊] is the shallow and obstinate practice of the inferior scholars. Achieving evenness–equality by leaving things uneven–unlike [*buqi erqi* 不齊而齊] is the superb discourse of the superior philosophers. (Zhang 1986, 61)

Zhang Taiyan seemed to take himself as a steadfast devotee to Zhuangzi's ideas. He considered that such assumptions as universal principles (*gongli*

公理) and Mozi's idea of the will of heaven (*tianzhi* 天志) were restrictive of the human mind by the excuse of universality and fell far short of Zhuangzi's wisdom of achieving equality by leaving things uneven.

According to Zhang, *qi* 齊 has the implication of "treating things in accordance with what they are" (Zhang 1986, 61: 因物付物，所以為齊). His exegesis of the *Qiwulun* starts as follows:[73]

> The *Qiwu* [齊物] is a discourse on equality. If one delves into its actual signification, one would find that it means not only that one should treat all sentient beings with equality without making differentiations regarding superiority and inferiority. "It is only when one is detached from speech, detached from words, and detached from the mind taking objects as its causal conditions" [離言說相，離名字相，離心緣相] that one can see that things are always equal, and this coincides with the signification of the *Qiwu*. (Zhang 1986, 48–49; cf. 1985, 262)

For Zhang Taiyan, *qiwu* implies achieving equality by leaving things uneven.

On the one hand, Zhang Taiyan emphasizes that equality refers to the state of the myriad things before any naming practices appear (cf. 2.4.7). Instead of taking equality as a certain final objective to be achieved, Zhang Taiyan regards it as the original "truth" of the world. On the other hand, he does not evade addressing the varying divergences among things. Differences are the actual ways of being of things. So long as one does not enforce any superficial "equality" by trying to obliterate differences, but instead accepts differences without imposing a fixed general criterion, the equality of things shows forth in all their differences.

It seems that the *Qiwulun* offers Zhang Taiyan a unique notion of equality that transcends the ideal of equality as abstract and utopian egalitarianism. It is beyond the antinomy between sameness and difference. More importantly, it annuls the presumably abysmal gap between humans and other sentient beings. As Zhang Taiyan remarks in another work,[74]

> What modern people call equality [*pingdeng* 平等] refers to the equality between human beings. Thus, they leave human beings and birds, beasts, grass, and trees unequal. The notion of equality in Buddhism equalizes human beings with birds and beasts. Zhuangzi goes one step further in equalizing [human beings] with things. Even so he does not remain contented. He considers that the tendency to making judgments concerning rightness and wrongness [*shifei* 是非] is a sign of inequality. One

can only achieve equality after one gets rid of such tendency. Just before his death, Zhuangzi says, "Using criteria that are unequal in order to obtain equality, such presumed equality is not equal." This is a footnote to his notion of equality. (Zhang Taiyan 1987, 64–65)[75]

Zhuangzi's notion of equality deals not only with sentient beings in the life world but also with terms such as good and evil, right and wrong.[76] One has to remain vigilant of the fact that one's criteria of values are constrained by one's (hidden) presuppositions, and hence, one should not stick to a fixed value system in weighing right and wrong. However, this does not mean that there can be neither rightness nor wrongness, but that one should proceed from the actual situation of a particular thing, and treat things as what they are.[77] Zhang Taiyan (1995, 14–15) cites Laozi to further explicate this point (chapters 64 and 49 of the *Laozi*). He comments that Laozi meant to say one should not bring to situations one's preconceptions concerning good and evil, right and wrong, and on this basis impose an apparently true but yet fake equality. Rather, one should acknowledge the dissimilarity between things, keep alert of the limitation of one's value judgments, proceed from the natural characteristics of things, and comport oneself in constant correspondence with the actual situation, just as the hinge of a door keeps on opening and closing according to need.

In his opening commentary on the title of the *Qiwulun*, Zhang Taiyan mentions in particular the story about Yao 堯 asking Shun 舜 (both being legendary ancient sage-kings) whether he could launch a war against three supposedly backward states. The story goes,[78]

故昔者堯問於舜曰：「我欲伐宗、膾、胥敖，南面而不釋然。其故何也？」舜曰：「夫三子者，猶存乎蓬艾之間。若不釋然，何哉？ 昔者十日並出，萬物皆照，而況德之進乎日者乎！」(2.6.1)

In ancient times, Yao asked Shun, "I want to attack Zong 宗, Kuai 膾, and Xu'ao 胥敖, for though I sit facing south on the throne, still I am not at ease. Why is this?" Shun said, "Though these three may continue to dwell among the grasses and brambles, why should this make you ill at ease? Once upon a time, ten suns rose in the sky at once, and the ten thousand things were all simultaneously illuminated. And how much better are many Virtuosities than many suns!" (Ziporyn)

Guo Xiang explains as follows:[79]

> Although the sun and the moon have no selfish preference in their illumination, yet there are still things beyond their range. But in virtue there is nothing unhappy. If one attempts to change the aspiration of the people who live in the mug world and the brushwood and to compel them to follow one's self, one is not in agreement with the comprehensiveness of *dao* . . . Let everything enjoy its own nature, and have its own satisfaction. No matter whatever and wherever things may be, leave them alone each in its own proper sphere. Then they are content and we also are happy.

In Zhang's exegeses, he cited from Guo Xiang's comments, "[This story] refers to the great sage [*dasheng* 大聖] in order to reveal the principle of equality–evenness (*qiyi* 齊一)";[80] and he elaborates, "Where one feels at ease, there is no meanness. Hence, the weeds are the wonderful dwelling-places for the three kingdoms" (Zhang 1986, 39). Different states are located in different environments. One cannot impose one's own criteria to draw the conclusion that the states that take their dwelling-places among weeds are uncivilized. Worse than that, one cannot use this as an excuse to smite them and try to adapt them to the "civilization" of the middle country. To do this can be compared to feeding a seagull with luxurious banquet, and entertaining a bird with magnificent music (Zhang 1986, 100).

Different states have divergent (literally "uneven" *buqi* 不齊) customs; what is called civilization and what is called barbarism ascribe value to different things. However, they all remain at ease with their own customs and do not bring in hindrance to one another, just as the ten suns do not affect one another. Virtue is supposed to be greater than the sun, so a virtuous king such as Yao should have no problem in allowing the coexistence of the three states. This is real equality. We can consider Zhang Taiyan's interpretation as a proto-daoist version of multiculturalism.[81] The will of trying to civilize the three states arises from the prejudice that considers them as unequal with the middle country.

Zhang Taiyan goes ahead to explain that one should not be restrained by words, names/terms, and mind, and thus fails to perceive the pre-originary evenness of things. Neither should one try to impose a fake facade of equality on things. Instead, one should return to hollowness (*xu* 虛), just as the pipes of *tian* are no-thing and belch forth breath without any partiality, and just as the mind of Ziqi who has emptied his own self (2.1.2) and who lets things remain uneven according to their own capacity. Only in this way can one see the evenness of things.

Both Western and Chinese theorists on multiculturalism can learn from Daoism on at least two points on the basis of the daoist insight of *buqi erqi*. First, there are no strict boundaries between things and between various ethnic groups, in particular those who have been living side-by-side for a long time, and so have *mutually* influenced one another. Second, one should not theorize by taking one's own position (as a member of the dominating majority) as the universal position,[82] and then treat other cultures as a certain object to be evaluated, tolerated, absorbed, or to be kept at distance. It is better to avoid using such determinations as majority versus minority, which are misleading and entail unequal evaluations.

We conclude that Zhang Taiyan has rightly pointed out, via Zhuangzi, that the tendency to making judgments concerning *shifei* (right or wrong) is a sign of inequality.

Chapter 10

Afterthoughts

We call this chapter "Afterthoughts" because it differs from chapters 7 to 9 in that those chapters are primarily based on the text of the inner chapters of the Zhuangzi. In this chapter we address two questions arising from Zhuangzi's text in relation to contemporary concerns in philosophy (which are not necessarily relevant to Zhuangzi's time).

Do the Ruists and Mohists Really Disagree?

In this section, we focus on the question of whether Ruists and Mohists "really" disagree with each other and whether the debate is pointless and therefore futile. The relevant passage is as follows (here *shi* and *fei* are used as verbs):

> 故有儒墨之是非，以是其所非，而非其所是。欲是其所非，而非其所是，則莫若以明。(2.3.5)

> And so we have the *shiing* and *feiing* of the Confucians and the Mohists, whereby one *shis* what the other *feis* and *feis* what the other *shis*. If you want to *shi* what the other *feis* and *fei* what the other *shis* then nothing is better than using clarity. (Hansen 1983b, 45, emphasis added)

Zhuangzi was not the first to refer to the dispute between Ruists and Mohists. Cheng Xuanying recounts (34),

> In the past, there is someone in the Kingdom of Zheng 鄭 whose name was Huan 緩. He studied for three years and became a Ruist. . . . His brother was called Di 翟. Huan let his brother be educated and he became a Moist. . . . But although Huan and Di were blood brothers, they followed different teachings and, moreover, they disputed [*shifei*] with one another. Huan regretted about his brother and died in remorse (sadness). The dispute about *biwo* and *shifei* has already got a long history. It reached its epitome with these two sages. Hence they are referred to as the head of chaos [亂臺之帥]. Hence we know that only when *dao* is lost and word is hidden do people start to pursue *shi* and *fei*.

According to this story, it is different courses of education and of development that have brought about *shifei* debates.¹

For Zhuangzi, the futility of *shifei* debates not only is an obvious problem for the debates between Ruists and Mohists, but also becomes evident in other contexts (see 2.6.6 already cited) and the following:

其或是也，其或非也邪？其俱是也，其俱非也邪？我與若不能相知也，則人固受黮闇，吾誰使正之。(2.6.18)

Is one of us right and the other wrong? Are both of us right or are both of us wrong? If you and I don't know the answer, then other people are bound to be even more in the dark. Whom shall we get to decide what is right?

Zhuangzi also noted the problem of assessing changing views over time.

孔子行年六十而六十化，始時所是，卒而非之，未知今之所謂是之非五十九非也。(27.2.1; G81, 102; cf. 25.8.1)

Confucius has been going along for sixty years and he has changed sixty times. What at the beginning he used to call right he has ended up calling wrong. So now there's no telling whether what he calls right at the moment is not in fact what he called wrong during the past fifty-nine years. (Watson)

Perhaps under the influence of Zhuangzi, the observation concerning the apparently irresolvable disagreement between Ruists and Mohists often appears in some other early texts. For example,

將誰使定儒、墨之誠乎？(Hanfeizi 50.1.3)

Whom could one ask to decide the real facts of the case of the Mohists and Confucians? (Harbsmeier in TLS)

Who is going to determine genuineness as between the Literati and the Mohists? . . . It is impossible to determine whether the Literati or the Mohists are right. (Liao 1959, 298–99)

However, the doubt voiced in the *Hanfeizi* is only entertained with respect to the historical distance to the original disputants.

孔、墨不可復生，將誰使定世之學乎？孔子、墨子俱道堯、舜，而取舍不同。皆自謂真堯、舜，堯、舜不復生，將誰使定儒、墨之誠乎？(Hanfeizi 50.1.3)

Since Confucius and Mòzǐ cannot be brought to life again whom is one to set to decide on the learning of our time. Both Confucius and Mòzǐ followed the Way of Yáo and Shùn, but their preferences were not the same, though they all called themselves true followers of Yáo and Shùn. Since Yáo and Shùn cannot be brought to life again whom is one to set to decide the truth between Confucians or the Mohists? (Harbsmeier in TLS)

In the *Hanfeizi*, we find the concern that historical distance may constitute an unavoidable hurdle to accessing the disagreement of Mohists and Ruists. It is assumed that there is a fact of the matter concerning what is *shi* and what is *fei*; the only problem is that we do not (and cannot) know it with respect to the teachings of the sages. This leaves open the possibility that there are "really true" (historical) "facts," although we cannot know them. Because of distance of time, we cannot decide any more who is right and who is wrong. Even if at one time all the one hundred schools would agree with one another, at another time this may not be the case. A somewhat similar view is expressed in the *Huainanzi*.[2]

天下是非無所定，世各是其所是，而非其所非。所謂是與非各異，皆自是而非人。(Huainanzi 11.27.1)

In the world, "right" and "wrong" have no determinate basis. Each generation affirms what it deems right and rejects what it deems wrong. What each calls right and wrong is different. This is due to the fact that each deems itself right and the other wrong. (Liu An, adapted)

Here it seems to be assumed that one can know the content of *shifei* judgments at different times.[3] However, the issue of accessibility or difference over time is not the core of Zhuangzi's doubts concerning the significance of *shifei* debates. Even if different *shifei* debates are accessible and known, they are still futile because Ruists and Mohists use "incommensurable" standards for their *shifei* judgments. This seems to be the correct explanation, in particular if we may assume that Zhuangzi is commenting on contemporaneous *shifei* debates and the issue of inaccessibility due to time distance does not arise.

The question "Do the schools *really* disagree?" hides a number of issues on which there can be disagreement; but, first of all, we should stress that the discussion of this issue is taking place in a language that contains quasi-universals as recognized by all the parties concerned (Ruists, Mohists, Zhuangzi, we, our readers). Remember (§1a) that quasi-universals are *not* universals: it is not a matter of *shared* meanings, but of family resemblances between the respective understandings of the words (quasi-universals) in the meta-language. Perhaps one could use the word "shared" for the similar understanding of different parties, but it is better to distinguish this similarity in principle from the more general claim that for interpretation to be possible one must share a language—a view that we oppose. What must be assumed are mutually recognizable human practices and quasi-universals for describing these practices, but nothing "identical" needs be shared.

Two questions are rather straightforward: Who disagrees with whom? About what do they disagree? More fundamentally: What stances are presupposed concerning language? How to understand *shifei* and *bian*? Is the disagreement about goal, about stance, or about method, or does the disagreement already starts at the level of the meanings of words? According to the later Mohists, only one party in a disagreement can be right (or both are wrong).[4] However, their understanding of disputation presupposes the ideal language assumption. According to the theory of interpretation we advocate, in the meta-language in which we talk about *shifei* debates, meanings and opinions are subject to the indeterminacies of interpretation (§1a). Hence, meanings and/or opinions that are ascribed to another scholar always remain underdetermined and/or undetermined.

The usual understanding of 2.3.5 by many scholars early and late is that the "who" of the disagreement are the Ruists and the Mohists. But we should also consider the possible disagreement between Zhuangzi and other schools (Ruists, Mohists, for instance), and disagreement between Zhuangzi and us.[5]

Now consider the question: About *what* do they disagree? There can be disagreement at different levels, for example, disagreement about funeral rituals, about the meaning of *ren* 仁 and *yi* 義, and about the meaning of *shifei*. Meanings cannot be separated from commitments and other factors.[6] Hence, there is no strict demarcation between meanings of words and judgments of the situation except in "block worlds."[7]

Trying to sort out meanings can only work, at best, for simple and decontextualized cases. It would work for "the cat sat on the mat" and the modern Chinese utterance *mao zai xizi shang* 猫在席子上. The latter is "true even if the cat has never before now sitten on the mat, false if it sat on a cloth mat" (Graham 1992, 65). It seems that bilingual speakers would agree on the truth or falsity of both the English and the Chinese version in every situation. But "cloth mat" is a family-resemblance-concept. It has no sharp boundaries. Hence, bilingual speakers may still disagree about concrete cases. This would be even more so for complicated cases because of irresolvable disagreement. Bilingual speakers may agree on a number of quasi-universals, but they may also resolutely disagree on the (in)correctness of certain actions that are described in terms of these quasi-universals.

The most fundamental issue concerning the notion of disagreement is that disagreement is only possible against the background of agreement (§1a). Simple examples of differences (for example, concerning cats sitting on mats) can only work provided that there is substantial mutual recognition of animal and human practices. If Zhuangzi would not agree that there are some things on which he and his interlocutors agree, he cannot even know that he and "they" have (apparent) disagreement or have different stances. Zhuangzi, Mohists, Ruists, and their commentators all acknowledge an "everyday" (commonsense) quasi-universal of *shifei*. It is only against such a background that Guo Xiang can say that there is neither *shi* and nor *fei* (Feng Youlan 1928, 44; Ziporyn 2009a, 144).[8] Zhuangzi can only "criticize" Ruists and Mohists because he and they have a similar "thin" understanding of *shifei*. Zhuangzi cannot make any evaluative comment concerning their contestations if he and they do not agree on the meaning of *some* words and the correctness of *some* opinions. This accords with the principle of charity.[9]

Graham says that Ruists and Mohists "can never reach agreement" (G81, 4). He also suggests: "competing thinkers do not really disagree" (G69, 144). Asking whether the Ruists and Mohists "really" agree or disagree only makes sense if there is already some agreement among Ruists, Mohists, Zhuangzi, the readers of our book and of Zhuangzi's text, and us, for example, some agreement concerning the fact of death or the process of dying.¹⁰ That is to say, there is agreement on some quasi-universals (in terms of family-resemblance-concepts grounded in the family resemblance of forms of life). Zhuangzi's stance on "death" is radical, but it still presupposes agreement on a large number of (value-)facts concerning human beings dying. This makes disagreement possible.¹¹ Although there is disagreement concerning their significance and relevance, there is agreement on the conventional commonsense meaning of *shifei* disagreement. We can perhaps criticize Zhuangzi for having overlooked the possibility that a continuing debate between scholars may not be completely pointless because there is always agreement on some everyday quasi-universals.

Commentators disagree on the answer to the question: on what meanings do Ruists and Mohists disagree? Graham suggests that Ruists and Mohists "differ radically" on the meaning of *yi* 義.¹² Sturgeon disagrees with him because for him *yi* 義 and other relevant notions are "nominally shared," and hence both Ruists and Mohists can invoke (and they did invoke) many of the "broadly similar basic goods" as justification.¹³ Graham and Sturgeon may both be right, either focusing on a "thick" or a "thin" meaning of *yi* 義. We agree with Sturgeon when he remarks that Zhuangzi would be suspicious of the values "nominally shared by Confucian and Mohist" (2015, 908) such as benevolence and righteousness (*ren* 仁 and *yi* 義).

Billeter (1998, 21) writes: "[Zhuangzi's] fundamental intuition seems to have been that the polemics to which the schools of thought of that time devoted themselves were essentially futile, because these schools *did not speak the same language*" (emphasis original). This can only be true if we presuppose that both schools are committed to the idea of rigidly fixed meanings (which is not an unreasonable assumption).¹⁴ As has already been stated, we may also assume that Ruists and Mohists agree on some minimal commonsense meaning of *shifei*.

Billeter also writes (1998, 21),

> What mattered to [Zhuangzi] was not that one opinion was as good as another, but that our opinions, prejudices, and habits of language—our "ready-made mentality" {*esprit fait*}—cut us off from the living sources of effective action, whether in word or in deed. He is quite different from a "relativist."

We agree with Billeter (and Wittgenstein) concerning the intertwinement of meanings, opinions, and action. Using language entails deploying meanings that function as quasi-universals, even if only momentarily.

However, according to our definition of quasi-universals, they only apply, for the time being, to concrete interaction between two or only a few traditions or languages (Ma and van Brakel 2015, 53–54). Hence, they are not universals as defined in cognitive science and mainstream analytic philosophy.

Hansen seems to hold in some places that there is real disagreement between Ruists and Mohists (cf. Coutinho 2015, 172). He also assumes that meanings are fixed for a community. This is apparent from remarks such as the following:[15]

> Community coherence allows that two discussants might disagree about the meaning, but that in such a case, one of them should be wrong. Neither faction can change the meaning of a term in their language by fiat, definition or intention. (Hansen 2015)

Because Ruists and Mohists belong to the same community (in Hansen's sense), "by definition" they speak the same language. Hansen's view entails that yi 義 and shifei have the same meaning for Ruists and Mohists. However, if we do not accept Hansen's stipulation of community coherence, meanings are *not* fixed in a community. Of course, one can still claim that they speak "more or less" the same language in practice.

Coutinho points out, correctly, that the issue for Zhuangzi is not disputes *between* Ruists and Mohists about what is *shi* and what is *fei* but about making such distinctions in the first place (2015, 183). Guo Xiang already made such a point.

> That there is a distinction of right and wrong is what the Confucianists and the Mohists affirm. That there is no such distinction is what they deny. To affirm what they deny and to deny what they affirm is to show there is no such distinction. (Cited in Feng Youlan 1928, 44)

Guo Xiang continues.

> To affirm what they negate and negate what they affirm, we must illuminate the sense in which there is no *shi* and *fei*. The best way to do this is to use the Confucians and Mohists to illuminate each other, to see each in the light of the other. Then we see how what each affirms as right is also not right and how what each considers wrong is also not wrong. The rights are not right

and the wrongs are not wrong, so there is no *shi* and *fei*. (cited in Ziporyn 2009a, 144–45)

When Guo Xiang is saying that *shi* is also not-*shi*, this is not a contradiction. It means that what the Ruists regard as *shi* (according to their criteria), the Mohists regard as not-*shi* (according to the Mohist criteria), and vice versa. The criteria needed to make *shifei* judgments are not the same for the Ruists and Mohists.

There is real difference between the stances of the Ruists, Mohists, *and* Zhuangzi (as seen from our perspective).[16] Zhuangzi's stance concerning death is radical (G81, 23–25). Yet, his disagreement with Ruists and Mohists is "real" disagreement because all human beings are aware of the fact–value of death. We can imagine that Ruists and Mohists agree on all the relevant meanings concerning death, mourning, and so on, but still disagree on the appropriate mourning period or other aspects of the process of mourning. One may argue that it cannot be said that Ruists and Mohists disagree (owing to the incommensurability of different stances). However, even then, there can be pragmatic disagreement by tacitly dropping the assumption of fixed meanings. Assuming a language with determined meanings leads to incommensurability and relativism. Dropping this assumption allows a form of pragmatism that leaves room for relativities, but this does not lead to relativism (cf. chapter 8).

Our interpretation of Zhuangzi's comments concerning *shifei* debates in 2.3.4 and elsewhere can be summarized as follows:

1. We should be aware that the issues surrounding 2.3.4 have to be discussed in a meta-language, which presupposes that there are at least some quasi-universals (that is, meanings and opinions) acknowledged by Ruists, Mohists, Zhuangzi, their commentators, we, and our readers—although each quasi-universal is understood (somewhat) differently by each party concerned.

2. In light of the theory of interpretation we advocate (§1a), disagreement is only possible against the background of agreements that are embedded in mutually recognized human practices. There *must* be some agreement in order for there to be disagreement. (This follows from the principle of charity.)

3. Only when a strict ideal language is presupposed is it possible for one to argue that neither agreement nor disagreement is possible because of incommensurability. However, such an

argument can only be made in a language, which is *not* an ideal language, but an everyday "ordinary" language. Perhaps one can say that incommensurability (assuming fixed meanings) amounts to irresolvable disagreement in everyday terms.

4. One can consider that intellectual schools such as the Ruists and Mohists either speak or do not speak the same language depending on whether one assumes that meanings are fixed or not. If meanings are fixed in terms of an ideal language for each party, the language of the other party is incommensurable and therefore meaningless. On the other hand, if meanings are not fixed, there would always be some quasi-universals concerning mutually recognized human practices. However, we suggest that in the time of Zhuangzi most of the schools were in conflict because of their respective assumptions of an ideal language and fixed meanings. Zhuangzi's claim that meanings are unfixed (*weiding*) is an exception.

5. Zhuangzi has always acknowledged and taken into account the existence of mutually recognized human practices (as his many stories and parables testify), which presupposes that one is attentive to another's position as a member of a community. Denying *any* kind of quasi-universals, or simply refusing communicative interaction, would block communicative interaction and make one's own sayings meaningless for others. This may have been the actual situation concerning the relation of Zhuangzi and other schools. Denying any form of quasi-universals (hence: denying any mutually recognizable human practices) is a performative contradiction because understanding the utterance expressing this denial in the first place presupposes quasi-universals.

6. On the basis of the assumption that meanings are not fixed (since we can construct quasi-universals on the basis of family-resemblance-concepts), we could distinguish between two possibilities (which are separated only by a vague and flexible border). The first possibility is that discussion between two parties makes sense because of the complexity of meanings and opinions that are involved. Clarifications may help understand one another better. The second possibility is that two parties disagree on particular central utterances, which

both can understand (more or less) in terms of the quasi-universals used in formulating the utterance. However, as Zhuangzi points out, in practice humans have a tendency to fall back on assuming rigid meanings and opinions.

7. When *shifei* is deconstructed and removed from stage, it can be seen that mutually recognizable human practices serve as background of an ordinary language (without fixed meanings), which contains such "vague" notions as good and bad (*hao'e*). If there is a cross-cultural family resemblance of *hao'e* and good/bad, {*hao'e* ⇔ good/bad} can be a quasi-universal.

8. Even if the disagreement concerning what is "correct" (*ke* 可, *shi* 是, *zheng* 正, and so on) and/or "appropriate" (*yi* 宜) seems to be irresolvable, discussion may still continue surrounding quasi-universals that both parties acknowledge. For communicative interaction to be possible, there *must* be these quasi-universals.

9. Careful use of everyday language may lead to success in "walking-two-roads." However, Ruists and Mohists are not walking-two-roads. Instead, being "inferior scholars," they walk the road of disputing the supposedly incommensurable stance of one another.

Is Zhuangzi's Stance Amoral?

When Zhi Dun (支遁, 314–366, also called Zhi Daolin 支道林) was having a discussion with other scholars concerning their reading of the first chapter of the *Zhuangzi*, someone said: "Everyone following his own nature is to be considered as (wandering) at leisure." Zhi objected strongly.[17]

> This is not true. The nature of (the tyrant) Jie [桀] and (the robber) Zhi [*Dao Zhi* 盜跖] was to destroy and to harm, and if one regards following one's nature as the realization (of perfect freedom), then (their way of life) would consequently also be wandering at leisure.

As Machek (2010, 118) remarks, Zhi Dun "was well aware of the dangerous implications of Guo Xiang's identification of spontaneity with morality, a move that might justify a great deal of violence and moral indifference." The disagreement between Guo and Zhi is not surprising if we take into account that allegedly Guo Xiang wanted to reconcile the spontaneity proposed by daoist classics with moral norms advocated by the Ruist school and by Guo Xiang himself.[18] According to Machek (113), Guo Xiang advocated

> the superiority of Confucius, who is considered a true sage over Zhuangzi, who is said to »have understood the root {of all things}« (*zhi ben* 知本), but whose words »were of no use« (*wuyong* 無用), and he was merely »the best of the hundred philosophers« (*baijia zhiguan* 百家之冠).

How interpretations of Zhuangzi can fit into moral and political discourse is a complicated issue. We will make a few comments on recent publications, and draw the conclusion that no progress has been made concerning this issue. This may be inherent to the human condition.

In his book *The Moral Fool: A Case for Amorality* (2009), Moeller argues against the validity of ethical distinctions. "If one begins to look at the world and oneself in moral terms, this is already turning away from the Dao" (32).[19] The moral fool does not dismiss "good deeds," but these are a matter of practice, not of principles. According to Moeller, the moral fool would deny (when pressed in all seriousness) that the Nazis' actions were morally wrong, but he or she (and Moeller) would also deny that they were morally right or morally permissible. The moral fool (moral error theorist), being morally blind, would not acknowledge that they were morally *anything*.

Ziporyn (2010) has written a sympathetic review of Moeller's book. His only critical remark concerns their disagreement about the meaning of "critique of relativism" and "radical relativism." The meaning of these words is not our concern. However, we would like to point out an important difference between the two scholars, which is evident in the following remarks:

> There can never be a simple, universal, stable, unequivocal consensus about what the relevant morality is, even within a given society, even at a given time and place. That is, there is no such thing as a univocal context: there are always multiple contexts, and hence multiple applicable standards of right and wrong. There are as many views of the matter as there are perspectives upon it, and even those within a given society cannot all have an identical perspective at all times. Right and wrong are relative not to an abstract something called "the present society,"

but to each moment of anybody and everybody's multifarious experience. (Ziporyn 2010)

The problem is not so much that all moral judgments are relative to context—the *Zhuangzi* does not deny this—but that these judgments are held so dearly within their respective contexts that they may lead to all kinds of moral beliefs and, possibly, destructive deeds. (Moeller 2009, 32)

It seems that Ziporyn stands more on the side of rigid standards than Moeller. Moreover, Ziporyn uses a sophisticated notion of context while Moeller considers context to be a secondary issue and emphasizes human inclinations in general. However that may be, either resorting to sophisticated context or appealing to awareness of human inclinations is not of much help when dealing with conflicting stances.

In contemporary (analytic) philosophy, the problem raised by Zhi Dun appears under the name of the "Daoist-Nazi problem" (Sturgeon 2015, 908).[20] The *daos* of the Ruists and Mohists are "reasonable" *daos*, but a Nazi-*dao* is *not* a "reasonable" *dao*. Hansen, Fraser, and Sturgeon offer many suggestions about how to counter the claim that all *daos* (including the Nazi-*dao*) are equal because they can only be contingently justified. However, in what follows we argue that their attempts to neutralize the Nazi-*dao* are not successful.

Fraser writes: "What keeps us from oppressing them, if anything does, is not doubt about the status of our way, nor our inability to convince them to adopt it. It is some form of appreciation, consideration, or respect for theirs" (2009, 453). But what if this view is not acknowledged (or considered ridiculous) by "the Other"? Fraser continues: "We must recognize them as potentially viable, with their own usefulness (and corresponding deficiencies), even if we ourselves do not follow them. They reveal aspects of the world and ways of life that our own do not" (454). Such a positive view concerning "the other" is not universally shared, and it is not clear whether Fraser is saying that the Nazi-*dao* must also be recognized as "potentially viable." Fraser also remarks,

A racist *dào* is deeply "deficient" in that it excludes the value of entire other races and their practices. Also, it is likely to prove less useful, even by the racist's own lights, than a non-racist *dào*, since it will tend to evoke resistance from members of other races and thus create obstacles for its adherents. (455n41)

Surely this is not the way things look from the Nazi perspective.

As an example, Sturgeon (2015, 908) considers the claim that "killing innocent babies for fun is wrong." However, the Nazi may well agree that it is wrong to kill *innocent* babies *for fun*. Moreover, if we drop the modifiers (the emphasized words in the previous sentence), it is not the case that all of humanity would agree that in all circumstances "killing babies is wrong." Sturgeon also remarks: "We should condemn a Nazi Dao follower, not because his actions, commitments, or Dao are 'wrong' in any absolute sense, but rather because he is stupid in failing to see important perspectives on his situation" (910). However, the Nazi would not consider these perspectives to be relevant. Sturgeon acknowledges that

> The value of diverse practices need not entail regarding them all as equally justified. Some might be more justified than others, because they realize or acknowledge more value, cohere better with other, everyday values, or prove more useful to those who follow them. (910)

This is simply stating the values of a variant of liberal democracy, which would have no impact on the Nazi. The Nazi would not agree with Sturgeon's specification of "everyday values."

Hansen's view is somewhat similar to that of Fraser and Sturgeon except that he draws more explicitly on Zhuangzi's text. He says that Zhuangzi "does *not endorse*, but *questions* the valuation of the natural. . . . Zhuangzi would, no doubt, condemn Nazi skills from *many* of the perspectives he *regularly* adopts" (1992, 290, emphasis added). But Hansen does not provide textual evidence for these *many* perspectives Zhuangzi *regularly* adopts. In support of the suggestion that "all doctrines are equally *the pipes of heaven*," Hansen (2015) says, "all the existing 道 *dao*^{guides} are *natural* in virtue of being actual." However, according to him, Zhuangzi "rejects the 'natural' to 'acceptable' inference." For support Hansen refers to his note 82: "I take this to be the implication of the 'pipes of heaven' passage." However, he offers no further explanation for "acceptable," neither does he consider alternative interpretations of the "pipes of heaven [*tian*]" passage.

Hansen, Fraser, and Sturgeon suggest that Zhuangzi's meta-level insight encourages us to learn from others and to be tolerant, and to develop our own way to perfectionism. But this cannot be justified. If one assumes that *dao*-learning belongs to skill acquirement that is amoral, then one cannot avoid reaching the extreme comparison that the *dao* of butchering an ox is the same as that of "butchering people" (Eno 1996, 142). Hansen, Fraser, and Sturgeon fail to give an account of the difference between butchering an ox and butchering people. The Nazi-*dao* is also the result of *dao*-learning. The robber Zhi (*Dao Zhi* 盜跖) also follows a *dao*. Sturgeon, Fraser, and Hansen's attempts at resolving the "Daoist-Nazi problem" and to ascribe the "solution" to Zhuangzi turn out to be abortive.[21]

Huang Yong (2010) has ascribed an "ethics of difference" to Zhuangzi. However, respecting the differences of things would require treating the Nazi in the way a Nazi would like to be treated, which does not seem to be a good solution to a clash between a Nazi and a "normal" form of life. The Nazi would not be willing "to get rid of one's pre-conceived opinions" (80) and one's "opinionated mind or prejudice, *cheng xin* 成心" (79). A mirror that merely *reflects* (Yearley 1983, as cited approvingly by Huang Yong 2010, 79n14) achieves no "dissolution" by reflecting the Nazi's "as they are" (81).

In §9e we already mentioned the brief exchange between Yao and Shun concerning the three kingdoms "in the weeds and brush" (2.6.1). Feng Youlan commented, following Guo Xiang.

> This shows the equality of civilization and barbarism. There is a variety in the ways of living, just as there is a variety in things. These different ways are of equal value. (Feng Youlan 1928, 51)

This stance does not seem to exclude a Nazi-variant of barbarism. The equality advocated does not seem to differ from a relativistic variant of multiculturalism (according to which a Nazi-*dao* is as good as any other *dao*).

If somebody objects that it is not fair to confront Zhuangzi with a (perfect) Nazi, one could point to the following passage from the *Liezi*:[22]

> 越之東有輒木之國，其長子生，則鮮而食之，謂之宜弟。其大父死，負其大母而棄之，曰：「鬼妻不可以同居竿。」楚之南有炎人之國，其親戚死，咼其肉而棄，然後埋其具，乃成為孝子……此上以為政，下以為俗。而未足為異也。(Liezi 5.7/2–3)

> East of Yue [越] is the country of Zhemu [輒木]. When a first son is born they cut him up and eat him; and they say that this will make the mother more fertile. When a grandfather dies, they carry off the grandmother on their backs and abandon her, saying: "It is not right to live with the wife of a ghost." South of Chu [楚] is the country of Yanren [炎人]. When a parent or kinsman dies, they have failed in their duty as filial sons unless

they strip off the flesh and throw it away before burying his bones. . . . These are official practices of the government and established customs among the people, but there is no need to find them strange. (G80, 104)

Williams (2017b, 7) cites this passage and remarks: "One could reasonably respond that the *Zhuangzi* would not advocate the practices in this *Liezi* passage, but the point is that he cannot, prima facie, consistently denounce them." But Williams does not offer any further comments concerning this "untamed value pluralism." We are afraid that it is the same case with other publications that mention this passage from the *Liezi*.

Perhaps we should not criticize Zhuangzi for not having resolved the problems that twentieth-century "great" philosophers confront with irresolvable difficulties. Consider the debate between the American philosophers Putnam and Rorty.[23] Both started their careers in analytic philosophy and later turned to American pragmatism. They agree on a number of points. Both presuppose a commonsense notion of good and bad, and consider the notion of absolute incoherent. They agree that our norms and standards reflect our interests and ever-evolving values and that translation is interest-relative.

We think that the major disagreement of Rorty and Putnam is well captured in the following remark by Rorty (1993, 451):[24]

> Putnam sees me as relativistic because I can appeal to no "fact of the matter" to adjudicate between the possible world in which the Nazis won, inhabited by people for whom the Nazis' racism seems common sense and our egalitarian tolerance crazy, and the world in which we won and the Nazis' racism seems crazy.
>
> I cannot, indeed, appeal to such a "fact of the matter," any more than a species of animal that is in danger of losing its ecological niche to another species, and thus faces extinction, can find a "fact of the matter" to settle the question of which species has the right to the niche in question. But neither, as far as I can see, can Putnam.

Rorty acknowledges and emphasizes that his view is ethnocentric.[25] He would be tolerant and sympathetic with respect to Chinese philosophy because that is what his particular ethnocentrism requires. Perhaps Rorty would say that Zhuangzi's stance that equality (*buqi erqi*, as explained in

§9e) is required is also an ethnocentric view. Rorty is responding to the contemporary world and Zhuangzi to his contemporaneous world.

We suggest that Zhuangzi is closer to Rorty's stance than to Putnam's, assuming that Rorty's appeal to evolution can be brought into harmony with features of Zhuangzi's so-called naturalism.[26] There is no fact of the matter concerning "correct" *shifei* judgments. Putnam remarks: "we are *thinkers*, and that *as* thinkers we are committed to there being *some* kind of truth, some kind of correctness which is substantial. That means that there is no eliminating the normative" (Putnam 1983, 246). According to Rorty, this statement shows that Putnam requires, in principle, necessary and sufficient conditions for normativity, but such a requirement is not possible. On this point, Zhuangzi would agree with Rorty. Nevertheless, Rorty has overlooked the fact that Putnam's "principles" keep evolving. They are not as rigid as what is presented by Rorty.

According to Putnam, all values (including facts) are founded in what the Greeks called *eudaimonia*. The most abstract specification of *eudaimonia* could be an all-in assessment of the quality of human lives. Perhaps this could be claimed to be a quasi-universal as far as Zhuangzi is concerned because he seems to have a clear stance concerning how to live (free and easy wandering, *wuwei*, accept death as a natural part of cosmic changes, and so on). Zhuangzi would certainly disagree with any further specification of *eudaimonia*. For example, it has been suggested that *eudaimonia* includes intellectual pursuits, artistic pursuits, health, beauty, wealth, honor, friendship, intellectual ability, justice, and so on.[27] However, such a set of Western-tilted specifications is not acceptable to Zhuangzi. It cannot claim universal validity.

Zhuangzi presents a strong case for the deconstruction of *shifei*.[28] Our stance tends toward Zhuangzi's, except that we consider that *shifei* conflicts are not always pointless. Moreover, *shifei* conflicts can be "real" in the real world in the sense that a conflict may develop toward a forced choice between surrender or fight in order to survive. This brings us back to Rorty's evolutionary argument. *Shifei* is a human contribution, but it derives from the natural necessity of making distinctions. Every living being must make distinctions in order to survive. Even plants and microbes respond to the difference of night and day. Similarities and differences in "the world out there" are responded to before there is language. Perhaps some sages can do without making distinctions, but this is not relevant to human beings who favor survival. Notwithstanding Zhuangzi's radical views concerning life and death, he displays a positive attitude toward survival.[29] However, for Zhuangzi, no matter how situations develop, doubt would always remain.

This is similar to the position of the arch-empiricist analytic philosopher van Fraassen. As he states (1986, 221),

> Our language, our world, our self are the domain of radical incompleteness, vagueness, darkness. So be it; it will be no solution to deny it.

Despite the fact that Zhuangzi's stance consists in doubt, walking-two-roads, and achieving equality by leaving things uneven (*buqi erqi*), one cannot avoid the possible escalation of irresolvable conflicts arising from the enthrallment of one's own *shifei* distinctions. In the modern world, more sophisticated forms of survival may have been developed. However, success cannot be guaranteed.

Appendix

The *Zhuangzi*—Key Notions

In the subsidiary sections that follow, we elaborate on some of the key notions in the inner chapters of the *Zhuangzi*. Some of our suggestions may appear to be speculative and tentative. Hence, the sections of the appendix are comparable with working notes that serve as background for our discussion of more specific issues in the main chapters of the present book.

In §A1, we make a few remarks concerning the "identity" of the text of the *Zhuangzi*. In this book we limit our textual basis to passages from the inner chapters (chapters 1–7 of the *Zhuangzi*) and a few related passages in the outer and miscellaneous chapter (chapters 8–3 of the *Zhuangzi*), which, according to Graham, are "related to the inner chapters" (G81, 100–11).

In §A2, we introduce the topic of the first chapter of the *Zhuangzi*: *Xiaoyaoyou* 逍遙遊. We discuss the early (Guo Xiang and Zhi Dun 支遁) and still existing disagreement concerning the relative importance of the big and the small (the opening story of the mythical bird Peng 鵬 and the small dove and cicada), and we extend the discussion to the issue of equality. This section can serve as background for §8c ("relativism"), §9e (*buqi erqi* 不齊而齊), and §10b (is Zhuangzi's stance amoral?).

Since most citations in this book are from chapter 2 of the *Zhuangzi*, in §A3 we discuss the title of chapter 2, namely *Qiwulun* 齊物論, and we propose that *wu* 物 is the main topic of the *Qiwulun*.

In §A4, we list the various sages that figure in the inner chapters of the *Zhuangzi*. We suggest that the differently named sages (such as *zhenren* 真人 and *shengren* 聖人) exhibit different features of a "sage" that serves as a role model for ordinary people and plays a central role in Zhuangzi's notion of walking-two-roads (§9c). Like *dao*, the notion of sage is, strictly speaking, inexpressible—an extreme case where meaning is not fixed (*weiding* 未定, §9b).

In §A5, we provide a short description of the preconceptual notions of *dao* 道, *tian* 天, and "the One" (*yi* 一), and we suggest that these notions should not be identified with a form of mysticism.

In §A6, we start with some brief remarks concerning the notion of *ziran* 自然 and Graham's translation of *ziran* as "spontaneous." *Ziran* is a central concept in daoism, but it occurs only twice in the inner chapters of the *Zhuangzi*. We suggest, following Ames, that Zhuangzi's notion of *hundun* 渾沌 is closer to the Western notion of spontaneity.

In the *Zhuangzi*, binomes containing the negation *wu* 无 often have a "positive" association, for example, the suggestion that *dazhi* 大知 (1.1.6, 2.2.1) is to be associated with *wuzhi* 无知 (2.6.2, 4.1.3), whereas *xiaozhi* 小知 is trapped in *shifei* distinctions (§8d). Another example is the suggestion that uselessness (*wuyong* 无用) is *dayong* 大用 (4.4.6). In §A7 we argue that Zhuangzi's positive remarks in the inner chapters about uselessness should be understood as part (or a variant) of Zhuangzi's stance with respect to the well-known daoist notion of *wuwei* 无為. Uselessness (*wuyong*) is a sign of non-dependence.

Zhuangzi's Text(s): What Are the Authentic Chapters?

Interpretation is highly undetermined. It is so not only because of underdetermination of any interpretation (see §1c) but also because of uncertainties concerning corruption and reconstruction of the text as well as complications about author(s). In the case of the *Zhuangzi*, there seems to be no other option but starting with the edition of Guo Xiang 郭象 (252–312). The history of the text before Guo's edition is hardly known.

The secondary literature tends to assume that the titles of the inner chapters reflect their content. Some commentators claim that Guo Xiang assigned the titles to the inner chapters (Machek, 114n1). According to Graham, it was one of the syncretists rather than Guo (G89, 257) who did this. According to Billeter, it might have been Zhuangzi (ca. 369–86 BCE) himself. Munro suggests that the chapter headings were gradually assigned over a period of time.[1] Klein (2010) raises doubts about the authorship and structure of the inner chapters. Wang Baoxuan 王葆玹 has given reasons for the claim that the *Qiwulun* might be the sole chapter that Zhuangzi authored himself (cited in Billeter 2016, 114). According to him, during the Han dynasty, the inner chapters had two-character titles, for example: *Qiwu* instead of *Qiwulun*. In earlier times they might not have titles at all. The title *Qiwu* originating from the Han dynasty may have been in use until the Tang dynasty (Billeter 2016, 115), while the title *Qiwulun* is only indirectly related to the content of chapter 2 (see §A3). This phrase itself does not occur in the *Qiwulun*.[2]

Graham (G81) has reconstructed the text and suggested that about twenty passages from the traditional chapters 23–27 and chapter 32 are passages related to the inner chapters.[3] He also added brief passages from chapters 14, 24, and 32 to chapters 2 and 3. When the phrase "inner chapters" is used in this book, its reference includes these "related" passages. We accept Graham's reconstruction insofar as it suits our wish to limit our discussions to Zhuangzi himself as much as possible.[4]

Liu Xiaogan (1994; 2015c) has carried out a detailed study concerning the *Zhuangzi* chapters. Most of his disagreement with Graham concerns the outer and miscellaneous chapters. Both agree that the inner chapters (chapters 1–7) are earlier, and that therefore this part of the *Zhuangzi* can be mainly ascribed to a historical person named Zhang Zhou 莊周. Although, as Liu puts it, "we are not on firm ground when we try to fill any of the gaps in the Inner chapters with scraps from the Outer and Miscellaneous chapters, as Graham tried to do" (177), we will consult several passages from the later chapters, which according to Graham are "related to the inner chapters" (G81, 100). These passages connect well with the inner chapters and, as yet, have not received much attention. Nevertheless, we must admit that nobody can make any conclusive claim simply owing to the paucity of relevant supporting materials.

Commentators widely disagree on the plausibility of corruptions and possible "corrections." Consider Graham's decision to move the beginning of chapter 14 (14.1.1) to chapter 2 (this move has hardly been noticed by other commentators).[5] According to Billeter (1998, 6), Graham restored the continuity of the text by inserting a passage into chapter 2, which can be interpreted as an explicit answer to Yancheng Ziyou's 顏成子游 question (2.1.8): "May I ask about the piping of Heaven?" (敢問天籟). What follows is Billeter's translation of the following inserted passage (14.1.1–3):[6]

> The sky turns around. The earth stands still.
> Sun and moon chase after one another.
> But what is it that controls this? What governs it all?
> What is it that, without exhausting itself, imparts movement to it all?
> Or is there, perhaps, some spring within that acts in a continuous manner?
> Or else, maybe, all turns of itself, coming to no term?
> Clouds produce rain,
> Rain clouds.

But what is it that makes all this come forth?
What, that without exhausting itself, unleashes this overflowing of joy?
Winds rise in the north,
Blow east, blow west,
Or, whirling around, mount up aloft.
But what is it that thus breathes out and in?
What is it, that without effort, sets all in motion, makes all submit to its action?
Let me ask you that!

According to Billeter, Graham's reconstruction is correct without himself being aware of the specific significance of this move.[7] Billeter comments: "This idea is so simple and so logical that it is hard to understand why no one had it before him" (1998, 8). But few other translators have followed Graham and Billeter; instead, they hold that "heavenly piping is not a piping as other pipings are, but a piping-enabling power."[8]

There are hundreds of ways of reading the *Zhuangzi*. Even if there were such a thing as authorial intention, the history of the extant text guarantees enormous indeterminacy or underdetermination (§1c). In addition to uncertainties about the extant Chinese original of the text, translations (into, say, French or modern Chinese) increase indeterminacy or cover up important nuances.[9] Translators disagree about which characters are corrupted. They add clarifications, leave out phrases, parse the text differently, and in general offer widely diverging translations of the most underdetermined passages, if only because of the highly condensed nature of (written) classical Chinese. Consider the following translations resulting in different speculative interpretations:[10]

大弢曰：是因是也。(25.9.2; G81, 108)

Ta T'ao said, "It fitted the facts." (Watson)

Ta T'ao said, "It was a case of doing what we thought acceptable in the circumstances." (G69, 144)

"It was the 'That's it' which goes by circumstances," said Ta T'iao. (G81, 108)

As the original has only four characters, and knowledge about their senses and grammar is limited, translation can only be highly speculative. To embed the characters in larger chunks of text may not help much, because there could be many choices involved in interpreting the textual surroundings, and because the original text itself *is* highly underdetermined with respect to interpretation. However, many passages, in particular the "stories" (parables, metaphors, analogies) can easily make sense if we draw on mutually recognizable human practices. For example, the story of Hui Shi and the large gourd in chapter 1; the story of Zhuang Zhou dreaming that he is a butterfly in chapter 2; the story of cook Ding in chapter 3, and so on. This does not mean that these stories are completely transparent and that every detail is easy to be translated. But it does mean that the gist of the story (whatever it is) seems to be not much different in either the classical Chinese or modern language versions. The same is true of early Chinese poetry in the *Shijing* 詩經 (Chia Fu-Shiang 2008). A text such as the inner chapters of the *Zhuangzi* may contain inconsistencies or locally incomprehensible language, but it does make sense because the text can be interpreted as utterances of an "intelligent person," and because a large amount of circumstantial evidence is available.

In general, we follow Graham's interpretative approach to the text except for the following modifications. We agree with Graham that Zhuangzi uses terminology from the later Mohist *Canons*, but we disagree with his assumption that the Mohists offered "direct answers to Chuang-Tzu's criticisms or disputation" (G69, 139). Instead, we suggest that Zhuangzi was well aware of the arguments of the Mohists and provided sophisticated rejoinders. Graham says that Zhuangzi uses argumentation only against "logicians." We consider that Zhuangzi uses (logical) argumentation as part of his rhetoric whenever it works to get his views across. As Graham himself says, Zhuangzi's style is a blend of (elliptic) argumentation, analogical reasoning, poetry, and other literary styles (148). Therefore, some statements by Graham may sound to be too extreme, for example, when he contrasts the "rational" Hui Shi with the "mystical" Zhuangzi (139), or when he says that Zhuangzi uses poetic metaphor for his positive views (148). Generally speaking, Zhuangzi would neither oppose nor embrace a particular position categorically, because he knows these positions thoroughly and realizes that there is some sense in all of them. We consider that Zhuangzi's primary opponents come from all the other schools.[11]

然則儒墨楊秉四，與夫子為五。(24.5.8; G81, 101)

Well then, there are the Confucians, the Mohists, the Yangists, the Bingists, and yourself. (Ziporyn)[12]

Graham noted that Zhuangzi often first puts forward an idea and then revises it or attacks it (G69, 138). This may constitute an internal dialogue of the author with himself, as is the case with Wittgenstein's *Philosophical Investigations*. We should also note the numerous (double) rhetorical and speculative questionings. For Zhuangzi, doubt regarding what seem to be his positive views always remains (see §9d).

Graham presents the following characteristics of the *Zhuangzi*, which is obviously intended as a compliment:

> the intricacy of its texture of contrasting yet reconciled strands, irreverent humor and awe at the mystery and holiness of everything, intuitiveness and subtle, elliptical flights of intellect, human warmth and inhuman impersonality, folkiness and sophistication, fantastic unworldly raptures and down-to-earth observation, a vitality at its highest intensity in the rhythms of the language which celebrates death, an effortless mastery of words and a contempt for the inadequacy of words, an invulnerable confidence and bottomless skepticism. (G81, 4)

This is an insightful description of Zhuangzi's text. Even if this assessment is not totally true, it shows that there is no ground for taking any utterance in the *Zhuangzi* at face value.

The Big (*Da* 大) and the Small (*Xiao* 小): Early Interpretations and Disagreements

Disagreement about the interpretation of the inner chapters in the *Zhuangzi* go back a long way. Perhaps it was Zhuangzi's intention to write an ambiguous text that does not present a systematic and consistent doctrine. In this section we present one example of an early disagreement concerning the interpretation of chapter 1, which remains an issue today among commentators. We assume that interpreters agree that the topic of the first chapter is freedom in a certain sense, which is what is meant by the title of chapter 1, *Xiaoyaoyou* 逍遙遊, which Graham translates as "Going Rambling without a Destination."[13] The title of chapter 1 seems to give the same advice to every creature, whether small or big: "Enjoyment in Untroubled Ease" (Legge's title of chapter 1), "soaring above the restricted viewpoints of the worldly. Escape the fixed routes to worldly success and fame, defy all approaches that you are useless, selfish, indifferent to the good of the Empire" (G81, 43).

Interpretations over the centuries have been dominated by Guo Xiang's commentary. Many of his comments suggest what today is called "relativism." Regarding the bird Peng 鵬 and the small dove and cicada in the first chapter, Guo says in his very first statement, which is a comment on the title of chapter 1:

> Although the small and the big are different, yet if they are released where they fulfill their inclinations, then all things follow their nature, their tasks correspond to their ability, each is suited to his lot in life, and in their freedom they are the same. How can there be any concept of superiority and inferiority between them? (Arendrup, 313)

Zhi Dun 支遁 (also called Zhi Daolin 支道林) disagreed with Guo concerning the notion of freedom and equality in chapter 1. According to Guo Xiang, big and small are on the same footing in relation to freedom, and their juxtaposition is devised to illustrate their underlying equality. While for Guo both big and small are equally free, for Zhi they are not equally free since the small birds' ways of life are in some way defective (Machek 2010, Zürcher 1959).[14]

Much later Lin Xiyi 林希逸 (1193–1270?) also objected to Guo Xiang's symmetry thesis. The bird Peng transcends the "petty quarrels of the vulgar world" (Machek 2010, 126), as represented by the two small creatures. Lin's view is strongly supported by Machek with reference to the following passages: the long-lived trees versus short-lived mushrooms, Hui Shi's narrow-minded handling of the big gourd versus Zhuangzi's grand wisdom (*dazhi* 大知); the superior hermit Xu You 許由 versus emperor Yao 堯; the wise master Lian Shu 連叔 versus the pedestrian and unbelieving Jian Wu 肩吾; the mighty yak versus the nervous weasel. All these cases seem to support the privileging of the perspective of the big over the small rather than symmetry of the two perspectives. The contrast between small and great understanding–knowledge clearly undermines the symmetry thesis.[15]

The rather long story about the birds ends as follows:

斥鴳笑之曰：「彼且奚適也？我騰躍而上，不過數仞而下，翱翔蓬蒿之間，此亦飛之至也。而彼且奚適也？」此小大之辯也。(1.1.10)

The little quail laughs at him, saying, "Where does he think he's going? I give a great leap and fly up, but I never get more than ten or twelve yards before I come down fluttering among the weeds and brambles. And that's the best kind of flying anyway! Where does he think he's going?" Such is the difference between big and little. (Watson; cf. Arendrup, 333)

The last clause seems to stop at the difference of the big and little,[16] but Guo Xiang argues,

> The support the small thing needs does not have to be big, whereas the support the big thing uses necessarily cannot be small. Therefore, even though the principles of nature lay out ultimate divisions, and things are each regulated by definite rules, so long as they are fit for the tasks at hand, all things are equal in that they all can accomplish themselves. (Guo Xiang, cited in Lian Xinda 2009, 237)

According to Lian Xinda, Guo Xiang is insinuating into readers' mind the idea that the small birds are so free that the degree of freedom Peng enjoys is called into question.

Zürcher, who gives a detailed account of Zhi Dun's teachings (1959, 123–30), seems to agree with Machek, but he gives the contrast between the big and the small a Nietzschean twist.[17]

> contrast between the great and the small, the supreme freedom of the Daoist adept and the narrow views of those who suffer from "mental blindness and deafness" . . . It is a glorification of the Daoist *Übermensch* as opposed to the "small man" of the world. (128)

Many of the early disagreements appear in almost the same form today. In a detailed analysis of the history of discussions concerning Peng, Lian Xinda (2009) shows that there are many admirers for the bird Peng in Western language literature, some considering Peng as a model of a sage or of a perfect person. However, the following passage constitutes a problem for all the interpreters:

> 風之積也不厚，則其負大翼也无力。故九萬里，則風斯在下矣，而後乃今培風，背負青天而莫之夭閼者，而後乃今將圖南。(1.1.4)

> If wind is not piled up deep enough, it won't have the strength to bear up great wings. Therefore, when the P'eng rises ninety thousand li, he must have the wind under him like that. Only then can he mount on the back of the wind, shoulder the blue sky, and nothing can hinder or block him. Only then can he set his eyes to the south.

The admirers of Peng do not seem to have noticed this passage. Lian points out that Mair goes so far as to simply leave out this passage in his translation (1994, 240n9).[18] Guo Xiang, as one may expect, stresses Peng's dependence on the wind.

> If there is enough to suit their nature, then the Peng has no reason to think itself superior to the small birds, and the small birds have no need to yearn for the Heavenly Lake [the Peng journeys to]. Therefore, though the great and the small are different in size, the freedom they enjoy in their wanderings are the same. (Guo Xiang, cited in Lian Xinda 2009, 236)

> If one depends on something, then even if one is as light and graceful as Liezi, one will not be able to move about without the support of the wind. Only after one obtains the support on which one depends is the free wandering possible. How much more so is this the case with the big Peng! (Guo Xiang, cited in Lian Xinda, 237)

To overcome the difficulty (with his interpretation) of Zhuangzi's apparent criticism of the dove and cicada, Guo Xiang claims that by the question "what do these two creatures understand?"[19] Zhuangzi means that Peng and the little dove are just naturally what they are and do not know why they are so. However, there seems to be nobody who agrees with Guo Xiang on this point.[20] As modern scholar Pu Jiangqing 浦江清 puts it, if a simple sentence can be twisted in such a way as Guo has done, then it would be impossible to read the *Zhuangzi* (cited in Lian Xinda, 238).

Given the degree of underdetermination, it is impossible to arrive at a definite choice for or against Guo's interpretation. Lian says these two camps may be seen as complementing one another. A recent commentator, Zhao Ming 趙明, takes a somewhat tangential position relative to both camps and argues that the many remarks about dependence in chapter 1 show that the main idea of the *Xiaoyaoyou* chapter is that no "free and easy wandering" is possible, because everything depends on something (according to Lian Xinda, 240).[21] Common sense seems to support this. But perhaps the ideal of *Xiaoyaoyou* is something one can strive for.

We suggest that the consequences of the wing–wind passage (more than the conclusion of the story) make it difficult to consider the Peng and the two little creatures as equals, contrary to what Guo Xiang assumes. However, this does not mean that the Peng models a sage or a perfect person. Perhaps the distinction between the Peng and the dove and cicada should be considered as analogous to, for example, the contrast between the gentleman and the petty man.[22] They are differently valued. However, the gentleman would turn out to be the petty man when faced with Heaven.

故曰，天之小人，人之君子；人之君子，天之小人也。(6.6.10)

So it is said, the petty man of Heaven is a gentleman among men; the gentleman among men is the petty man of Heaven.

The *Qi* 齊 and *Lun* 論 of *Wu* 物

Chapter 2 of the *Zhuangzi*, the *Qiwulun*, opens with the state of losing one's self and ends with the idea of transformation of things, as embodied in the famous butterfly story, and thus abolishes the stark opposition between thisness and thatness, and between affirmation and negation.[23] All things share pre-originary equality, despite their great divergence.[24] Furthermore, one should detach from speech, words, and mind in order to recognize the pre-originary equality of things.

At the beginning of the *Qiwulun*, Ziqi of Nanguo 南郭子綦 claims that he has lost his own self such that his body is like withered wood and his heart dead ashes. He says that Yancheng Ziyou has only heard the pipes of men but not the pipes of earth and the pipes of *tian*.[25]

夫大塊噫氣⋯⋯ (2.1.4)

子綦曰：夫吹萬不同，而使其自已也，咸其自取，怒者其誰邪！(2.1.9)

The no-thing (*dakuai* 大塊) blows out breath. . . .

Ziqi replies, "The wind blows on the ten thousand things that are never the same (*chuiwan butong* 吹萬不同), so that each can be itself—all take what they want for themselves, but who does the sounding?"

Zhang Taiyan (whom we follow—cf. §9e) points out that Ziqi of Nanguo starts his description of the pipes of earth with reference to wind that comes out of an invisible no-thing. As Guo Xiang defines, "*dakuai* is no-thing (*wuwu* 無物).[26] It belches forth breath, so is there any thing?"[27] This no-thing does not have any sound of its own and does not depend on other things (including humans); nevertheless, it makes possible the sounding of the pipes of earth by blowing into the ten thousand hollows. This no-thing is actually the pipe(s) of *tian*. It corresponds with the common sense that the wind always blows evenly, instead of unevenly, on everything without regard of their difference in shape or their status according to human valuations.

Zhang Taiyan explains that the *Qiwu* chapter is based on an examination of names/terms and forms and their union in mind. The wind is a metaphor for different kinds of cognition of things in the mind. The ten thousand hollows burst out howling and yet their sounds are different and thus constitute the pipes of earth. This parallels the fact that there are different names and discourses in the world that voice different views, just as a domestic hen and a wild magpie sing in different ways in expressing themselves, and just as floating dust makes up different shapes in rising up to the heaven (Zhang Taiyan 1986: 65). The ten thousand hollows have different shapes and produce enormously divergent types of sound. In this respect, they seem to be uneven (*buqi* 不齊). However, because each of them produces its own music within the limit of its own capacity, it cannot be said that they are uneven. (See also §9e.)

There are a great variety of translations of the title of the *Qiwulun* 齊物論. The most popular translation is: "A Discussion (Discourse, Commentary) on the Equality of Things" (Chen Guying, Feng Youlan, Mair, Schipper, Muller, and Callahan 1998, 184).[28] Occasionally we find "Identity of Things" instead of equality (Levi), or "Uniformity of All Things" (Wang Rongpei). Often a process aspect is added: "Making All Things Equal" (Watson, Eno), or "Equalizing Things" (Kjellberg, Cleary), "Smoothing Things" (Internet Encyclopedia of Philosophy, Coutinho 2004, 2), "Evening Things Out" (Graham, Fraser), or "Leveling All Things" (Lin Yutang, Cook 2003, 66). Graham adds the word sorting (to render *lun*): "The Sorting which Evens Things Out."

Only rarely is the focus not directly on things, but on equalizing of theories, discourses, or assessments, which leads to more sophisticated translations: "Equalizing Assessments of Things" (Ziporyn); "Things, Theories—Sorting Themselves Out" (Wu Kuang-ming); to recognize the equal validity of discourses on things (Billeter).[29]

The older translators each chose their own idiosyncratic title: "The Identity of Contraries" (Giles); "The Adjustment of Controversies" (Legge); "Universal Harmony" (Wieger); "Equalization of the Worldview" (Wilhelm).[30] Sometimes a subtitle is added: "Making the Spirit Equal and Getting Rid of Self-Centered Patterns" (Chen Guying 2016, 16); "The Music that Comes Out of Emptiness" (Levi).[31]

Having reviewed the various proposals for the translation of the title of chapter 2, we suggest that the central topic of the *Qiwulun* is *wu* 物. In English, a thing is usually not thought of as an organism, whereas arguably organism is the paradigmatic example of *wu* 物 in classical Chinese.[32] In classical Chinese, *wu* has a much wider scope than Western "object" or "thing." It includes organisms and abstract entities, and perhaps everything that could be classified by human languages.[33] Furthermore, *wu* is enmeshed in the debate about Hansen's "mass noun hypothesis" (Ma Lin and van Brakel 2016a, 160–64). Still, it may be acceptable to consider *wu*/object–thing as a quasi-universal because both *wu* and object (or thing) are "theoretical" terms relative to a perspective.

Recently Kwok Sai Hang (2016) has proposed an outline of "Zhuangzi's philosophy of thing," which is built on the suggestion that according to Zhuangzi "the concept of thing is just a linguistic construction" (294; cf. 298) because "things are so because they are called so" (2.4.2). The view ascribed to Zhuangzi shows similarities with reflections in the Western tradition. For example, Quine writes,

> The very notion of an object at all, concrete or abstract, is a human contribution, a feature of our inherited apparatus for organizing the amorphous welter of neural input. (1992, 6)

> I see all objects as theoretical. (1981, 20)

Quine's view that "object" is a theoretical notion is not idiosyncratic. Other Western philosophers have made similar points, emphasizing the relativity of the notion of object or thing to human interests. For example, according to Chomsky (1995, 30),

> What is a thing, and if so what thing it is, depends on specific configurations of human interests, intentions, goals and actions, an observation as old as Aristotle.

The remarks by Quine and Chomsky would not be much different if we replace "object" (or "thing") by "*wu*" in the citations. However, Quine and Chomsky would not consider a human being, for instance, as a thing.

All *wu* are dependent on *dao*, but they are independent in their being-so. The *wu* depend on one another without there being a hierarchy. The *wu* are interconnected, unified, and equalized, but diversity (distinctive identities) remains. The difference between the *wu* is not eradicated by their equalization. Concerning the relation of *wu* and language, Billeter writes, the appearance of the distinct and stable entities we term "things" *wu* 物 within this reality is an artifact of language. It is language that by introducing into reality demarcations, distinctions, oppositions, and suchlike, has created "things" at the same time as giving them names and establishing logical relations between them. (1998, 28)

Usually, commentators have been keen to interpret the *Qiwulun* by looking for three single (English) concepts, each corresponding to one of the three characters respectively. However, this is achieved at the expense of ignoring the embedment of, for example, *lun* in the clusters of other concepts.[34] Billeter (1998, 6) distinguishes between the use of *lun* as a verb and a noun respectively.

1. As a verb, *lun* is used to judge things by means of placing them in a particular order of preference;

2. As a noun, *lun* is used to designate a discourse in which items are arranged in such a way as to make plain the differentiated value judgments about these items.

Ziporyn (2009a, 9n1) extends the second meaning further as

a discourse that weighs relevant factors with much or little argument and explanation, but generally with the intent of rendering a judgment and expressing a position on what is so and what is right.

We agree that Zhuangzi's use of *lun* can be understood as being motivated by ordering things with *little* argument and explanation, but we disagree that we can understand Zhuangzi's *lun* in terms of phrases such as "expressing a position on what is so and what is right."[35]

Graham says that Zhuangzi "always" uses *lun* in a favorable sense (G81, 48; G91, 296) and proposes the following brief characterization of *lun*: "the coherent thought and discourse which arranges things in their proper relations" (as distinct from "disputation [辯] over posed alternatives") (G89, 189). Graham elaborates this with reference to 2.5.7, which is the *only* occurrence of *lun* in the inner chapters.

六合之外，聖人存而不論；六合之內，聖人論而不議；春秋經世先王之志，聖人議而不辯。(2.5.7)

> As to what is beyond the Six Realms, the sage admits its existence [cun 存] but does not discuss [lun 論] it. As to what is within the Six Realms, he discusses [lun] it but does not express an opinion [yi 議]. In the case of the *Spring and Autumn*, the record of the former kings of past ages, the sage discusses [lun 論] it but does not discriminate [bian 辯] it. (Watson, translation modified)

Translators agree that the three characters, *lun, yi, bian*,[36] form a gradation,[37] but it seems to be a different classification from possible classifications in English. Graham translates the three characters in this passage as sort out, assess, argue over, respectively; Billeter translates them as comment, judge, dispute; Watson as theorize, debate, discriminate; Alt (2000) and Cleary as discuss, deliberate, debate. Chan Wing-tsit as discuss, pass judgment, argue; and Mair as discuss, deliberate, dispute. All these translations make some sense, but it is difficult to distinguish between the alternative classifications in English and to relate them to either of the classifications in Chinese (namely, *lun, yi*, and *bian*). However, it is obvious that Chinese and English gradations do not deploy the same concepts.

Some commentators have pointed out systematic ambiguities in the title of chapter 2 in connection with different parsings of *Qiwulun*. We propose the following interpretation. The subject of the *Qiwulun* is *wu* (*wanwu* 萬物, myriad of *wu*), which is investigated from two perspectives (*lun* and *qi*) at the same time.[38]

1. *lun* 論: to arrange the *wu*(s) in their proper places and relations (without presupposing strict rules or classifications).

2. *qi* 齊:[39] to equalize the *wu*(s) that have been sorted; "equalize" in the sense as explicated by Zhang Taiyan (§9e): treating things in accordance with what they are.

For example, positions of Mohists and Ruists (2.3.5) are different and can be sorted, and thereby can be ordered (*lun*); at the same time, their stances must be equalized (*qi*): "What the Confucians and Mohists consider right is considering something right and considering something else wrong. Not considering anything right or wrong is what they consider wrong."[40]

Typically, the arranging and equalizing of *wu* 物 is followed in Zhuangzi's text by doubt concerning what has been said concerning *wu*. The dream passages offer typical examples of raising doubt. In ordinary sorting, we may distinguish between dreaming and being awake, but we cannot be sure whether we are dreaming or are awake: first *lun* and then doubt (see also §9d).

Equalizing different *wu* is possible because, in their original state before there were classifications and *shifei* judgments, they were equal (because in the original state the *wu* are without any ordering or evaluation).

惡乎至？有以為未始有物者，至矣，盡矣，不可以加矣。其次以為有物矣，而未始有封也。(2.4.7)

其次以為有封焉，而未始有是非也。(2.4.8; cf. 23.7.1)

How far did it go? To the point where some of them believed that things have never existed—so far, to the end, where nothing can be added. Those at the next stage thought that things exist but recognized no boundaries among them. Those at the next stage thought there were boundaries but recognized no right and wrong.

Zhuangzi does not deny the human habit of categorizing. Being engaged in *lun* is how the human world fares. It is part of everyday life and ordinary language.[41] Sages equalize *shi* and *fei*, and at the same time merge with the everyday. This is illustrated by the story of the monkeys and the number of acorns they get from the monkey keeper, the gist of which is called "walking-two-roads" (§9c).

The Sages

Graham lists the following important characteristics of the sage featuring in the *Zhuangzi* (G89, 186–88, 383–87), proceeding from his own sympathy for the daoist idea of spontaneity (cf. §A6):

1. The sage is perfectly aware of all the viewpoints, and let inclinations settle before acting.[42]

2. Hence, the sage attends to the total situation, and mirrors the particular situation without forcing it into rigid classifications.

3. The sage unlearns self-made divisions and classifications, and returns to the course that originates from heaven–nature (*tian*);

4. The sage follows no rules or principles, refrains from making distinctions, and walks two roads.

In the inner chapters, many other characteristics of "the sage" are mentioned. In this section we highlight some features we consider to be especially relevant to the theme of *shifei*. Zhuangzi often raises doubts about the features he has just proposed. Not all the features mentioned are equally trustworthy.[43] However, we assume that (some features of) sages serve as a role model for humans.

The first difficulty is how to distinguish between a more literal and a more metaphorical reading of features such as "tucking the universe under his arm" (2.6.11). Scholars under the influence of Hansen (1992) suggest that we must distinguish between features that are intelligible, relevant, and conceivable *for us*—"us" being the modern us of today—and those that are not. In accordance with such a distinction, such things as "not depending on anything" (1.1.13) and "not getting burned by entering fire" (6.1.4) may be inconceivable for "us" (if we take the statement literally). But this would not seem to be so obvious if the extension of "us" is broadened.

Zhuangzi uses many characters to modify *ren* 人 (usually translated as human, people, person, and formerly as "man"). One would not expect Zhuangzi to favor pigeonholing different kinds of *ren* into ten or more different kinds of *ren* (cf. Levi 2012, 115–16). However, in the first chapter of the *Zhuangzi*, a hierarchy is suggested consisting of ordinary humans, petty officials bound by social obligations, and the "higher" *ren* in the likes of Song Rongzi 宋榮子, who is indifferent to the praise or blame by the masses.[44] Further above is Liezi 列子, who, riding on the wind, is almost free from any attachment but is still not entirely free. On the top of the hierarchy, we find the one who rambles around without limitations and does not depend on anything (1.1.11–13).[45]

In the following paragraphs, we introduce the different kinds of "sages" that occur in the inner chapters, including the terms often translated as sage(s), as well as other varieties. The distinction between the sages and the humans is not as strict as is sometimes suggested by the translations. The sages are also a kind of *ren* 人. According to Guo Xiang, the term sage is "simply a name for someone who attains his nature" (cited in Arendrup 1974, 343). What we can say for certain is that the Zhuangzian sage is different from the Ruist sage. The Ruist sage, but not the Zhuangzian sage (who collects pieces of wisdom), is not treated sympathetically in the *Zhuangzi*.

The *shengren* 聖人 (usually translated as sage) often occurs in the inner chapters, and we have cited the passages involving the *shengren* in the main chapters.[46] The sage of Graham's characterizations of the sage listed at the beginning of this section is referred to in the index of his book as "Sage. *See Sheng* 'sage' . . . (For all schools the ideal of the wisest man)" (G89, 493–94). Hence, Graham uses the English word "sage" to refer to the *shengren* exclusively. The first occurrence of the *shengren* is in chapter 1, together with the *shenren* 神人 and the *zhiren* 至人.

> 至人无己，神人无功，聖人无名。(1.1.13)

> The perfect person (*zhiren* 至人) has no self; the divine person (*shenren* 神人) has no merit; the sage (*shengren* 聖人) has no fame. (Watson, translation modified)

The *shenren* (divine person, also translated as Spirit Man and Holy Man), occurs only a few times in the inner chapters.[47] Graham translates *shen* 神 as "daimon, god." We will exclude the *shenren* from the list of "standard" sages, because he or she is too different from humans by too great a disparity to serve as a role model. See the following description of the *shenren*:[48]

> 藐姑射之山，有神人居焉，肌膚若冰雪，淖約若處子。不食五穀，吸風飲露，乘雲氣，御飛龍，而遊乎四海之外……孰弊弊焉以天下為事！之人也，物莫之傷，大浸稽天而不溺，大旱金石流土山焦而不熱。是其塵垢粃糠，將猶陶鑄堯舜者也。(1.2.7–9)

> There is a Holy Man [*shenren* 神人] living on faraway Ku-she Mountain [姑射之山, Guye Mountain], with skin like ice or snow, and gentle and shy like a young girl. He doesn't eat the five grains, but sucks the wind, drinks the dew, climbs up on the clouds and mist, rides a flying dragon, and wanders beyond the four seas. . . . Why should he wear himself out over the affairs of the world? There is nothing that can harm this man. Though flood waters pile up to the sky, he will not drown. Though a great drought melts metal and stone and scorches the earth and hills, he will not be burned. From his dust and leavings alone you could mold a Yao or a Shun.

The *zhiren* (perfect person) is mentioned in a number of chapters.[49] He has been characterized as perfected sage, highest person, ruler, real person, and consummate person. On one occasion, Wang Ni (possibly a sage) says that the perfect *zhiren* is godlike (2.6.8: 至人神矣).[50] Therefore, we do not consider the *zhiren* as a role model for humans either. Kongzi (Confucius) certainly has not reached the stage of becoming a perfect person (5.3.4).

The *zhenren* 真人 (true person) occurs mainly in chapter 6.[51] Some passages suggest that the *zhenren* is not much different from the *shengren*

(6.8.8–9). However, the *shengren* has no *qing* 情 (cf. §7d), whereas the *zhenren* "is chilly like autumn, balmy like spring, and his *joy and anger* prevail through the four seasons. He goes along with what is right for things and no one knows his limit" (Watson, emphasis added).[52] Although the *zhenren* "breathes with his heels" (6.1.5), we count him as a variant of the sage, or as a role model for humans in contrast with the "mass of men" (*zhongren*).

> 古之真人，其狀義而不朋，若不足而不承；與乎其觚而不堅也，張乎其虛而不華也；邴邴乎其似喜乎！崔乎其不得已乎！滀乎進我色也，與乎止我德也；(6.1.12)

> This was the True Man of old: his bearing was lofty and did not crumble; he appeared to lack but accepted nothing; he was dignified in his correctness but not insistent; he was vast in his emptiness but not ostentatious. Mild and cheerful, he seemed to be happy; reluctant, he could not help doing certain things; annoyed, he let it show in his face; relaxed, he rested in his virtue.

> 何謂真人？古之真人，不逆寡，不雄成，不謨士。若然者，過而弗悔，當而不自得也。(6.1.3)

> What do I mean by a True Man? The True Man of ancient times did not rebel against want, did not grow proud in plenty, and did not plan his affairs. A man like this could commit an error and not regret it, could meet with success and not make a show.

The *quanren* 全人 (complete person) occurs only twice (5.5.1; 23.10.1) and the *wumingren* 无名人 (nameless person) only once (7.3.3).[53] It is strange that the *shengren* is "skilled in what pertains to Heaven but clumsy in what pertains to man," whereas the *quanren* is "skilled in Heavenly affairs and good at human ones as well" (23.10.1).[54]

It can be seen from the above list that there seem to be gradations, perhaps even a hierarchy, between different kinds of sages,[55] but it is also clear that there are no strict borders. We assume that the features of some sages should function as a role model for humans. Hence, the title of this section is "The Sages." Those sages who are completely on the side of *tian* (and perhaps should not be referred to as a kind of *ren*) are not relevant to the sage as a role model for "ordinary" humans. We suggest that humans can only reach the stage of "true person" (*zhenren*) or of sage (*shengren*), and perhaps the stage of *quanren*. It is not clear whether Zhuangzi himself has reached that stage. We have assumed that all the "wise men" listed above are "higher" than the gentleman (*junren* 君人) and worthy person (*xianren* 賢人), who are again "higher" than the ordinary human or commoner (*zhongren* 眾人) and the petty man (*xiaoren* 小人).[56]

There are many individuals in the stories from the inner chapters who would seem to be sages or other forms of complete or perfect persons without a specific label being attached to them, but they are not sages to the same degree. For example, although Yao and Shun are both considered as sages (sage-kings), the hermit Xu You 許由 is said to be "higher." Yao first preferred giving the empire to Xu You; Shun was the second choice (Ziporyn 2009a, 6n13). Nevertheless, even Xu You could not forget his self-identity. Shi Deqing 釋德清 comments: "only the Spirit-Man [*shenren* 神人] on Mt. Guye [1.2.7: 姑射之山] is the one who forgets everything without exception."[57] Also consider the story of Jixian 季咸 (a *wu* 巫),[58] Liezi (a daoist), and Huzi 壺子 (Liezi's teacher) in chapter 7 (7.5.1–12). Surely Huzi must be a sage. Other persons who exemplify features of sages include the monkey keeper, Wang Ni (2.6.2–5), and Wang Tai 王駘 (5.1.1).

As already remarked, we have to be careful with the features assigned to sages because some features mentioned cannot be taken at face value. A description of the sage's features may be followed by its immediate denial or doubt, and even further doubt. This happens, for example, in 2.6.9–16 where divergent descriptions of the features of a sage are presented. The first description of the sage is offered by Kongzi (Confucius), as reported by Qu Quezi 瞿鵲子 when talking to Chang Wuzi 長梧子.

聖人不從事於務，不就利，不違害，不喜求，不緣道；无謂有謂，有謂无謂，而遊乎塵垢之外。(2.6.9)

The sage does not occupy himself with the affairs of the world. He neither seeks gain, nor avoids injury. He has no pleasure in seeking. He does not purposely adhere to *Tao*. He speaks without speaking. He does not speak when he speaks. Thus he roams beyond the limits of this dusty world. (Feng Youlan)

Kongzi himself regards such a description as "wild and flippant words" (孟浪之言).[59] To the contrary, Qu Quezi considers that these words refer to the working of the mysterious Way (*miaodao* 妙道).[60]

In response, Chang Wuzi says that even Huangdi 黃帝 (the Yellow Emperor; ?–2598? BCE) would be confused by these words,[61] and he gives an alternative description of the sage.[62]

旁日月，挾宇宙，為其吻合，置其滑涽，以隷相尊。眾人役役，聖人愚芚，參萬歲而一成純。萬物盡然，而以是相蘊。(2.6.11–12)

The sage leans on the sun and moon, tucks the universe under his arm, merges himself with things, leaves the confusion and muddle as it is, and looks on slaves as exalted. Ordinary men strain and struggle; the sage is stupid and blockish. He takes part in ten thousand ages and achieves simplicity in oneness. For him, all the ten thousand things are what they are, and thus they enfold each other.

After some digression, Chang Wuzi suggests that all the three of them may be dreaming and the words used to characterize sages may be just a Supreme Swindle (*diaogui* 弔詭). Finally, Chang suggests that after a very long time a great sage (*dasheng* 大聖) may arrive and explain these words, and that this would also be a case of a great awakening (*dajue* 大覺).[63]

Hence, there are no definitive characteristics of sages. Perhaps they are inexpressible, as in the case of *dao*. Graham says: "Sagehood can no more be put into words than the knack of the carpenter" (G89, 187). Prima facie a "knack" is not mysterious because we can have similar "ordinary" experiences, even if we may not be able to have such achievements as cook Ding has. It is a matter of mutual recognition of human practices.[64] We can recognize what is at stake from cook Ding's narration concerning his knack with dissecting an ox.

Dao 道, *Tian* 天, and "the One"

Dao can be translated as "way" (or sometimes "method"),[65] but perhaps not as "The Way." We should allow for many *daos*, but definitely not translations like God or Reason (which were common renditions in the past).[66] We are sympathetic to the suggestion of translating it as *daos* rather than *dao*. Even if we sometimes render it as singular, we still understand it as multi-perspectival. Graham's seminal book, *Disputers of the Tao*, could have had the title: *Disputers of Divergent Daos*. If *daos* are taken to be plural (and different), then different sages may follow different *daos* (§A6).

Billeter has suggested that the word *dao* in the *Zhuangzi* is not a consecrated or sacred word but may have as many as twenty meanings in different places in the text (2015, 37). That the word *dao* is not mysterious is consistent with Zhuangzi's stance with respect to language. Concerning the story of cook Ding, Billeter translates as follows:

臣之所好者道也，進乎技矣。(3.2.3)

What interests your servant is the functioning of things [*dao*], not merely the technique. (Billeter 2015, 15)[67]

Virtually all other translators render *dao* as "the Way" in this passage (for example, Watson, Graham, and Mair). Billeter suggests that how things function does not need a mysterious *dao*. *Dao* may be inexpressible (2.5.9),[68] but this is not because it is a "mysterious" word, but because it functions to reiterate that meanings are unfixed (§9b). Being inexpressible may be seen as an extreme case of being unfixed (*weiding*). Other knack stories, apart from that of cook Ding, may be able to provide even stronger evidence, but they do not appear in the inner chapters.

Tian 天 has been translated as Heaven and nature. Its important combinations with other characters are as follows:[69]

1. The light of Heaven, *yutian* 於天 (2.3.7);[70] sometimes paraphrased as being guided by the way in which things manifest themselves (Billeter).[71]

2. Heavenly Equality, *tianni* 天倪 (2.6.21; 27.1.1/4/7); also translated as the "grindstone of nature" (Coutinho 2004: 158).

3. Heaven the Equalizer, *tianjun* 天鈞 (2.4.6; 23.4.1) or *tianjun* 天均 (27.1.7); also rendered as the celestial potter's wheel.[72]

4. Heavenly Reservoir, *tianfu* 天府 (2.5.10); also translated as celestial storehouse (Cleary, Graham) or store of nature (Chan Wing-tsit), in which things are both kept and hidden.

5. Heavenly Gruel, *tianyu* 天鬻 is the food of Heaven (5.5.4).

As Graham notes, *tianjun* and *tianni* are the same (天均者天倪也): "The 'Potter's Wheel of Heaven' is the whetstone of Heaven" (G81, 107; 27.1.7). Both *tianjun* and *tianni* can mean equal(ize). Perhaps they should be associated with the *qi* 齊 ("equalize") in the title given to chapter 2 (cf. §A3). *Tian* is the source of *yiming* 以明. Hence the "source" of *qi* 齊 may also be located in *tian*, as it is engaged in the process of equalizing (*tianni*).

The following passage (2.6.17–22) first raises doubt and then points to the equalizing "by" *tian*.[73]

既使我與若辯矣，若勝我，我不若勝，若果是也，我果非也邪？……和之以天倪。(2.6.17, 2.6.21)

Suppose you and I have had an argument [辯]. If you have beaten me instead of my beating you, then are you necessarily right and am I necessarily wrong? (2.6.17)

... Harmonize them all [that is, the judgments of who is right and who is wrong] with the Heavenly Equality. (2.6.21)

Roughly speaking, humans sort/classify; *tian, dao*, and sages do not; they equalize, but the distinction of *ren* (humans) and *tian* (heaven–nature) is not separated by a strict border.

Billeter (2015, 46) has suggested that Zhuangzi uses the word *tian* to indicate the regime of action that is spontaneous and "necessary" in distinction from the human regime of intentionality.

In the inner chapters Zhuangzi remarks a number of times that all things are one.[74] Not only the sage "stops at the one, the whole, and the simple" (Feng Youlan 2.6.12; Watson: "achieves simplicity in oneness"), but also humans are encouraged to "keep to the One" and "enter into the pure, the divine, the One."[75] This easily leads to associations with some transcendent(al) One. The One is primarily associated with the sage. It is not easily accessible to humans unless they can achieve the status of sage.

According to Graham, Zhuangzi's "claim that everything is one is self-contradictory" (G69, 138). He refers to the following passage:

既已為一矣，得有言乎？既已謂之一矣，且得无言乎？一與言為二，二與一為三。(2.5.5)

If then all things are One, what room is there for speech? On the other hand, since I can say the word 'one' how can speech not exist? If it does exist, we have One and speech—two; and two and one—three. (Lin Yutang)

We have already become one, so how can I say anything? But I have just said that we are one, so how can I not be saying something? The one and what I said about it make two, and two and the original one make three. (Watson)

Now that we are one, can I still say something? Already having called us one, did I succeed in not saying something? One and the saying makes two, two and one make three. (Graham)

There are other passages that, in some translations, may support Graham's ascription of inherent contradiction to the unitary thesis of the One.

不言則齊，齊與言不齊，言與齊不齊也，故曰无言。(27.1.4)

As long as I do not say anything about them ["all things in the Heavenly Equality"], they are a unity. But the unity and what I say about it have ceased to be a unity. Therefore I say, we must have no-words [*wuyan* 无言]! (Watson)[76]

If you refrain from saying, everything is even; the even is uneven with saying, saying is uneven with the even. Hence the aphorism "In saying he says nothing." If in saying you say nothing, all your life you say without ever saying, all your life you refuse to say without ever failing to say. (G81, 107)

If the unitary thesis is inherently self-contradictory, then perhaps it should not be taken so seriously? It is not a contradiction in the "standard" negative sense, as Graham seems to suggest (G69, 138). A contradiction may be used (rhetorically) to say something non-contradictory (§9d). The One contrasts with distinctions among the myriad of *wu* (*wanwu* 萬物). Contradictions do not apply to the pre-originary where there are no distinctions. Rules of logic do not apply there. *Dao* and the One are preconceptual notions (like form[s] of life). Because the notions of *dao* and the One refer to a state of the universe before there are *wu*, Zhuangzi says, "If the Way is made clear, it is not the Way."[77]

Support for mysticism can be found in many places in the inner chapters,[78] but the contradiction mentioned above raises doubt about the coherence of a claim for a metaphysical, absolute One beyond the world of distinctions. Furthermore, if all perspectives are equally arbitrary (or equally right), this also applies to "all is One" (cf. Hansen 2015; Chinn 1997, 211).

Ziran 自然 and *Hundun* 渾沌

Spontaneity is central to Graham's interpretation of the *Zhuangzi*,[79] but one wonders whether this word is the best translation of *ziran* 自然.[80] *Ziran* occurs only twice in the inner chapters, which is rendered by Watson as: "follow along with things the way they are" (7.3.3).[81] *Ziran* is a common binome in classical Chinese, but this is not the case in the inner chapters.

Hansen summarizes the relation of *dao*, spontaneity, and other central concepts as follows (expressing a stance which he criticizes):

Following that inner *dao* amounts to following one's inner nature and acting spontaneously. One who has cultivated her skills to the highest point requires no conscious thought to act. The actions just spontaneously flow out of her. She unites mystically in her actions with a universal force that fills the entire universe. (1992, 195)

Connecting spontaneous with the mystical entails the assumption that spontaneity is also inexpressible.

We suggest that the best starting point for understanding Zhuangzi's notion of spontaneity is Ames's interpretation of the story of Hundun at the very end of chapter 7.[82]

南海之帝為儵，北海之帝為忽，中央之帝為渾沌。儵與忽時相與遇於渾沌之地，渾沌待之甚善。儵與忽謀報渾沌之德，曰人皆有七竅以視聽食息，此獨无有，嘗試鑿之。日鑿一竅，七日而渾沌死。

The ruler of the North Sea was "Swift," the ruler of the South Sea was "Sudden," and the ruler of the Center was "Hundun 渾沌, or Spontaneity." Lords Swift and Sudden had on several occasions encountered each other in the territory of Lord Spontaneity, and Spontaneity had treated them with great hospitality. Swift and Sudden, devising a way to repay Spontaneity's generosity, remarked that: "Everyone has seven orifices through which they can see, hear, eat, and breathe. Spontaneity alone is without them." They then attempted to bore holes in Spontaneity, each day boring one hole. On the seventh day, Spontaneity died.

If we read the *hundun* passage from a cosmological perspective, there is some similarity with Peirce's claim that chance is a factor in the universe: "When we gaze upon the multifariousness of nature we are looking straight into the face of a living spontaneity."[83] Ames provides the following interpretation of the *Hundun* passage:[84]

Hundun is the integral indeterminacy honeycombing all construals of order that is necessary for the spontaneous emergence of novelty in a continuing present. . . . Hundun is a partner in the continuing production of significance rather than some independent primordial source of order. . . . In fact, not only have Lords Swift and Sudden killed Lord Hundun, they have for all intents and purposes, committed suicide themselves.

Hundun refers to the situation when there are no distinct entities yet. Ames suggests that by killing Lord Hundun, a crucial contribution to the "spontaneous emergence" of significance and novelty is denied. However, although the hundunic indeterminacy is *necessary* for novelty, there could be different possibilities for what emerges. That is to say: what may emerge cannot be a *particular* unique thing when the requirement of spontaneity was fulfilled.

Wuwei 无為 and *Wuyong* 无用

Wuwei 无為 (which is related to the natural spontaneity of *ziran*) often occurs in the *Zhuangzi*.[85] There is an extensive literature on the interpretation of *wuwei* and its possible similarity to Western notions, for example, Heidegger's (1955) notion of *Gelassenheit* (which is also difficult to translate into English).[86] However, the focus of such literature most often falls on the *Laozi*, and *wuwei* is claimed to mean something like: non-purposive action and yet do act, doing nothing with nothing left undone, effortless action, following the veins of nature, acting free from desires, and similar expressions trying to capture some non-passive sense of not-doing (Liu Xiaogan 2015d, 82–87).[87] Several commentators suggest that *wei* in the expression *wuwei* should be interpreted as *not* to act according to social conventions.

In contrast, Zhuangzi's use of *wuwei* seems to have somewhat different meanings in different contexts.[88] Moreover, it is often the case that the persons that figure in the stories in the inner chapters are literally doing nothing as distinct from skilled and/or spontaneous action. Instead of reflecting on the "abstract" notion of *wuwei*, we prefer illustrating it with examples. The examples are clear enough. The first occurrence of *wuwei* is at the end of chapter 1, when Hui Shi complains about an unusable tree.

> 吾有大樹，人謂之樗。其大本擁腫而不中繩墨，其小枝卷曲而不中規矩，立之塗，匠者不顧。(1.3.6)

> I have a big tree of the kind men call *shu* [樗]. Its trunk is too gnarled and bumpy to apply a measuring line to, its branches too bent and twisty to match up to a compass or square. You could stand it by the road and no carpenter would look at it twice.

Zhuangzi replies,

> 今子有大樹，患其无用，何不樹之於无何有之鄉，廣莫之野，彷徨乎无為其側，逍遙乎寢臥其下。不夭斤斧，物无害者，无所可用，安所困苦哉？(1.3.8)

> Now you have this big tree and you're distressed because it's useless [*wuyong* 无用]. Why don't you plant it in Not-Even-Anything Village, or the field of Broad-and-Boundless, relax and do nothing [*wuwei* 无為] by its side, or lie down for a free and easy sleep under it? Axes will never shorten its life, nothing can ever harm it. If there's no use for it, how can it come to grief or pain?

Hui Shi is advised to *wuwei*, "to relax and do nothing." The exchange concerning the useless tree is similar to the previous exchange (1.3.1–5) where Hui Shi complains about a calabash being too big to be of any use. Zhuangzi replies,

> 今子有五石之瓠，何不慮以為大樽而浮乎江湖，而憂其瓠落无所容？則夫子猶有蓬之心也夫！(1.3.5)

> Now you had a gourd big enough to hold five piculs. Why didn't you think of making it into a great tub so you could go floating around the rivers and lakes, instead of worrying because it was too big and unwieldy to dip into things! Obviously you still have a lot of underbrush in your head!

The phrase *wuwei* is not used in the last citation, but "floating around the rivers and lakes" is an example of *wuwei*. We suggest that Zhuangzi's positive remarks in the inner chapters concerning uselessness (*wuyong*) can be understood as part of his sympathy for *wuwei*.

In chapter 4, Zhuangzi points out that it is the uselessness of "unusable" trees that protects them from being cut down and therefore let them live out the years given to them by nature (*tian*). Because it is wretched (useless) timber, the tree can live out the years nature gave it. As the sacred oak in chapter 4 puts it,[89]

> 且予求无所可用久矣，幾死，乃今得之，為予大用。使予也而有用，且得有此大也邪？(4.4.6)

> As for me, I've been trying a long time to be of no use, and though I almost died, I've finally got it. This is of great use to me. If I had been of some use, would I ever have grown this large?

Feng Youlan (1931, 64) comments, "To be useless is the way to preserve one's life." And that is the way in which Zhuangzi's parables concerning "uselessness" have been interpreted by commentators over the ages (including many poets).[90]

Useful trees end their lives prematurely.

桂可食，故伐之；漆可用，故割之。(4.7.4)

The cinnamon can be eaten and so it gets cut down; the lacquer tree can be used and so it gets hacked apart.

故未终其天年，而中道已夭于斧斤，此材之患也。(4.5.4)

They [catalpas, cypresses and mulberries] never get to live out the years Heaven gave them, but are cut down in mid-journey by axes. This is the danger of being usable.

In chapter 1, when complaining that the tree and the big gourd (calabash) are useless, Hui Shi adds, "Your words, too, are big and useless." Zhuangzi points out that Hui Shi's rigid thinking leaves no room for seeing the "uselessness of the useful" ("the use of the useless"). The theme of the use of uselessness in the *Zhuangzi* occurs several times and is the focus of Heidegger's interest in Zhuangzi (van Brakel 2014). Heidegger cites Zhuangzi twice at length and shows familiarity with the tree passages in chapters 1, 4, and 26.[91] In 1962 he cites the passage concerning the big tree (1.3.6–8) at the end of chapter 1 (Heidegger 1962, 131/7). In 1944/45, Heidegger cites the passage concerning the necessity of the useless in chapter 26 (156/239).[92]

惠子謂莊子曰：子言无用。(26.7.1; G81, 100)

Hui Tzu said to Chuang Tzu, "Your words are useless!"

莊子曰：知无用而始可與言用矣。夫地非不廣且大也，人之所用容足耳。然則廁足而墊之致黃泉，尚有用乎？(26.7.2)

Chuang Tzu said, A man has to understand the useless before you can talk to him about the useful. The earth is certainly vast and broad, though a man uses no more of it than the area he puts his feet on. If, however, you were to dig away all the earth from around his feet until you reached the Yellow Springs, then would the man still be able to make use of it?

The crevice dropping into the Underworld in chapter 26 (G81, 100) is mirrored in Heidegger's text when he speaks of "the emptiness that seems to gape around us when we wait on the pure coming" (1944/45, 149/229).

When Heidegger writes: "The useless has is own greatness and determining power since it does not let anything be made out of it" (1962, 131/8), he may have borrowed from Wilhelm's translation of *wusuokeyong* 无所可用 in the story of the village tree in chapter 4.[93] Heidegger may also have appreciated the end of chapter 4:

人皆知有用之用，而莫知无用之用也。(4.7.4)

All men know the use of the useful, but nobody knows the use of the useless! (Watson)

Nobody knows how useful [*nützlich*] it is to be useless [*nutzlos*]. (Wilhelm)

Probably this passage inspired Heidegger to write that we must learn "to know the necessity of the unnecessary and, as learners, teach it to the peoples [*Völkern*]."[94]

Graham classifies the passages in the *Zhuangzi* that bear on "uselessness" as part of his identification of Zhuangzi's "own words" (see tables in Graham 1980, 59–69). We do not agree with Graham when he speaks of the "unqualified praise" for uselessness in the inner chapters as contrasted with chapter 20 where Zhuangzi is "represented as balancing judiciously between the talented and untalented [*cai* 材 and *bucai* 不材]" (Graham 1980, 73).[95] In chapter 20, Zhuangzi's disciples questioned him, saying,[96]

昨日山木之木，以不材得終其天年；今主人之雁，以不材死；先生將何處？ (20.1.3)

Yesterday there was a tree on the mountain that gets to live out the years Heaven gave it because of its worthlessness [*bucai* 不材]. Now there's our host's goose that gets killed because of its worthlessness. What position would you take in such a case, Master?

However, this passage is not part of the inner chapters. Moreover, Zhuangzi's reply is usually cited as

莊子笑曰：周將處夫材與不材之間。(20.1.4)

Chuang Tzu laughed and said, "I'd probably take a position halfway between worth and worthlessness."

This leads to Graham's view just cited. However, if we look at how the text continues, Zhuangzi dismisses the "halfway" position. In addition, he may have lost interest in the specifics of trees and geese and may have moved on to more abstract matters.

材與不材之間，似之而非也 故未免乎累。若夫乘道德而浮遊則不然。无譽无訾，一龍一蛇，與時俱化，而无肯專為。(20.1.4)

But halfway between worth and worthlessness, though it might seem to be a good place, really isn't—you'll never get away from trouble there. It would be very different, though, if you were to climb up on the Way and its Virtue and go drifting and wandering, neither praised nor damned, now a dragon, now a snake, shifting with the times, never willing to hold to one course only.

Notes

Introduction

1. A conceptual scheme is a cluster of concepts. Because of the holism of concepts, strictly speaking, a concept is already a conceptual scheme.

2. How to find a text in TLS using the sequence number? For example, to look for 32.12.4 from the *Zhuangzi*, go to the page "Standard Search." On the third line choose "contains" and insert 莊子. Insert the numbers 32, 12, and 4 on the lines for Sequence No. 1, 2, and 3, respectively. Click "Perform Search."

3. A serious weakness of TLS is that it fits classical Chinese into the pigeonholes of classifications that are common in modern cognitive science (assumed to be universally valid).

4. Translators: John S. Major, Sarah A. Queen, Andrew Seth Meyer, and Harold D. Roth; but in Works Cited listed under Liu An 劉安 (ca. 179–122 BCE), King of Huainan.

5. Makeham (2012) has diagnosed this problem, citing numerous Chinese sources for support. We have discussed the general features of what has been called "transcendental pretense" elsewhere (Ma Lin and van Brakel 2016a, 215–18). An example is the projection of the (recent) Western concept of semantic truth onto classical Chinese texts (§2a).

6. {*yi* 宜 ⇔ fitting} is to be read as: there is a family resemblance between *yi* 宜 and fitting. Such a quasi-universal has two sides: *yi* 宜 and fitting. From the English side, fitting can be extended to encompass a large part of the conceptual range of *yi* 宜; from the Chinese side, *yi* 宜 can be extended to encompass a large part of the conceptual range of fitting.

7. See the "notes on referencing" for an explanation of the convention of using an en dash in phrases such as language–meaning.

8. We will use the English word sage to cover both *shengren* 聖人 and *zhenren* 真人, in particular, who may serve as a role model for humans. See for these and other "sages" §A4.

9. As will be discussed in §4c, *zhen* 真 is perhaps the most common higher-order standard of correctness. Our notion of "higher-order" refers to a higher

"meta-level" at which one speaks about a lower "object-level." Higher-order standards in our sense should be clearly distinguished from the "higher viewpoint of the Tao," which "transcends shapes and features" (Feng Youlan 1947, 67).

10. These are his translations in Graham (1981)—a translation of the parts from the *Zhuangzi*, whose original text he has edited. In a later work he slightly modified these translations: "a 'this' according to what one goes by" and "a 'this' which deems" (G89, 179).

11. 章太炎 (1868–1936), also called Zhang Binglin 章炳麟.

Chapter 1

1. See Ma Lin and van Brakel (2016a). See also Ma Lin and van Brakel (2015) on quasi-universals; Ma Lin and van Brakel (2016b) on mutually recognizable human practices and principle of mutual attunement; and Ma Lin and van Brakel (2018) on hermeneutic relativity.

2. Our notion of a Wittgensteinian variant of "family-resemblance-concepts" diverges from all other uses of "family resemblance" in the secondary literature (Ma Lin and van Brakel 2016c), and from other related phrases such as "vagueness" as well (on vagueness, see, for example, Hall and Ames 1995, 165–70). In particular, we do not propose the family-resemblance-principle only as a useful *tool*, which is common in Chinese and comparative philosophy, but as a *necessary condition* of interpretation.

3. See Ma Lin and van Brakel (2016a, 165–73) on form(s) of life. There is no precise explanation of forms of life. A form of life is a given unjustified and unjustifiable pattern of human activity. It is the ultimately unsystematizable complex of actual societal life on which any provisionally formulable regularities or rules of behavior are based. Hansen remarks that form of life "is a very tempting translation of *dao*^{way}" (1992, 383n46; cf. 72, 75, 84). Fraser articulates a similar idea: "In the context of classical Chinese thought, agency is manifested through the activity of following a dào, a way or form of life" (2014, 555). Both *li* 禮 and *li* 理 could be said to be congeners of form(s) of life as well (Ma Lin and van Brakel 2016a, 340n54) despite their many differences.

4. We follow Rosemont (1988, 55–57, 66) in focusing on human beings only. However, not much can be fixed by restricting the discussion to humans. For example, Rosemont refers positively to the work by Ekman as well as by Rosch and Mervis that has allegedly shown that all humans share the same basic emotions and the same basic color terms (58n32). But this is not true (Ma Lin and van Brakel 2016a, 56–58, 77–85).

5. A speech act is an utterance that has a performative function in language and communication. We consider "utterance" to be a primitive pragmatic concept. Theoretically speaking, utterances include assertions, questions, imperatives, predicates, strings of characters, and so on (cf. Wittgenstein 2009).

6. In Ma Lin and van Brakel (2016a, chapter 3), we present an extensive discussion of "universalism and relativism."

7. See Ma Lin and van Brakel (2016a, chapter 2 and passim).

8. Aristotle, *De Interpretatione* 16a3–9. Of course, there are alternative translations of this passage. Sallis (2002, 48) points out that in the original text, the Greek word for "word" does not occur.

9. For a discussion of the frame problem and the problem of complete description, see van Brakel (1992). Cf. "the very ideas of a complete expression and of a signifier that would cover exactly the signified are both inconsistent" (Merleau-Ponty 1973, 29). See also Kim Myeong-seok (2014, 51), who refers to the frame problem when discussing the work of Wong (2006).

10. Different descriptions (say of Zhuangzi) can be compared in terms of "correctness," primarily understood in the sense of fitting, which is explained in §6b. However, disagreement as to what fits may eventually lead to a clash or an irresolvable disagreement, as discussed in §10a.

11. The phrase "metaphysical realism" is also borrowed in the context of Chinese philosophy. See, for example, an article titled, "The Daoist Conception of Truth: Lao Zi's Metaphysical Realism vs. Zhuang Zi's Internal Realism." Liu JeeLoo (2003).

12. See, for example, Slingerland (2013).

13. A "meta-language" is a (natural) language just like any other language, except that it is used specifically to speak *about* one or more other languages. Hence, any translation or interpretation of a classical text is to be given in a meta-language relative to the language of the classical text. We propose that such meta-languages focus on the construction of quasi-universals (as distinct from commitment to the ideal language assumption).

14. The earlier meaning of *lan* 藍 is the appearance of indigo dye (from the indigo plant).

15. See §A2 on the bird Peng.

16. The TLS lists uses of *cang* in different syntactic and semantic contexts. In all cases it is rendered as "blue" or "azure." This may have been caused by the fact that the TLS classifies *cang* in the synonymy group of BLUE. *Qing* is also listed in six out of seven cases under the synonymy group of BLUE. In modern Chinese, the blue sky is also called *lantian* 蓝天.

17. There are more differences in the translations of the first clause of this citation than in the case of the blue sky because of uncertainties concerning the character *mang* 莽; it may stand on its own and perhaps mean "weeds," whereas *mangcang* 莽蒼 is a set expression, which may mean, for example, shrubbery (TLS).

18. Other reported meanings of *cang* include: azure/blue, green-azure, celestial blue, dark blue/green; bluey-green, gray-green, green color of the sea (and hence gloomy); the "green" aspect of life (in French: *verdoyant*); graying (of hair). *Cangsheng* 蒼生 refer to ordinary people who have black hair (nobles wear hats). According to the *Erya*, *cang* "means" *zhui* 騅 (piebald: horse of mixed gray and white color); according to the *Shuowen jiezi*, *cang* is the *se* 色 (appearance) of grass.

19. See for modern *qing* 青 also Ma Lin and van Brakel (2016a, 213, 328n71, 349n13).

20. Other reported uses of *qing* include: green, green/blue, blue, dark blue; brown/black, dark gray; indigo (dye), blackish (color of the earth), freshly green and living, tender green (color of plants in spring), purple (color of the east).

21. *Xuan* occurs once in the *Zhuangzi*: *xuan gong* 玄宮 "dark palace" (ZH 6.3.4).

22. The *Kangxi zidian* defines *cang* as "dark *qing* 青."

23. See Ma Lin and van Brakel (2016a, 212, 349n13; cf. 77–84).

24. Possibilities are also limited by the constraints of the English language. The French language already offers different options. The options in modern Chinese are again different.

25. The underdetermination of a theory or interpretation by the data (the evidence) is sometimes called the Quine-Duhem thesis. It holds that every theory (and hence every interpretation) is underdetermined by the evidence in the sense in which there is always the possibility of finding an alternative interpretation (theory) that fits the data equally well. The word "indeterminacy" is used in comparative and Chinese philosophy for a range of purposes. See, for example, Chiu Wai Wai (2015) and Coutinho (2015). As far as our understanding of the relevant terms is concerned, Zhuangzi's *weiding* 未定 (§9b) includes both underdetermination and indeterminacy.

26. For more detailed discussion of these notions, see Ma Lin and van Brakel (2016a, 255–60).

27. Epistemic virtues are the properties a good interpretation (or theory) should have, such as empirical adequacy and coherence with background knowledge (Ma Lin and van Brakel 2016a, 85–89).

28. See Ma Lin and van Brakel (2016a, 18–20).

29. Wang Zhongjiang, cited from Makeham (2012, 350).

30. Ames uses this expression five times in a recent interview (Tan Xiaoli and Huang Tianyuan 2015). Ames also used it in the title of his article "Indigenizing Globalization and the Hydraulics of Culture: Taking Chinese Philosophy on Its Own Terms" (Ames 2004). A similar slogan is: "Let the text speak itself" (Ames 1998, 9).

31. Similarly, Hall and Ames (1987, 1995) are using a meta-language that claims universals, including cosmos, defining, changing, wholeness of experience, intelligent practices, vital relationality, wisdom, order, patterns, event, aspects, and so on. Some of these concepts can be said to be quasi-universals, but certainly not all.

32. It can be argued that modern (philosophical) Chinese is closer to modern (philosophical) English than to classical (philosophical) Chinese.

33. "FR(. . .)" is to be read as: "family-resemblance-concept of . . ."

34. This is *not* a variant of the Gadamerian "fusion of horizons." The metalanguage is one hundred percent the language of the (modern) interpreter.

Chapter 2

1. English dictionaries list the following congeners of truth: correct, real, genuine, faithful, precise, accurate, reliable, trustworthy, sincere, and legitimate. This cluster could be considered as the pre-theoretical notion of truth (in English). The

pre-theoretical notion of truth should be contrasted with the theoretical notion of semantic truth, which is usually stipulated to be a property of descriptive compositional sentences (that is, not a property of objects or of persons).

2. According to the *correspondence theory of truth*, "truth" is found in the correspondence between what is said in a sentence and what is the case in the world; truth is correspondence to the facts. Cf. citation of Aristotle in §1b.

3. According to the *coherence theory of truth*, a sentence is true if it coheres with (a coherent system of) other sentences. One finds the coherence notion of truth in both the analytic and continental traditions of Western philosophy.

4. The theory of truth of the American pragmatists, mainly Peirce and James, emphasizes the interest in concrete practical aims: truth is what gets you along in the world. The only thing one can hope for is to produce sentences or utterances that are of use for certain aims (scientific, political, religious, . . .). *Both* correspondence *and* coherence are pragmatically relevant on this account.

5. For further discussions, see Rosemont (2014) and Ma Lin and van Brakel (2016a, 292).

6. More emphatically, "Chinese has no concept of truth" (Hansen 1985, 492, 494).

7. Hansen considers a sentence to be a free-standing utterance (1985, 498).

8. All references to Harbsmeier in this chapter without year of publication mentioned refer to Harbsmeier (1998). Harbsmeier (1989) is an earlier shorter version of his (1998).

9. For additional criticisms of Harbsmeier, see Robins (2010) and Fraser (2012).

10. Hansen also remarks that translating *dang* 當 ("hit-on") as "true" would be intelligible for some of the later Mohist *Canons* (such as B35 and B71). However, "instead of associating *dang* with 'is satisfied by' we may render it as 'is (appropriately) predictable of'" (1985, 509). Normally, we refer to the *Canons* using the numbering in Graham (1978), as we have just done.

11. Cf. *zhenzai* 真宰 true master; *zhenjun* 真君 true lord.

12. Originally, classical Chinese texts were written as a single continuous string of characters. Later editors parsed the text using punctuation. Different modern translations of, say, the *Zhuangzi*, may be based on different parsings of the text.

13. It is common to define semantic truth with reference to Tarski's work. However, Tarski showed that a natural language is inconsistent in the sense that contradictions can always be constructed (similar to the paradox of the Liar). Therefore, a truth definition for a natural language that is formally correct is not possible (Tarski 1931).

14. Modern interpreters change the punctuation as they see fit (as well as the separation of the text in paragraphs). Harbsmeier acknowledges that punctuation was later added to extant texts.

15. Harbsmeier's final example is Zhu Xi (1130–1200), who comments on a text by Xunzi 荀子 (ca. 310–c. 235 BCE): "These two sentences [*ju* 句] are well-said . . . 此二句說得好)" (cited by Harbsmeier: 184). Harbsmeier remarks that Zhu Xi "is absolutely right when he takes it that there are exactly two sentences." That

Zhu Xi and Harbsmeier think of it as sentences is not relevant. What is at issue is whether Xunzi would think of it as sentences.

16. Following Hansen, Robins (2010, 247–85) provides detailed arguments why *ci* should be translated as "phrase" and never as "sentence." For arguments supporting the view that there are explicit statements, if not sentences, in classical Chinese, see Harbsmeier (1989, 1998) and Roetz (1993, 78, 81). These scholars argue that (*translated*) phrases such as "I have heard it said that" (*guyue* 故曰) and "therefore (it is said that)" (*wuwenzhi* 吾聞之) are "expected to be filled in with statements rather than any other strings of words" (Harbsmeier, 181).

17. Fraser and Saunders assume that when Graham uses "saying" (*yan* 言) or "calling" (*wei* 謂) in his translations of the *Canons*, this indicates that assertions would follow; see, for example, A29–33, A79, B35. However, this is not self-evident.

18. Some may consider this citation from Brandom as a case of relativism (or as an exemplification of the coherence theory of truth).

19. For many years, Hansen (1983b–2015) has argued that Chinese theorizing about knowledge does not focus on beliefs or other sentential structures but rather on drawing action-guiding *shi-fei* distinctions.

20. See Graham (G59, G89, 408–12), Jullien (1989, 105), Reding (2004, 171). However, there may well be family resemblances between various functions of "to be" and particular Chinese characters (Ma Lin and van Brakel 2016a, 227–32).

21. According to the *Kangxi zidian*, the following characters may replace one another: *shi* 實, *shi* 是, *shi* 寔.

22. In English, trustworthy means "telling the truth" or "keep promises," that is, correspondence of words and intentions. But note that the Chinese concept of "person" is very different.

23. We give Roetz's English glosses in brackets (and we do the same in the case of other authors cited in this section). Our list is alphabetical and does not follow Roetz's numbered sequence.

24. Strictly speaking, we cannot compare the lists of Harbsmeier and Roetz, because, while Harbsmeier's list concerns "notions like 'is true'" (200), Roetz's list concerns "validity concepts" (85–96) that include rightness-related expressions and "validity claims with ontological implications" (in addition to [implying] truth claims) (85). According to Roetz, "none of the terms is used exclusively for one validity claim" (96).

25. In the "original" Chinese edition of the *Zhuangzi* used in TLS, the negation *wu* is written as 无, not as 無. We follow TLS in using 无 when citing the *Zhuangzi*.

26. The full synonym group consists of correct, earnest, faithful, genuine, perfect, prove, and true. Each item is defined in a specific way, for example: *true* means to *conform* to *reality*, or: *correct* means *appropriate* so as to *fit* the *facts* or the *principles perfectly*. All italicized words are defined in terms of each other.

27. The difference is subtle because Habermas can also be considered as a "pragmatist" (though not in the same sense that Hansen can be). Habermas aims to set out the universal pragmatic conditions of ideal consensus, drawing on a mixture of Peircean theory with speech act theory and social theory.

28. "One would not expect another culture, with a language unrelated to the Indo-European family, to have a word with the same range of ambiguities as our 'true'" (G91, 296).

29. The notion of cluster concepts (which Anne Cheng 2004 calls a "constellation" of concepts) is a familiar idea in Chinese and comparative philosophy. See, for example, Rosemont (1988, 61–64).

30. These choices are part of the interpreter's hermeneutic relativity (Ma and van Brakel 2018), which entails pluralism but not relativism.

31. It seems that *shi* 是 can be said of a wide range of things: a statement, assertion, person, principle of action, state of affairs, object, action, policy, and so on.

32. Elsewhere (Ma and van Brakel 2015) we have elucidated the notion of hybrid concept (as distinct from that of pseudo-homonym) in more detail. These merged, or blended, or mingled concepts are like other concepts, except that they have received no name yet. Merging concepts amounts to making *new* family-resemblance-concepts in the interpreter's language that can serve as quasi-universals to correspond with alien (perhaps polysemous) concepts. This idea has often been mentioned in passing (for example, Richards 1932, 4, Hall and Ames 1995, 168), but it has not yet received the theoretical attention it deserves.

33. Cf. Hall (2001, 296n7): "the meaning of the term in one context is always reinforced by and presupposes all of the alternative senses of the term."

34. Following Wittgenstein, we need to distinguish between fitting "in the small" and fitting "in the large" (Wittgenstein 2009, §66). Similarities in the small refer to prima facie similarities between the referents of family-resemblance-concepts. Similarities in the large refer to similar ways of fitting in the embedding forms of life.

35. Cf. contrasting opinions of Graham and Jullien: "Classical Chinese syntax is close to symbolic logic: it has an existential quantifier" (G89, 412). "And what verb is there in classical Chinese that expresses 'to exist'?" (Jullien 2014, 151).

36. In classical texts, *you* should perhaps be rendered as "presence" (not as existence) in most cases; see Hall and Ames (1995, 227). For a discussion of chapter 11 of the *Daodejing*, see Ma (2006).

37. For example, Hansen's explanations of his preferred translations are full of terms such as relativism and realism, while Graham, more cautiously, tends to place such words in scare quotes ("nominalist," "sophist").

38. Of course, philosophers from whatever tradition may introduce new "technical" terminology, but we believe that all philosophical problems can be discussed in an ordinary language. For example, to appreciate (or not to appreciate) Zhuangzi's remarks concerning death/dying and mourning do not require highbrow philosophical jargon. More sophisticated language can be built on the basis of ordinary languages (for which more "mutual recognition of human practices" can be expected). Of course, the issue of what is and what is not philosophy may lead to irresolvable disagreements (cf. §10a).

39. For a discussion of McLeod's book from a somewhat different perspective, see §4c.

40. See McLeod (2016, ix, xvi, 1, 5, 33–34, 74, 106, 161, 175, 183).

41. McLeod's overview shows that the most common character suggestive of the implicit use of the concept of truth seems to be *ran* 然.

42. See McLeod (2016, 10, 16, 20, 52–53, 66, 71, 98, 99, 106).

43. The author's speculations about *shi* 實 being a unifying second-order concept (2016, 149, 158, 160, 163–64) are interesting, but such suggestions can also be made (and have been made) with respect to other texts or characters, as the author acknowledges (65).

44. Numerous characters have been translated (in some contexts) as category: *lun* 倫, *chou* 儔, *yu* 域, *shu* 屬, *tu* 徒, *wu* 物, *ke* 科, and *zhong* 種. This may be partly due to the fact that psychologists use the word "category" when philosophers tend to use the word "kind." We suggest that no classical Chinese character should be translated as "category" in a philosophical context.

45. According to Cheng Xuanying (2011, 43), originally, *lei* meant "similarity across generations."

46. Roetz remarks that *bei* refers to the "inner logical structure of arguments" (1993, 96).

47. Geaney (1999) has criticized Graham's reconstruction of the later Mohist *Canons*. However, most anglophone commentators follow Graham's editing of the *Canons*, though alternative translations of specific passages vary widely.

48. Harbsmeier refers to A40 (and A73) on page 217 while citing A74, which he corrects on page 330. Harbsmeier explicitly identifies *fan* 仮 with being contradictory (330). Most reconstructions of the Mohist Canons are based on the "Taoist Patrology Text" (G78, 499–525), which reads for A74: 辯爭攸也辯勝當也. Different commentators propose different emendations of *you* 攸. Graham considers it to be a corrupted word deriving from *fan* 仮 (G78, 84). According to him, *fan* "was obsolete after the end of the Mohist school" (185); hence, it is liable to be corrupted. *Fan* 仮 may be one of the Mohists' technical terms derived from *fan* 反 (according to Graham, it meant something like "turn around"). For a detailed critique of Graham's emendations, see Saunders (2014, 220n6), who identifies A74 as 辯, 爭彼也。辯勝, 當也. Each alternative reading of A74 depends on decisions about how to read A73, B30, and B72.

49. B35, "謂辯無勝必不當，說在辯 [As for disputation: one calls something affirmatively, another calls it negatively. The one that matches wins]" (Coutinho 2004, 106). "To say that there is no winner in disputation necessarily does not fit the fact. Explained by: disputation" (G78, 402).

50. According to Graham, *fan* (being the converse of each other) is corrupted to 攸 or *bi* 彼 (G78, 318n187). (According to TLS, 攸 is a pre-classical pronoun.) Saunders uses *bi* in citing A74. Hansen (1985, 509n20) has correctly pointed out that "emending *bi* to *fan* disconnects the text from Zhuangzi's use of *bi*" (cf. §7b).

51. Cf. translation of A74 by Harbsmeier above and by Cheng Chungying in a note at the end of this section. The phrase *dang ye* 當也 has also been translated as "the fitting one" (Fraser 2012, 362). An alternative translation of *dang* in this context is "appropriate."

52. Coutinho (2004, 107) avoids the issue of "converse claims" versus "opposites" by translating the first characters of A74 as: "Disputation is contending over alternatives."

53. Saunders claims that A73 shows that *bi* applies to words, not to claims (A73, "彼，不可兩不可也。(彼)，凡牛，樞非牛，兩也。無以非也"). However, at this point, his text becomes a bit garbled. He says: "The idea that *bi* [fan?] are [sic] converse *claims* is a major motivating factor for glossing *dang* as truth in B74" (221). But there is no *dang* in B74. Perhaps he intends to refer to A74, but Saunders himself glosses *dang* in terms of fitting; only Cheng Chung-ying renders *dang* in terms of truth.

54. The various definitions of *dang* may form a semantic web such that the meaning of *dang* pervades throughout a series of English words such as: "equal," "compatible," "appropriate," "fit," "encounter," "match." Definitions of TLS restrict the meaning of *dang* to: fit the facts, be true; be correct; be fitting and right, be as it should be; be appropriate; be to the point; be the right thing in the right place; and adequate, justified.

55. Similarly, Cheng Chung-ying translates A74 as: "The purpose of it is to compete for the *truth* (*bi*). When an argument is won, it is because *truth* has been reached" (353, emphasis added). Cf. Cheng's translation of A32: "言，出舉也。" *Yan* (to say or speak of words) is to emit references; "言也者，諸口能，出民者也。民若畫虎也。言也謂言，猶名致也。" "Language is to make representation of reality possible . . . Since names are used to represent reality, *yan* is to use names to represent things for achieving objective truth by saying something about things named. Thus, *yan* is to say something about names" (353).

56. There are other characters that have been translated as "contradictory." In the *Guanzi* we find: "名物處違是非之分" (31.01.03) ("As contradictions arose between what people said and what they did, and distinctions emerged between right and wrong") (Rickett 1985, 413). English-language dictionaries (*OED*, *Merriam-Webster*) make a distinction between opposite (things in contrast or conflict), contrary (diametrical opposition), and contradictory (if one is true–valid the other is not), but sinologists are less precise in this respect. TLS defines *wei* 違 as: to be in contradiction with, or simply "contradict." But in a word list, TLS translates *wei* as: disagree, contrary. Many translations of *wei* occur. It may mean something like "oppose" or "avoid," perhaps "contrary," but not something formal such as "contradiction(s)."

57. It seems plausible to argue that at the time of the later Mohists and Zhuangzi, there was a keen awareness of the significance of avoiding "perversity" in the context of *bian*.

58. Some commentators have suggested that this "disproof" of skepticism or relativism shows that Zhuangzi is wrong. However, it is implausible that Zhuangzi would not have been aware of this "problem."

59. Both Graham (1969, 1981, 1989) and Coutinho (2004, 2015) emphasize that for Zhuangzi there is nothing wrong with contradictions. Nevertheless, Alt (2000: 5) disputes this point.

218 / Notes to Chapter 3

60. Similarly, Cheng Chung-ying (2003) translates B71 as: "To regard all sayings (*yan*) as false (self-contradictory) is self-contradictory. The explanation consists in the nature of the saying formulating this position" (353).

61. Graham also uses the word "illogical" as a translation of *bei* 誖 (G78, 199). For B71, B77, and B79, he translated *bei* as self-contradictory; for B8, self-refuting or self-contradictory (G78, 358n295); for B34, fallacious; for B76, fallacy. Some commentators translate it as inconsistent, as Graham did on at least one occasion (G89, 185). Another possible translation of *bei* is "confused."

Chapter 3

1. Other translations include: that's it and that's not, is and is not, (in)correct, (un)suitable, (dis)approve (approval and rejection), so and not-so, yes and no (affirm/deny), good/evil, justify/condemn.

2. Cf. note on referencing (placed after Acknowledgment) for details about translations.

3. Lai (2008, 57, 64, 148, 159, 285, 306).

4. "無是非" (literally: not [*wu* 無: lack of] *shifei*) occurs in a couple of sources, leading to various translations. For example: "[a person of talent] does not set himself up as judge over right and wrong" (Hanfeizi 6.3.1); "without any longer distinguishing between right and wrong" (Liezi 2.3/4; 4.6/2).

5. Cf. "無廉恥，不知是非" (Xunzi 4.4.1) "having neither scruples nor shame, not knowing right from wrong" (Knoblock 1, 188).

6. It is not the case that Rickett always translates Guanzi's *shifei* as true/false. "When the enlightened ruler establishes good order, he pays attention to right and wrong and investigates the facts, using procedures and measures to judge people" (Rickett 1998, 168; 明主之治也，審是非).

7. Xunzi (18.9.1–Knoblock 3, 46, already cited) makes a similar remark.

8. Xu Shen 許慎, the compiler of the *Shuowen jiezi*, says: "Men all use their private judgments, right and wrong has no standard, while clever opinions and slanted pronouncements have caused considerable confusion among scholars" (cited in Nylan 2016, 110).

9. The phrase "以是為非以非為是" also occurs in the *Liji* and the *Lüshi chunqiu*. There does not seem to be a good reason to alternate true/false and wrong/right in Crump's translation, as only *shi* and *fei* are reversed in the Chinese original.

10. *Shifei* and "order and anarchy" are often mentioned together; in such cases, usually *shifei* is translated as right and wrong. For example, Xunzi: "是非治亂" (6.1.1) ("wherein lies the distinction between right and wrong and between order and anarchy" (Knoblock 1, 223). "審於是非之實，察於治亂之情也" (Hanfeizi 14.5.4) ("[he] examines carefully the facts of right and wrong and he investigates the real facts of good government and chaos") (Harbsmeier in TLS).

11. There are many similar statements about *xin* in the *Liezi*.

12. Alternative translation: "discursive thinking of the mind is not sufficient to fix what is right and wrong" (Harbsmeier 1998, 197).

13. The "definition" of *zhi*/know versus ignorance follows a list of similar definitions. The two parts of the citation from the *Xunzi* are separately cited in the *Kangxi zidian* 康熙字典 as possible definitions of *zhi* 知 (knowing, wisdom) and *yu* 愚 (ignorant, stupid) respectively. The phrase 是是非非 also occurs in the *Lunheng* 33.5.3. Forke translates it as: "Both declare good to be good, and bad, bad."

14. Several writers mention the opposites "this and not-this," for example, Sturgeon (2014, 23; 2015, 907), Hansen (1992, 120), and Fraser (2011, 103). However, it rarely occurs in a concrete translation. Graham's is an exception when discussing canon B3: "What is deemed *fei* (not-this)" (*weifei* 為非); "is not being deemed not-this" *buweifei* 不為非) (G78, 354). In discussing B35, Graham mentions "not-this" as a possible translation of *fei* (117), but in the full text for B35 it reads: "it is not" (403; cf. G69, 142).

15. In the "lexeme entry attribution" of TLS, *shi* and *fei* in this passage are defined as "consider correct–true" and "regard as untrue."

16. *Chengran* 誠然 has been translated as "true indeed" (Xinlun 新論 3.24, trans. Pokora) and "in reality" (Liezi 1.9/6; G60). Cf. 語誠然乎哉 (Mengzi 5A4): "whether what is here said really took place" (Legge); "whether these words are authentic" (Levy).

17. The Chinese translation was a cooperative undertaking by Li Zhizao 李之藻 (1571–1630), a Chinese "Christian" scholar, and the Jesuit Francisco Furtado (1589–1653). According to the most recent investigations (Mynard 2017), the *Minglitan* was published in 1636 and contained translations and explanations of parts of Aristoteles's *Categoriae*, *Porphyrii*, and *Isagoge*.

18. Note that the highest standard in these classical Chinese texts is *zhen* 真, not *shi* 是 (cf. §4c).

19. That is to say, the same passage Wardy translates.

20. Wang Jianlu (2014, 174–83) contains a useful table listing English translations of the "technical" Latin terminology, their translation in the *Minglitan*, and the translation in modern Chinese.

21. There is no consensus as to whether Confucianism and Aristotelianism are strikingly different and "incompatible" (Mynard 2017, 62), or whether the *Minglitan* "refutes suggestions of a general incommensurability between Chinese and European ways of thinking" (Kurtz 2011, 341). For discussion of various reviews of Wardy (2000), see Ma Lin and van Brakel (2016a, 37–39).

22. "Now, if we accept the three generation theory, the statement about the excellent conduct must be wrong, and, if we declare the latter view to be correct, then we must dismiss the theory about the three generations as erroneous, for both are contradictory" (Forke 1, 452; "夫據三世，則浃備之說非；言浃備之說為是，則據三世之論誤。二者相伐" [Lunheng 28.1]).

23. Forke's translation is: "If words do not express the truth, the statement cannot be considered correct" (Forke 1, 103).

Chapter 4

1. Cf. translation of *ruoshi* 若是: if (that) is so; like this.
2. "Telle n'était pas la conduite d'un vrai noble" (Levy).
3. Perhaps we can consider the account in the *Grand Ricci* as the consensus among French sinologists. The *Grand Ricci* has "negation" instead of disapproval.
4. Probably *shi* 是 was first used as a copula in the *Mengzi* (1A7 and 6A15; see Kim Myeong-seok 2014, 72n23). Most current dictionaries give the (modern) meaning of *shifei* as (1) right and wrong; and (2) quarrel–dispute–trouble. Only some of the Oxford dictionaries add "truth and falsity." True and right are rarely mentioned together as alternatives; an example is Sturgeon (2014, 22): "true or right."
5. In the *Grand Ricci*, we find under the historical use of *ran*: being so, in this way, approve, conform to reality, conform to natural movement, appropriate, true, in fact, to see things how they are.
6. An example of translating *shi* as truth (and *fei* as falsehood) was given earlier in a citation from the *Liezi* (G60, 142).
7. Example of *shi* 是: "the alternatives in disputation, for example whether a thing is or is not an ox." Example of *ran* 然: "What is so rather than what it is. . . . being so that a man who climbs a tree is frightened and an ape is not" (G69, 139).
8. Cf. §7g; *ci* 此 is the opposite of *bi* 彼 (this and that).
9. Knoblock sometimes translates *ran* as "true" in the *Xunzi*. Occasional translations of *ran* as "true" occur in most Warring States sources from which we cite in this book.
10. The convention of writing true/right and false/wrong also occurs (Wardy 2000, 97).
11. When translating a comment by Guo Xiang, Ziporyn takes the liberty of translating Guo's *shi* and *fei* as, respectively, "'this' and 'right,'" and "'that' and 'wrong'" (2009a, 144).
12. To ascribe the meaning (in)correct to *shifei* is rather uncommon in anglophone literature.
13. "Does the philosophical significance of unwieldy technical apparatus such as "That's it, that's not it" justify the interruption that this kind of language imposes on the text?" (Ames 1983, 617). Later Graham changed his translation of *shifei* to "It's this, it's not" (G89, 278–79).
14. Fraser has argued, in connection with Mohist dialectics and truth, that *shi* "may overlap the role of truth at least partly" (Fraser 2012, 363), although he favors *dang* as the best candidate for the role of truth. Presumably most Western scholars assume that "truth" does not denote moral rightness.
15. Harbsmeier (1998, 197) remarks that the context suggests whether moral or epistemic rightness is meant (or left ambiguous).
16. Kim Myeong-seok explicitly considers right and wrong as applicable to "matters of morality" (2014, 53).

17. It is not always clear whether the translation "right and wrong" limits itself to *morally* right and wrong. Cf. Lloyd's (2004, 59) criticism of Harbsmeier (1998, 194).

18. Cf. also: Chuci 15.8; Huainanzi 6.7.14; Liezi 3.3/6, cf. 7.8/12; Linjilu 臨濟錄 3.1; Shiji 6.39.3; "古者謂是采真之遊 [The men of old called this the wandering of the Truth-picker]" (ZH 14.5.10); "此馬之真性也 [This is the true nature of horses]" (ZH 9.1.1).

19. A somewhat similar modifier is *zhi* 至. For example, 至是之是無非，至非之非無是 (Huainanzi 11.27.4) ("The right of perfect rightness is without wrongness, and the wrong of perfect wrongness is without rightness").

20. Cf. Legge: "If the covering them thus was indeed right." Levy: "If this is really the only thing to do [Si c'est vraiment la seule chose à faire]."

21. Cf. *zhengli* 正理 true–correct principle; *zhengfa* 正法 rectify laws or norms; *zhengdao* 正道 straight–correct Way. Citing a passage from the *Mengzi* (5B9 in Lau's translation): "臣不敢不以正對 [I dared not answer with anything but the truth]," Harbsmeier (1998: 201) speculates "that the concept of truth seems thus embedded in the concept of *zheng* as used on this occasion." (There seems to be a typing error in Harbsmeier: 以不正 should be 不以正.)

22. The passage Harbsmeier cites from the *Xunzi* is similar to a passage in Aristotle's *Metaphysica* 1011b26–27, but *not* to 1051b2–5 as Harbsmeier suggests. Also cf. *De Interpretatione*: 16a3–9, which we cited in §1b.

23. Elsewhere, Harbsmeier translates Xunzi 2.3.2 as: "Calling what is right right, and calling what is wrong wrong, that is called straightness" (Harbsmeier in TLS).

24. Rickett translates the binome *shixu* 實虛 in the *Guanzi* as: "reality and emptiness," "solid base or not," "abilities," or "degree of solidity." Elsewhere, truth-related translations of *shi* 實 include: fact, thing which happened; true, honest; in fact, actually; prove, show to be true; really, indeed so.

25. See §2d for a differently focused discussion of McLeod's proposals.

26. Hence, McLeod ascribes to Wang a kind of pluralism about truth grounded in the concept of *shi* 實, or "actuality" (2011, 38). In a study on "Truth in Mohism," Fraser makes a similar point (2012, 357): "The Moists thus seem to be employing a very basic, primitive conception of correctness." According to Fraser, all judgments (in particular in terms of *dang* and *ke*) can be seen as a matter of discriminating *shi* from *fei*. In contrast, McLeod assumes that "moral principles" and "what is the case" are subsidiaries of "being true" (2011, 52).

27. Cf. "以正道而辨姦，猶引繩以持曲直" (Xunzi 22.3.8) ("Using the correct Way to analyze pernicious doctrines is akin to stretching the marking line to test the crooked and straight") (Knoblock 3, 133).

Chapter 5

1. Putnam and Goodman use the words fact and value in the common sense *without* metaphysical association. They develop ideas of the early American

pragmatists (namely, Peirce, James, Dewey, and Mead). The ordinary language philosophers Austin and Ryle have also been understood as trying to uproot dichotomies or "dualisms." Heidegger and Wittgenstein may also be interpreted as subscribing to anti-Cartesianism and anti-dualist stances.

2. Other terms are used for other contrasts, the most famous one being "mind/body dualism." In sinology the preferred term seems to be "dichotomy," and we will go along with that. The following is an incomplete list of what we consider to be (Western) dichotomies: value and fact, ethics and science, ought and is, prescriptive and descriptive, emotion and reason, cultural–artifice–convention and natural, and perhaps also subjective and objective, pragmatic and metaphysical, metaphorical and literal, relativism and universalism, nominalism and realism, *phenomenon* and *noumenon*, cultural–anthropological and transcendental.

3. Such opposites led to the construction of paradoxical statements such as space-time paradoxes. Space-time paradoxes can be resolved by constructing a notion of continuity and/or comparison relative to a standard.

4. See also Hall and Ames (1995, 267; 1999, 191).

5. Evading the fact/value dichotomy seems to be "common to the Chinese tradition in general" (G89, 29; cf. 355). Graham has argued that his "quasi-syllogism" applies to all Chinese philosophers (G89, 383–88). He seems to believe that the Chinese tradition could help the Western tradition to see a way of bringing the world of fact and the world of value together. For Graham, values always arise from *spontaneous* inclinations and combine with "reason" as two inseparable components of decision-making and suchlike (Graham 1985). Because Graham draws heavily on the notion of spontaneity (although combined with "reason") for all his accounts of classical Chinese philosophy, he is sometimes misunderstood as imposing a daoist paradigm onto all Chinese philosophers.

6. Slingerland (2013) argues that there is a "weak" form of the mind/body dualism in classical Chinese, provided that mind and body are understood as *xin* 心 and *xing* 形 respectively.

7. The "two" refer to the pragmatic or normative issues versus the semantic or descriptive ones.

8. Sturgeon's two senses of *shifei* are not primarily descriptive/prescriptive, but subjective/objective. For example: "what is so or not so, rather than what individuals actually take as being so or not so" (2014, 24). Ames (2015, 102) speaks of the "coalescing" of the subjective and objective aspects of "knowing our way around."

9. The coinciding, collapsing, fusing, and so on, of factual and normative significance has also been said of the congeners of the "is true" predicate, for example, *cheng* 誠 (Harbsmeier 1998, 204).

10. In the translation of 2.6.5, Watson avoids the use of "ought": "Of these four, which knows how to fix the standard of beauty for the world? [四者孰知天下之正色哉？]."

11. Assuming that "right" is understood as "neutral" with respect to the fact/value dichotomy. (Cf. §6b on the quasi-universal [*yi* 宜 ⇔ fitting], a generic notion of rightness.)

12. According to Hansen, *shi* and *fei* "are both thin prescriptive *and* descriptive terms" (1992, 120). Whether it is the word for water or for benevolence, there is no difference in learning to use these words, both involving categorization and discrimination (126).

13. Chinese text follows Mei Yi-pao (1929), reproduced in CLT; the translation is from Knoblock and Riegel (2013, 250).

14. The citation from Zhang Dainian uses simplified characters. Zhang's wording of "yielding" is rather idiosyncratic; other translations of *cirang* 辞让 include modesty, respect, and reverence. There are many alternative translations of the passage(s) from Zhu Xi, but the four items cited by Zhang Dainian are almost always called emotions. For example, when translating an article by Chen Lai (2004, 92), Robert Forster has Zhu Xi say that compassion, shame, reverence, and sense of right and wrong are emotions. Chen Lai is citing Zhu Xi's *Yushan jiang yi*《玉山講義》(*Lectures delivered at Yushan*). But, of course, this Chinese source does not contain the English word "emotion(s)."

15. Mengzi, 2A6 and 6A6, cited and discussed in §7a.

16. Note that Zhang Dainian (1989, 197) uses the modern words *lizhi yu qinggan* 理智与情感 (reason and emotion).

17. Rorty (1982, 163) agrees with Putnam: "[T]here is no epistemological difference between truth about what ought to be and truth about what is, not any metaphysical difference between facts and values, not any methodological difference between morality and science." Davidson wrote: "The plainest practical reasoning requires the collusion of values and cognitive judgments" (2004, 15).

18. For references to the works of scholars mentioned in this paragraph, see van Brakel (1999). The same notion of objectivity may occur in nonscientific contexts as well, for example, in the mode of the omniscient narrator or in Rawls's notion of judgments that occur behind a veil of ignorance.

19. See Putnam (1981, 127–216; 1987, 41–86; 1990, 135–92; 1994, 151–220; 2002; 2004). What follows contains many paraphrases from Putnam's writings.

20. Cf. Graham's example of a cat sitting on a mat/*xi* 席 in §10a.

21. The arch-empiricist Quine wrote: "The lore of our fathers is a fabric of sentences. . . . It is a grey lore, black with fact and white with convention. But I have found no substantial reasons for concluding that there are any quite black threads in it, or any white ones" (1986, 132).

22. Cf. "To call a writer a hack, a scientific investigation slipshod, an athlete a clutch player, a driver reckless, or a proof valid is both to describe and to express an evaluation of the referent" (Elgin 2007, 3).

23. Translating *shifei* as (dis)approval may presuppose that *shifei* is a judgment based on "sentiments" (*qing* 情).

24. The community is the whole of humanity, not any particular community (associated with a relativistic stance). "Our interests shall *not* be limited. They must not stop at our own fate, but must embrace the whole community. This community, again, must not be limited, but must extend to all races of beings" (Peirce 1878, 611). Cf. Putnam (1987, 54).

25. *Hence*, this community must have a political structure that recognizes these "facts" about facts and values. Here Putnam (1987, 53–56) is following Habermas.

26. For more on *eudaimonia*, see the exchange between Putnam and Rorty reviewed in §10b.

Chapter 6

1. In our chapter 2, we have used "fit(ting)" to render *dang* 當 as used (copiously) in the later Mohist *Canons*.

2. This section contains many slightly rephrased sentences from Goodman's writings. See Goodman (1978, 1984); Goodman and Elgin (1988); Goodman's contributions in McCormick (1996). See also Elgin (2007).

3. While admitting the enormous difference in time and tradition, one can see a similarity between the views of Putnam and Goodman, on the one hand, and some of the ideas expressed in the second chapter of the *Zhuangzi*, on the other.

4. For Goodman, all worlds are "literally" worlds, not metaphors or possible worlds. However, a strict separation between what is a version and what is a world is not possible.

5. Cf. Ma Lin (2015).

6. See contributions in McCormick (1996). Occasionally one finds traces of Goodmanian terminology of many worlds (making) in the sinological literature. Perhaps unaware of Goodman's work, Billeter (1998, 29) also uses the stars as an example that "language has created 'things' and at the same time a 'world.'" Callahan (1998, 178) suggests in passing that many worlds correspond to many perspectives. Coyle (1998, 202) speaks of "worldmaking."

7. Goodman's example of a soldier saying something that is true but not right is somewhat similar to the Mohists' distinction between being accurate (*dang*) and being not acceptable (*buke* 不可).

8. Cf. Jullien (1999) on efficacy.

9. Cited from the author's twenty-six-page English version of the Italian original.

10. Elgin is not a sinologist. She was a one-time collaborator of Nelson Goodman and continues promoting his work.

11. The reason why one would prefer *not* to use "know(ledge)" is that for many philosophers "know(ledge)" is associated with "justified true belief," which association a pragmatist wants to avoid when studying classical Chinese sources.

12. Cf. Hansen (1983a, 6): "we judge the interpretation by how well it 'fits' the facts to be explained. There are no exhaustive and definitive criteria of the 'best fit' of a theory to a body of data."

13. As we have noted earlier, notwithstanding their disagreements, several interpreters agree with translating *dang* in the *Canons* such as A74, B35, and B71 as "fit the fact." For example, Fraser writes, "Besides utterances, a person's conduct can be characterized as *dang* (fitting) or not (both in the sense of fitting the facts and for characterizing a person's conduct)" (2012, 362).

14. Goodman does not address moral rightness, but he does not exclude the possibility that his notion of rightness can be used for moral rightness. "Any treatment of rightness may, of course, give rise to speculation concerning an application to moral rightness; but I willingly leave that to others" (Goodman 1987, 109).

15. It should be emphasized that the "content" of the quasi-universal fit/*yi* and *yi*/fit is not the same on both sides.

16. There are other verbs used in English to convey the commonsense notion of fitting, for example: "the sticking together of the parts of a thing" (Ziporyn 2013, 43).

17. This phrase occurs several times in the *Hanfeizi*, *Hanshi waizhuan*, *Lienüzhuan* 列女傳, *Mengzi*, *Shiji*, and other sources.

18. Cf. "以義變應，知當曲直故也" (Xunzi 3.5.2) ("His use of his sense of what is morally right to change in response to every situation is because of knowledge that is precisely fitting for every occasion, whether curved or straight") (Knoblock 1, 175).

19. See G89, 11, 45, 111, 242, and 255. See also Lloyd (1996, 11).

20. Cf. Ames's (2011, 201–5) discussion of the *paronomastic* association of *yi* 義 with its near homophone 宜. According to Ames, both characters reflect "one's best judgment on how one might dispose oneself in one's relation to others in order to accomplish the recommended action, and confidence that what one is doing is appropriate in the circumstances"; the outcome of a "negotiation between self and the specific context that requires broadmindedness, flexibility, and accommodation" (203), grounded in a fiduciary community. Elsewhere Hall and Ames (1999, 34, 194) suggest that *yi* 義 should not be identified with "right" but with "appropriateness," or perhaps with "aesthetic rightness" or "production and appropriation of what is fitting."

21. *Liji* 2.312 (Legge 1961). Cf. "*Yi* [義] focuses principally on what is right or fitting" (Cua 2003, 76, 371, 842); "right [義] as the socially fitting" (G89, 495); "*yi* [義] as appropriateness according to the situation" (Wong 2014, 224).

22. Cf. various "gray" sources on the internet: "that which is righteous is fitting and proper"; "to be 'righteous' is to be 'fitting and proper'"; "what is fitting to the circumstances." Cf. Cicero's "propriety," which is what is fitting and agreeable to an occasion or person.

23. Chinese text from CTP; translation from Wang Huaiyu (2009, 326).

24. Karlgren (1974, 85) lists as meanings of *yi* 宜: ought, to order aright, proper, right, and fit, and as meanings of *yi* 義 (82): "right" sense, signification, just(ice), righteous(ness), good, common to all, and patriotic.

Chapter 7

1. Some of these issues we addressed for the Warring States Period in chapter 4. Here we focus on the *Zhuangzi*.

2. Cao Chuji (2000, 18n9) remarks that Wen Yiduo 聞一多 (1899–1946) suggested that the middle part should actually be read as: "to affirm (*shi*) what

one takes to be right in order to deny (*fei*) what one takes to be wrong [以是其所是，而非其所非]."

3. Also note that the 4th to the 5th clauses and the 6th to the 7th clauses are identical except for the first character: *yi* 以, have or believe, or *yu* 欲, desire.

4. Coutinho (2004, 154–55) disputes the usual translation of 2.3.5. He translates the end of 2.3.5 as "If you desire to affirm what is denied and deny what is affirmed, then nothing is as good as *ming* illumination" (2015, 184). Coutinho prefers "to give prominence to the literal contradictoriness of the text."

5. Reding's dissertation is in French (Reding 1985) and he wrote a contribution for the *Encyclopédie philosophique universelle*.

6. We consider the authors who publish only in English as part of the anglophone academic community. We refer to scholars as francophone if they publish in French, which is presumably their native language. They may also publish in English, but they participate primarily in the francophone academic community.

7. Levi: "Ainsi se développent les querelles entre . . . Les uns tiennent pour vrai [true] ce que les autres tiennent pour faux [false] et inversement. Plutôt que de défendre l'un ou l'autre de ces points de vue, le mieux est . . ."

8. According to the Larousse dictionary: *vrai*: true, real, natural, authentic, not fake, correct, fitting; *faux*: incorrect (wrong), false, forged–fake, imitation, and unjustified; *erreur*: mistake; *le vrai*: to be true–right; and in Dutch (van Dale): *waar*: passend, echt, werkelijk, and waarachtig; *vals*: onwaar, and onecht.

9. Levi's translations are rather similar to the earlier renditions by Lafitte.

10. "Les distinctions entre justice et charité, entre bien et mal ne font que semer le désordre et la confusion."

11. "Zoals ik het zie geldt dat ook voor de principes van medemenselijkheid en gerechtigheid zowel als voor de verschillen tussen goed en kwaad. Die zijn zo verschrikkelijk verward."

12. In addition: *juste* for *shi* and *ne pas être cela* for *fei*.

13. "Les Chinois ont bien manié le jugement disjonctif: 'c'est ceci'/'ce n'est pas ceci' (*shi/fei*: vrai ou faux, bien ou mal)" (Jullien 2008).

14. This seems to be the case in view of the entry in the *Grand Ricci*.

15. André Levy is the translator of the *Mengzi*. Jean Levi is the translator of *Les Œuvres de Maître Tchouang*.

16. "La conscience du bien et du mal est le début de la sagesse" (Levy).

17. "Du sentiment de la connaissance vient du bien et du mal, la conscience" (Levy). "Le sentiment du bien et du mal tout homme possède en son Coeur" (Wieger).

18. Sometimes Levy uses *vrai* or *vraiment* when English translators use "good" or "indeed" respectively (Mengzi, 1A6, 3A5, 3B8).

19. "Sans conscience du bien et du mal, on ne serait plus une créature humaine."

20. "'Richtig' und 'Falsch.' Die Antwort auf eine Ja/Nein-Frage . . . und weiterhin 'Recht' und 'Unrecht.'"

21. "Yes and no" as translations of *shifei* also occur in earlier French translations: "oui et non" (Wieger, Lafitte).

22. According to the Langenscheidt dictionary, *richtig* means: right, correct, true, real, genuine, proper, appropriate. *Falsch* means: wrong, untrue, false,

artificial, fake, insincere, inappropriate, and unreliable. According to the Wahrig dictionary, *richtig* means: so geartet, wie es sein soll, wie es sich gehört, genau, stimmend, passend, den Tatsachen entsprechend, zutreffend; regelrecht, fehlerfrei; echt, eigentlich, and wirklich.

23. According to the Langenscheidt dictionary, *recht* means: right(ly), proper, suitable, true, real, and good; *unrecht*: wrong, injustice, mistaken, inopportune, unsuitable, and inconvenient. *Recht* is more literary than *richtig*.

24. Cheng Xuanying's paraphrase of 2.2.2 is: "[This passage] means that the arising of their ideas and their chasing after (following up) the situation is as speedy as the edge of an arrow; and when they administer things and try to expel disaster, they are as fierce as a bow-machine. They are only fixated upon *shi* and *fei*, and do not concern themselves with anything else" (27). All of 2.2.2: "小恐惴惴，大恐縵縵。其發若機栝，其司是非之謂也；其留若詛盟，其守勝之謂也。[Their little fears are mean and trembly; their great fears are stunned and overwhelming. They bound off like an arrow or a crossbow pellet, certain that they are the arbiters of right and wrong. They cling to their position as though they had sworn before the gods, sure that they are holding on to victory]."

25. "Pestes comme la détente de l'arbalête pour approuver ou condamner."

26. This citation comes from Billeter's discussion (1998, 17).

27. Feng Youlan: idem; Legge: idem; Ziporyn idem; Schipper: "wat is juist en wat is niet." The Dutch word *juist* corresponds to the French word *juste* and approximates the German word *richtig*. But there is no appropriate equivalent in English, though it can be translated as right or correct.

28. Feng Youlan, Lin Yutang, and Mair all share the same exception in translating *shifei* as affirm/deny (instead of right/wrong), when *shifei* occurs in the story of the monkeys getting three in the morning and four in the evening or the reverse. French and German translations also have affirm/deny in this case. Reding (1985, 285–86) translates *shifei* in the monkey story as: "juger 'c'est ainsi' ou 'ce n'est pas ainsi.' " That is to say, Reding translates *shifei* as so/not-so, the common translation of *ranburan* in English.

29. Graham uses approve/reject in his translation of the *Liezi* (G60, 130, 139).

30. There is no exact correspondence between true, *wahr*, and *vrai* in English, German, and French. However, they are tied together by close family resemblances, and in Western philosophy they are usually stipulated to mean the same. For example, with respect to the work by Heidegger, the academic community has stipulated that *Sein* is *Being*, *Être*, and *cunzai* 存在 (or *cunyou* 存有). That is to say: the foreign-language expressions convey whatever Heidegger's *Sein* or *Seyn* means.

31. See, for example, Cao Chuji (2000), Chen Guying (2007), Si Lü (2013), Zhang Gengguang (1993). An exception is Qin Xuqing and Sun Yongchang (2003).

32. Such suggestions had already been made in the Chinese commentarial tradition.

33. For the part in square brackets, see §7g.

34. ". . . und nimmt" "Dies" als das, was es ist. "Dies" ist auch "Das." "Das" ist auch "Dies" (Schuhmacher).

35. "Tout 'ceci' est donc un 'cela,' tout 'cela' est un 'ceci.' "

36. All the translations we have consulted give similar translations to the binome 彼是 (that/this, Das/Dies, cela/ceci), except that Graham translates it as "Other/it."

37. *Ci* 此 means "this" and, by extension, "here" and "now."

38. Cf. "Without them (the feelings mentioned above) there would not be I" (Chan Wing-tsit). Chan comments that we cannot be sure whether *bi* 彼 refers to the emotions, the True Lord, or the Way (1969, 181n4).

39. Some translators clarify "this" (*shi*) in terms of "subjective" or "Subject" (Lin Yutang, Schuhmacher) or add clarification in parentheses: "Everything is 'that' (another thing's other); everything is 'this' (its own self)" (Feng Youlan).

40. French *recevable* can be translated as: acceptable, admissible, applicable.

41. Schipper does the same by translating *ke* as "correct" (*juist*) and *shi* as "yes" (*wel*). Cleary translates *kebuke* as "right and wrong" (and *shifei* as affirming/denying). These examples and other French translations suggest that the difference between *kebuke* and *shifei* is not as large as is suggested by anglophone translations.

42. "Tout dénomination juste est en même temps fausse et, réciproquement, toute dénomination fausse est en même temps juste. Si bien que toute qualification est à la fois juste et fausse et fausse et juste" (Levi 2.3.7).

43. Some scholars presume that in the *Canons*, the later Mohists were refuting Zhuangzi's view. We think that it is rather the other way around. We surmise that Zhuangzi was aware of the views expressed in the *Canons* and that he presented a highly sophisticated alternative. Zhuangzi rejects the Mohists' dogmatism by arguing that "this" and "that" produce each other. "This" is also a "that." "That" is also a "this" (Ziporyn 2.3.8). The Mohists stipulated repeatedly that "you can call 'that' what I call 'this,' but only if you also call 'this' what I call 'that'" (B82; cf. B68 and B72; G78, 447, 455–57).

44. Compare: "Simultaneous affirmability [*ke*] is simultaneous negatibility, and vice versa. What is circumstancely right is circumstancely wrong and vice versa" (Ziporyn); "Possibility arises from impossibility, and vice versa. Affirmation is based upon denial, and vice versa" (Lin Yutang).

45. "Quand il s'agit de discuter de ce qui est et de ce qui n'est pas, ou de décider si une chose est ainsi plutôt qu'autrement, en approuvant ce que l'autre approuve, il devient impossible de faire la distinction entre le vrai et le faux bien qu'ils soient distincts; en disant que cela est ainsi quand l'autre juge que c'est ainsi, il devient impossible de discerner entre ce qui est ainsi et ce qui ne l'est pas, même s'ils sont différents." (Levi 2.6.21)

46. Alt (2000, 7) notices that for unexplained reasons, Graham reverses the order of the English equivalents of *shibushi* and *ranburan*.

47. This citation is also a rare occasion where *feibufei* 非不非 occurs.

48. For justification of Graham's translation, see G82, 30.

49. Legge also distinguishes between the two, but in terms of affirming and asserting an opinion.

50. There are a few occurrences in the outer chapters. 17.4.1: "然不然，可不可 [and proved that not so was so, {made (to appear) true what is not true};

that the unacceptable was acceptable {made (to appear) acceptable what was not acceptable}]" (Watson; text in braces: Harbsmeier in TLS); 12.9.1: "可不可然不然 [is admissible or it is inadmissible; it is so, or it is not so]."

51. In the *Lüshi chunqiu*, there are parallel constructions of *shi–ke*, *ke–ran*, and other combinations that do not occur in the *Zhuangzi*. See 12.6.1.3 (*shifei kebuku* [是非可不可]), 16.8.1.1 (*kebuke er ranburan, shibushi er feibufei* [可不可而然不然, 是不是而非不非]), 3.5.2.7 (*kebuke shanbushan* [可不可善不善]). We found one occurrence in the *Xunzi*: 不卹是非然不然之情 (8.3.3, repeated in 23.18.3): "in being indifferent to the real nature [*qing* 情] of truth and falsity and the true nature of what is the case and what is not" (Knoblock 2:71). The last passage can be compared with what is said in the citation from Cheng Xuanying at the end of this section.

52. This parallel construction occurs almost in the same way in 27.1.6 (G81, 107). Perhaps 2.3.7 can be interpreted as a parallel construction involving *ke* and *shi*.

53. Cf. Schipper: "There is nothing that is not such or so, nothing that is not correct or incorrect." ("无物不然，无物不可 [Er is niets dat niet zus of zo is en niets dat niet juist of onjuist is].")

54. *Shifei*, *biwo*, and *hao'e* are contrasts or "opposites"; *zeng* and *xian* are near-synonyms. Each of the 8 mentioned notions arise from *qing* 情.

55. Our interpretation is echoed in Billeter's brief remark (concerning his translation of the first part of the *Qiwulun*) that in the contexts where *shifei* can be rendered as "the opposition of true and false," the phrase actually means "*all oppositions between contrary terms that are inscribed in language*" (1998, 4n10; emphasis added; cf. 20). He does not specify which oppositions are of the "*shifei* type." Cf. Wang Youru (2003, 37): "life and death, big and small, fullness and emptiness, usefulness and uselessness, completion and destruction, and so on. All these pairs can be put under the category of 'this' and 'that,' namely, one thing and its other."

56. A few clauses down, Zhuangzi repeats the last clause of the citation (5.6.8). Kjellberg translates 好惡 as "good and bad" (5.6.6) on the first occurrence and "likes and dislikes" (5.6.8) on the second (followed by Van Norden 2011, 155), perhaps distinguishing *hao'e* (good/bad) and *haowu* (like/dislike), both written as 好惡.

57. "Diese Leidenschaften ist es nicht, die ich meine" (Wilhelm).

58. Waley adds a note saying: "The '—less' has dropped out of the original" (Waley 1939, 20).

59. "Wat jij hier noemt is niet wat ik onder 'gevoelens' versta" (Schipper).

60. Cf. Eifring (2004, 15).

61. "J'appelle 'sentiments' la faculté de juger" (Levi).

62. "Juger 'c'est ainsi' ou 'ce n'est pas ainsi,' voilà ce que j'appelle 'être essentiellement homme'" (Reding).

63. Hui Shi would presumably agree with Mengzi, who says explicitly that the one without *shifei* is not a human being: "Not to have a mind which calls things right and wrong is not human" (2A6, Pulleybank 1995, 86).

64. Although 5.5.5 may be more like an "objective" observation and 5.6.6 more like a "subjective" principle.

65. As already mentioned, 好惡 is said to be *hao'e* or *haowu* ("good and evil" or "love and hate" [like/dislike, preferences and aversions]). In both cases it is different from *shifei* (Fraser 2011, 103–4).

66. Also missing in the inner chapters are the binomes *bici* 彼此, *bufei* 不非, *cibi* 此彼, *ranfou* 然否, *shixu* 實虛, *shibi* 是彼, *xushi* 虛實.

67. Perhaps *xin* 信 differs from other modifiers: 大信稽之 (24.15.3; G81, 60): "great Trust" (Watson); "ultimately truthful" (Graham), "Great Dependable" (Ziporyn). Concerning a sage (7.1.2): "其知情信" ("His understanding was truly trustworthy") (Watson). ("His knowledge was real and untroubled by doubts") (Legge).

68. *Zheng* has been translated as: true or truth, right, real, correct, straight(en), aligned with, standard, proper, control. Ziporyn (2009a, 5n10, 218–19) says that in chapters 1 and 2 of the *Zhuangzi*, *zheng* is aligned with "true." To include "decide" among the translations of *zheng*, as Watson does in his translation of 2.6.18–19, may not be the best choice. Ziporyn translates *zheng* in this context as "straighten it out"; other translators choose "judge" as an alternative to "decide."

69. Feng Youlan renders *zhenwei* as "truth and error" (Feng 1947, 65).

70. Eno (1996, 133) is a rare English-language publication in which one finds *shifei* translated as true/false: "How do spoken words come to be obscured, such that they are subject to judgments of 'true' [*shi*] or 'false' [*fei*]'" (2.3.4). This bears similarity with Lü Huiqing's (呂惠卿; 1032–1111) comment (cited in Ziporyn 2009a, 145): "The Course is everywhere, so all words are the Course. How could the Course be so obscured that some words are true [*zhen*] and others are false [*wei*]? All things are the Course, so words are also the Course. How could words be so obscured that some words are right [*shi*] and others wrong [*fei*]?" It is interesting to note that Lü Huiqing considers that *zhenwei* applies to words.

71. This is the only occasion where Schuhmacher (perhaps following Wilhelm) translates *shifei* as "Recht" and "Unrecht," the words with explicit moral meanings; Mair has the usual "right and wrong." Wilhelm uses *Recht/Unrecht* more often than later translators; he also uses *Bejahung* and *Verneinung* (saying yes and saying no) but not *richtig* and *falsch*.

72. Guo Xiang (2011, 33), Cheng Xuanying (2011, 33). Note that Cheng substitutes *zhenfei* for *zhenwei*.

73. *Dao* is often associated with true/false, but also with right/wrong. "道者，萬物之始，是非之紀也" (*Hanfeizi* 5.1.1). "As for the Way, it is the beginning of the myriad things and the Guideline of right and wrong." Cf. Fraser (2012, 366): "the early Moists subsumed what we think of as questions of truth or falsity within the broader rubric of the proper *dao*."

74. *Huwen xianyi* 互文見義 or "interdependence" refers to homologous phrases that mutually support one another, which thus creates a hybrid to which both phrases contribute (homologous means the same grammatical environment).

75. In his translation of the *Lunheng*, Forke translated *zhenwei* as "truth and untruth" (1, 253); or "truth and falsehood" (1, 85).

76. In his notes to G81, Graham translates 是亦因彼……因是因非……亦因是也 as: "'It' likewise goes by 'Other' . . . If going by something else you affirm (judge

to be 'it') then going by something else you deny . . . This too is to affirm going by something else" (G82, 14–15). In changing the earlier translation (of adaptive and contrived *shi*), Graham has been influenced by his work on the *Canons*.

77. According to Billeter, *yin* in the sense of "according to the circumstances" should be understood as "embracing change." The *Grand Ricci* specifies *yin* as: following nature, based on reality (*suivre la nature; se fonder sur la réalité*).

78. In other sources (*Hanfeizi, Linjilu, Liezi, Mojing, Xunzi,* and *Zhanguoce*), *weishi* 為是 is rendered as: so, this, right, correct; for example, Xunzi (16.4.2): "treat right as right [是為是]."

79. *Yishi* 移是 occurs in 23.7.4–6. Ziporyn follows Graham: "The definition of what is right adopts the shifting rightness of 'this.'"

80. Translations of *yin'er* 因而 differ: follow, according, accede to circumstances; thereupon; therefore; on the basis of this, then (Harbsmeier in TLS); that is why, consequently (Ricci: *C'est pourquoi; en conséquence; par consequent*); rely on, accordingly (Rickett); CTP: take action accordingly.

81. Translations of *yinxun* 因循 (in the *Huainanzi*) do not differ much. The *Grand Ricci* translates: "to conform (for example, to circumstances when governing)." *Se conformer* (*p. ex.: aux circonstances pour gouverner*).

82. Graham remarked: "Sinologists have to make up their minds about the present hypothesis from the handling of the ten examples in the present translation." (G69, 143). But most translators have either followed Graham without giving any reason or, more often, provided their own translations without explaining why they are *not* following Graham.

83. Wu Kuang-ming (1990, 232–34) does not agree that *yinshi* can be considered as a technical term with a specific meaning.

84. It remains an option to separate *yin* and *shi*, treating *shi* as a demonstrative, and yin as "to rely on."

85. The distinction is not always clearly made. For example, "whichever *dao* proves to be the most efficacious for a given situation" (Williams 2017a, 183). Is it assumed that there are different *daos*, but only one unique *dao* for each unique situation?

86. Cf. "Good and bad depend not on fixed standards but on particular circumstances" (G89, 207).

87. Depending on whether one assumes that all sages act, feel, and so on, in the same way or not, there could arise either a universalistic or a pluralistic perspective.

88. Indirectly this issue is also addressed in §10a in terms of the question of whether the views of Ruists and Mohists are incommensurable. We think that the universalism/relativism seesaw is a non-issue in the sense that, *intrinsically*, Chinese and comparative philosophy cannot be completely exempted from *both* "universalistic" *and* "relativistic" features.

89. Zhong Tai 钟泰 (2008, 47) claims, if "one is imprisoned in [such distinctions as] *wu* 物 and *wo* 我 and [disputations concerning] *shi* and *fei*, then this would harm *dao* 道."

90. An example from other chapters is 6.8.2: "Yao has already tattooed you with benevolence and righteousness and cut off your nose with right and wrong [夫堯既已黥汝以仁義，而劓汝以是非矣]."

91. Translations of 2.6.12 differ widely.

92. See Harbsmeier (1992, 81, translating Lin Yunming's comment): "being 'this' also is what it is on the basis of 'that' [是亦因彼而然耳]."

93. "Tout 'cela' naît du 'ceci' et que tout 'ceci' suppose un 'cela.' De là découle la théorie de l'engendrement réciproque du 'ceci' et du 'cela'" (Levi).

94. "De redenering van het wederzijds voortbrengen van complementaire tegengestelden" (Schipper).

95. Hence it is said: "That comes out form this, this likewise goes by that, the opinion that 'it' and 'other' are born simultaneously" (G89, 179).

96. Cheng Xuanying: "彼此是非相因而有 'that' and 'this,' 'right' and 'wrong' come into existence on the basis of each other" (cited and translated in Harbsmeier 1992, 81).

97. Mair chooses "derives from" to translate *chu*. Billeter chooses "derives from" to translate *yin*.

98. An alternative way of reading the text (which is not considered by Graham) is to say that 是亦因彼 refers to a sage and 彼出於是 to commoners.

99. B could be said to *underlie* A.

100. It may be a case of *huwen xianyi* 互文見義.

101. In different sources, one finds a whole range of possible translations of *wei* 為: do or make, for the sake of (perhaps most common), do or consider what is right/correct, counts as, satisfy a condition of being deemed X, "do" in the strong sense of "to accomplish an act," "to posit something."

102. Translations of the occurrence of *weishi* in 2.4.3, 2.4.4, and 2.5.6 are rather similar; 2.4.3: thus, therefore, for this reason, so let's take, hence; 2.4.4: therefore, because of, for this reason, so, this being the case; 2.5.6: because of, hence, this being the case, for this reason.

103. See also §7b for discussion of the context of 2.3.7.

104. Cf. Ziporyn's translation of Liu Xianxin 劉咸炘 (1896–1932): "Going by the rightness of the present 'this' means following along with each one, affirming it as right. What is eliminated is only the tendency for self and other to negate and criticize each other" (2009a, 146).

105. Some have wondered whether it is not odd for a daoist text to read *yi* 已 as "stop." Others have argued that *yi* 已 is only added for tone.

106. Chan 2.4.5: "This is to let it (Nature) take its own course." Alternative translations (Chan, 184n24): "he stops with this" and "this is because he relies on this (that is, Tao)." And the next phrase: "He has arrived at this situation." Another translation (Chan 184n25): "He has stopped."

107. This passage contains the only occurrence of *yinfei* 因非 in the *Zhuangzi*.

108. "Toute qualification est à la fois juste et fausse et fausse et juste" (Levi).

109. Schumacher: "'Dies' und 'Das' sind voneinander abhängig; Richtig und Falsch sind ebenfalls voneinander abhängig."

110. "Omdat er een 'wel' is is er ook een 'niet,' en tegenover het 'niet' staat altijd weer een 'wel'" (Schipper).

111. Could this be Zhuangzi's intention? (cf. §9d). Wu Kuang-ming gives the following "literal" translation: "As following-on *yes*, so following-on *no*; as following-on *no*, so following-on *yes*. With this holy man not by and illuminates them from heaven. Also following-on (*this-*) *yes*."

Chapter 8

1. See contributions in Kjellberg and Ivanhoe (1996), two contributions by Coutinho and Liu Xiaogan in the *Dao Companion to Daoist Philosophy* (Liu Xiaogan 2015a), Kjellberg (2007), and Allinson (2015).

2. The situation with skepticism is somewhat better, but not much. Scholars distinguish between epistemological, methodological, therapeutic, and rhetorical skepticism. See §8d.

3. In Ma Lin and van Brakel (2016a, chapter 3), we present an extensive discussion of "universalism and relativism."

4. The passages Liu Xiaogan cites are mainly from the *Qiwulun*, and also from chapter 5, including 2.3.6–7, 2.4.2–4, 2.6.2–6, and 5.1.1–5. Other passages that have been cited in support of ascribing relativism to Zhuangzi include: 2.1.7, 2.3.5, and 2.6.17–18. Hansen (1983b) argues at length that all these passages in context support a relativistic stance. He points out that the character *dao* occurs thirteen times in the *Qiwulun*, among which eleven times "the claim about taos is introduced, followed, or explained by a claim about *yan*/words: language, *wei*/call: say, or the paradigmatic linguistic distinctions *shi-fei*" (37).

5. 2.4.2: *dao tong wei yi* 道通為一.

6. See §§A4–6 for a brief exposition of these notions.

7. Liu Xiaogan suggests that the passages he cites can be considered as "a critical and necessary technical stage from which to advance toward detachment from the earthly world and achieve spiritual freedom, or carefree wandering" (2015b, 210).

8. But as we can see below (§8d), contemporary relativistic interpretations are actually more nuanced. Confer Feng Youlan's phrase "equally natural, equally good," and Hansen's modification to: "all are equally 'right'—at least equally 'natural'" (Hansen 1983b, 39).

9. We specify *zhi* in this way because we consider that *zhi* is first of all a matter of understanding.

10. The expressions closest in meaning to perspective are: *jian* 見 (literally "view" and hence opinion or doctrine) and *suo* 所 (literally "place" and hence "standpoint"). There are numerous other characters to which the English word "perspective" has been added in translation, including broad (*bo* 博), good (*xian* 賢), limited (*ju* 拘), narrow (*xia* 狹), fair (*shu* 恕), and distant (*yuan* 遠).

11. Of necessity, all the natural languages contain paradoxes (Tarski 1931), such as the paradox of the liar. Hence, universalism would always be inherently "self-refuting," unless one is prepared to eradicate all the natural languages.

12. Literally, "incommensurability" means "cannot be measured on the same scale." See Ma Lin and van Brakel (2016a, 49–51, 68–72, and 152–55).

13. See Ma Lin and van Brakel (2016a, 135–39).

14. See Ma Lin and van Brakel (2015, 482–83).

15. "Counter-intuitive" is a typical term from analytic philosophy. It actually means: being counter-intuitive as sensed by scholars educated in anglophone philosophical academic circles. Hence, what is considered "counter-intuitive" is nothing universal.

16. Wong's model assumes that different traditions rank supposedly shared (universal) moral values in different manners. For example, the value of community and the value of individuality are both universal values, but they are ranked differently in different traditions. Different moralities "are simply different prioritizations of the same universe of values" (Xiao Yang and Huang Yong 2014, 17). Thus, the difference between the Ruists and the Mohists is a matter of "weighing" (setting different priorities) *given* shared "real values" (Wong 2006, 234).

17. The "problem of the criterion" refers to an argument to the effect that we are unable to justify any of our beliefs. It was first raised by Sextus Empiricus.

18. Putnam (1981, 1987) has argued at length for this distinction.

19. Many authors warning against relativism may not be aware that some of the most important discoveries in modern physics concern relativities. For example, motion and the mass of an object is "relative to a variable frame of reference" (Boghossian: 13). However, in contrast with the relativities physics deals with, it is not easy to come up "with a satisfactory characterization of the 'standards' to which moral or epistemic judgments are to be relativized" (37). It is not even clear whether it is the same notion of "being relative to . . ." as that in physics.

20. Consider, for example, one *chi* 尺 is about 23 cm. One *ren* 仞 is about eight *chi*.

21. The distinction between "natural" and "conventional" features of Chinese characters raises more complicated issues.

22. The SP was defended in the 1980s by, for example, Barnes and Bloor (1982), as well as Hesse (1980).

23. SP-ers also study the so-called pseudoscience, such as parapsychology, and claim there is no principled difference between science and pseudoscience.

24. An example is Coutinho (2015).

25. In the conclusion of (1983b, 51), Hansen classifies Zhuangzi as a relativist and a skeptic.

26. Hansen's critical concern, which is directed at the tradition that considers Zhuangzi as a mystical monist, is perhaps more important than his positive interpretation in terms of increasingly elaborate versions of relativism and skepticism.

27. Graham also speaks of "the relativism of 'The sorting which evens things out'" (G81, 25).

28. For Graham's own view in this respect, see Graham (1985).

29. A list of these passages was given at the beginning of this chapter.

30. As Graham points out (G69, 141), by the time of Xunzi, conventionalism concerning language has been generally accepted: 約定俗成謂之宜 (22.2.8). "The agreement becomes fixed, the custom is established, and it is called 'appropriate' [宜]" (Knoblock 3, 130).

31. Like other passages involving *shifei*, this passage also brings out the disagreement between different translators. As to *shi* in the phrase "publicly accepted *shi*," Watson translates it as "right," Graham translates it as either "it" (in "That's it") or "this" (in "It's this"), Reding (1985) translates it as *c'est ainsi*. Many translations of *c'est ainsi* are possible, for example: "so that's it," "this is," "it is," "this is so," and "this is how."

32. Reding characterizes it as the *impossibility* of debate (1985, 286; "l'impossibilité du débat"), citing (in his translation) 24.5.3 (G81, 101): "S'il n'y a pas de 'c'est ainsi' commun à tous dans le monde et si chacun considère son 'c'est ainsi' comme le seul vrai . . ."

33. That is to say: conventions are presupposed in addition to a shared ordinary language with "unfixed" meanings.

34. Peterman (2008, 373): "If we hold that we do not know anything, then we must hold that we do not know that we do not know anything."

35. According to Ivanhoe (1993), Zhuangzi's therapeutic proposals are meant to undermine our confidence in proposals. This "in no way threatens his belief in an intuitive, ineffable sense of or knack for the Dao" (649). Therefore, he is neither a skeptic nor a relativist.

36. Sextus Empiricus (1976, 201 [79]); see a similar translation in Mates (1996).

37. In using the word deconstruction, we follow Ames's "deconstruction of polar opposites" (1998, 3) and Wang Youru's idea that "deconstruction of self or self-identity is the core of Zhuangzi's deconstruction of all linguistic-conceptual hierarchies" (2003, 44). Sometimes, deconstruction is associated with postmodernism. However, as Wang Youru points out, Zhuangzi "would probably criticize the latter's view as one-sided, namely, as privileging many over one" (64, 51).

38. *Zhi* 知 in classical Chinese has been translated as: knowledge, know it, know what is going on, be sure of, know all about (it), know the identity of; know oneself; know that, know of, know about, know whether; be known. Translators render *zhi* in the inner chapters about 60 percent as knowing and about 30 percent as understanding. Other translations include wisdom and vision. 故夫知效一官 (1.1.11): "Therefore a man who has wisdom enough to fill one office effectively." 唯達者知通為一 (2.4.4): "Only the man of far-reaching vision knows how to make them into one." Recently it has been suggested that translating *zhi* as realize may be better.

39. Hansen (2015) remarks: "Stories of surprises, gestalt shifts and dreams all play a skeptical role." Exposure to the unexpected may be therapeutic or may widen one's views, so why call it skepticism?

40. Chang Tzu-li (2016) adds that *zhi* also means: the ability to judge right and wrong, to judge what one ought to do and what one ought not to do. Cf. Mengzi's four sprouts.

41. Cf. Hansen (2015): "The text naturally implies that we are to learn (come to know) something from these stories. This knowing about knowing is valuable. Ignoring it would be bad *from many, if not all, points of view*" (emphasis original).

42. Some scholars have associated *dazhi* with *zhenren* 真人 (true person) in chapter 6 of the *Zhuangzi*.

43. We assume that *dazhi* is knowledge/*zhi* in the sense that it is (like *zhi*) subject to "fitting experience" and "fitting (or opposing) earlier knowing" (about *dao*). See Ma Lin and van Brakel (2016a, 117–19).

44. As Sturgeon points out (2014, 156), Zhuangzi does not promote "epistemological nihilism." He "can offer wide-ranging practical advice on how to improve our own epistemic situation, while at the same time warning us of the ultimate limits of what we can come to know." That is to say, he is skeptical about our ability to know a privileged class of ultimately correct ways of drawing distinctions (*guoshi* 果是 and *guofei* 果非), but he does not question our ability to know how to distinguish things in an ordinary situation.

45. There are many passages where translating *zhi* as either knowing or understanding would make a difference. Consider 2.5.9: "Therefore understanding that rests in what it does not understand is the finest [故知止其所不知，至矣]."

46. Translations of *wuzhi* include: without knowledge, know nothing, lacking awareness.

47. Cf. 聞以有知知者矣，未聞以无知知者也 (4.1.32) ("You have heard of the knowledge that knows, but you have never heard of the knowledge that does not know"). See also 2.6.2 and 7.2.3.

48. This phrase can also be found in the *Guanzi*, *Lüshi chunqiu*, and *Shangjunshu* 商君書. The passage 1.1.6 concerns the observation that the short-lived cannot come up to the long-lived (and it is the same case with *dazhi* and *xiaozhi*); cf. §A2.

49. In support of ascribing relativism to Zhuangzi, 2.6.4–5 have been cited; in support of skepticism, 2.6.2–3 have been cited. The beginning of 2.6.2 is repeated in 7.1.1: "Four times he asked a question and four times Wang Ni said he didn't know [四問而四不知]."

50. TLS comments concerning 2.6.2 that these questions are rhetorical; they are aimed at emphatically affirming the assumed answers; concerning 2.6.4/5, TLS remarks that it is a "way of expressing something by playfully creating an appearance of claiming its opposite, typically assuming one's playfulness to be understood by the intended audience."

51. "The question 'how do I know that knowing is not ignorance' is not answerable" (G89, 182).

52. Wang Fuzhi 王夫之 (1619–1692) points out that Zhuangzi may refute his main point in advance "lest it become something fully formed" or "to show that it is not to be taken as any one definite theory" (cited by Ziporyn 2009a, 153).

53. Fraser remarks: "Wang Ni must accept the implicit premise that the diverse practices he cites all meet some minimal standard of justification or qualify for some form of equal consideration" (2009, 439).

54. For a different interpretation, see Kwok Sai Hang (2016).

55. According to modern discourse, these distinctions between animals and humans are self-evident. We assume that the examples can also be read as either concerning *only* different animals or concerning *only* different groups of humans.

56. Moreover, humans and monkeys or apes can be "in agreement" about what is the best place to sleep (for humans and monkeys, respectively). They can even agree that some apes and some humans sleep on the ground and in trees, respectively.

Chapter 9

1. An exception is Wong's (2005, 102) saying that interrogative skepticism "embodies a stance, not a set of claims," a stance is "not a set of conclusions or beliefs." According to Wong, it is mistaken to read the text as containing some final doctrines. The text is an *enactment* of the skeptical virtue (of the Zhuangzian *dao*).

2. An example is Ni Peimin (2016, 139): "Conflicting truth claims about metaphysical facts cannot all be true, but competing visions of excellence may co-exist like different styles of art."

3. The *Oxford Thesaurus* lists the following cluster of notions that share some family resemblances with attitude: view, viewpoint, outlook, perspective, stance, standpoint, position, inclination, orientation, approach, reaction; opinion, idea, conviction, feeling, and thinking; in brief: a settled way of thinking and/or feeling

4. Whether the reader agrees with ascribing these attitudes to Zhuangzi or not is not relevant. All the statements used in the examples can be negated and still express an attitude or stance.

5. Metaphorical use of language undermines the conventional distinction between the logical and the paradoxical.

6. See van Fraassen (2002, 47–49, 62–64, 141–43; 2004).

7. Assuming that transformations (*wuhua* 物化) are exceptional.

8. Notwithstanding Zhuangzi's often negative remarks concerning (small) knowledge, he knows the literature of his time on a wide range of subjects.

9. Cf. Wu Kuang-ming (1990, 231).

10. Cf. "而未知吾所謂之其果有謂乎，其果无謂乎" (2.5.3): "But I don't know whether what I have said has really said something or whether it hasn't said something."] "夫道未始有封，言未始有常" (2.5.6): "The Way has never known boundaries; speech has no constancy" (cf. the opening line of the *Daodejing*). Schipper translates the first clause of 2.5.6 as: "As yet the *Dao* has never been defined [De Tao is nog nimmer gedefinieerd]."

11. For an elaborate defense of this point, see Wang Youru (2003, 97–102 and passim). According to this author, Zhuangzi eschews any reifying appropriation of *dao* and maintains the prescriptive and pragmatic character of his *dao* (80; cf. 48). Zhuangzi is against the disputatious use of language, not against language *per se*.

12. According to Shi Deqing 釋德清 (1546–1623), words that are without any deliberate or fixed position are the words of the sage (cited in Ziporyn 2009a, 139).

13. Lin Shuen-fu defines *zhiyan* 卮言 as: "speech that is natural, unpremeditated, free from pre-conceived values, always responding to the changing situations in the flow of discourse, and always returning the mind to its original state of emptiness as soon as a speech act is completed (cited in Chong Kim-chong 2006, 376). As Chong points out, Zhuangzi's stance is closely connected to his use of *zhiyan*. *Zhiyan* is often translated as "goblet words" (Chong Kim-chong 2006, Griffith 2017, Wang Youru 2004, Møllgaard 2014) and considered to be the most important and most characteristic type of language in the *Zhuangzi*. Graham calls them "spill-over" saying, "a fluid language which keeps its equilibrium through changing meanings and viewpoints" (G81, 107). Imputed words or sayings from a lodging place, *yuyan*, is taking the standpoint of the other party in the debate and arguing from it (*argumentum ad hominem*). Weighted saying, *chongyan*, has the weight of the speaker's experience behind it (cf. G82, 31).

14. Lloyd (2002, 120) argues that Zhuangzi's *yuyan*, *zhiyan*, and *chongyan* refer to different degrees of semantic stretch. These sayings do not privilege the literal, not even in a specific context. Lloyd's notion of semantic stretch is somewhat similar to our idea of extension of family-resemblance-concepts.

15. See Billeter, Feng Youlan, Graham, Watson, Mair, Ziporyn, and Lin Yutang.

16. Translations of *weiding* include: unfixed, undecided, not fixed, uncertain, unsettled, not (yet) sure or secure, never certain, not yet established, underdetermined, undetermined, and lastly: not definite.

17. We would say that the passage "prepares" the criticism of the *shifei* debates, separating it from the later discussion concerning this and that (2.3.7–8). Eno combines 2.3.3–5 into one paragraph.

18. Guo Xiang, as cited in Ziporyn (2009a, 144). Guo's "self and other" probably refers back to 2.2.4.

19. Our interpretation has been influenced by our comparison of Zhuangzi and the later Wittgenstein.

20. Cf. on indeterminacy Ma Lin and van Brakel (2016a, 255–57).

21. "We do indeed have the feeling that we are talking of realities that exist outside of language, but are obliged to recognize that since the form of these realities is determined by the form of our language, they are in themselves undetermined. This is the starting-point" (Billeter 1998, 21).

22. See Malinowski (1935, 9) and (1923, 307). See also Voloshinov (1930, 95).

23. Coutinho writes: "The boundaries between affirmation and denial, the distinction between what is so and what is not, are not clearly and sharply determined" (2015, 186).

24. Cf. Ma Lin and van Brakel (2016a, chapter 4).

25. Cf. Wang Youru (2003, 35), who remarks that Zhuangzi uses reason to show that there is no fixed reason.

26. Graham writes: "we should avoid contradiction by refusing to make this distinction" (G69, 141). This passage does not occur in Graham's later work.

27. Alt points out that Eno, Loy, Yearly, and Coyle follow Graham in considering that *shifei* has a wider scope than morally right/wrong.

28. See §7b for a discussion of a longer passage from 2.3.7.

29. Compare: "to put two contraries into opposition is to lose sight of something" (Billeter 1998, 30).

30. See Graham's comments on canons A50 and A88 (G78, 299, 341).

31. Paraconsistent logic rejects $\neg(p \wedge \neg p)$, that is to say, it denies the validity of the law of non-contradiction (Priest 1995). That a contradiction might be true seems to be a threatening idea. However, the truth (and falsity) conditions of, for example, negation and conjunction, work just as one would expect them to work; $\neg \alpha$ is true if and only if α is false; and vice versa. Similarly, $\alpha \wedge \beta$ is true if and only if both conjuncts are true, and false if at least one conjunct is false. Further, if α is both true and false, so is $\neg \alpha$, and so is $\alpha \wedge \neg \alpha$. Hence, a contradiction can be true (though false as well).

32. *Yiming* is a common phrase in classical Chinese. It has been translated in a variety of ways. Watson translates *ming* 明 as clarity (2.3.5, 2.3.8, 2.4.9–11, 6.8.1), bright (5.2.3, 6.4.6), enlightened (7.4.1–3). Ziporyn (2009a, 217–18) emphasizes that the binome *yiming* does not refer to the transcendental but to attentiveness to the surface. In the latter sense, it is related to the Heavenly Reservoir (*tianfu* 天府) and the Shadowy Splendor (*baoguang* 葆光) in 2.5.10 and to the Radiance of Drift and Doubt (*guyi zhiyao* 滑疑之耀) in 2.4.11.

33. According to Graham, *tianjun* and *tianni* are the same (G81, 107; 27.1.7). Cf. §A5.

34. We borrow the phrase *xiashi* 下士 from Zhang Taiyan (cf. §9e). It does not occur in the inner chapters, but Zhuangzi uses *xia* 下 (and *shang* 上) to refer to inferior (and superior), provided that it fits the context; see, for example, 4.1.13: 以下拂其上者也 "used their positions as ministers to oppose their superiors."

35. Perhaps the remarks in the inner chapters regarding the various sages are not wholly consistent. We exclude those characterizations that could not be taken as a role model for humans (see §A4). Our discussion mainly concerns a sage who walks two roads.

36. The idea of walking-two-roads also exists in the Western tradition. For example, see Heraclitus fragment 102: "To god all things are beautiful and good and just, but men have thought that some things are unjust, others just" (cited in Lloyd 2005, 117).

37. Guo Xiang claims that the controversy concerning *wu* and *wo* is already raised by Ziqi 子綦 in 2.1.2 ("Now I have lost myself" 今者吾喪我).

38. Or perhaps already in 2.4.4 when *yong* 庸 is first mentioned.

39. Watson: "The monkeys were all delighted. There was no change in the reality behind the words, and yet the monkeys responded with joy and anger. Let them, if they want to [眾狙皆悅。名實未虧，而喜怒為用，亦因是也]" (2.4.6). Schipper translates this occurrence of *shi* and *fei* as so and not so (*zo en niet zo*).

40. See the translations of Chan Wing-tsit, Eno, Feng Youlan, Graham, Harbsmeier, Liu Xiaogan, Lin Yutang, Mair, Muller, and Wu Kuang-ming. Cleary: "double efficiency" [sic]! Schipper's translation is somewhat different: "to see the matter from two sides [*de zaak van twee kanten zien*]."

41. For example, Legge: "His two proposals were substantially the same, but the result of the one was to make the creatures angry, and of the other to make them pleased—an illustration of the point I am insisting on. Therefore, the sagely man brings together a dispute in its affirmations and denials, and rests in the equal fashioning of Heaven. Both sides of the question are admissible." Wilhelm provides a similar translation.

42. Taking the position on the *daoshu* could be considered as a stance without a point of view, where *shi* and *fei* are no longer dependent on one another. Cf. Luo Miandao 羅勉道: "This is called right and wrong both proceeding and not being in contradiction with each other" (cited and translated in Harbsmeier 1992, 105).

43. See translations of Billeter, Chan Wing-tsit, Feng Youlan, Graham, Harbsmeier, Legge, Lin Yutang, Mair, Kjellberg, Watson, and Ziporyn.

44. From a Zhuangzian stance, the "position" on the *daoshu* is not a *perspective*. To put it in contemporary terms, one could say that it is a lateral stance (Merleau-Ponty 1964, 120, 139).

45. Following Cheng Xuanying (2011, 42).

46. *Yong* 庸 has been translated as the constant (Watson), lodging places in the usual (Graham), the common (Feng Youlan, Lin Yutang), the everyday function of each thing (Ziporyn), the ordinary (Legge, Fraser 2015; Peterman 2008, 372), ordinary practice (Eno 1996, 133–36), the customary (Harbsmeier), the commonplace (Muller), and "ordinary" daily life (Wu Kuang-ming 1990, 199). In other sources, *yong* has been translated as perfectly ordinary, usual, common, and also as mediocre, unremarkable. Fraser (2015, 11) says that, according to an ancient annotation incorporated into the text, "the ordinary" refers to "pragmatic efficacy in pursuing the values at play in some context."

47. On the basis of the parsing: 庸也者，用也 (2.4.4), *yong* 庸 may just mean *yong* 用 (use[ful]?).

48. According to some interpreters, Zhuangzi's suggestion that the sage following the torch of chaos and doubt may be the expression of a preference for confusion, disorder, and anarchy instead of (perfect) harmony. That is to say, when Zhuangzi uses the notion of *he* 和 (harmony) in 2.4.6, this may have to be understood as subject to the principle of chaos and doubt. Hence, "(perfect) harmony" may not be the best translation of *he* (in the case of the *Zhuangzi*). Cf. Coutinho's (2004, 159n) suggestion that "perhaps, with polytonality and dissonance we rediscover more ancient possibilities of harmonization."

49. "Le saint se méfie de tout éclat louche et trouble."

50. Perhaps Zhao Yifu 趙以夫 (1189–1256) may have given a positive reading. Ziporyn translates him as saying: "It is from drifting chaos and doubt-wracked confusion that the illumination emerges. This alone is esteemed by the sage" (2009a, 151).

51. Original: "所以，迷乱人心的炫耀是圣人所要摒弃的。所以，圣人不用个人的才技辩说夸示于人，而是寄寓在事物的自然规律中，这就叫做"以明" (Si Lü 2013: 22).

52. Cited in Chen Guying (2007, 86).

53. Translation problems (also into modern Chinese) are aggravated because of uncertainties concerning the meaning of a number of characters. For example, *gu* 滑

has been rendered as confusion, disturbance, disorder, slippery, chaos. . . . According to Cao Chuji (23n16), *guyi* 滑疑 means glib or good at speaking and arguing; it can confuse people concerning *shifei* and concerning sameness and difference.

54. The uses of *yi* 宜 as "appropriateness in the light of circumstances" can perhaps be understood as pointing to *yong*. Cf. citations in §6b from *Liji* 10.1/7 and *Shiji* 6.58.8, 97.10.7. Cf. ZH 6.1.8: 與物有宜而莫知其極. "He goes along with what is right for things and no one knows his limit."

55. Bradley mentions more unusual examples of walking-two-roads (2015, 66, 12, 16), for example, using words to undermine words, and embracing the equality *and* inequality of all things.

56. Cf. Guo Xiang (2011, 132) and Cheng Xuanying (2011, 132). See also Cheng Xuanying (42): "The sages are those whose virtue is integral with heaven and earth [*tiandi* 天地], whose illumination is as even as the sun and the moon."

57. According to Lin Xiyi, "right and wrong only appear as a result of 'self' versus 'other'" (Ziporyn 2009a, 147). Probably Lü Huiqing is correct in saying that self/other and right/wrong should be discarded together (Ziporyn 2009a, 155).

58. In our reading of 6.1.2, this is Zhuangzi's "normal" doubt (see §9d); 23.10.1 is more extreme.

59. "De allerhoogste mens heeft lak aan de hemel in het algemeen, en lak aan de hemel van de mensen in het bijzonder."

60. Graham remarks that *tian/ren* is "the last and most obstinate dichotomy" in the *Zhuangzi* (G81, 106).

61. "It may have been his intent to provoke uncertainty about uncertainty and skepticism about skepticism" (Kjellberg 2007, 281).

62. For detailed analyses of Zhuangzi's (alleged) skepticism (or relativism) in comparison with Western thinkers and assessments of the story of Cook Ding, see Kjellberg and Ivanhoe (1996), in particular contributions by Eno, Ivanhoe, Kjellberg, Raphals, and Schwitzgebel. Different authors reach different conclusions. However, there seems to be near-consensus that Zhuangzi does not present skeptical *arguments* or *recommendations*.

63. *Zheng* 徵 resists easy translation. Translations for (*bu*)*ping* (不)平 and (*bu*)*zheng* (不)徵 include: (un)even and (not) verified (Mair), (un)even and (un)certain (Legge), (un)even and (not) right (Giles), (un)planned and (un)proven (Wieger and Levi), (un)fair and proof(less) (Watson).

64. Therefore, we do not know which Chinese character leads to the English word doubt in Graham's translation. The character *yi* 疑, often translated as doubt, is quite common in classical Chinese texts, but it occurs only once in the inner chapters in the phrase "torch of chaos and doubt" (in 2.4.11: 是故滑疑之耀). A more common character for "chaos" is *luan* 亂. It occurs in 2.6.6 and is usually translated, in the *Zhuangzi*, as "confusion."

65. This "knowing" is not ascribed to any particular kind of sage. The passage serves to introduce Zhuangzi's "difficulty" in 6.1.2.

66. *Cheng* 盛: flourish, superior, abundant, full; *zhiyi* 至矣: arise, arrive, perfection, supreme, utmost, fulfill, reach, attain. Watson translates *cheng* in 2.5.9 as "the finest," in 6.1.1 as "peak," and in 7.5.2 as "perfect."

67. There are a number of other Western-biased phrases in Sturgeon (2015; emphasis added): "*absolutely* correct action-guiding distinctions" (893); "being *ultimately* right" (910); "to know in an *absolute* sense" (902).

68. Some commentators argue that invoking true knowledge, or perfect knowledge, or no-knowledge (*buzhi* 不知) can be considered as resorting to mysticism.

69. Translations of *ji* 幾 include: just about to succeed, just about to achieve one's ends; be near perfect; get close to success; approaching.

70. According to Billeter (1998, 16): "The questioning mode does not express doubt or uncertainty here, but rather the suspension of judgment."

71. Concerning 2.3.8, TLS comments that these are open unanswerable alternative questions.

72. When Zhang Taiyan was in jail from 1903 to 1906, he engrossed himself in studies of Buddhist scriptures, specifically those of the "Consciousness-Only Yogācāra School" (唯識瑜伽行派). But his reading of the *Laozi* and the *Zhuangzi* started much earlier in his life, and he directly remarked that Laozi and Zhuangzi's ideas are loftier when compared with Buddhism (Zhang 1995, 6).

73. Zhang's citation comes from the *Discourse on the Awakening of Faith in the Mahāyāna*《大乘起信論》. Translation of this citation follows Murthy (2011, 210).

74. The modern Chinese word *pingdeng* 平等 that translates the modern notion of equality was formerly employed to convey Buddhist ideas. One can see that Zhang Taiyan's idea of equality via his interpretation of Zhuangzi is rather radical.

75. Zhang Taiyan does not give a reference for his citation from the *Zhuangzi*.

76. Cf. discussion of *wu* 物 in §A3.

77. This notion is similar to Graham's explanation of the "technical term" *yinshi*.

78. In Watson's translation, there is the phrase "little dwellers," but in the Chinese text there is no character that would suggest "little."

79. Cited in Feng Youlan (1928, 49). Feng himself comments (51): "This shows the equality of civilization and barbarism. There is a variety in the ways of living, just as there is a variety in things. These different ways are of equal value." Wang Fuzhi wrote: "If Yao insists on comparing right and wrong with these three who are dwelling in the grasses and brambles, he is just another bit of grass and bramble himself" (translated and cited in Ziporyn 2009a, 157).

80. The expression *qiyi* 齊一 does not occur in the inner chapters. It occurs only once in the outer chapters (in 14.3.5).

81. Zhang Taiyan's interpretation of Zhuangzi's text has been related to cultural pluralism in terms of equality between different cultures as affiliated to different countries, in particular between Chinese (Han) culture and Western culture in general (Wang Yuhua 2004; Wong Young-tsu 2010, 142–43). Ma Lin (2017) brings Zhang's interpretation into the debate on multiculturalism.

82. Unfortunately, most theorists seem to come from the majority groups in their countries.

Chapter 10

1. Zhuangzi himself told this story as well, although in a somewhat different form (32.2.1; G81, 108). See for discussion also G82, 31–32.

2. We have adapted the English translation of Liu An (417), which renders *shi* 世 as age(s); translating it as world or generation may be better. We have also changed "immutable" to "indeterminate."

3. This view leaves it open to state that the stances of the sage-kings are the correct ones because it is assumed that their views, although different, can be known. On the other hand, the "generations" in the citation may be restricted to a period of a few hundred years before the time of writing.

4. B35: "To say that there is no winner in disputation necessarily does not fit the fact" (G78). This has already been cited in §2d.

5. Coutinho (2004, 185) interprets the "who" as follows: "Zhuangzi implies that we ought to affirm what we deny and deny what we affirm." This does not seem to be Zhuangzi's advice. His advice is that we refrain from making *shifei* judgments or, when achieving the state of walking-two-roads, go along with things but not take *shifei* distinctions seriously.

6. Graham suggests that some of Zhuangzi's examples show that the bitterest disagreement may arise when different meanings are assigned to words (G81, 102). This can be true of everyday disagreement. But because of the intertwinement of opinions and meanings (and the holism of language), conflicts are not resolvable by asking participants to "define their terms."

7. Block worlds are simple and closed "ideal language" worlds. They are fully defined so that complete description is possible.

8. In fact, Zhuangzi never made such a claim. Ascribing to him the view that there is neither *shi* nor *fei* was meant as a criticism of Zhuangzi.

9. For the principle of charity, see Ma and van Brakel (2016a, 275–84; 2016b).

10. A minimalistic notion of death is shared with those people who believe in an afterlife or reincarnation.

11. Zhuangzi's disagreement with other scholars on the issue of mourning presupposes agreement on the commonsense meaning of "appropriate behavior at the death of a relative or a friend." There may be disagreement about how to respond to the death of persons; nevertheless, it only makes sense to speak of disagreement provided that there is agreement concerning quasi-universals such as death or dying.

12. See G89, 177; cf. G69, 142, 144; G81, 11.

13. But this is not enough "to determine an entire ethical system," which is grounded in "fundamentally opposed" and "incompatible" values, says Sturgeon (2015, 908).

14. Graham may call this taking a *weishi* stance (cf. §7f).

15. In addition, Hansen (2015) suggests that, in order to interpret the entire linguistic community, we should be making a judgment as Zhuangzi's contemporaneous

(not contemporary) philosophers did. "Any inference that the passages are incoherent must follow *in ancient Chinese* terms" (emphasis original).

16. Even if, *per impossibile*, we make no distinctions (of "different" *wu*), there would be differences in practice.

17. Cited and translated in Zürcher (1959, 128–29).

18. "Guo's essentially non-moral conception of a society, in which every member is justified to lead any kind of life, provided that his actions agree with his natural talents and inclinations, obviously militates against the Buddhist picture of a universe dominated by moral law" (Zürcher, 129).

19. Such perspectives are "unwarranted, unnecessary, and often unhelpful" (30).

20. The non-analytic philosophers may be less concerned about the Nazi-*dao* because they may assume that *dao* is intrinsically a positive term for morality.

21. Coutinho (2015, 175) correctly points out that if flexibility is a value of our meta-discourse, this meta-discourse is not value neutral (it would favor *daos* that are flexible). They do not bring us any further in "re/dis-solving" the problem Zhi Dun has raised.

22. One may speculate that the passage from the *Liezi* was written by somebody who would like to criticize Zhuangzi's "amoral" stance, as Zhi Dun had done (cf. §A2).

23. We primarily draw on Putnam (1990, 18–26) and Rorty (1993), but both of them address the issue of relativism and each other's views in other publications.

24. Note that survival allows for many perspectives, all "workable" in practice.

25. Rorty also calls himself an ironist. Van Norden (2016) has suggested that Zhuangzi is ultimately an "ironist" in Rorty's sense (9–10, 15). But cf. Wang Youru (2003, 218n76).

26. The word naturalism can have many different meanings. We use it in the senses of De Caro and Macarthur (2010).

27. There are slightly different lists in the Western literature. Nussbaum's (2000) proposals for a common humanity and the existence of associated functions—the realization of which constitute common marks of the human good—cannot claim to apply to all human practices. Her list of "capabilities" is full of "American" value judgments. Even those who are sympathetic to Nussbaum's views note: "our ability to recognize a common humanity is apt to outstrip any list of criteria that theorists are likely to come up with" (Wolf 1995, 109).

28. Zhuangzi's deconstruction of *shifei* yes/no-debates could well apply to the community of Zhuangzi interpreters (as well as almost all the discourses in academic disciplines).

29. For example, in the recurrent occurrence of uselessness as protection for a long life—a theme taken up by recluse poets such as Xi Kang (Ji Kang) 嵇康 (223–62) and Tao Yuanming 陶淵明 (365–427). Cf. Major (1975), Radice (2001), and van Brakel (2014).

Appendix

1. According to Liu Xiaogan (1994, viii).

2. In the *Zhuangzi*, *qi* 齊 usually is the name of the geographical area of Qi. Cf. different translations of 1.1.2: *Qixie*《齊諧》*The Universal Harmony* (Watson, presumably the title of a book; similarly, Ziporyn: *Equalizing Jokebook*) or G81, *Tall stories of Ch'i*. There is a rare occurrence of *qi* meaning equal(ity) in the inner chapters: 子齊執政乎？ "Do you think you're the equal [齊] of a prime minister?" (5.2.2); cf. also: 子之先生不齊 "Your master is never the same!" (7.5.7).

3. See G81, 100–11.

4. We agree with the commentators who state that chapters 1 to 7 in the *Zhuangzi* form an interconnected "whole."

5. See for his justification of this move G82, 13–14.

6. Mark Elvin translated Billeter's original French edition (Billeter 1994) of the first part of chapter 2 of the *Zhuangzi* into English (Billeter 1998). Billeter's translation of classical Chinese into French is also in Billeter (2016, 117–22). The translations by Levi, Mair, Graham, and Watson of 14.1.1–3 are similar, taking into account the fact that the original is a poem. Watson presents a shortened version. Original: 天其運乎？ 地其處乎？ 日月其爭於所乎？ 孰主張是？ 孰維綱是？ 孰居无事推而行是？ 意者其有機緘而不得已邪？ 意者其運轉而不能自止邪？ 雲者為雨乎？ 雨者為雲乎？ 孰隆施是？孰居无事淫樂而勸是？ 風起北方，一西一東，有上彷徨，孰噓吸是？ 孰居无事而披拂是？ 敢問何故？

7. For a detailed critique of Graham's reordering of the *Zhuangzi*, see Lin Shuen-Fu (2003); for the move of the passage from chapter 14 to chapter 2, see Lin's page 278.

8. Wu Kuang-ming remarks (cited in Stevenson 2008, 241): "Many commentators follow Guo Xiang in saying that there is in fact no heavenly piping, which is a literary expression of a collective mutuality of earthly and heavenly pipings."

9. Graham (1976) considers that translations of the *Zhuangzi* suffer from unending verbiage without direction, which he calls the "rambling mode," and he lists seven causes for this. He remarks that scholarly expertise and literary acumen is not enough to translate this "extraordinary hotchpotch" (G81, 30).

10. Reminder: our citations from one of the outer or miscellaneous chapters are "passages related to the inner chapters" (according to Graham).

11. Cf. Si Lü (2013, 17n8): "the disputes over *shi* and *fei* between Ruists, Mohists, and other schools have all proceeded from their own fixed and subjective views so that they affirm what the other denies and deny what the other affirms."

12. There is no agreement as to who the Bingists are (Ziporyn 2009a, 103n).

13. Ziporyn: "Wandering Far and Unfettered." Kjellberg: "Wandering Round and About."

14. In §10b we addressed Zhi Dun's critique of Guo Xiang's essentially nonmoral conception of a society in which every member is justified to lead any kind of life.

15. "小知不及大知，小年不及大年 [Those of little understanding cannot come up to great understanding; the short-lived cannot come up to the long-lived]" (1.1.6).

16. Last clause 1.1.10: 此小大之辯也.

17. From the perspective of Zürcher, Zhuangzi's perfect person shows affinities with Nietzsche's *Übermensch*. Dutch and German dictionaries give a fair rendition to

Übermensch in Zürcher's sense: perfect, ideal, god-like human, being without faults or weaknesses, *transcending good and evil,* or at least developing in that direction (emphasis added).

18. See ellipsis on page 4 of Mair (1994).

19. 之二蟲又何知 (1.1.5).

20. In defense of Guo Xiang, it can be pointed out that "these two little creatures" fulfill a positive role in 7.2.3: 而曾二蟲之无知! "Have you got less sense than these two little creatures?"

21. Uselessness (§A7) is a sign of non-dependence.

22. Coutinho (2004, 70) takes a middle position, which could provide a compromise: Peng is a recluse ("higher" than ordinary humans, but not a sage). But this would not satisfy Guo Xiang.

23. Hansen (2015, relativistic skepticism) and Allinson (1989, spiritual transformation) both provide sophisticated and detailed analyses and interpretation of all the passages in the *Qiwulun* that suggest superficially either relativism or spiritual transformation (mysticism).

24. For the purpose of the present exposition, we understand "pre-originary" in the sense of either the cosmos before (human) distinctions have been introduced and/or the necessary preconditions of talking about the myriad of things. Cf. 2.4.7 cited in §A3.

25. We follow Watson's translation with modification. Graham renders *dakuai* 大塊 as "That hugest of clumps of soil." Watson renders it as "The Great Clod." Both have missed the actual meaning as no-thing, as Wu Kuang-ming reports (1990, 157–58), following Guo Xiang (24). Graham (G81, 49) comments on the *dakuai*: "That hugest of clumps of soil [. . .] seems to conjure up an image of the universe so far in the distance that it is no bigger than a clod you could hold in your hand." Such relativity of perspective fits the *Qiwulun*'s central theme of "evening out all things." Wu Kuang-ming (155) says the *dakuai* "is either earth . . . or between heaven and earth." *Dakuai* occurs in 2.1.4, 6.2.3, and 6.5.9.

26. Translations of *wuwu* 無物 include: nothing, no thing, not, not a thing/being.

27. Guo Xiang (2011, 24). *Wuwu* occurs in the *Laozi*, but not in the *Zhuangzi*.

28. Schipper: "Verhandeling over de gelijkheid der dingen." Schuhmacher: "Über die Gleichheit der Dinge."

29. Alternatively: "Consider as equivalent all discourses concerning things" (Billeter 2016, 115 ["Considérer comme équivalents tous les discours sur les choses"]).

30. Wieger: "Harmonie universelle"; Wilhelm: "Ausgleich der Weltanschauung."

31. "Discours sur l'identité des choses ou La musique qui sort du vide."

32. In modern Chinese, animals are referred to as moving *wu* (*dongwu* 动物) and human beings as *renwu* (人物). Plants are *zhiwu* (植物) and inorganic things such as rivers and mountains can constitute *jingwu* (景物). Both the butterfly and Zhuang Zhou are referred to as *wu* 物 in 2.7.3, and the interchange between them is called *wuhua* (物化). See for details Ma Lin (2015, 816).

33. Wang Youru (2003, 36): "The word 'thing (*wu*)' refers to different pairs of things, qualities, functions, feelings, views, and so forth." Schipper restricts *wu* to "all creatures on earth."

34. *Lun* has been translated as discourse, judge, considered opinion, sort out and discuss, pass judgment on, assess, investigate, adjudicate.

35. It is somewhat ambiguous whether Billeter and Ziporyn are commenting on the use of *lun* 論 in various sources in the Warring States Period, or whether they are commenting specifically on Zhuangzi's usage. This is a problem for most commentators. We cannot exclude the possibility that Zhuangzi's use of characters was perhaps idiosyncratic in his time.

36. In a list of "eight virtues," just before the passage cited, the following "virtues" are listed: *youzuo* 有左, *youyou* 有右, *youlun* 有倫, *youyi* 有義, *youfen* 有分, *youbian* 有辯, *youjing* 有競, *youzheng* 有爭 (2.5.6). "There is left, there is right, there are theories, there are debates, there are divisions, there are discriminations, there are emulations, and there are contentions." The characters of the first two items have been doubted. Watson translates them as "there is left and right." Graham translates the characters as "you can locate as there and enclose by a line." Perhaps left and right refer to protocol of where to stand at court, but Graham considers it as a case of corrupted characters (G82, 15).

37. Considering it as a gradation is already an interpretation because there is no sharp distinction between the last three binomes.

38. The distinction of *lun* and *qi* may seem to echo that of *xiaozhi* 小知 and *dazhi* 大知, but, as Zhang Taiyan has shown, *qi* allows for inferior as well as superior interpretations. See discussion in §9e on Zhang Taiyan's distinction between trying to even out what is not equal (*qiqi buqi* 齊其不齊) and achieving evenness by leaving things uneven (*buqi erqi* 不齊而齊).

39. *Qi* 齊 has many translations, including: orderly, ordinary (egalitarian), together (jointly), uniform, along with, equal(ity), the same, level, of equal height, regulate, put in order; order, command, complete, entire, very fast, nimble; limit, boundary, to limit, to impose a boundary on, distinguish, separate, central, swirl, vortex. We assume that when taking equal(izing) and level(ing) as the central meaning of *qi* 齊, it still contains other shades of meaning in its connotation. Hence, it is a hybrid concept. It is arrived at by *yiming* 以明: "rather than defending the point of view that the other side rejects, or rejecting the point of view that the other side defends, it is better to have a clear understanding" (Billeter 2.3.5).

40. Guo Xiang, cited in Ziporyn (2009a, 144–45); cf. Feng Youlan (1928, 44).

41. Zhuangzi uses everyday sorting words that can be rendered in English as monkey, deer, centipede, snake, food, taste, beautiful, catch, fly or run away, and so on.

42. "The ideal sage will for all Chinese schools be the man perfectly aware of all viewpoints, with the spontaneous desire and the ability to benefit all by orderly government" (G89, 384). Hansen (1992, 428) perceptively remarks: "'respond with awareness' seems to have a built-in *shi-fei*. How Zhuangzi can disapprove

of distinctions and accept 'sorting' without making a distinction between them remains a mystery to me."

43. Cf. 6.2.6: "If he can serve as a model for men" (人猶效之). We disagree with Guo Xiang when he says: Do not imitate sages. It is "good" for humans to try to walk two roads, and in this way he/she could become a sage.

44. Zhuangzi (1.1.11): "The whole world could praise Sung Jung-tzu [Song Rongzi] and it would not make him exert himself; the whole world could condemn him and it would not make him move."

45. See 1.1.13: "If he [Liezi] had only mounted on the truth of Heaven and Earth, ridden the changes of the six breaths, and thus wandered through the boundless, then what would he have had to depend on?" (若夫乘天地之正，而御六氣之辯，以遊无窮者，彼且惡乎待哉?) Even then, as Shi Deqing 釋德清 remarks: "although the sage may be vast, he is still confined to the realm of limited forms, with his own particular body" (cited in Ziporyn 2009a, 130–31). A vast consciousness and vast duration are also bounded and limited. As long as one uses concepts, one is dependent on something (Schipper 2007, 79n70).

46. The *shengren* appears close to ten times in chapter 2 (2.3.7, 2.3.8, 2.4.11, 2.4.6, 2.5.7, 2.5.8, 2.6.9, and 2.6.12; all of them already cited in the main chapters), and also, occasionally, in chapters 4 to 7.

47. The *shenren* occurs in 1.1.13, 1.2.7, 4.5.3, and 4.5.5. The *tianren* 天人 does not occur in the inner chapters (it does occur in chapters 27 and 33).

48. The *shenren* does not try to be friendly with the crowd (24.13.7; G81, 110); he shows interest in the unusableness, which he makes use of: 嗟乎神人，以此不材! (4.5.3. "Aha!—it is this unusableness that the Holy Man makes use of!") The *shenren* finds the "men with piles" "auspicious" (4.5.5). According to Puett (2003, 249), the *shenren* "does not distinguish objects in terms of what is the usable and unusable for sacrifices." Shi Deqing identifies the *shenren* with a "great sage" *dasheng* 大聖 (cited in Ziporyn 2009a, 134). The *dasheng* is mentioned once in the inner chapters (2.6.16).

49. The *zhiren* 至人 occurs in 1.1.13, 2.6.8, 4.1.8, 5.3.4–5, 5.4.11, and 7.6.2.

50. "王倪曰：「至人神矣！大澤焚而不能熱，河漢沍而不能寒, 疾雷破山，飄風振海而不能驚。若然者，乘雲氣，騎日月，而遊乎四海之外。死生无變於己，而況利害之端乎！」[Wang Ni replied, "The Perfect Man is godlike. Though the great swamps blaze, they cannot burn him; though the great rivers freeze, they cannot chill him; though swift lightning splits the hills and howling gales shake the sea, they cannot frighten him. A man like this rides the clouds and mist, straddles the sun and moon, and wanders beyond the four seas. Even life and death have no effect on him, much less the rules of profit and loss!"] (2.6.8). This makes the *zhiren* rather similar to the *shenren*.

51. For an elaborate discussion of the *zhenren*, see Coyle (1998).

52. Original: 淒然似秋，煖然似春，喜怒通四時，與物有宜？而莫知其極 (6.1.8). Perhaps instead of Watson's "right for things," a better translation is "appropriate for things," given that the character *yi* 宜 is used. We assume that "joy and anger" belong to *qing* 情.

53. The Nameless Person said (7.3.3), "Let your mind wander in simplicity, blend your spirit with the vastness, follow along with things the way they are, and

make no room for personal views then the world will be governed [无名人曰：汝遊心於淡，合氣於漠，順物自然而无容私焉，而天下治矣]." Perhaps the *wumingren* can also be considered a role model, but not enough is said in 7.3.3 to gather its meaning.

54. We have cited from 23.10.1 before, but one cannot be too confident about this passage. Watson translates the *quanren* 全人 as "normal men" in 5.5.1 and as "complete man" in 23.10.1. In chapter 5, the *quanren* is the complete person in contrast with deformed people. That is to say, being complete refers to the body being complete. Certainly, having a complete body is not sufficient to be considered a sage. Wang Tai (5.1.1), who has lost a foot and has more followers than Kongzi, would seem to be a sage. The text in chapter 23 may suggest that the *quanren* is similar to a sage. There are too few occurrences to decide whether the *quanren* should be counted as a role model for humans.

55. Using *zhe* 者 instead of *ren* 人 also indicates a person. Therefore, we could add more kinds of sages, for example, the "person of virtue" (*dezhe* 德者), which occurs in chapters 4 and 5, and the "person of far-reaching understanding" (*dazhe* 達者) in 2.4.4.

56. Watson translates *zhongren* 眾人 in the *Zhuangzi* as everybody, ordinary men, common herd, mob, common (run of men), or mass of men.

57. Cited in Ziporyn 2009a, 133; cf. citation of 1.2.7 in §A4.

58. It is difficult to locate the *wu* 巫 (shaman, physician-witch) on the scale of different *ren*; he/she could be a "lower" sage.

59. This is Watson's translation. Chan Wing-tsit translates it as: "rough description" (of the sage). There is also disagreement concerning the translation of 不緣道 in 2.6.9. It seems to be saying that the sage does not follow the Way (Watson). Perhaps we should understand this as: the sage conforms to the Way spontaneously but not intentionally (which is a specifically human feature).

60. Lü Huiqing comments that both Kongzi and Ju Quezi are wrong and offers his own "definition" of a sage: "The sage knows nothing of benefit and harm, so he neither seeks nor avoids anything. He is ever satisfied, so he seeks no happiness. He knows everything is the course, so he follows no specific course. His saying something is how he says nothing, and his saying nothing is how he says something" (Ziporyn 2009a, 159). The sage is completely free of fixed intentions.

61. Hansen (2015) considers that this confusion of the Yellow emperor illustrates that the "perfected people" are "unintelligible and irrelevant to us."

62. Graham translates it as follows (acknowledging that it is a poem):

> Go side by side with the sun and moon,
> Do the rounds of Space and Time. . . .
> Common people fuss and fret,
> The sage is a dullard and a sluggard. . . .

63. The expression *dajue* occurs in the continuation of the story paraphrased in this paragraph: "且有大覺而後知此其大夢也 [And someday there will be a great awakening when we know that this is all a great dream]" (transl. Watson; last phrase of 2.6.14 in TLS). Chiu Wai Wai (2015, 264) remarks: "Great awakening is

elusive in the sense that no one, not even a sage, can be certain that it has been attained." Even a great sage cannot judge what is ultimately right. Zhang Binglin 章炳麟 (Zhang Taiyan) remarks that "the great awakening from the great dream means that one knows life to be a dream" (cited in Ziporyn 2009a, 159), Hence, both life and death are dreams.

64. For a contrary view, see Yearley (1993).

65. Schipper (2007, 68n64) considers that the numerous occurrences of *dao* 道 in the *Zhuangzi* refer to (various) methods. Billeter makes a similar remark (2015, 37).

66. Concerning the debates between the Ruists and the Mohists, Feng Youlan translates: "If we are to affirm what these two schools both deny, and to deny what they both affirm, there is nothing better than to use *the light of reason*" (2.3.5; emphasis added).

67. "Ce qui intéresse votre serviteur, c'est le fonctionnement des choses, non la simple technique."

68. There is an extensive literature on the inexpressibility of *dao*, but it isconcerned mainly with the *Laozi*. For Zhuangzi's remark in 2.5.9, see, for example, Feng Youlan (1947, 70).

69. *Yutian* often occurs in classical texts. *Tianni* 天倪, *tianjun* 天鈞, and *tianjun* 天均 are rare and rather unique to the *Zhuangzi*. These three are usually translated as being equal; 鈞 and 均 are variants.

70. *Yutian* also occurs in 5.1.7, 5.5.4, and 6.6.10. *Yutian* in 2.3.7 is translated as: light of Heaven (Watson, Graham, Feng Youlan, Kjellberg, and Muller), Heavenly (nature) [Legge], Heaven (Nature) [Lin Yutang], light of nature (Mair), daylight of Heaven (Ziporyn), illuminated by Heaven (Levi).

71. Normally, *yu* 於 is explained as a preposition or has the function of adding a syllable for ease of reading. Hence, we might also translate *yutian* 於天 as heaven.

72. Translations of *jun* 均: harmony, standard, equal, same, all; translation of *jun* 鈞: equal, (potter's) wheel, weight measures.

73. This may be achieved by using goblet words (*zhiyan* 卮言); see 27.1.4 (G81: 106–7).

74. Consider also *weiyi* 為一: make into one; see 1.2.8, 2.4.3–5, 2.5.4, 5.3.5. We assume as a minimalistic meaning of *dao* that it indicates natural functioning and the absence of strict borders. This already leads to: "Dao makes all into one" (2.4.3, 道通為一).

75. The translations are from Lin Yutang. In both cases it concerns advice of Kongzi 孔子 (551 BCE–479 BCE) to his disciple Yan Hui 顏回. Apparently, Graham assumes that Kongzi is not talking on behalf of Zhuangzi because, according to Graham, Zhuangzi never directly declares that everything is one; he would always speak of *the sage* treating everything as one (G81, 56). Translations of Lin Yutang and Watson suggest that Zhuangzi is advising that "everybody" enters into Oneness. Lin Yutang: 一宅而寓於不得已 (4.1.31) "make oneness your house and live with what cannot be avoided." Watson: "then you can enter the mysterious oneness of Heaven" (6.7.6：乃入於寥天一). Note that Watson adds the word mysterious.

76. Watson translates *wuyan* 无言 as "not say" in chapters 2 and 4.

77. Original: 道昭而不道 (2.5.9).

78. There is an extensive literature on Zhuangzi's (alleged) mysticism. For example, Roth (2000) finds support for a "greater form" of "intuitive knowledge" that comes with what he calls extrovertive mystical experience. See also Billeter (1998, 7–16) on Ziqi's "meditation" (2.1.2). Some commentators will consider the "far and carefree wandering," which indicates a state of non-dependence, as a mystical state. According to Yearley (1983), Zhuangzi's radical, intrawordly mysticism is very different from "Western" and "Indian" mysticism; it "aims to see the world in a new way" (131). Some of Zhuangzi's more "bizarre" views should be understood as a rhetorical device of exaggeration or as asking you "to deal with everything [for example, death] the way you deal with aesthetic objects" (136). Yearley (1996, 174) argues that Zhuangzi uses "portraits of skills" to point to the "ultimate spiritual state."

79. *Dao* guides spontaneous action. For detailed expositions, see Graham (1983, 1985). See also the discussion in §7f concerning Graham's *yinshi* and spontaneity.

80. Graham (G89, 499): "*Tzu* 自 [*zi*] 'of itself, spontaneously' and *Tzu jan* [*ziran*] 'so of itself, spontaneous.'" A more common translation of *ziran* is "natural(ly)" or "by itself." It has also been translated as "effortless" (cf. *wuwei* 无為 in next section).

81. See also 5.6.6: 常因自然而不益 "He just lets things be the way they are and doesn't try to help life along."

82. 7.6.3–4: translation from Ames (2005, 55–56); slightly different translation in Hall and Ames (1995, 230).

83. CP 6.553. Peirce uses a cluster of phrases relating spontaneity to (absolute) chance (CP, passim): fortuitous (CP 1.403, 6.297, 6.401), indeterminacy (CP 1.399, 6.13), arbitrary determination (CP 6.46), lawless originality (CP 1.407), and sporadic spontaneous irregularity (CP 1.156). The citations are from Peirce (1931–58), the *Collected Papers* (CP).

84. Ames (2005, 56); see also Hall and Ames (1995, 230–34); Stevenson (2008).

85. *Wuwei* occurs 47 times in the *Zhuangzi* and 6 times in the inner chapters.

86. It has been documented that Martin Heidegger has displayed interest in the *Laozi* or the *Zhuangzi* (in German translations) on at least 13 occasions (Ma Lin 2006).

87. An early characterization of *wuwei* can be found in the *Shiji* (CTP): "The *Daojia* is inaction [*wuwei* 無為], but it also says that nothing is left undone. Its essentials are easy to practice, but its speech is difficult to understand. Its techniques are based on emptiness and non-existence; its usage is based on following and compliance [*yinxun* 因循]; it has no complete tendency, no constant form. Therefore, it is capable of investigating the facts of all things. It does not put itself ahead of things; it does not place itself behind things; that is why it can be the master of things" (*Shiji* 130, cited by Chen and Sung 2015, 250).

88. Watson's translations of *wuwei* in the inner chapters are: do nothing (1.3.8), does not care (5.4.6), without action (6.3.1), nonbeing (6.5.1), inaction (6.6.7), do not be (7.6.1).

89. This is the only occurrence of *dayong* 大用 in the *Zhuangzi*. It has been suggested that Zhuangzi's uselessness (*wuyong*) in the inner chapters can be understood as "great use" (*dayong* 大用 [4.4.6]).

90. The image of the useless tree was well known among the so-called recluse poets, as illustrated by the rhymed essay *Rongmufu* 榕木賦 ("Rhapsody on the Banyan Tree") by Li Gang (Li Kang) 李綱 (1083–1140).

91. For references to Heidegger's work, we will give the page number of the English translation followed by the page number of the German original, separated by a slash.

92. See Ma Lin (2008) for a wide-ranging discussion of "Heidegger and Asian Thought."

93. Wilhelm: *daß sich aus ihm nichts machen läßt*.

94. Heidegger (1944/45, 155/237, and 143/220f).

95. In the inner chapters, *wuyong*, including *wusuokeyong*, is used in a context of "preferring the useless." When the subject is timber, *bucai* 不材 or *sanmu* 散木 are used. Graham does not mention *sanmu* in his classification, and he characterizes *bucai* as "preferring untalented to talented." *Cai* can mean either talent or (good) timber (or both). *Sanmu* occurs in 4.4.3, 4.4.6; *bucai* occurs in 4.4.3, 4.5.3, and 20.1.1.

96. On the passage "comparing" the tree and the goose in chapter 20, see also the discussion in Chong Kim-Chong (2006, 379).

Works Cited

Allinson, Robert E. 1989. *Chuang-Tzu for Spiritual Transformation: An Analysis of the Inner Chapters.* Albany: State University of New York Press.
———. 2015. "Of Fish, Butterflies and Birds: Relativism and Nonrelative Valuation in the Zhuangzi." *Asian Philosophy: An International Journal of the Philosophical Traditions of the East* 25 (3): 238–52.
Alt, Wayne. 2000. "Zhuangzi, Mysticism, and the Rejection of Distinctions." *Sino-Platonic Papers* (100).
Ames, Roger T. 1983. "Book Review Graham (1981, 1982)." *Journal of Asian Studies* 42 (3): 615–17.
———. 1998. "Introduction." In *Wandering at Ease in the Zhuangzi*, edited by Roger T. Ames, 1–14. Albany: State University of New York Press.
———. 2004. "Indigenizing Globalization and the Hydraulics of Culture: Taking Chinese Philosophy on Its Own Terms." *Journal of Globalizations* 1: 171–80.
———. 2005. "Collaterality in Early Chinese Cosmology: An Argument for Confucian Harmony (*he* 和) as Creatio in Situ." *Taiwan Journal of East Asian Studies* 2 (1): 43–70.
———. 2011. *Confucian Role Ethics: A Vocabulary.* Hong Kong: Chinese University Press.
———. 2015. "Reading the *Zhongyong* "Metaphysically."" In *Chinese Metaphysics and Its Problems*, edited by Chenyang Li and Franklin Perkins, 85–103. Cambridge, UK: Cambridge University Press.
———, ed. 1998. *Wandering at Ease in the Zhuangzi.* Albany: State University of New York Press.
———, and Henry Rosemont, trans. 1998. *The Analects of Confucius: A Philosophical Translation.* New York: Random House.
Arendrup, Birthe. 1974. "The First Chapter of Guo Xiang's Commentary to Zhuangzi: A Translation and Grammatical Analysis." *Acta Orientalia* 6 (1): 129–48.
Barnes, Barry, and David Bloor. 1982. "Relativism, Rationalism, Sociology of Knowledge." In *Rationality and Relativism*, edited by Martin Hollis and Steven Lukes, 21–47. Oxford, UK: Blackwell.

Baxter, William H. 1983. "A Look at the History of Chinese Color Terminology." *Journal of the Chinese Language Teachers Association* 18: 1–25.
Berthrong, John. 2011. "Neo-Confucianism." In *The Oxford Handbook of World Philosophy*, edited by Jay L. Garfield and William Edelglass, 82–94. New York: Oxford University Press.
Billeter, Jean François. 1994. "Tchouang-Tseu, Ts'i Wou-Louen: Que tous les discours se valent. Chapitre 2 du Tchouang-Tseu (Premiere Partie)." *Philosophie* 44: 5–11.
———. 1998. "Stopping, Seeing and Language: An Interpretation of Zhuangzi's Qi Wulun." Translated by Mark Elvin. *East Asian History* 15/16: 1–32.
———. 2002. *Leçons Sur Tchouang-Tseu*. Paris: Allia.
———. 2016. *Études Sur Tchouang-Tseu*. Paris: Allia.
Boghossian, Paul. 2006. "What Is Relativism?" In *Truth and Relativism*, edited by Patrick Greenough and Michael Lynch, 13–37. Oxford, UK: Clarendon Press.
Boucher, S. C. 2014. "What Is a Philosophical Stance? Paradigms, Policies and Perspectives." *Synthese* 191: 2315–32.
Bradley, Scott P. 2015. *All Is Well in the Great Mess*. Bradenton, FL: BookLocker.
Brandom, Robert. 1983. "Asserting." *Noûs* 17 (4): 637–50.
———. 1994. *Making It Explicit*. Cambridge, MA: Harvard University Press.
Bullock, Jeffrey S. 2011. *Yang Xiong: Philosophy of the Fa yan*. Highlands, NC: Mountain Mind Press.
Callahan, William A. 1998. "Cook Ding's Life on the Whetstone: Contingency, Action, Inertia in the *Zhuangzi*." In *Wandering at Ease in the Zhuangzi*, edited by Roger T. Ames, 175–94. Albany: State University of New York Press.
Cao Chuji 曹础基, ed. 2000. *Zhuangzi qianzhu*《庄子浅注》[A Didactic Annotation to the *Zhuangzi*]. Beijing, China: Zhonghua shuju.
Chakravarty, Anjan. 2004. "Stance Relativism: Empiricism versus Metaphysics." *Studies History and Philosophy of Science* 35: 173–84.
Chan Wing-tsit. trans. 1969. *A Source Book in Chinese Philosophy*. Princeton: Princeton University Press.
Chang Tzu-li. 2016. "Re-Exploring Wang Yangming's Theory of *Liangzhi*: Translation, Transliteration, and Interpretation." *Philosophy East and West* 66 (4): 1196–217.
Chen Guying. 2016. *The Philosophy of Life: A New Reading of the Zhuangzi*. Leiden, The Netherlands: Brill.
Chen Guying 陈鼓应. trans. 2007. *Zhuangzi jinzhu jinyi*《庄子今注今译》[A Contemporary Annotation to the *Zhuangzi* with (modern Chinese) Translation]. Beijing, China: Shangwu chubanshe.
Chen Lai. 2004. "The Discussion of Mind and Nature in Zhu Xi's Philosophy." In *Chinese Philosophy in an Era of Globalization*, edited by Robin R. Wang, 75–98. Binghamton: State University of New York Press.
Chen, L. K., and Hiu Chuk Winnie Sung. 2015. "The Doctrines and Transformation of the Huang-Lao Tradition." In *Dao Companion to Daoist Philosophy*, edited by Xiaogan Liu, 241–64. Dordrecht, The Netherlands: Springer.
Chen Yinchi 陈引弛. 2016. *Wuwei and xiaoyou: Zhuangzi liu zhang*《无为与逍遥: 庄子六章》[*Wuwei* and *Xiaoyao*: Six Chapters on the *Zhuangzi*]. Beijing: Zhonghua shuju.

Cheng, Anne. 2004. "The Status of *Qing* in Philosophical Texts of Ancient China." In *Expressions of States of Mind in Asia*, edited by Paolo Santangelo, 49–72. Napoli: Università degli Studie di Napoli "L'Orientale."
Cheng Chung-ying. 2003. "Language and Logic." In *Encyclopedia of Chinese Philosophy*, edited by Antonio S. Cua, 343–55. New York and London: Routledge.
Cheng Xuanying 成玄英. 2011. "Subcommentary on the Zhuangzi." In *Zhuangzi Zhusu*《莊子注疏》[*Zhuangzi*: Commentary and Subcommentary]. Beijing, China: Zhonghua shuju.
Chinn, Ewing Y. 1997. "Zhuangzi and Relativistic Scepticism." *Asian Philosophy: An International Journal of the Philosophical Traditions of the East* 7 (3): 207–20.
Chiu Wai Wai. 2015. "Goblet Words and Indeterminacy: A Writing Style That Is Free of Commitment." *Frontiers of Philosophy in China* 10 (2): 255–72.
Chomsky, Noam. 1988. *Language and Problems of Knowledge*. Cambridge, MA: MIT Press.
———. 1995. "Language and Nature." *Mind* 104: 1–61.
Chong Kim-chong. 2006. "Zhuangzi and the Nature of Metaphor." *Philosophy East and West* 56: 370–91.
———. 2010. "Zhuangzi and Hui Shi on *Qing* 情." *Tsing Hua Journal of Chinese Studies, New Series* 40 (1): 21–45.
———. 2011. "The Concept of *Zhen* 真 in the *Zhuangzi*." *Philosophy East and West* 63 (2): 324–46.
Chu Boxiu 褚伯秀. 2014. *Zhuangzi yihai zhuanwei*《莊子義海纂微》[Selected Collation from the Sea of Meaning of the *Zhuangzi*]. 2 vols. Shanghai, China: Huadong shifan daxue chubanshe.
Cleary, Thomas. 1999. *The Collected Translations of Thomas Cleary: The Taoist Classics*. Vol. 1. Boston, MA: Shambhala.
Connolly, Tim. 2011. "Perspectivism as a Way of Knowing in the Zhuangzi." *Dao: A Journal of Comparative Philosophy* 10: 487–505.
Cook, Scott, ed. 2003. *Hiding the World in the World: Uneven Discourses on the Zhuangzi*. Albany: State University of New York Press.
———. 2003. "Harmony and Cacophony in the Panpipes of Heaven." In *Hiding the World in the World: Uneven Discourses on the Zhuangzi*, edited by Scott Cook, 64–87. Albany: State University of New York Press.
Coutinho, Steve. 2004. *Zhuangzi and Early Chinese Philosophy: Vagueness, Transformation, and Paradox*. Aldershot, UK: Ashgate.
———. 2015. "Conceptual Analysis of the *Zhuangzi*." In *Dao Companion to Daoist Philosophy*, edited by Xiaogan Liu, 159–91. Dordrecht, The Netherlands: Springer.
Coyle, Daniel. 1998. "On the *Zhenren*." In *Wandering at Ease in the Zhuangzi*, edited by Roger T. Ames, 197–210. Albany: State University of New York Press.
Crump, J. I., trans. 1979. *Chan-Kuo Ts'e*. San Francisco, CA: Chinese Materials Center.
Cua, Antonio S., ed. 2003. *Encyclopedia of Chinese Philosophy*. New York and London: Routledge.
Davidson, Donald. 2004. *Problems of Rationality*. Oxford: Clarendon Press.

De Caro, Mario, and David Macarthur, eds. 2010. *Naturalism and Normativity*. New York: Columbia University Press.
Dewey, John. 1922. *Human Nature and Conduct: An Introduction to Social Psychology*. New York: Henry Holt.
Eifring, Halvor. 2004. "Introduction: Emotions and the Conceptual History of *Qing* 情." In *Love and Emotions in Traditional Chinese Literature*, edited by Halvor Eifring, 1–36. Leiden, The Netherlands: Brill.
Ekman, Paul. 1980. *The Face of Man: Expressions of Universal Emotions in a New Guinea Village*. New York: Garland.
———. 1992. "An Argument for Basic Emotions." *Cognition and Emotion* 6: 169–200.
Elgin, Catherine Z. 2007. "The Fusion of Fact and Value" *Iride* 20: 83–101.
Eno, Robert. 1996. "Cook Ding's Dao and the Limits of Philosophy." In *Essays on Skepticism, Relativism and Ethics in the Zhuangzi*, edited by Paul Kjellberg and Philip J. Ivanhoe, 127–51. Albany: State University of New York Press.
———, trans. 2010. *Zhuangzi: The Inner Chapters*. Bloomington: Indiana University. http://www.indiana.edu/~p374/Zhuangzi.pdf.
———, trans. 2016. *Mencius: An Online Teaching Translation*. Bloomington: Indiana University. http://www.indiana.edu/~p374/Mengzi.pdf.
Feng Gia-Fu, and Jane English, trans. 1974. *Chuang Tsu: Inner Chapters*. New York: Random House.
Feng Youlan. [1928] 1989. *Chuang-Tzu*. Beijing, China: Foreign Languages Press.
———. 1931. *A Short History of Chinese Philosophy*. Beijing, China: Foreign Language Press.
———. 1947. *The Spirit of Chinese Philosophy*. London: Routledge & Kegan Paul.
Feyerabend, Paul. 1999. *A Conquest of Abundance: A Tale of Abstraction versus the Richness of Being*. Chicago, IL: University of Chicago Press.
Fodor, Jerry A. 1975. *The Language of Thought*. Cambridge, MA: Harvard University Press.
———. 1983. *The Modularity of Mind*. Cambridge, MA: MIT Press.
Forke, Alfred, trans. 1907. *Lun-Hêng*. London: Luzac & Co.
Fox, Alan. 2003. "Reflex and Reflection: *Wuwwei* 無為 in the *Zhuangzi*." In *Hiding the World in the World: Uneven Discourses on the Zhuangzi*, edited by Scott Cook, 207–25. Albany: State University of New York Press.
Frank, Manfred. 2003. "Are There Rationally Undecidable Arguments?" *Common Knowledge* 9 (1): 119–31.
Fraser, Chris. 2009. "Skepticism and Value in Zhuangzi." *International Philosophical Quarterly* 49 (4): 439–57.
———. 2011. "Emotion and Agency in Zhuangzi." *Asian Philosophy: An International Journal of the Philosophical Traditions of the East* 21 (1): 97–121.
———. 2012. "Truth in Mohist Dialectics." *Journal of Chinese Philosophy* 39 (3): 351–68.
———. 2014. "Wandering the Way: A Eudaimonistic Approach to the Zhuangzi." *Dao: A Journal of Comparative Philosophy* 13: 541–65.

———. 2015. "Zhuangzi and the Heterogeneity of Value." In *New Visions of the Zhuangzi*, edited by Livia Kohn. St. Petersburg, FL: Three Pines Press, preprint pages 1–21.
Frege, Gottlob. 1892. "Über Sinn Und Bedeutung." *Zeitschrift für Philosophie und Philosophische Kritik* 100: 25–50.
Furtado, Francisco (Fu Fanji 傅汎濟), and Li Zhizao 李之藻. 1631 [1959]. *Minglitan*《名理探》[An Inquiry in Names and Principles]. Beijing, China: Sanlian shudian.
Geaney, Jane M. 1999. "A Critique of A. C. Graham's Reconstruction of the 'Neo-Mohist Canons.'" *Journal of the American Oriental Society* 119 (1): 1–11.
Giles, Herbert A., transl. 1889. *Chuang Tzu*. London: Bernard Quaeitch.
Goodman, Nelson. 1978. *Ways of Worldmaking*. Indianapolis, IN: Hackett.
———. 1984. *Of Mind and Other Matters*. Cambridge, MA: Harvard University Press.
———, and Catherine Z. Elgin. 1988. *Reconceptions in Philosophy and Other Arts and Sciences*. Indianapolis, IN: Hackett.
Goulding, Jay. 2007. "New Ways toward Sino-Western Philosophical Dialogues." *Journal of Chinese Philosophy* 34 (1): 99–125.
Graham, A. C. 1959. "'Being' in Western Philosophy Compared with *Shih/Fei* and *Yu/Wu* in Chinese Philosophy." *Asia Major* 7 (1/2): 79–112.
———, trans. 1960. *The Book of Lieh-Tzu: A Classic of the Tao*. New York: Columbia University Press.
———. 1969. "Chuang-Tzu's Essay on Seeing Things as Equal." *History of Religions* 9 (2/3): 137–59.
———. 1976. "Chuang Tzu and the Rambling Mode." In *A Companion to Angus C. Graham's Chuang Tzu–the Inner Chapters*, edited by Henry Rosemont, 141–56. Honolulu: University of Hawai'i Press.
———. [1978] 2003. *Later Mohist Logic, Ethics and Science*. Hong Kong: Chinese University Press.
———. [1980] 2003. "How Much of Chuang Tzu Did Chuang Tzu Write?." In *A Companion to Angus C. Graham's Chuang Tzu–the Inner Chapters*, edited by Henry Rosemont, 58–103. Honolulu: University of Hawai'i Press.
———, trans. 1981. *Chuang-Tzu: The Inner Chapters*. Indianapolis, IN: Hackett.
———. 1982. "Textual Notes to Chang Tzu: The Inner Chapters." In *A Companion to Angus C. Graham's Chuang Tzu—The Inner Chapters*, edited by Henry Rosemont, 5–57. Honolulu: University of Hawai'i Press.
———. 1983. "Taoist Spontaneity and the Dichotomy of 'Is' and 'Ought'" In *Experimental Essays on Chuang-Tzu*, edited by Victor H. Mair, 3–23. Honolulu: University of Hawai'i Press.
———. 1985. *Reason and Spontaneity*. London: Curzon Press.
———. 1989. *Disputers of the Tao: Philosophical Argument in Ancient China*. La Salle, IL: Open Court.
———. 1991. "Reflections and Replies." In *Chinese Texts and Philosophical Contexts. Essays Dedicated to Angus C. Graham*, edited by Henry Rosemont, 267–322. La Salle, IL: Open Court.

———. 1992. "Conceptual Schemes and Linguistic Relativism in Relation to Chinese." In *Unreason within Reason: Essays on the Outskirts of Rationality*, edited by Angus C. Graham, 59–83. La Salle, IL: Open Court.
Griffith, Jeremy. 2017. "From Leaky Pots to Spillover-Goblets: Plato and Zhuangzi on the Responsiveness of Knowledge." *Dao: A Journal of Comparative Philosophy* 16: 221–33.
Guo Weiwei. 2007. "Le *Canon mohiste* et la logique." *Études chinoises* 26: 267–83.
Guo Xiang 郭象. 2011. "Commentary on the Zhuangzi." In *Zhuangzi Zhusu*《莊子注疏》 [Zhuangzi: Commentary and Subcommentary]. Beijing: Zhonghua shuju.
Haack, Susan. 1998. *Manifesto of a Passionate Moderate*. Chicago, IL: University of Chicago Press.
Hall, David L. 2001. "Just How Provincial Is Western Philosophy? 'Truth' in Comparative Context." *Social Epistemology* 15 (4): 285–97.
———, and Roger T. Ames. 1987. *Thinking through Confucius*. Albany: State University of New York Press.
———, and Roger T. Ames. 1995. *Anticipating China: Thinking through the Narratives of Chinese and Western Culture*. Albany: State University of New York Press.
———, and Roger T. Ames. 1999. *The Democracy of the Dead: Dewey, Confucius, and the Hope for Democracy in China*. Chicago: Open Court.
Hansen, Chad. 1983a. *Language and Logic in Ancient China*. Ann Arbor: University of Michigan Press.
———. 1983b. "A *Tao* of Tao in Chuang-Tzu." In *Experimental Essays on Chuang-Tzu*, edited by Victor H. Mair, 24–55. Honolulu: University of Hawai'i Press.
———. 1985. "Chinese Language, Chinese Philosophy, and 'Truth.'" *Journal of Asian Philosophy: An International Journal of the Philosophical Traditions of the East* 44: 491–518.
———. 1992. *A Daoist Theory of Chinese Thought: A Philosophical Interpretation*. New York: Oxford University Press.
———. 2007. "Prolegomena to Future Solutions to 'White-Horse Not Horse.'" *Journal of Chinese Philosophy* 34: 473–91.
———. 2015. "Relativistic Skepticism in the Zhuangzi." *http://www.philosophy.hku.hk/ch/Skeptic.htm*.
Harbsmeier, Christoph. 1989. "Marginalia Sino-Logica." In *Understanding the Chinese Mind: The Philosophical Roots*, edited by Robert E. Allinson, 125–66. Oxford University Press.
———. 1992. *An Annotated Anthology of Comments on Zhuangzi: Qiwulun*. Edited by Christoph Harbsmeier, *Serica Osloensia*. Vol. 2. Oslo, Norway: University of Oslo.
———. 1993. "Conceptions of Knowledge in Ancient China." In *Epistemological Issues in Classical Chinese Philosophy*, edited by Hans Lenk and Gregor Paul, 11–30. New York: State University of New York Press.
———. 1998. *Language and Logic*. Edited by Joseph Needham. Vol. 7: 1, *Science and Civilization in China*. Cambridge, UK: Cambridge University Press.
———, and Jiang Shaoyu. 2013. "An Historical and Comparative Encyclopaedia of Chinese Conceptual Schemes."

Hawkes, David, trans. 1985. *The Songs of the South: An Ancient Chinese Anthology of Poems by Qu Yuan and Other Poets*. Harmondsworth, UK: Penguin Books.

Heidegger, Martin. [1944/45] 1995. *Feldweg-Gespräche*. Vol. 77, *Gesamtausgabe*. Frankfurt am Main, Germany: Vittorio Klostermann. See translated version in citation below.

———. 2010. *Country Path Conversations*, translated by Bret W. Davis. Bloomington: Indiana University Press.

———. 1955. "Gelassenheit." In *Reden und andere Zeugnisse eines Lebensweges 1910–1976*, 517–29. Frankfurt am Main, Germany: Vittorio Klostermann (2000). Memorial address: Discourse on Thinking, 43–57, New York: Harper and Row.

———. [1957] 1994. "Grundsätze des Denkens." In *Bremer und Freiburger Vorträge*, 77–166. Frankfurt am Main, Germany: Vittorio Klostermann.

———. [1962] 1989. *Überlieferte Sprache und technische Sprache*. St. Gallen, Switzerland: Erker. See translated version in citation below.

———. 1998. "Traditional Language and Technological Language." *Journal of Philosophical Research* 23: 129–45.

Hesse, Mary B. 1980. *Revolutions and Reconstructions in the Philosophy of Science*. Hassocks, UK: Harvester.

Hightower, James Robert, trans. 1952. *Han Shih Wai Chuan*. Cambridge, MA: Harvard University Press.

Huang Yong. 2010. "The Ethics of Difference in the *Zhuangzi*." *Journal of the American Academy of Religion* 78 (1): 65–99.

Ivanhoe, Philip J. 1993. "Zhuangzi on Skepticism, Skill, and the Ineffable Dao." *Journal of the American Academy of Religion* 61 (4): 639–54.

———. 1996. "Was Zhuangzi a Relativist?" In *Essays on Skepticism, Relativism and Ethics in the Zhuangzi*, edited by Paul Kjellberg and Philip J. Ivanhoe, 196–214. Albany: State University of New York Press.

———, and Bryan W. Van Norden, eds. 2001. *Readings in Classical Chinese Philosophy*. New York: Seven Bridges Press.

Jullien, François. 1989. *Un sage est sans idée, ou l'autre de la philosophie*. Paris: Seuil.

———. 1999. *The Propensity of Things: Toward a History of Efficacy in China*. New York: Zone Books.

———. 2008. *De l'universel, de l'uniforme, du commun et du dialogue entre les cultures*. Paris: Librairie Arthème Fayard.

———. 2014. *On the Universal, the Uniform, the Common and Dialogue between Cultures*. Cambridge, UK: Polity Press.

Jung Hwa Yol. 2013. "Wang Yangming and the Way of World Philosophy." *Dao: A Journal of Comparative Philosophy* 12: 461–86.

Karlgren, Bernhard. 1974. *Analytic Dictionary of Chinese and Sino-Japanese*. New York: Dover.

Kim Myeong-seok. 2014. "Is There No Distinction between Reason and Emotion in Mengzi?" *Philosophy East and West* 64 (1): 49–81.

Kjellberg, Paul. 1996. "Sextus Empiricus, Zhuangzi, and Xunzi." In *Essays on Skepticism, Relativism and Ethics in the Zhuangzi*, edited by Paul Kjellberg and Philip J. Ivanhoe, 1–25. Albany: State University of New York Press.

———, trans. 2001. *Zhuangzi*. In *Readings in Classical Chinese Philosophy*, edited by Philip J. Ivanhoe and Bryan W. Van Norden. New York: Seven Bridges Press.
———. 2007. "Dao and Skepticism." *Dao: A Journal of Comparative Philosophy* 6: 281–99.
———, and Philip J. Ivanhoe, eds. 1996. *Essays on Skepticism, Relativism, and Ethics in the Zhuangzi*. Albany: State University of New York Press.
Klein, Esther. 2010. "Were There "Inner Chapters" in the Warring States? A New Examination of Evidence About the Zhuangzi." *T'oung Pao* 96 (4/5): 299–369.
Knoblock, John, trans. 1988. *Xunzi: A Translation and Study of the Complete Works*. Vol. 1. Stanford, CA: Stanford University Press.
———, trans. 1990. *Xunzi: A Translation and Study of the Complete Works*. Vol. 2. Stanford, CA: Stanford University Press.
———, trans. 1994. *Xunzi: A Translation and Study of the Complete Works*. Vol. 3. Stanford, CA: Stanford University Press.
———, and Jeffrey Riegel, trans. 2013. *Mozi*. Berkeley, CA: Institute of East Asian Studies.
Kurtz, Joachim. 2011. *The Discovery of Chinese Logic*. Leiden, The Netherlands: Brill.
Kwok Sai Hang. 2016. "Zhuangzi's Philosophy of Thing." *Asian Philosophy: An International Journal of the Philosophical Traditions of the East* 26 (4): 294–310.
Lacey, Hugh. 1999. *Is Science Value Free? Values and Scientific Understanding*. London: Routledge.
Lafitte, Jean-Jacques, trans. 1994. *Tchouang-Tseu: Le rêve du papillon*. Paris: Albin Michel.
Lai, Karyn. 2008. *An Introduction to Classical Chinese Philosophy*. Cambridge, UK: Cambridge University Press.
Lau Dim Cheuk, trans. 1963. *Tao Te Ching*. Hong Kong: Chinese University Press.
———, trans. 1983. *Mencius*. Hong Kong: Chinese University Press.
Legge, James, trans. 1869. *The Chinese Classics*. London: Trubner.
———, trans. 1891. *The Writings of Kwang-Tze [Zhuangzi]*. In *The Sacred Books of the East*, edited by F. Max Müller. Vol. XL. Oxford: Oxford University Press.
———, trans. 1885. *Li Ki [Liji* 禮記*]*. In *The Sacred Books of the East*, edited by F. Max Müller. Vol. XXVIII. Oxford: Oxford University Press.
Levi, Jean, trans. 2010. *Les Œvres de Maître Tchouang*. Paris: Éditions de l'encyclopédie des nuisances.
Levi, Jean. trans. 2012. *Écrits de Maître Wen* [文子, 道玄真經]. Paris: Les Belles Lettres.
Levy, André, trans. 2003. *Mencius*. Paris: You-Feng.
Li Gang 李綱. 2004. "Rongmufu 榕木賦 [Rhyme prose on the Banyan tree]." In *Quanji* 《全集》 [Complete Works (by Li Gang)], 19–20. Changsha, China: Yuelu shushe.
Lian Xinda. 2009. "Zhuangzi the Poet: Re-Reading the Peng Bird Image." *Dao: A Journal of Comparative Philosophy* 8: 233–54.
Liao, W. K. 1939. *The Complete Works of Han Fei Tzu*. London: Arthur Probsthain.
———. 1959. *The Complete Works of Han Fei Tzu*. Vol. II. London: Arthur Probsthain.

Lin Shuen-Fu. 2003. "Transforming the Dao: A Critique of A. C. Graham's Translation of the Inner Chapters of the *Zhuangzi*." In *Hiding the World in the World: Uneven Discourses on the Zhuangzi*, edited by Scott Cook, 263–90. Albany: State University of New York Press.

Lin Yutang 林語堂, trans. 1957. *The Chuang Tzu*. Taipei, Taiwan: Shijie shuju. http://www.terebess.hu/english/chuang.html.

Liu An (King of Huainan), John S. Major, Sarah A. Queen, Andrew Seth Meyer, and Harold D. Roth, trans. 2010. *The Huainanzi: A Guide to the Theory and Practice of Government in Early Han China*. New York: Columbia University Press.

Liu JeeLoo. 2003. "The Daoist Conception of Truth." In *Comparative Approaches to Chinese Philosophy*, edited by Bo Mou, 278–93. Aldershot, UK: Ashgate.

Liu Xiaogan. 1994. *Classifying the Zhuangzi Chapters*. Dordrecht, The Netherlands: Springer.

———, ed. 2015a. *Dao Companion to Daoist Philosophy*. Dordrecht, The Netherlands: Springer.

———. 2015b. "Zhuangzi's Philosophy: A Three Dimensional Reconstruction." In *Dao Companion to Daoist Philosophy*, edited by Xiaogan Liu, 193–220. Dordrecht, The Netherlands: Springer.

———. 2015c. "Textual Issues in the *Zhuangzi*." In *Dao Companion to Daoist Philosophy*, edited by Xiaogan Liu, 129–58. Dordrecht, The Netherlands: Springer.

———. 2015d. "Laozi's Philosophy: Textual and Conceptual Analyses." In *Dao Companion to Daoist Philosophy*, edited by Xiaogan Liu, 71–100. Dordrecht, The Netherlands: Springer.

Lloyd, Geoffrey Ernest Richard. 1996. *Adversaries and Authorities*. Cambridge, UK: Cambridge University Press.

———. 2002. *The Ambitions of Curiosity: Understanding the World in Ancient Greece and China*. Cambridge, UK: Cambridge University Press.

———. 2004. *Ancient Worlds, Modern Reflections: Philosophical Perspectives on Greek and Chinese Science and Culture*. New York: Oxford University Press.

———. 2005. *The Delusions of Invulnerability: Wisdom and Morality in Ancient Greece, China and Today*. London: Duckworth.

Ma Lin. 2006. "Deciphering Heidegger's Connection with the *Daodejing*." *Asian Philosophy: An International Journal of the Philosophical Traditions of the East* 16: 149–71.

———. 2008. *Heidegger on East-West Dialogue: Anticipating the Event*. New York: Routledge.

———. 2015. "Thinking with Zhuangzi and Su Shi against Heidegger on Artwork." *Philosophy East and West* 65 (3): 809–45.

———. 2017. "Taking Zhang Taiyan into Multiculturalism: Achieving Equality by Leaving Things Uneven (Buqi Erqi 不齊而齊)?" *Dao: A Journal of Comparative Philosophy* 16: 73–93.

———, and Jaap van Brakel. 2014. "Out of the Ge-Stell? The Role of the East in Heidegger's *das andere Denken*." *Philosophy East and West* 64: 527–62.

———, and Jaap van Brakel. 2016a. *Fundamentals of Comparative and Intercultural Philosophy*. Albany NY: State University of New York Press.
———, and Jaap van Brakel. 2016b. "A Theory of Interpretation for Comparative and Chinese Philosophy." *Dao: A Journal of Comparative Philosophy* 15: 575–89.
———, and Jaap van Brakel. 2016c. "Revisiting Wittgenstein on Family Resemblance and Colour(s)." *Philosophical Investigations* 39 (3): 254–80.
———, and Jaap van Brakel. 2018. "On the Interpreter's Choices: Making Hermeneutic Relativity Explicit." *Dao: A Journal of Comparative Philosophy*. 17: 455–78.
Machek, David. 2010. "Is Freedom in Necessity or in Happiness? Guo Xiang's and Lin Xiyi's Controversial Readings of Zhuangzi's "Free Rambling." *Studia Orientalia Slovaca* 9 (2): 111–28.
———. 2015. ""Emotions That Do Not Move": Zhuangzi and Stoics on Self-Emerging Feelings." *Dao: A Journal of Comparative Philosophy* 14: 521–44.
Mair, Victor H., ed. 1983. *Experimental Essays on Chuang-Tzu*. Honolulu: University of Hawai'i Press.
———, trans. 1994. *Wandering on the Way*. New York: Bantam Books.
Major, John S. 1975. "The Efficacy of Uselessness: A Chuang-Tzu Motif." *Philosophy East and West* 25 (3): 265–79.
Makeham, John. 2012. "Epilogue: Inner Logic, Indigenous Grammars, and the Identity of Zhongguo Zhexue." In *Learning to Emulate the Wise: The Genesis of Chinese Philosophy as an Academic Discipline in Twentieth-Century China*, edited by John Makeham, 347–72. Hong Kong: Chinese University Press.
Malinowski, Boris. 1923. "The Problem of Meaning in Primitive Languages." In *The Meaning of Meaning*, edited by C. K. Ogden and I. Richard, 315–36. London: Routledge and Kegan Paul.
———. 1935. *The Language of Magic and Gardening*. London: Allen & Unwin.
Malmqvist, Göran. 1971. *Studies on the Gongyang and Guliang Commentaries I*. Kungsbacka, Sweden: Elanders.
Marchal, Kai. 2013. "Moral Emotions, Awareness, and Spiritual Freedom in the Thought of Zhu Xi (1130–1200)." *Asian Philosophy: An International Journal of the Philosophical Traditions of the East* 23 (3): 199–220.
Mates, Benson, transl. 1996. *Sextus Empiricus: Outlines of Pyrronism*. New York, Oxford, UK: Oxford University Press.
McCormick, Peter J., ed. 1996. *Starmaking: Realism, Anti-Realism, and Irrealism*. Cambridge, MA: MIT Press.
McLeod, Alexus. 2011. "Pluralism about Truth in Early Chinese Philosophy: A Reflection on Wang Chong's Approach." *Comparative Philosophy* 2 (1): 38–60.
———. 2015. "Replies to Brons and Mou on Wang Chong and Pluralism." *Comparative Philosophy* 6 (1): 169–84.
———. 2016. *Theories of Truth in Chinese Philosophy: A Comparative Approach*. London: Rowman & Littlefield.
Mei Yi-pao, trans. 1929. *The Ethical and Political Works of Motse*. London: Probsthain.
Merleau-Ponty, Maurice. 1964. *Signs*. Evanston: Northwestern University Press.

———. 1973. *The Prose of the World*. Evanston, IL: Northwestern University Press.
Moeller, Hans-Georg. 2009. *The Moral Fool: A Case for Amorality*. New York: Columbia University Press.
Møllgaard, Eske. 2007. *An Introduction to Daoist Thought. Action, Language, and Ethics in Zhuangzi*. London and New York: Routledge.
———. 2014. "Zhuangzi's Word, Heidegger's Word, and the Confucian Word." *Journal of Chinese Philosophy* 41 (3–4): 454–69.
Mou Bo. 2015. "Rooted and Rootless Pluralist Approaches to Truth: Two Distinct Interpretations of Wang Chong's Account." *Comparative Philosophy* 6 (1): 149–67.
Muller, A. Charles, trans. 2016. *Zhuangzi*. http://www.acmuller.net/con-dao/zhuangzi.html.
Murthy, Viren. 2011. *The Political Philosophy of Zhang Taiyan: The Resistance of Consciousness*. Leiden, The Netherlands; Boston, MA: Brill.
Mynard, Thierry. 2017. "Aristotelian Works in Seventeenth-Century China: An Updated Survey and New Analysis." *Monumenta Serica: Journal of Oriental Studies* 65 (1): 61–85.
Ni Peimin. 2016. "*Gongfu* Method in the *Analects* and Its Significance Beyond." In *Chinese Philosophy Methodologies*, edited by Sor-hoon Tan, 127–42. London: Bloomsbury.
Nivison, David S. 1991. "Hsun Tzu and Chuang Tzu." In *Chinese Texts and Philosophical Contexts. Essays Dedicated to Angus C. Graham*, edited by Henry Rosemont, 129–42. Chicago and La Salle, IL: Open Court.
Nussbaum, Martha C. 2000. *Women and Human Development. The Capabilities Approach*. Cambridge, UK: Cambridge University Press.
Peirce, Charles Sanders. 1878. "The Doctrine of Chances." *Popular Science Monthly* 12: 604–15.
———. 1905. "What Pragmatism Is." *The Monist* 15 (2): 161–81.
———. 1931–58. *The Collected Papers of Charles Sanders Peirce*. 8 vols. Eds. C. Hartshorne, P. Weiss (vols. 1–6) and A. Burks (vols. 7–8). Cambridge, MA: Harvard University Press.
Peterman, James. 2008. "Why Zhuangzi's Real Discovery Is One That Lets Him Stop Doing Philosophy When He Wants To." *Philosophy East and West* 58 (3): 372–94.
Pokora, Timoteus, trans. 1975. *Hsin-Lun (New Treatise) and Other Writings by Huan T'an*. In *Michigan Papers in Chinese Studies* (20).
Puett, Michael J. 2003. "'Nothing Can Overcome Heaven': The Notion of Spirit in the *Zhuangzi*." In *Hiding the World in the World: Uneven Discourses on the Zhuangzi*, edited by Scott Cook, 248–62. Albany: State University of New York Press.
———. 2004. "The Ethics of Responding Properly: The Notion *Qing* 情 in Early Chinese Thought." In *Love and Emotions in Traditional Chinese Literature*, edited by Halvor Eifring, 37–68. Leiden, The Netherlands: Brill.
Pulleybank, Edwin G. 1995. *Outline of Classical Chinese Grammar*. Vancouver: University of British Columbia Press.

Putnam, Hilary. 1981. *Reason, Truth, and History*. Cambridge, UK: Cambridge University Press.
———. 1987. *The Many Faces of Realism*. La Salle, IL: Open Court.
———. 1988. *Representation and Reality*. Cambridge, MA: MIT Press.
———. 1990. *Realism with a Human Face*. Cambridge, MA: Harvard University Press.
———. 1994. *Words & Life*. Cambridge, MA: Harvard University Press.
———. 2002. *The Collapse of the Fact/Value Dichotomy*. Cambridge, MA: Harvard University Press.
———. 2004. *Ethics without Ontology*. Cambridge, MA: Harvard University Press.
Qin Xuqing, 秦旭卿, and Sun Yongchang 孙雍长, trans. 2003. *Zhuang Zi*《庄子》[Zhuangzi (in modern Chinese)]. Changsha, China: Hunan renmin chubanshe.
Quine, Willard V. O. 1981. *Theories and Things*. Cambridge, MA: Harvard University Press.
———. 1986. *The Ways of Paradox and Other Essays*. Cambridge, MA: Harvard University Press.
———. 1992. "Structure and Nature." *Journal of Philosophy* 89:5–9.
Radice, Thomas. 2001. "Clarity and Survival in the Zhuangzi." *Asian Philosophy: An International Journal of the Philosophical Traditions of the East* 11 (1): 33–40.
Raphals, Lisa. 1996. "Skeptical Strategies in the *Zhuangzi* and *Theaetetus*." In *Essays on Skepticism, Relativism and Ethics in the Zhuangzi*, edited by Paul Kjellberg and Philip J. Ivanhoe, 26–49. Albany: State University of New York Press.
Reding, Jean-Paul. 1985. *Les fondements philosophiques de la rhétorique chez les sophistes grecs et chez les sophiste chinois*. Neuchâtel, Brussels: Peter Lang.
———. 2004. *Comparative Essays in Early Greek and Chinese Rational Thinking*. Aldershot, UK: Ashgate.
Ricci. 2001. *Grand dictionnaire Ricci de la langue chinoise*. 7 vols. Paris/Taipei: Desclée de Brouwer.
Richards, Ivor Armstrong. [1932] 1997. *Mencius on the Mind: Experiments in Multiple Definition*. London: Curzon.
Rickett, W. Allyn, trans. 1985. *Guanzi: Political, Economic, and Philosophical Essays from Early China*. Vol. 1. Princeton, NJ: Princeton University Press.
———, trans. 1998. *Guanzi: Political, Economic, and Philosophical Essays from Early China*. Vol. 2. Princeton, NJ: Princeton University Press.
Robins, Dan. 2010. "The Later Mohists and Logic." *History and Philosophy of Logic* 31 (3): 247–85.
Roetz, Heiner. 1993. "Validity in Chou Thought: On Chad Hansen and the Pragmatic Turn in Sinology." In *Epistemological Issues in Classical Chinese Philosophy*, edited by Hans Lenk and Gregor Paul, 69–113. New York: State University of New York Press.
Rorty, Richard. 1982. *Consequences of Pragmatism (Essays: 1972–1980)*. Brighton, UK: Harvester Press.
———. 1993. "Putnam and the Relativist Menace." *Journal of Philosophy* 90 (9): 443–61.

Rosch, Eleanor, and Carolyn B. Mervis. 1975. "Family Resemblances: Studies in the Internal Structure of Categories." *Cognitive Psychology* 7 (4): 573–605.

Rosemont, Henry. 1988. "Against Relativism." In *Interpretation across Boundaries: New Essays in Comparative Philosophy*, edited by Gerald James Larson and Eliot Deutsch, 36–70. Princeton, NJ: Princeton University Press.

———. 1992. "Remarks on the Quasi-Syllogism." *Philosophy East and West* 42 (1): 31–35.

———. 2014. "Truth as Truthfulness." *Confluence: Online Journal of World Philosophies* 1: 151–57, 205–12.

———. 2016. "Translating and Interpreting Chinese Philosophy." In *The Stanford Encyclopedia of Philosophy*, edited by Edward N. Zalta. http://plato.stanford.edu/archives/sum2016/entries/chinese-translate-interpret/.

Roth, Harold D. 2000. "Bimodal Mystical Experience in the "Qiwulun" Chapter of Zhuangzi." *Journal of Chinese Religions* 28 (1): 31–50.

———. 2003. *A Companion to Angus C. Graham's Chuang Tzu–The Inner Chapters*. Honolulu: University of Hawai'i Press.

———. 2008. "Against Cognitive Imperialism: A Call for a Non-Ethnocentric Approach to Cognitive Science and Religious Studies." *Religion East and West*, 1–26.

Sallis, John. 2002. *On Translation*. Bloomington IN: Indiana University Press.

Saunders Jr., Frank. 2014. "Semantics without Truth in Later Mohist Philosophy of Language." *Dao: A Journal of Comparative Philosophy* 13: 215–29.

Schipper, Kristofer, trans. 2007. *Zhuang Zi: de volledige geschriften: het grote klassieke boek van het Taoïsme*. Amsterdam, The Netherlands: Uitgeverij Augustus.

Schuhmacher, Stephan, trans. 2006. *Zhuangzi: Das Buch der Spontaneität*. Oberstdorf, Germany: Windpferd.

Schwitzgebel, Eric. 1996. "Zhuangzi's Attitude toward Language and His Skepticism." In *Essays on Skepticism, Relativism and Ethics in the Zhuangzi*, edited by Paul Kjellberg and Philip J. Ivanhoe. Albany: State University of New York Press.

Sellmann, James D. 1998. "Transformational Humor in the *Zhuangzi*." In *Wandering at Ease in the Zhuangzi*, edited by Roger T. Ames, 163–74. Albany: State University of New York Press.

Sextus Empiricus. 1976. *Outlines of Pyrrhonism*. London: Heinemann.

Si Lü 思履, ed. 2013. *Zhuangzi quanshu*《庄子全书》[Complete Works by Zhuangzi (in modern Chinese)]. Beijing: Zhongguo huaqiao chubanshe.

Siddiqui, Farheen, and M. Afshar Alam. 2011. "Web Ontology Language Design and Related Tools: A Survey." *Journal of Emerging Technologies in Web Intelligence* 3 (1): 47–59.

Singh, Danesh. 2016. "Epistemic Perpectivism and Living Well in the Thought of Nietzsche and Zhuangzi." *Journal of East-West Thought* 6 (4): 1–17.

Slingerland, Edward. 2013. "Body and Mind in Early China: An Integrated Humanities–Science Approach." *Journal of the American Academy of Religion* 81 (1): 6–55.

Smith, Huston. 1980. "Western and Comparative Perspectives on Truth." *Philosophy East and West* 30 (4): 425–37.
Stevenson, Frank W. 2008. "The Question of the Wind in Zhuangzi." In *China-West Interculture: Toward the Philosophy of World Integration: Essays on Wu Kuang-Ming's Thinking*, edited by Jay Goulding. New York: Global Scholarly Publications.
Sturgeon, Donald James. 2014. "Knowledge in Early Chinese Thought." PhD dissertation, the University of Hong Kong. http://hdl.handle.net/10722/198813.
———. 2015. "Zhuangzi, Perspectives, and Greater Knowledge." *Philosophy East and West* 65 (3): 891–917.
Tan Xiaoli, and Huang Tianyuan. 2015. "Translating Chinese Philosophy on Its Own Terms: An Interview with Professor Roger T. Ames." *Asia Pacific Translation and Intercultural Studies* 2 (2): 139–49.
Tarski, Alfred. [1931] 1956. "The Concept of Truth in Formalized Languages." In *Logic, Semantics, Metamathematics*, edited by Alfred Tarski, 152–278 (Polish original 1931; German translation 1936). Oxford, UK: Clarendon.
Tjan Tjoe Som, trans. [1949] 1952. *Po Hu T'ung. The Comprehensive Discussions in the White Tiger Hal.* Westport, CT: Hyperion Press (Leiden, The Netherlands: Brill).
Unger, Ulrich. 2000. *Grundbegriffe der altchinesischen Philosophie: Ein Wörterbuch für die klassische Periode*. Darmstadt, Germany: Wissenschaftliche Buchgesellschaft.
van Brakel, Jaap. 1992. "The Complete Description of the Frame Problem." *Vivek (Bombay)* 5 (3): 11–16; also available as *Psycoloquy* 3 (60) (1992) at http://www.cogsci.ecs.soton.ac.uk/cgi/psyc/newpsy?3.60.
———. 1999. "We." *Ethical Perspectives* 6: 224–35; also translated into Chinese: *Zhexuejia* 哲學家 2009: 167–82.
———. 2014. "Heidegger on Zhuangzi and Uselessness." *Journal of Chinese philosophy* 41 (3–4): 387–406.
———, and Ma Lin. 2015. "Extension of Family Resemblance Concepts as a Necessary Condition of Interpretation across Traditions." *Dao: A Journal of Comparative Philosophy* (4): 475–97.
van Fraassen, Bas C. 1986. "The World We Speak of, and the Language We Live In." In *Philosophy and Culture: Proceedings of the 17th World Congress of Philosophy (Montreal, 1983)*, 213–21. Montreal, QC: Editions du Beffroi.
———. 2002. *The Empirical Stance, The Terry Lectures*. New Haven, CT: Yale University Press.
———. 2004. "Replies to Discussion on the Empirical Stance." *Philosophical Studies* 121: 171–82.
Van Norden, Bryan W., trans. 2001. *Mengzi (Mencius)*. In *Readings in Classical Chinese Philosophy*, edited by Philip J. Ivanhoe and Bryan W. Van Norden. New York: Seven Bridges Press.
———. 2011. *Introduction to Classical Chinese Philosophy*. Indianapolis, IN: Hackett.
———. 2016. "Zhuangzi's Ironic Detachment and Political Commitment." *Dao: A Journal of Comparative Philosophy* 15 (1): 1–17.

Voloshinov, Valentin Nikolaevich. [1930] 1986. *Marxism and the Philosophy of Language*. Cambridge, MA: Harvard University Press.
Waley, Arthur. 1939. *Three Ways of Thought in Ancient China*. London: Allen & Unwin.
Wang Huaiyu. 2009. "The Way of Heart: Mencius' Understanding of Justice." *Philosophy East and West* 59 (3): 317–63.
Wang Jianlu 王建鲁. 2014. *Minglitan yu Bianzhengfa daquan zhushu bijiao yanjiu* 《名理探》与《辩证法大全注疏》比较研究 [A Comparative Study of the *Minglitan* and *In Universam Dialekticam Aristotelis*]. Beijing, China: Zhongguo shehui kexue chubanshe.
Wang Rongpei 汪榕培, trans. 2003. *Zhuang Zi* 《庄子》. Changsha, China: Hunan renmin chubanshe.
Wang Youru. 2003. *Linguistic Strategies in Daoist Zhuangzi and Chan Buddhism*. London: RoutledgeCurzon.
———. 2004. "The Strategies of 'Goblet Words:' Indirect Communication in the *Zhuangzi*," *Journal of Chinese Philosophy* 31 (2): 195–218.
Wang Yuhua 王玉华. 2004. *Duoyuan shiye yu chuantong de helihua: Zhang Taiyan sixiang de chanshi* 《多元视野与传统的合理化：章太炎思想的阐释》 [An Interpretation of Zhang Taiyan's Thought: A Pluralistic Perspective and the Rationalization of Tradition]. Beijing: Zhongguo shehui kexue chubanshe.
Wardy, Robert. 2000. *Aristotle in China. Language, Categories and Translation*. Cambridge, UK: Cambridge University Press.
Watson, Burton, trans. 1968. *The Complete Works of Chuang Tzu*. New York: Columbia University Press.
———, trans. 1993. *Records of the Grand Historian by Sima Qian*. New York/Hong Kong: Columbia University Press.
———, trans. 2003. *Xunzi: Basic Writings*. New York: Columbia University Press.
Wieger, Léon, trans. 1913. *Œvres de Tchoang-Tzeu*. http://www.inlibroveritas.net: numerous editions.
Wilhelm, Richard, trans. 1920. *Dschuang-Dsi. Das wahre Buch vom südlichen Blütenland*. Jena, Germany: Diederichs.
Williams, John R. 2017a. "The Vanishing Wild Card: Challenges and Implications of Ziporyn's Zhuangzi." *Philosophy East and West* 67 (1): 177–91.
———. 2017b. "The Radiance of Drift and Doubt: Zhuangzi and the Starting Point of Philosophical Discourse." *Dao: A Journal of Comparative Philosophy* 16:1–14.
Wittgenstein, Ludwig. 2009. *Philosophical Investigations*. Oxford: Blackwell. 4th ed., translated by G. E. M. Anscombe, P. M. S. Hacker, and J. Schulte. Oxford, UK: Wiley-Blackwell.
Wolf, Susan R. 1995. "Commentary on Martha C. Nussbaum: Human Capabilities, Female Human Beings." In *Women, Culture, and Development: A Study of Human Capabilities*, M.C. Nussbaum and J. Glover, 105–15. Oxford, UK: Clarendon Press.
Wong, David B. 2005. "Zhuangzi and the Obsession with Being Right." *History of Philosophy Quarterly* 22 (2): 91–107.

———. 2006. *Natural Moralities: A Defense of Pluralistic Relativism*. New York: Oxford University Press.

———. 2014. "Reply to Hansen." In *Moral Relativism and Chinese Philosophy: David Wong and His Critics*, edited by Yang Xiao and Yong Huang, 215–40. Albany: State University of New York Press.

Wong Young-tsu. 2010. *Beyond Confucian China: The Rival Discourses of Kang Youwei and Zhang Binglin*. London and New York: Routledge.

Wu Kuang-ming. 1990. *The Butterfly as Companion: Meditations on the First Three Chapters of the Chuang Tzu*. Albany: State University of New York Press.

Xiao Yang, and Huang Yong, eds. 2014. *Moral Relativism and Chinese Philosophy: David Wong and His Critics*. Albany: State University of New York Press.

Yearley, Lee H. 1983. "The Perfected Person in the Radical Chuang-Tzu." In *Experimental Essays on Chuang-Tzu*, edited by Victor H. Mair, 125–39. Honolulu: University of Hawai'i Press.

———. 1996. "Zhuangzi's Understanding of Skillfulness and the Ultimate Spiritual State." In *Essays on Skepticism, Relativism and Ethics in the Zhuangzi*, edited by Paul Kjellberg and Philip J. Ivanhoe, 152–82. Albany: State University of New York Press.

Zhai Jiangyue, trans. 2005. *The Spring and Autumn of Lü Buwei*. Guilin, China: Guangxi Normal University Press.

Zhang Dainian. 1989. *Zhongguo gudian zhexue gainian fanchou yaolun*《中国古典哲学概念范畴要论》[An Essential Introduction to the Concepts and Categories in Classical Chinese Philosophy]. Beijing, China: Zhongguo shehui kexue chubanshe. See translated version in citation below.

———. 2002. *Key Concepts in Chinese Philosophy*. New Haven, CT, London: Yale University Press.

Zhang Gengguang 张耿光, trans. 1993. *Zhuangzi quanyi*《庄子全译》[A Complete Translation of the *Zhuangzi* (into modern Chinese)]. Guiyang, China: Guizhou renmin chubanshe.

Zhang Taiyan. 1985. "*Paiman pingyi* 排滿平議 [On repelling the Manchu's]." In *Zhang Taiyan quanji*《章太炎全集》[Complete Works by Zhang Taiyan], 262–70. Shanghai, China: Shanghai renmin chubanshe.

———. 1986. "*Qiwulun shi* 齊物論釋 [A commentary on the *Qiwulun*]." In *Zhang Taiyan quanji*《章太炎全集》[Complete Works by Zhang Taiyan], 1–58 and 59–124. Shanghai, China: Shanghai renmin chubanshe.

———. 1987. *Guoxue gailun*《國學概論》[Introduction to National Learning]. Chengdu, China: Bashu shushe.

———. 1995. "Lun fofa yu zhongjiao, zhexue yiji xianshi zhi guanxi 論佛法與宗教、哲學以及現實之關係. [On the Relation between Buddhism and Religion, Philosophy and Reality]." In *Zhang Taiyan ji, Yangdu ji*《章太炎集、楊度集》[Selected Works by Zhang Taiyan and Yang Du], 5–17. Beijing, China: Zhongguo shehui kexue chubanshe.

Zhong Tai 鐘泰. 2008. *Zhongguo zhexueshi* 中國哲學史 [A History of Chinese Philosophy]. Beijing, China: Dongfang chubanshe.

Ziporyn, Brook. 2008. "Form, Principle, Pattern, or Coherence? Li 理 in Chinese Philosophy." *Philosophy Compass* 3 (3): 401–22.

———, trans., 2009a. *Zhuangzi: The Essential Writings* Indianapolis, IN: Hackett.

———. 2009b. "Zhuangzi as Philosopher." Indianapolis, IN: Hackett. https://www.hackettpublishing.com/zhuangziphil.

———.2010. Review of "Hans-Georg Moeller, *The Moral Fool: A Case for Amorality*," *Dao: A Journal of Comparative Philosophy* 9: 481–85.

———. 2013. *Beyond Oneness and Difference: Li and Coherence in Chinese Buddhist Thought and Its Antecedent.* Albany: State University of New York Press.

Zürcher, Erik. 1959. *The Buddhist Conquest of China.* Leiden, The Netherlands: Brill.

Name Index

Alam, M. Afshar, 4
Allinson, Robert E., 122, 233n1, 246n12
Alt, Wayne, 80, 138–40, 192, 217n59, 228n46, 238n27
Ames, Roger T., 10, 15, 42, 64, 180, 202, 210n2, 212n30–32, 212n36, 220n13, 222n4, 222n8, 225n20, 251n82, 251n84
Arendrup, Birthe, 185, 194

Baxter, William H., 7
Berthrong, John, 51
Billeter, Jean François, xvi, 68–76 passim, 88, 93, 95–96, 100, 102, 135, 137, 139, 147, 154, 166, 180–82, 190–92, 198–200, 231n77, 232n97, 238n15, 238n21, 239n29, 240n43, 242n70, 245n6, 246n29, 247n35, n39, 250n65, 251n78
Boghossian, Paul, 234n19
Boucher, S. C., 132
Bradley, Scott P., 241n55
Brandom, Robert, 17, 214n18
Bullock, Jeffrey S., xvii, 88

Callahan, William A., 60, 189, 224n6
Cao Chuji 曹础基, xvi, 83, 225n2, 227n31, 241n53
Chakravarty, Anjan, 132
Chan Wing-tsit, xvi, 52, 68, 87, 95–97, 100–4, 142, 144–45, 192, 199, 228n38, 239n40, 240n43, 249n59
Chang Tzu-li, 235n40
Chang Wuzi 長梧子, 197–98
Chen Guying 陈鼓应, xvi, 77, 103, 189, 227n31, 240n52
Chen Lai, 223n14
Chen Qitian 陈启天, 104
Chen Shen 陈深, 91–92
Chen, L. K., 251n87
Chen Yinchi 陈引弛, 6
Cheng Chungying, 22, 217n53, n55, 218n60
Cheng Xuanying 成玄英 (fl. 630–60), xvi, 76, 81, 87–88, 92, 96, 105, 120, 135–36, 146, 161, 216n45, 229n51, 230n72, 232n96, 240n45, 241n56
Cheng, Anne, 84, 215n29
Chinn, Ewing Y., 201
Chiu Wai Wai, 139, 212n25, 249n63
Chomsky, Noam, 4, 190
Chong Kim-chong, 83, 129, 238n13, 252n96
Chu Boxiu 褚伯秀, 146
Cleary, Thomas, xvi, 68, 76, 87, 95–98, 101, 103, 189, 192, 199, 228n41, 239n40
Confucius. See *Kongzi*
Connolly, Tim, 111
Cook, Scott, 189
Coutinho, Steve, xvii, 68, 79–80, 93, 95–96, 109, 119, 137–41, 167, 189,

272 / Name Index

Coutinho, Steve (*continued*)
  199, 212n25, 216n49, 217n52, n59, 226n4, 233n1, 234n24, 238n23, 240n48, 243n5, 244n21, 246n22
Crump, J. I., xvii, 33, 218n9
Cua, Antonio S., 225n21

Dao Zhi 盜跖 (Robber Zhi), 170, 174
Davidson, Donald, 223n17
De Caro, Mario, 244n26
Dewey, John, 10, 54, 222n1
Di 翟 (brother of Huan 緩), 162
Ding (cook Ding) 丁, 121, 133, 183, 198–99, 241n62

Eifring, Halvor, 229n60
Elgin, Catherine Z., 59–61, 223n22, 224n2, n10
English, Jane, xvi, 80
Ekman, Paul, 210n4
Eno, Robert, xvi, xvii, 52, 71, 97–98, 102–4, 143, 173, 189, 230n70, 238n17, 238n27, 239n40, 240n46, 241n62

Feng Gia-Fu, xvi, 80
Feng Youlan, xvi, 5–6, 52, 68, 72, 76, 79–82, 87, 97–103, 111, 113–14, 139, 143–45, 148, 165, 174, 189, 197, 200, 204, 210n9, 227n27–28, 228n39, 230n69, 238n15, 239n40, 240n43, 240n46, 242n79, 247n40, 250n66, 250n68, 250n70
Feyerabend, Paul, 112
Fodor, Jerry A., 4
Forke, Alfred, xvii, 23, 43–44, 46, 89, 219n13, 219n22, 219n23, 230n75
Fraser, Chris, 17–18, 28, 41, 50, 53, 60, 172–74, 189, 210n3, 213n9, 214n17, 216n51, 219n14, 220n14, 221n26, 224n13, 230n65, 230n73, 236n53, 240n46
Frege, Gottlob, 3
Fu Fanji 傅汎際. *See* Furtado, Francisco

Furtado, Francisco (1589–1653), 37, 219n17

Geaney, Jane M., 216n47
Giles, Herbert A., xvi, 73, 82, 102–3, 189, 241n63
Goodman, Nelson, xxii, 49, 57–65, 221n1, 224–25
Graham, A. C., xiv, 89–95 passim
Griffith, Jeremy, 238
Guo Weiwei, 27
Guo Xiang 郭象 (252–312), xvi, 24, 85, 87, 91, 96, 103, 105, 110–11, 114, 117, 120, 135–36, 146–48, 153, 157–58, 165–71, 174, 179–80, 184–88, 194, 220n11, 230n72, 238n18, 239n37, 241n57, 245n8, 245n14, 246–48

Haack, Susan, 109
Hall, David L., 19, 215n33. *See also* Ames
Hanfeizi 韓非子 (c. 280–233 BCE), xvii, xxi, 31–32, 63–65, 122, 163, 218n4, 218n10, 225n17, 230n73, 231n78
Hansen, Chad, xiii, xxiii, 15–17, 19, 28, 40–42, 50, 52, 60, 68, 89, 109, 111, 113, 118, 161, 167, 172–73, 194, 201, 210n3, 213n6, 213n7, 213n10, 214n16, 214n19, 214n27, 216n50, 219n14, 223n12, 224n12, 233n4, 233n8, 234n25, 235n39, 236n41, 243n15, 246n23, 247n42, 249n61
Harbsmeier, Christoph, xiii, 15–19, 25–28, 32, 36–38, 41, 47, 63–65, 91–92, 95, 99, 102–5, 122, 143, 145–46, 152, 163, 213n8, 213n9, 213n14, 213n15, 214n16, n24, 216n48, 216n51, 218n10, 219n12, 220n15, 221n17, 221n21, 221n22, 221n23, 222n9, 229n50, 231n80, 232n92, 232n96, 239n40, 240n42, 240n43, 240n46

Name Index / 273

Hawkes, David, xvii, 43, 45–46
Heidegger, Martin, xix, xvi–xvii, 205–6, 222n1, 227n30, 251n86, 252n92, 252n98
Hesse, Mary B., 234n22
Hightower, James Robert, xvii, 33, 39, 45, 123
Huan 緩 (brother of Di 翟), 162
Huang Tianyuan, 212n30
Huang Yong, 174, 234n16
Huangdi 黃帝 (Yellow Emperor; 2698?–2598? BCE), 197
Hui Shi 惠施 (370–310 BCE), 82–84, 131, 183, 203–5, 229n63
Huizi 惠子. See Hui Shi
Hundun 渾沌, 131, 201–2
Huzi 壺子, 197

Ivanhoe, Philip J., 121, 233n1, 235n35, 241n62

James, William, 213n4, 222n1
Jian Wu 肩吾, 185
Jiang Shaoyu, xiii
Jiang Xichang 蔣錫昌, 146
Jiao Hong 焦竑 (1540–1620), 91, 142
Jie 桀 (1728?–1675? BCE), 32, 170
Jullien, François, 70, 214n20, 215n35, 224n8, 226n13
Jung Hwa Yol, 21

Karlgren, Bernhard, 225n24
Kim Myeong-seok, 10, 38, 211n9, 220n4, n16
Kjellberg, Paul, xvi, 51–52, 75–77, 83, 95–97, 100–3, 121, 139, 143–55 passim, 189, 229n56, 233n1, 240n43, 241n61, 241n62, 245n13, 250n70
Klein, Esther, 180
Knoblock, John, xvii, 32–35, 44–48, 64, 123, 218n5, 218n7, 218n10, 220n9, 221n27, 223n13, 225n18, 229n51, 235n30

Kongzi 孔子 (Confucius, 551–479 BCE), 22, 162–63, 171, 195, 197, 249n54, 249n60, 250n75
Kurtz, Joachim, 37, 219n21
Kwok Sai Hang, 190, 236n54

Lacey, Hugh, 55
Lafitte, Jean-Jacques, xvi, 69, 226n9, 226n21
Lai, Karyn, 218n3
Lau Dim Cheuk, xvi–xvii, 71
Legge, James, xvi–xvii, 39, 45, 63, 65, 71, 73, 79, 82, 87, 95–97, 100–3, 139, 143, 150, 189, 219n16, 221n20, 225n21, 227n27, 228n49, 230n67, 240n41, 240n43, 240n46, 241n63, 250n70
Levi, Jean, xvi, 68–69, 73, 75–78, 80, 83, 87, 95–98, 100–2, 143, 145, 150, 189, 194, 226n7, 226n15, 228n42, 228n45, 229n61, 232n93, 232n108, 241n63, 245n6, 350n70
Levy, André, xvii, 39, 70–71, 219n16, 220n2, 221n20, 226n15–n18
Li Gang (Li Kang) 李綱 (1083–1140), 252n90
Li Ji 麗姬 (Lady Li), 126
Li Zhizao 李之藻 (1571–1630), 37, 219n17
Lian Shu 連叔, 185
Lian Xinda, 187–87
Liao, W. K., xvii, 64–65, 163
Liezi 列子 (450–375 BCE), xiv, 31, 33–35, 42, 123, 174–75, 187, 194, 197, 218n4, n11, 219n16, 220n6, 221n18, 227n29, 231n78, 244n22, 248n45
Lin Shuen-Fu, 238n13, 245n7
Lin Xiyi 林希逸 (1193–1270?), 91, 105, 185, 241n57
Lin Yunming 林雲銘 (1628?–1697?), 96
Lin Yutang 林語堂, xvi, 24, 52, 72, 75–76, 80, 83, 95–99, 101–4, 139, 143–45, 189, 200, 227n28, 228n39,

Lin Yutang (continued)
  228n44, 238n15, 239n40, 240n43,
  240n46, 250n70, 250n75
Liu An 劉安 (ca. 179–122 BCE),
  (King of Huainan), xvii, 33–35, 44,
  164, 209n4, 243n2
Liu JeeLoo, 211n11
Liu Xianxin 劉咸炘 (1896–1932),
  232n104
Liu Xiaogan, xvii, 96, 103, 110,
  143, 153, 181, 203, 233n1, 233n4,
  233n7, 239n40, 244n1
Lloyd, Geoffrey Ernest Richard, 41,
  225n19, 238n14, 239n36
Lü Huiqing 呂惠卿 (1032–1111),
  230n70, 241n57, 249n60
Luo Miandao 羅勉道 (fl. ca. 1270), 91,
  240n42

Ma Lin, xix–23 passim
Macarthur, David, 244n26
Machek, David, 84, 170–71, 180,
  185–86
Mair, Victor H., xvi, 6, 52, 68, 71–72,
  75–77, 79–80, 83, 87, 94–98, 100–1,
  103, 139–40, 143, 145–46, 150, 187,
  189, 192, 199, 227n28, 230n71,
  232n97, 238n15, 239n40, 240n43,
  241n63, 245n6, 246n18, 250n70
Major, John S., 209n4, 244n29
Makeham, John, 209n5, 212n29
Malinowski, Boris, 137, 238n22
Malmqvist, Göran, 65
Mao Qiang 毛嬙 (Mao-ch'iang), 126
Marchal, Kai, 53
Mates, Benson, 235n36
McCormick, Peter J., 61, 224n2,
  224n6
McLeod, Alexus, 18, 22–23, 43, 47,
  50, 215n40, 216n42, 221n26
Mei Yi-pao, 223n13
Mengzi 孟子 (Mencius, 372–289 BCE),
  xvi–xvii, 22, 31, 34, 39, 42, 45, 53,
  70–71, 73, 219n16, 220n4, 221n21,
  223n25, 225n17, 226n15, 226n18,
  229n63
Merleau-Ponty, Maurice, 211n9,
  240n44
Mervis, Carolyn B., 210n4
Meyer, Andrew Seth, 209n4
Moeller, Hans-Georg, 171–72
Møllgaard, Eske, 238n13
Mou Bo, 22
Mozi 墨子 (470–391 BCE), xvii, 22,
  52, 163
Muller, A. Charles, xvi, 6, 97, 100–4,
  143, 189, 239n40, 240n46, 250n70
Murthy, Viren, 242n73
Mynard, Thierry, 219n17, n21

Ni Peimin, 237n2
Nie Que 齧缺, 125, 127
Nivison, David S., 50
Nussbaum, Martha C., 244n27
Peirce, Charles Sanders, xxiv, 60, 150,
  202, 213n4, 214n27, 222n1, 223n24,
  251n83
Peng 鵬 (bird), 5, 123–24, 179,
  185–88, 211n15, 246n22
Peterman, James, 93, 116, 235n34,
  240n46
Pokora, Timoteus, xvii, 219n16
Pu Jiangqing 浦江清, 187
Puett, Michael J., 83, 248n48
Pulleybank, Edwin G., xvii, 34, 40, 45,
  71, 229n63
Putnam, Hilary, xxii, 49, 54–58, 112,
  175–76, 221n1, 223n17, 223n19,
  223n24, 224n25–26, 224n3, 234n18,
  244n23

Qin Xuqing 秦旭卿, xvi, 104, 227n31
Qu Quezi 瞿鵲子, 197
Queen, Sarah A., 209n4
Quine, Willard V. O., 190, 212n25,
  223n21

Radice, Thomas, 244n29

Raphals, Lisa, 121, 241n62
Reding, Jean-Paul, xvii, 18, 36, 68–69, 84, 214n20, 226n5, 227n28, 229n62, 235n31–32
Richards, Ivor Armstrong, 215n32
Rickett, W. Allyn, xvii, 33, 45–46, 63, 65, 122, 217n56, 218n6, 221n24, 231n80
Riegel, Jeffrey, xvii, 223n13
Robber Zhi. *See* Dao Zhi
Robins, Dan, 213n9, 214n16
Rosch, Eleanor, 210n4
Roetz, Heiner, xvii, 18–19, 42, 87, 214n16, n24, 216n46
Rorty, Richard, 112, 175–76, 223n17, 224n26, 244n23, n25
Rosemont, Henry, 10, 50, 113, 210n4, 213n5, 215n29
Roth, Harold D., 92–93, 209n4, 251n78
Russell, Bertrand, 4

Sallis, John, 211n8
Saunders Jr., Frank, 17, 26, 214n17, 216n48, 216n50, 217n53
Schipper, Kristofer, xvi, 69–70, 76, 83, 87, 96–97, 101, 103, 127, 148, 189, 227n27, 228n41, 229n53, 229n59, 232n94, 233n110, 237n10, 239n39, 246n28, 247n33, 248n45, 250n65
Schuhmacher, Stephan, xvi, 72, 77, 83, 227n34, 228n39, 230n71, 246n28
Schwitzgebel, Eric, 135, 241n62
Sellmann, James D., 93
Sextus Empiricus, 121, 150, 155, 234n17, 235n36
Shi Deqing 釋德清 (1546–1623), 197, 237n12, 248n45, 248n48
Shi Kuang 師曠, 146
Shun 舜 (2233?–2184? BCE), 157, 163, 174, 195
Si Lü 思履, xvi, 84, 105, 145–46, 227n31, 240n51, 245n11
Siddiqui, Farheen, 4

Slingerland, Edward, 92, 211n12, 222n6
Song Rongzi 宋榮子, 194, 248n44
Stevenson, Frank W., 245n8, 251n84
Sturgeon, Donald James, xiii, 18, 36, 40, 42, 51, 111, 122, 152, 166, 172–74, 219n14, 220n4, 222n8, 236n44, 242n67, 243n13
Su Dongpo 蘇東坡 (also called Su Shi), 58
Su Shi 蘇軾 (also called Su Dongpo), 58
Sun Yongchang 孙雍长, xvi, 104, 227n31
Sung Hiu Chuk, Winnie, 251n87
Tan Xiaoli, 212n30
Tarski, Alfred, 5, 17, 213n13, 233n11
Tjan Tjoe Som, xvii, 35–36, 63

Unger, Ulrich, 71–72

van Brakel, Jaap, xix–23 passim
van Fraassen, Bas C., xxiii, 129–34, 177, 237n6
Van Norden, Bryan W., xvii, 71, 153, 229n56, 244n25
Voloshinov, Valentin Nikolaevich, 238n22

Waley, Arthur, xvii, 83, 229n58
Wang Baoxuan 王葆玹, 180
Wang Chong 王充 (27–100? CE), xvii, 16, 22, 47
Wang Fuzhi 王夫之 (1619–1692), 236n52, 242n79
Wang Huaiyu, 225n23
Wang Jianlu 王建鲁, 219n20
Wang Ni 王倪, 125–27, 195, 197, 236n49, n53, 248n50
Wang Rongpei 汪榕培, xvi, 68, 77, 87, 95–98, 100–1, 103, 144–45, 189
Wang Tai 王駘, 197, 249n54
Wang Youru, 134, 229n55, 235n37, 237n11, 238n13, 238n25, 244n25, 247n33

Wang Yuhua 王玉华, 242n81
Wang Zhongjiang, 212n29
Wardy, Robert, 37, 219n19, n21, 220n10
Watson, Burton, xvi, xvii passim
Wen Yiduo 闻一多 (1899–1946), 225n2
Wieger, Léon, 189, 226n17, n21, 241n63, 246n30
Wilhelm, Richard, xvi, 72, 82, 102–3, 189, 206, 229n57, 230n71, 240n41, 246n30, 252n93
Williams, John R., 60, 175, 231n85
Wittgenstein, Ludwig, 4, 138, 166, 210n5, 215n34, 222n1, 238n19
Wolf, Susan R., 244n27
Wong Young-tsu, 242n18
Wong, David B., 113, 211n9, 225n21, 234n16, 237n1
Wu Kuang-ming, 95–97, 101, 143, 189, 231n83, 233n111, 237n9, 239n40, 240n46, 245n8, 246n25

Xiao Yang, 234n16
Xu Shen 许慎, 218n8
Xu You 許由, 185, 197
Xunzi 荀子 (310?–235?), xvii, 11, 22, 31–35, 44–47, 64, 123, 152, 213n15, 218n5, 218n7, 218n10, 219n13, 220n9, 221n22, n23, n27, 225n18, 229n51, 231n78, 235n30

Yancheng Ziyou 顏成子游, 188
Yang Xiong 揚雄 (53 BCE–18 CE), 28
Yao 堯 (2356?–2255? BCE), 90, 120, 157–58, 163, 174, 185, 195, 197, 232n90, 242n79
Yearley, Lee H., 174, 250n64, 251n78

Zhai Jiangyue, xvii, 79, 90
Zhang Binglin 章炳麟. See Zhang Taiyan
Zhang Gengguang 张耿光, xvi, 227n31
Zhang Taiyan 章太炎 (1868–1936), xxiv, 155–59, 188–89, 192, 239n34, 242n72, 242n75, 247n38, 250n63
Zhao Ming 趙明, 187
Zhao Wen 昭文, 146, 154
Zhao Yifu 趙以夫 (1189–1256), 240n50
Zhi Dun 支遁 (314–366), 170, 172, 179, 185, 244n21, 244n22
Zhi Daolin 支道林. See Zhi Dun
Zhong Tai 鐘泰, 142, 231n89
Zhu Xi 朱熹 (1130–1200), 53, 213–14, 223n14
Zhuang Zhou 莊周. See Zhuangzi
Zhuangzi 莊子 (369?–286? BCE), 109–208 passim
Ziporyn, Brook, xiii, xvi, 5–7, 24, 41–42, 51–51, 67–68, 72, 75–78, 80, 83, 87, 90, 94–103, 111, 122, 134, 137, 142–43, 145–47, 149, 157, 165, 168, 171–72, 183, 189, 191, 197, 220n11, 225n16, 227n27, 228n43, 228n44, 230n67, 230n68, 230n70, 231n79, 236n52, 237n12, 238n15, 238n18, 239n32, 240n43, 240n46, 240n50, 241n57, 242n79, 245n2, 245n12, 245n13, 247n35, 247n40, 248n45, n48, 249n57, 249n60 250n63, 250n70
Ziqi 子綦 (of Nanguo), 141, 158, 188, 239n37
Zürcher, Erik, 185–86, 244n17, 244n18, 245n17

Subject Index

acceptability, 102
adequacy, empirical, 212n27
admissibility, 19
affection. See emotions
amoralism, xxiv, 117, 155, 170–77
anarchy, 33, 218n10, 240n48
anger. See joy and anger
appropriateness, 63–64, 225n21, 241n54
argument(ation): ad hominem, 86, 238n13; logical structure of, 216n46; rhetorical, xxiv, 88, 132, 149–54, 201. See also bian 辯
assertions, 17, 26, 131
attunement, mutual (principle of), 2, 133, 210n1
authentic(ity), 16–17, 180, 219n16
axis of dao, 142–44

baby birds, 115, 136–37, 141
barbarism, 158, 174, 242n79
be, to be, possible congeners of to be in classical Chinese, 18, 214n20. See also ran 然; shi 是; you 有
beauty (standard of), 86, 126; and ugliness, 35
Being, 31, 227n30
Bejahung, 77, 230n71
benevolence. See ren 仁
big and small, 185
binaries, contrasting, 49
binomes, 47, 74, 84, 86–87, 180, 230n66

birth/death, 102, 104, 139, 153, 157, 168, 176, 243n10, 248n50, 250n63
bivalence, 140–41, 154
black and white, 52
BLUE, 5, 211n16. See also qing 青; cang 蒼
Book of Rites. See Liji
Buddhism (Buddhist), 156, 242n72, 244n18
boundaries, strict, 89, 112, 159

Canons, the, 25–30. See also Mohists
capabilities (Nussbaum), 244n27
cat. See mao
Categoriae (Aristotle), 219n17. See also Minglitan
category (or "kind"), 24, 216n44. See also lei
certainty, 19
chance, 202, 251n83. See also spontaneity; hundun 渾沌
charity, principle of, 165, 168, 243n9
circumstancely, 103, 228n44
civilization. See barbarism
clarity (clear understanding), 68, 93, 110, 142–45, 161, 239n32
cluster: of concepts, xxi, 20–21, 26, 61, 73, 132, 212n1, 215n29, 251n83; of shifei 是非, shibi 是彼, and kebuke 可不可, 77–78
cognition: flowing, 92; fixated, 92

coherence: second-order, 65; principle of, 167; and theory of truth, 15, 213n3, 214n18. See also fitting
color(s): appearance and, 5–8; basic color terms, 210n4; COLOR, 8
common sense, 9, 221n1. See also ordinary, the; everyday, the
common, the. See ordinary, the
commonality, 97, 146
commoners, 21, 94, 142, 146, 232n98
completeness, 151–52, 177
comprehensiveness, 158
concept(s), xiv, xv, 17; hybrid, xviii, 21, 38, 69, 122, 215n32, 247n39; innate, 3, 4. See also category; cluster
conceptual schemes, 1–2. See also incommensurability
conditions (necessary) of possibility, 1–3, 16, 214n27; not-so-necessary preconditions of interpretation, 2
contradiction, 25, 68, 80, 104–5, 134, 138–41, 200–1, 213n13, 217n56,n59, 239n31, 240n42; performative, 169. See also paradoxes
constant, the, 97, 144–46, 240n46. See ordinary, the
contraries, 73, 141
conventionality, of language, 120
converse, 26–27, 216n50, 217n52, n53
copula(e), 220n4
correctness, 15, 18, 37, 43, 62, 165, 176, 209n9, 211n10, 221n26; correct/false, 32, 68–69; correct/incorrect, xxi, 68–69
correspondence, 37, 227n30; theory of truth, 15, 27, 213n2; with facts, 61. See also isomorphy thesis
Course, the. See dao
customary, the, 240n46. See also the ordinary
credibility, 61, 116
CTP (Chinese Text Project), 13

dao, 198–99, 237n10; DAO, 89, 90, 171; daos, 89, 93, 172, 198, 231n85, 244n21; prescriptive and pragmatic character of, 237n11. See also dao 道
De interpretatione (Aristotle), 211n8, 221n22
deconstruction, xx, 141, 176, 235n37, 244n28
demarcations. See distinctions
demonstrative: shi 是 as, 39–41, 70, 231n84
dénomination (naming), 69, 75, 77, 102, 228n42
dependence, mutual, 101; non-dependence, 180, 246n21, 251n78
description: of how the world is, 4; problem of complete description, 3, 151, 243n7; descriptive/prescriptive, 50, 55. See also fact-value
designation (designation), 75, 77
dichotomies, xviii, 49–58; of description/prescription, 50; of fact/value, xx, xxii, 50–56; no dichotomies in classical Chinese of descriptive/evaluative, 54; of rationality/spontaneity, 49; of reason/emotion, xxii; of subject(ive)/object(ive), 49–53
dictionaries: Langenscheidt, xiv, 226n22; 227n23; Larousse, xiv, 226n8; OED, 217n56; van Dale, xiv, 226n8; Wahrig, xiv, 227n22; Merriam-Webster, xiv, 217n56. See also Erya 爾雅; Ricci
discourse, argumentative, 133
disputation. See bian 辯
distinctions, 46, 50, 53–54, 60, 76, 81, 85, 90, 98, 102, 130, 138–39, 142, 144, 176–77, 180, 191, 201; action-guiding shifei, 214n19
diversity, 2, 95, 120, 190
doubt, 138, 149–53; the undoubted, 150–51. See also torch of chaos and doubt

dualism, mind/body, 222n2, n6

earnestness, 21
effectiveness (efficacious), 60, 231n85
egalitarianism, 156
emotions: basic, 210n4. See also joy and anger; *qing* 情
epistemology. See knowledge; virtues, epistemic
equality, 158, 166, 179–82, 198–99, 201, 203, 209, 212–13, 223–25; equalizing, 20, 24, 157, 216–17, 269; achieving equality by leaving things uneven, 134, 156, 177. See also *qi* 齊
essentialization, 22, 54; essentials, 83
ethics, of difference, 174
ethnocentrism, 175
Être. See Being
eudaimonia, 56, 176, 224n26
everyday, the, function of each thing, 98, 240n46

fact/value: dichotomy, 49–58
facts: accordance with, 18; factitious, 57; fact-value (value-facts), 37, 168
family resemblance, xv, xx, 1, 210n2; across traditions, xxi, 20; concepts, 1, 10, 135, 165–66; extensions of, 19, 238n14; in the large and in the small, 71, 215n34; principle of, 2, 210n2
faux, le, 31–32, 69, 70, 73, 76, 87–88, 226
feelings. See emotions
fitting, 57–61; rightness and fitting, 57–65; and *yi* 宜, 62–65
fool, moral, 171
form(s) of life, 210n3
FR. See family resemblance
frame problem. See problem of complete description
freedom, 92, 131, 170, 184–87, 233n7

fusion of horizons, 212n34

games: and *youxi* 游戏, 1–2
Gelassenheit, 203. See also *wuwei* 无為
genuine(ness), 16, 18, 20–21, 43–44, 163, 212n1, 226n22; and false, 87
germs (Mengzi). See sprouts
globalization, 2
good: the good, 56, 93, 118; good/bad, xxi, 1, 38, 170, 229n56; good/evil, 218n1; *le bien et le mal*, 69; *goed en kwaad*, 69, 226n11. See also *hao'e* 好惡
grindstone of nature, 199. See also *tianni* 天倪

Hansen-Harbsmeier dispute, 15–18
harmonization, 240n48
heaven: companion of, 147; heaven-nature, xxiii, 142, 147, 149, 193, 200; the Equalizer, 143, 199; heavenly equality, 142, 199–201. See also *tian* 天
holism, 209n1, 243n6
goblet words. See *zhiyan* 卮言
human practices, mutually recognizable, 1, 11, 112, 114, 122, 133, 141, 164, 169–79, 183, 210n1
hybrid, xviii, xxi, 10, 20–21, 26, 38

identity, 9, 19, 141
illumination, 68, 158, 226n4, 240n50, 241n56. See also clarity
impromptu (words). See *zhiyan* 卮言
incommensurability, xxiv, 8 112, 114, 168–69, 219n21, 234n12
indeterminacy: of reference, 8; of translation, 8. See also underdetermination
indexicals. See this/that; other/I
inequality, 156, 159, 241n55. See also equality
integrity, 18, 21

interaction, communicative, 169–70
interdependence, xxiv, 67, 96, 230n74
irrationality, 117, 131; bridled, 132
irrealism, 58
irresolvability, 27, 142
isomorphy (thesis), 3–4

joy: and anger, 99, 196, 239n39, 248n52; and sorrow, 35
juste/faux, 32
justice, 46, 69–70, 72, 176, 226n10, 227n23

know(ledge), xv; completeness of (perfection of, ultimately correct), 151–52; as justified true belief, 121, 133, 224n11; know(ing) how/that/of, xv, 125–26, 235n38; not knowing something, 123–24; propositional, 131. See also doubt; understanding

language: anti-language, 135, 137; common, 2, 235n33; everyday, 170; ideal language assumption, 3–8; logically regimented, 133; natural, 3–5, 138, 211n13; 213n13, 233n11; ordinary, 22, 54, 141, 169–70, 193, 215n38, 222n1; of thought, 4
lateral relation (Merleau-Ponty), 240n44
law: English, 131; of non-contradiction, 239n31; Prussian, 131
light of Heaven. See *yiming* 以明
likes/dislikes, 73
lodging place (sayings from a), 97, 146, 238n13
logic: logical analysis, 25–26; paraconsistent, 141, 239n31; principles of, 8, 27; symbolic, 215n35

man. See person
meaning: being unfixed-indeterminate, 235n33; double, xxi, 41; *double entendre*, 41; fixed (precise), xxiii, 3, 133, 135–41, 166, 168–70; theory of, 138. See also concepts; words; *weiding* 未定
men. See people
meta-language, 5, 50–51, 53, 114, 164, 168, 211n13, 212n31
metaphor, 1, 47, 61, 68, 92, 129, 133, 183, 189, 194, 222n2, 237b5
Metaphysica (Aristotle), 47, 221n22
metaphysics (metaphysician), 4, 15, 22, 49–50, 54, 109, 129–32, 202, 211n11, 221n1, 222n2, 223n17, 237n2
mind, the, 34, 53, 144, 156, 238n13
mirror metaphor. See isomorphy thesis
model: sage as a role model for humans, 149, 179, 194–96, 209n8, 239n35, 249n53–54
modifiers: in classical Chinese, 43–48; of *shi* 是 in the *Qiwulun*, 85–89
modularity (of mind), 4
Mohists, xxiv, 16–17, 22, 27, 129, 133, 140; later Mohist *Canons*, xiv, xv, xxi, xxiv, 3, 17, 25–29, 183, 213n10, 216n47–48, 224n1; Ruists and Mohists, 25, 68, 81, 90, 94–95, 110, 112, 119, 121, 135, 138, 142, 161–70
monkey(s), 40, 247n41
mood(s), 76, 129, 137
morality: identification of morality with spontaneity, 56, 170; moral norms, 171
multiculturalism, 158–59, 174, 242n82
mysticism, xx, 180, 201, 242n68, 246n23, 251n78

naturalism, 176, 244n26
Nazi-*dao*, 172–74
needs, human, 54–55
negation, 69–70, 87, 239; in classical Chinese, 180, 188, 214n25; double, 44

no-thing, 158, 188–89, 246n25. See also *wuwu* 無物
non-dependence, 180, 251n78
notions, preconceptual, xxii, 180, 201

object: linguistic construction of, 190; theoretical notion of, 190. See also *wu* 物
OED (*Oxford English Dictionary*), 217n56
One, the (Oneness, into one), 95, 97–98, 110, 198, 200, 235n38, 250n74–75
opposites, xxii, 26, 34, 40, 67–81, 96, 144, 217n52, 219n14, 229n54, 235n37. See also this/that (not-this); good/bad; other/I
oracle bones, 40, 70
ordinary (everyday), the, xxiv, 98, 130, 142, 144, 146, 193, 240n46. See also *yong* 庸
other/self (that/me, other/I), 1, 96, 228n36, 241n57; It and Other, 153
oughtness, 76; and isness, 75, 212

paradoxes, 48, 92, 156, 237, 246, 257, 261
people, companion of, 147–48; ordinary, 94–95, 142, 179, 197, 211n18
person (human, "man"): complete, 196, 249n54; divine (holy), 219, 224, 257, 272; nameless, 220, 272; perfect (consummate, real, highest, godlike), 141, 172, 186, 195, 219, 245n17, 248n50; true (real, genuine, whole), 16, 148 195; worthy, 197. See also sages
perspectivism, 135, 142
pluralism, 113, 175, 215n30, 221n26, 242n81
postmodernism, 235n37. See also deconstruction
postulate: of symmetry, 116–17

potter's wheel of heaven, 143–44, 149, 199
pragmatism (American), 54; pragmatist theory of truth, 15, 213n4. See also Ames; Dewey; Goodman; James; Peirce; Putnam
preconditions. See conditions
prejudice(s). See pre-conception; relativity, hermeneutic
pretense: in projecting theories of truth, 21–25; transcendental pretense, xxi, 22–23, 25–26, 29, 209n5
problem: of complete description, 3, 151–52, 211n9; of the criterion, 234n17; Daoist-Nazi, 172, 174
punctuation, xvi, 213n12, n14. See also parsing
parsing, xvi, 68, 75, 240n47

quarrels, 68–70, 81, 110, 135, 185
quasi-universals, xv, xx–xxii, 2, 26
questions, rhetorical, 149–54
Quine-Duhem thesis. See underdetermination

racist. See problem, Daoist-Nazi
radiance of drift and doubt. See torch of chaos and doubt
rationality: and morality, 56; epistemic, 130; instrumental, 54; universal, 117. See also virtues, epistemic; reason
realism, internal, 112, 211n11; metaphysical, 4, 211n11
reality (the really given), 19
reasonableness, 83
reason/emotion (cognitive/affective), xxii, 49–50, 53–54
Recht/Unrecht, 254
rectitude, 69
relativism, 109–20; being self-refuting, 126; indexical, 118; relativistic interpretations of the *Zhuangzi*, 109–

relativism (continued)
  18; moral, 113, 119; skeptical, 118; and universalism, 222n2. See also incommensurability; universalism
relativity, hermeneutic, 2, 9–10, 29 113, 210n1, 215n30; relativities (versus relativism), xxiii, 114–18, 126, 168, 234n19
relevance, 55, 59–61, 153
rhetoric. See questions
Ricci, Grand Ricci (Le Grand Dictionnaire Ricci), xiv, 40, 64, 70, 220n3, n5, 226n14, 231n71, 231n80–81
richtig/falsch, 71–72
rightness, 57–65; being right, 20, 61–62; instead of truth, 57–61; moral, 43, 49, 220n14, 225n14; normative, xxi, 18, 42–43, 62; right is not right, 78; right/true, 37–38; right-true-correct, xxiii, 142; right/wrong, xix. See also fitting, shifei
righteousness. See yi 義
rites (decorum, propriety). See li 禮
Ruists (Confucians): do Ruists and Mohists really disagree, 161–69
rules (rigid, strict), 117–18, 192

sage(s), 193–98; great, 93, 158, 198, 248n48, 250n63; Ruist sage, 194; sage-kings, 43, 130, 157, 197, 243n3
scholars; inferior, xxiii, 95, 142, 155, 170; superior, 155, 185
science, justification of. See virtues, epistemic
Sein, das. See Being
self (the), 75. See also other/I
self-contradiction, 49; perverse, 49–52
self-deception, 174
self-realization, 45
self-refutation, 135, 138
semantic(s), and concept of truth, 15–17, 25, 62, 209n5, 213n1, n13; semantic stretch, 238n14
sensibilities, 133

sentence: being a linguistic universal, 16–17
sentiments. See emotions
simplicity, 61, 95, 198, 200, 248n53
sincerity, 18–21; and "cheng," 21. See also cheng 誠
situations. See circumstances
skepticism, and zhi 知, 121–28; therapeutic, 121, 233n2
skill (ability), 121, 130, 173
small. See big and small; similarity (large and small)
so (being so): so, correct (shi 是), 18, 40; so is not so, 78; so, this way (ran 然), 18, 40. See also ran 然
SP (Strong Program), 116–18
speech: ideal speech situation, 19; speech act theory, 137, 210n5
spontaneity, 49, 93, 119, 170–71, 180, 193, 201–3, 222n5, 251n79, 251n83
sprouts (Mengzi), 34, 73, 235n40
stance, instead of perspective or set of beliefs, 129–34
standardization, 4, 22, 73
standards, higher-order, xxi, 43–44, 46–48, 67, 85–89, 209n9
stars: being made, 58, 224n6
straight(forwardness) (uprightness), 21, 47
suspension of judgment, 121, 242n70

term(s): "on its own terms," 9–11; thin/thick, 165–66 223n12
that's it/that's not, 20, 33
that/this, this/that, 1, 77, 82, 96, 228n36
things: going along with (following the course of), 100, 105; myriad of, 156, 192, 201, 230n73, 246n24. See also object
this/not-this, 38, 41
this/right, 41; this:right, 41; this:right: assent, 41
TLS (Thesaurus Linguae Sericae), xiii
Topic-comment, 80, 139

torch of chaos and doubt, 145, 240n48, 241n64
translations: in English (anglophone); in French (francophone), 67–74. In Dutch, *see* Schipper; in German, *see* Schuhmacher, Wilhelm
trees, 122, 126, 203–6, 252n90
trustworthiness. *See* faithfulness
truth (concept of): absolutely true, 44, 46; factual and moral rightness, 49; IS TRUE, 19; not being a shared concept of human thought, 21–25; objective, 22, 27, 217n55; possible congeners in classical Chinese, 18–21; projection of truth onto classical Chinese 15–30; true-correct, 221n21; TRUE, 19; truth as a subsidiary of generic rightness, xxii, 57–61; truth-candidate, 18. *See also* Harbsmeier-Hansen dispute; semantics; *shi* 是; universals

unbridgeable, 114–15
underdetermination, 8–9. *See also* indeterminacy
understanding, great, 92, 214n15; versus knowledge, xviii, 57, 60–61, 111, 122, 127, 185, 233n9, 235n38, 236n45. *See also yiming* 以明
unfixed (*weiding*), xxiii, 135, 169, 199. *See* indeterminacy, underdetermination
universalism and relativism, 109–20. *See also* ideal language; isomorphy (thesis); relativism
universals, 2, 4, 10, 21–22, 167, 212n32. *See also* quasi-universals
usefulness, 61; practical use, 117. *See also* uselessness
uselessness, 204, 228–30, 253, 268, 270, 276
usual, the. *See* ordinary, the
utterance, 210n5
utility, 79, 84, 188, 162, 186

vagueness, 156, 162, 201, 234
validity, 43, 83, 86, 195, 200, 213, 238, 263
values: value-fact, 37; *See also* epistemic virtues; fact/value dichotomy
veracity, 42
vérité, 69
Verneinung, 77, 230n71
version (Nelson Goodman), 57–59
virtues (values): being also values, 55, 109; epistemic, 2, 9, 42, 54, 57, 61, 212n27. See also *de* 德
vrai, le, 31, 70, 226n8, 228n45; *vrai/faux*, 56, 87–88

walking-two-roads (*liangxing* 兩行), 141, 165, 167, 171–72, 203, 263, 265
Way, the. *See dao*
weishi 為是, as contrived *shi* 是; translation of, 97–99. See also *yinshi* 因是
wisdom, 36, 53, 70, 73, 122, 156, 185, 194, 235n38
words: meaning of, being part of action, 137. *See also* concepts
work of art, 3, 58
world(s): block worlds, 165, 243n7; making worlds, 58–61, 224n6; possible worlds, 224n4; ready-made world, 117; worldview, 132, 189; a world, 58–59
wrong: wrong/false, 37; wrong-false-incorrect, xxiii, 142

Yangists, 183
yes/no, 20, 38, 71, 244n28

Zhuangzi, and relativism, 109–27; his stance being amoral? 170–77; his stance, 129–59; his text(s), 180–84
Zhuangzi, the, inner chapters (passages related to), xvi, 181

www.ingramcontent.com/pod-product-compliance
Lightning Source LLC
Chambersburg PA
CBHW071829230426
43672CB00013B/2793